DESIGN AND ANALYSIS OF ALGORITHMS

AUTHOR (S)

Dr. Hari Prabhat Gupta, Ph.D.
Associate Professor,
Dept. of Computer Science & Engineering,
IIT (BHU) Varanasi, India.

Dr. Rahul Mishra, Ph.D.
Assistant Professor,
Dept. of Computer Science & Engineering,
IIT Patna, India.

REVIEWER

Dr. R. S. Singh
Associate Professor
Dept. of Computer Science & Engineering,
IIT (BHU) Varanasi, India

KHANNA BOOK PUBLISHING CO. (P) Ltd.
4C/4344, Ansari Road, Darya Ganj, New Delhi, India

All India Council for Technical Education
Nelson Mandela Marg, Vasant Kunj, New Delhi, India

Dear Readers,

To prevent the piracy, this book is secured with HIGH SECURITY HOLOGRAM on the front title cover. In case you don't find the hologram on the front cover title, please write us to at contact@khannabooks.com or whatsapp us at +91-99109 09320 and avail special gift voucher for yourself.

Specimen of Hologram on front Cover title:

Moreover, there is a SPECIAL DISCOUNT COUPON for you with EVERY HOLOGRAM.

How to avail this SPECIAL DISCOUNT:

Step 1: Scratch the hologram

Step 2: Under the scratch area, your "coupon code" is available

Step 3: Logon to www.khannabooks.com

Step 4: Use your "coupon code" in the shopping cart and get your copy at a special discount

Step 5: Enjoy your reading!

ISBN: 978-93-5538-670-0

Book Code: UG432EN

Design And Analysis Of Algorithms

by Dr. Hari Prabhat Gupta, Ph.D
and Dr. Rahul Mishra, Ph.D

First Edition: 2026

Originally Published by:
All India Council for Technical Education, Ministry of Education, GOI

Exclusively Published & Distributed by:
Khanna Book Publishing Co. (P) Ltd.
4C/4344, Ansari Road, Daryaganj,
New Delhi (INDIA)

Visit us at: **www.khannabooks.com**
Write us at: **contact@khannabooks.com**

To view complete list of books,
Please scan the QR Code:

Printed in Bharat.

प्रो. टी. जी. सीताराम
अध्यक्ष
Prof. T. G. Sitharam
Chairman

सत्यमेव जयते

अखिल भारतीय तकनीकी शिक्षा परिषद्
(भारत सरकार का एक सांविधिक निकाय)
(शिक्षा मंत्रालय, भारत सरकार)
नेल्सन मंडेला मार्ग, वसंत कुंज, नई दिल्ली–110070
दूरभाष : 011–26131498
ई–मेल : chairman@aicte-india.org

ALL INDIA COUNCIL FOR TECHNICAL EDUCATION
(A STATUTORY BODY OF THE GOVT. OF INDIA)
(Ministry of Education, Govt. of India)
Nelson Mandela Marg, Vasant Kunj, New Delhi-110070
Phone : 011-26131498
E-mail : chairman@aicte-india.org

FOREWORD

Engineers are the backbone of any modern society. They are the ones responsible for the marvels as well as the improved quality of life across the world. Engineers have driven humanity towards greater heights in a more evolved and unprecedented manner.

The All India Council for Technical Education (AICTE), have spared no efforts towards the strengthening of the technical education in the country. AICTE is always committed towards promoting quality Technical Education to make India a modern developed nation emphasizing on the overall welfare of mankind.

An array of initiatives has been taken by AICTE in last decade which have been accelerated now by the National Education Policy (NEP) 2020. The implementation of NEP under the visionary leadership of Hon'ble Prime Minister of India envisages the provision for education in regional languages to all, thereby ensuring that every graduate becomes competent enough and is in a position to contribute towards the national growth and development through innovation & entrepreneurship.

One of the spheres where AICTE had been relentlessly working since past couple of years is providing high quality original technical contents at Under Graduate & Diploma level prepared and translated by eminent educators in various Indian languages to its aspirants. For students pursuing 2nd year of their Engineering education, AICTE has identified 87 books, which shall be translated into 12 Indian languages - Hindi, Tamil, Gujarati, Odia, Bengali, Kannada, Urdu, Punjabi, Telugu, Marathi, Assamese & Malayalam. In addition to the English medium, books in different Indian Languages are going to support the students to understand the concepts in their respective mother tongue.

On behalf of AICTE, I express sincere gratitude to all distinguished authors, reviewers and translators from the renowned institutions of high repute for their admirable contribution in a record span of time.

AICTE is confident that these outcomes based original contents shall help aspirants to master the subject with comprehension and greater ease.

(Prof. T. G. Sitharam)

ABOUT THE AUTHOR

Hari Prabhat Gupta is working as faculty in the Department of Computer Science and Engineering, IIT (BHU) Varanasi. Previously, Hari was a Technical Lead in Samsung R&D Bangalore, India. Hari received his Ph.D. and M.Tech. degrees in Computer Science and Engineering from Indian Institute of Technology Guwahati; and his B.E. degree in Computer Engineering from Govt. Engineering College Ajmer, India. Hari has elevated to the grade of Senior Member of IEEE in June 2020 based on his significant contributions to the profession. Hari successfully organized short-term courses under Quality Improvement Programme, courses under Global Initiative of Academic Networks (GIAN), VRITIKA training program, and other continuing education programs in the domain of smart sensing, machine learning, and wireless sensing. Hari has published three Indian patents and more than 150 research papers in journals and conferences. Hari was awarded TCS research fellowship, Samsung spot awards, and best teacher awards. Hari has finished various research projects sponsored by different government and private organizations.

Rahul Mishra currently holds a position as a faculty member in the Department of Computer Science and Engineering at IIT Patna. Prior to this role, he served as an assistant professor at DA-IICT, Gandhinagar. His professional journey also includes a tenure as a Research Associate at the Department of Computation and Data Science, Indian Institute of Science, Bangalore, India. His research focus centers around machine learning and deep learning, particularly in the context of system deployment. Notably, he has delved into real-world deployment challenges with a specific emphasis on federated learning perspectives. Additionally, he has actively pursued applications in the practical domain, with a keen interest in areas involving drones and edge computation. Rahul Mishra's academic background includes being a research scholar at the Department of Computer Science and Engineering, IIT (BHU) Varanasi, where he successfully completed his Ph.D. His doctoral research spanned the broad domain of sensor data analytics and applied artificial intelligence, integrating deep learning and federated learning methodologies.

ACKNOWLEDGEMENTS

The authors are grateful to AICTE particularly Prof. T. G. Sitharam, Chairman; Prof. Abhay Jere, Vice-Chairman; Prof. Rajive Kumar, Member-Secretary; and Dr. Sunil Luthra, Director and Reena Sharma, Hindi Officer Training and Learning Bureau, for their meticulous planning and execution to publish the technical book for Engineering and Technology students. We sincerely acknowledge the valuable contributions of the reviewer of the book Prof. R. S. Singh, Dept. of CSE, IIT (BHU) Varanasi for making it students' friendly and giving a better shape in an artistic manner. This book is an outcome of various suggestions of AICTE members, experts and authors who shared their opinion and thoughts to further develop the engineering education in our country. It is also with great honour that we state that this book is aligned to the AICTE Model Curriculum and in line with the *guidelines* of NEP-2020. Towards *promoting education in regional languages*, this book is being translated in scheduled Indian regional languages. Acknowledgements are due to the contributors and different workers in this field whose published books, review articles, papers, photographs, footnotes, references and other valuable information enriched us at the time of writing the book. We affectionately dedicate this book to them.

Hari Prabhat Gupta
IIT (BHU) Varanasi, India

Rahul Mishra
IIT Patna, India

PREFACE

The book titled ***Design and Analysis of Algorithms*** is an outcome of our extensive experience in teaching and researching programming languages. It commences with a thorough introduction to algorithm analysis, encompassing various techniques for algorithm design. The content aligns with the recommendations provided by AICTE, offering a systematic and simple approach.

Beginning with the foundational concepts of algorithm design and analysis, the book meticulously illustrates the practical applications of each concept. The major content covers AICTE-suggested topics and delves into algorithm design techniques, starting with algorithm analysis. Subsequently, it explores graph and tree data structures and the associated algorithms, fostering students' critical thinking and logical skills. The book incorporates a diverse range of questions, including both long and short-answer types, adhering to the lower and higher orders of Bloom's taxonomy. This approach facilitates a progressive learning journey, starting with understanding, remembering, and applying basic concepts and gradually advancing to higher-order skills such as creativity, analysis, and evaluation. To enhance practical application, each chapter concludes with experiments, enabling students to apply the acquired knowledge. Additionally, references and recommended readings are provided for further exploration of theoretical and practical aspects of the content. Throughout the writing process, the authors leveraged ChatGPT and DALL·E2 artificial language systems to generate effective and easily comprehensible text, accompanied by illustrative figures.

The authors earnestly hope that the book serves as a source of motivation for students to delve into the practical applications of algorithm design, contributing to research and development in the engineering field. Constructive comments and suggestions from readers are welcomed to improve future editions of the book. It is with great pleasure that the authors present this book to teachers and students alike, anticipating its positive impact on the learning journey.

Hari Prabhat Gupta
IIT (BHU) Varanasi, India

Rahul Mishra
IIT Patna, India

OUTCOME BASED EDUCATION

For the implementation of an outcome based education the first requirement is to develop an outcome based curriculum and incorporate an outcome based assessment in the education system. By going through outcome based assessments evaluators will be able to evaluate whether the students have achieved the outlined standard, specific and measurable outcomes. With the proper incorporation of outcome based education there will be a definite commitment to achieve a minimum standard for all learners without giving up at any level. At the end of the programme running with the aid of outcome based education, a student will be able to arrive at the following outcomes:

PO1. **Engineering knowledge**: Apply the knowledge of mathematics, science, engineering fundamentals, and an engineering specialization to the solution of complex engineering problems.

PO2. **Problem analysis**: Identify, formulate, review research literature, and analyze complex engineering problems reaching substantiated conclusions using first principles of mathematics, natural sciences, and engineering sciences.

PO3. **Design / development of solutions**: Design solutions for complex engineering problems and design system components or processes that meet the specified needs with appropriate consideration for the public health and safety, and the cultural, societal, and environmental considerations.

PO4. **Conduct investigations of complex problems**: Use research-based knowledge and research methods including design of experiments, analysis and interpretation of data, and synthesis of the information to provide valid conclusions.

PO5. **Modern tool usage**: Create, select, and apply appropriate techniques, resources, and modern engineering and IT tools including prediction and modeling to complex engineering activities with an understanding of the limitations.

PO6. **The engineer and society**: Apply reasoning informed by the contextual knowledge to assess societal, health, safety, legal and cultural issues and the consequent responsibilities relevant to the professional engineering practice.

PO7. Environment and sustainability: Understand the impact of the professional engineering solutions in societal and environmental contexts, and demonstrate the knowledge of, and need for sustainable development.

PO8. Ethics: Apply ethical principles and commit to professional ethics and responsibilities and norms of the engineering practice.

PO9. Individual and team work: Function effectively as an individual, and as a member or leader in diverse teams, and in multidisciplinary settings.

PO10. Communication: Communicate effectively on complex engineering activities with the engineering community and with society at large, such as, being able to comprehend and write effective reports and design documentation, make effective presentations, and give and receive clear instructions.

PO11. Project management and finance: Demonstrate knowledge and understanding of the engineering and management principles and apply these to one's own work, as a member and leader in a team, to manage projects and in multidisciplinary environments.

PO12. Life-long learning: Recognize the need for, and have the preparation and ability to engage in independent and life-long learning in the broadest context of technological change.

COURSE OUTCOMES

After course completion, the students will be able to:

CO-1: A comprehensive understanding of the fundamentals involved in the analysis and selection of algorithms

CO-2: Discussions on the analysis of algorithms. Moreover, For a given algorithms analyze worst-case running times of algorithms based on asymptotic analysis and justify the correctness of algorithms.

CO-3: Discussions various algorithm designing techniques. Moreover, it covers the following outcomes:

- Describe the greedy paradigm and explain when an algorithmic design situation calls for it. For a given problem develop the greedy algorithms.
- Describe the divide-and-conquer paradigm and explain when an algorithmic design situation calls for it. Synthesize divide-and-conquer algorithms. Derive and solve recurrence relation.
- Describe the dynamic-programming paradigm and explain when an algorithmic design situation calls for it. For a given problems of dynamic-programming and
- Develop the dynamic programming algorithms, and analyze it to determine its computational complexity.
- For a given model engineering problem model it using graph and write the corresponding algorithm to solve the problems.

CO-4: An in-depth understanding of computational problems, exploring their fundamental concepts and characteristic

CO-5: Comprehend the concepts of Approximation algorithms and randomized algorithms, highlighting their significance in algorithmic solutions. It covers the following outcomes:

- Explain the ways to analyze randomized algorithms
- Explain what an approximation algorithm is. Compute the approximation factor of an approximation algorithm

Course Outcome	Expected Mapping with Programme Outcomes (1- Weak Correlation; 2- Medium correlation; 3- Strong Correlation)											
	PO-1	PO-2	PO-3	PO-4	PO-5	PO-6	PO-7	PO-8	PO-9	PO-10	PO-11	PO-12
CO-1	3	-		1	-	-	1	3	3	-	3	3
CO-2	3	3	3	2	3	2	1	-	3	2	3	3
CO-3	3	3	3	3	3	3	1	-	3	2	3	3
CO-4	3	2	3	3	3	3	1	-	3	2	3	3
CO-5	3	2	2	3	3	3	1	-	3	2	3	3

GUIDELINES FOR TEACHERS

Outcome Based Education (OBE) aims at improving student's skills and knowledge. Therefore, it becomes the teacher's responsibility to implement OBE in an appropriate and systematic way. Following are some responsibilities (not limited to) are given below:

- The teachers must provide the exercise so that students can explore more and more.
- The teachers must try to enhance the student's skills and logical skills while pursuing the course.
- Every student must be accoutred with quality of education appended with competence after they finalized their education.
- They must always motivate the students to enhance their quintessential performance by their capabilities.
- The teachers must promote and motivate the team work as it creates the interest and curiosity amongst the students.
- They must ensure Bloom's taxonomy as shown in Figure I during the assessment and evaluation of the students. The detailed explanation of Bloom's Taxonomy is given in Table I.

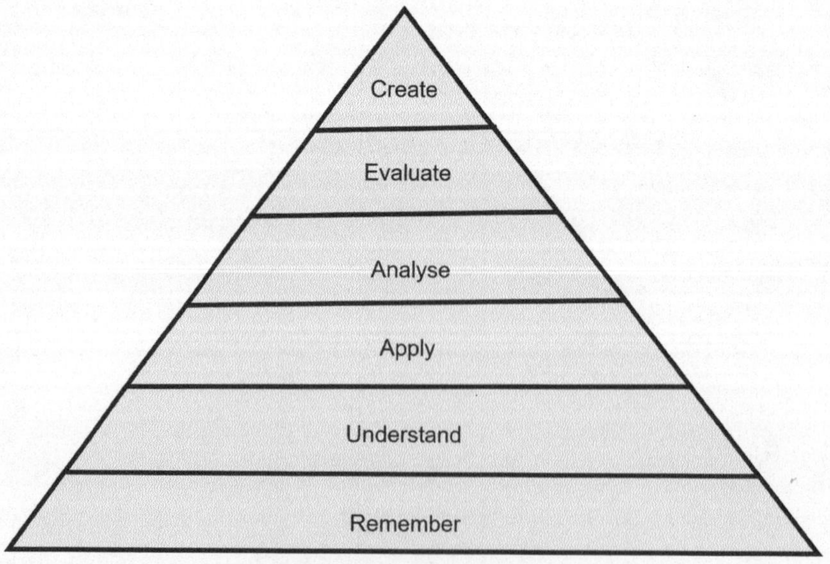

Figure I: Bloom's taxonomy

Table I: Bloom's Taxonomy

Level	Teacher should check the student's ability to	Student should be able to	Possible Mode of Assessment
Create	create	design or fabricate or simulate	Mini or major project
Evaluate	justify	secure or defend	Assignment
Analyse	distinguish	characterize or distinguish	Project/lab methodology
Apply	use information	operate or illustrate	Technical presentation/ illustration
Understand	explain the ideas	explain or describe	Presentation/seminar
Remember	define (or remember)	define or remember	Quiz

GUIDELINES FOR STUDENTS

Students must opt for equal responsibility for simulating the OBE. Following are some responsibilities (not limited to):

- Students must be familiar with each unit outcome before starting the new unit.
- Students must be familiar with each course outcome before starting the course.
- Students must be familiar with each programme outcome before starting the programme.
- Students must properly apply the concept to practical problems.
- Student's learning must be related to practical and real life consequences.
- Students must be familiar with their competency at every level of OBE.

List of Figures

List of Tables

Table of Content

1 Introduction to Algorithms

UNIT SPECIFICS

This unit covers the following aspects:

- *About the characteristics of algorithms*
- *Algorithms designing techniques*
- *Organization of the book*

This unit initiates the discussion by outlining the fundamental necessity of algorithms. It then delves into critical considerations in algorithm design and selection, focusing on aspects such as time complexity, space complexity, computation complexity, approximation, failure probability, robustness, error handling, scalability, and parallelization. The unit then explores various algorithm designing techniques, including brute-force methodology, backtracking, greedy algorithms, dynamic programming, divide-and-conquer, NP-completeness, and randomized algorithms. The unit involves exploring the organization of book, focusing on an overview of the next units, and offering readers a glimpse into the structured journey ahead. The link given in the QR code provides supplementary material of this unit.

UNIT OUTCOMES

The outcomes of the unit are as follows:

U1-O1: About the algorithms

U1-O2: Algorithm design and selection

U1-O3: Algorithms designing techniques

U1-O4: Organization of the book

Unit-1 Outcomes	EXPECTED MAPPING WITH COURSE OUTCOMES (1- Weak Correlation; 2- Medium correlation; 3- Strong Correlation)				
	CO-1	**CO-2**	**CO-3**	**CO-4**	**CO-5**
U1-O1	3	2	-	-	-
U1-O2	2	2	-	-	-
U1-O3	3	2	-	-	-
U1-O4	3	2	-	-	-

1.1 About the Algorithms

Before we dive into the intricate world of algorithms, let us start on a journey – not just any journey, but a road trip from Varanasi to Delhi. Imagine you are using the myriad paths connecting these two vibrant cities with your trusty car. The task is to find the shortest route, minimizing the travel distance. This scenario serves as our backdrop to explore the concept of algorithms and their profound role in problem-solving.

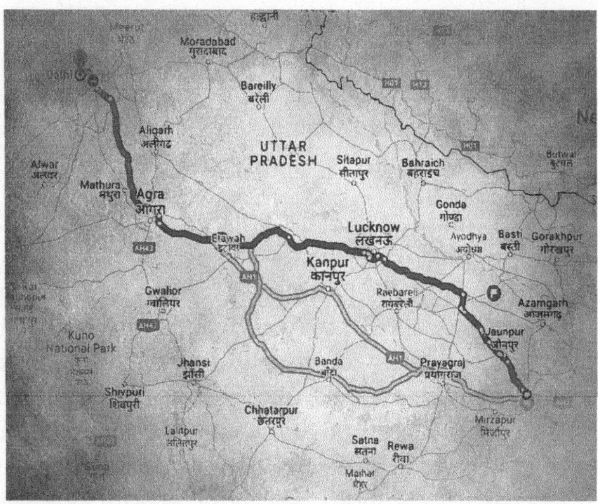

Our first step is to map out the starting point (Varanasi) and the destination (Delhi). The map becomes our canvas, and the cities, nodes in a vast network waiting to be connected. The possibilities unroll as we contemplate routes – Varanasi to Lucknow to Agra to Delhi or Varanasi to Prayagraj to Agra to Delhi. Multiple options lay before us; the challenge is choosing the most efficient path. In this journey, efficiency is paramount. We aim to save travel distance, and hence, we seek the shortest path. The question that arises is, how do we determine the shortest path among the multitude of options? One pragmatic solution involves manually calculating the distance for each path, comparing, and selecting the shortest. However, this method is laborious, especially when dealing with numerous points or a lack of time and resources. Moreover, while this manual approach holds merit, its drawbacks become apparent, particularly when faced with real-world complexities: (i) Numerous Points: In scenarios where the number of cities or waypoints increases, the manual calculation process becomes unwieldy and time-consuming. (ii) Resource Constraints: The manual approach demands significant time and effort, making it impractical when faced with time constraints or a lack of resources. (iii) Subjectivity: Human bias and subjectivity may inadvertently influence the selection process, leading to inconsistencies or errors in determining the shortest path.

This brings us to the crux – the need for a methodology, a systematic approach that eliminates manual calculations. This methodology becomes the algorithm, a set of instructions to efficiently solve problems. We aim to automate finding the shortest path, especially when faced with large datasets or time constraints. An algorithm, in the context of problem-solving, can be defined as a step-by-step procedure or set of rules designed to perform a specific task. It transforms the manual, time-consuming process into an automated, efficient solution. Whether in medical science, construction, or car running, algorithms provide the systematic approach needed to tackle complex problems. Algorithms are not confined to a specific domain; they are ubiquitous. In medical science, they help match DNAs; in construction, they calculate vibration levels, and in transportation, they optimize routes. The essence lies in their ability to streamline problem-solving across diverse fields. More formally, an algorithm is a step-by-step procedure or a set of rules designed to perform a specific task or solve a particular problem. It is a precise and unambiguous sequence of instructions that, when executed, produces the desired output or achieves a specific goal.

1.2 Critical Considerations in Algorithm Design and Selection

The design and selection of algorithms are pivotal aspects of computational problem-solving, influencing efficiency of solutions, reliability, and accuracy. Several key factors demand careful consideration to ensure that the chosen algorithm aligns with the specific requirements and constraints of the problem. Let us explore some important key factors that need to be considered while designing and selecting an algorithm for a given problem [1-4]. In this context, we extend our exploration to the road trip from Varanasi to Delhi.

a) **Time complexity:** The first factor influencing the choice of algorithms is the time complexity of the selected algorithm. Time complexity is a quantitative measurement that evaluates the efficiency of an algorithm in terms of the amount of time it requires to execute as a function of the input size. It provides insights into how the running time of the algorithm increases or decreases with the growth of the input size. In simpler terms, time complexity answers the question: "How does the execution time increase with the input size of the algorithm?" It focuses on understanding the fundamental relationship between the efficiency of algorithm and the magnitude of the problem it seeks to solve. Opt for algorithms with lower time complexity for swift execution, especially in critical real-time processing scenarios. Let us consider the time complexity of our Varanasi to Delhi road trip. Imagine we are tasked with determining the most time-efficient algorithm for finding the shortest route. In this scenario, time complexity would be crucial because the efficiency of algorithm directly impacts how quickly we can plan our journey.

b) **Space complexity:** Moving to the second crucial factor in algorithm evaluation, space complexity measures the amount of memory an algorithm requires with its input size. The emphasis here is on selecting algorithms with minimal space complexity to efficiently utilize memory resources, especially in environments where memory constraints are a significant concern. Imagine we are developing a navigation app that recommends the optimal route based on real-time traffic data. In this context, space efficiency is critical, especially for mobile devices with limited memory capacity.

c) **Computation complexity:** Computation complexity is a comprehensive metric, encapsulating time and space complexities, offering a holistic perspective on an overall resource utilization of algorithm. Striking a balance between time and space complexities becomes imperative, considering the unique demands of the problem at hand and the available computational resources. Let us extend our exploration to the Varanasi to Delhi road trip, where computational efficiency is crucial for real-time navigation through varying traffic conditions. Our goal is to find an algorithm that not only minimizes planning time (time complexity) but also operates within the memory constraints of our navigation system (space complexity).

d) **Approximation:** Some problems are computationally hard or even intractable. In such scenarios, approximation algorithms emerge as valuable tools, providing near-optimal solutions within a reasonable computational timeframe. These algorithms play a crucial role when achieving exact solutions becomes impractical, offering a delicate equilibrium between precision and computational efficiency. Approximation algorithms are typically assessed in terms of their approximation ratio, quantifying how close the output of algorithm is to the optimal solution. A lower approximation ratio signifies a more accurate approximation. Let us apply the approximation concept to our Varanasi to Delhi road trip, where finding the shortest route may be computationally challenging due to the dynamic nature of traffic conditions. The goal is to identify an algorithm that can swiftly produce a route that is sufficiently close to the optimal solution.

e) **Failure probability:** In algorithmic decision-making, some approaches introduce an element of randomness, leading to varying outcomes. Evaluating the acceptable level of failure probability becomes a critical consideration. Deterministic algorithms are the preferred choice when determinism is paramount and precise results are non-negotiable. However, probabilistic algorithms may present advantageous solutions in scenarios where uncertainty is acceptable and computational speed is a priority. The level of failure probability in probabilistic algorithms is often quantified and considered in terms of the success rate of the algorithm and the reliability of its outcomes. Let us relate the concept of failure probability to our Varanasi to Delhi road trip, where unforeseen circumstances such as sudden road closures or unexpected traffic incidents may introduce an element of unpredictability. Consider a deterministic algorithm that meticulously plans the route based on historical traffic data and predefined road conditions. While this approach ensures a predictable and precise solution, it may struggle to adapt swiftly to unexpected events, as it relies on a static set of parameters.

f) **Robustness and error handling:** The robustness of an algorithm refers to its ability to gracefully handle unexpected inputs or errors without causing a system crash or failure. Prioritizing algorithms with robust error-handling mechanisms becomes crucial, especially in real-world scenarios where input data may exhibit noise, incompleteness, or errors. A robust algorithm is one that can continue functioning effectively and provide meaningful outputs even in the presence of uncertainties or irregularities in the input data. This is achieved through the implementation of error-checking mechanisms, boundary validations, and strategies to gracefully recover from unexpected situations. Let us relate the concept of robustness and error handling to our Varanasi to Delhi road trip, where the navigation system must contend with imperfect or unreliable data sources, such as fluctuating GPS signals, incomplete road information, or sudden changes in traffic conditions. Consider an algorithm that meticulously plans the route based on accurate and complete map data. While this deterministic approach might work well under ideal conditions, it could face challenges in the real world where data inconsistencies or unexpected events are common. A lack of robust error handling in such an algorithm may lead to system crashes or suboptimal routes when faced with unexpected disruptions.

g) **Scalability:** Scalability is a critical aspect of algorithmic evaluation, emphasizing on ability of algorithm to maintain efficiency as the size of the input or problem scales. It involves assessing how well an algorithm performs when confronted with an increase in the magnitude of the data or problem it needs to handle. Scalability is paramount, particularly in applications dealing with large datasets or experiencing a growing user base. A scalable algorithm can efficiently adapt to the increasing complexity and demands associated with larger input sizes, ensuring consistent performance without a significant degradation in efficiency. Let us apply the concept of scalability to our Varanasi to Delhi road trip, considering a navigation system that must accommodate an expanding database of cities, roads, and traffic information. Imagine an algorithm that plans routes based on a fixed set of cities and roads, optimized for a specific region. While this algorithm may work well for smaller areas, its efficiency could diminish when faced with a larger geographical scope, incorporating more cities and intricate road networks. The lack of scalability in such an algorithm might result in slower route planning times and decreased performance as the dataset expands.

h) **Parallelization and concurrency:** Algorithms that support parallelization can execute multiple tasks simultaneously, enhancing overall performance. In an era dominated by multicore processors and distributed systems, it becomes essential to prioritize algorithms that exploit parallelization to harness computational power efficiently. Parallelization involves breaking down a computational task into smaller subtasks that can be processed concurrently, either by utilizing multiple cores within a processor or by distributing tasks across different processors or nodes in a network. Let us explore the concept of parallelization and concurrency in the context of our Varanasi to Delhi road trip, where real-time navigation demands swift processing of complex route planning tasks. On the other hand, a parallelizable algorithm can break down the route planning task into parallel subtasks. Each processor or core can independently explore different portions of the road network, significantly speeding up the overall route-planning process. This parallel approach leverages the computational power of multicore processors or distributed systems to handle complex scenarios efficiently.

While not inherently linked to computational complexity, it is advisable to prioritize algorithms with transparent, maintainable code, simplifying troubleshooting, updates, and collaborative efforts. Furthermore, ethical considerations play a crucial role, encompassing the assessment of societal impact, fairness, and privacy implications associated with algorithmic decisions. It is imperative to evaluate algorithms ethically, especially in applications where decisions may impact individuals or communities.

1.3 Algorithms Designing Techniques

Algorithm design techniques refer to systematic approaches and strategies for creating algorithms to solve specific computational problems. These techniques guide the process of transforming problem statements into efficient and effective step-by-step procedures that a computer can execute. The choice of algorithm design technique often depends on the nature of the problem, the desired properties of the solution, and the efficiency requirements. Algorithm design techniques can be classified into categories based on underlying principles and strategies. We discuss some common algorithm-designing techniques:

a) **Brute-force methodology:** The brute-force methodology is the most simple algorithm design approach, systematically exploring all possible solutions until the correct one is identified. This exhaustive method considers every potential solution without employing any optimization or pruning strategies. A classic example of brute-force is the search for an element in an unsorted list, where each element is examined individually until a match is found. Despite its simplicity, brute force can be computationally expensive and may not be suitable for large-scale or complex problems.

b) **Backtracking:** Backtracking is a systematic strategy employed in algorithmic problem-solving to explore all possible solutions in a structured manner. The algorithm thoroughly searches for potential solutions and backtracks when it discerns that the current path cannot lead to a valid solution. This approach is particularly effective in scenarios where a trial-and-error method is suitable. A classic illustration of backtracking is observed in the N-Queens problem, where the objective is to place N queens on a chessboard in a way that none of them attacks each other. The backtracking algorithm systematically explores different arrangements of queens, abandoning paths that lead to conflicts. This methodical exploration ensures the algorithm exhaustively evaluates all potential solutions while avoiding invalid configurations.

c) **Greedy algorithms:** Greedy algorithms operate by making locally optimal choices at each step, aiming to achieve a global optimum. At each decision point, the algorithm selects the best possible choice without considering the future consequences of its selections. The coin change problem is an illustrative scenario, where the algorithm consistently picks the largest coin available at each step. While Greedy algorithms are simple and efficient for certain problems, they may not always guarantee the globally optimal solution and require careful consideration of the problem's characteristics.

d) **Dynamic programming:** Dynamic programming dissects a complex problem into simpler overlapping subproblems, ensuring that each subproblem is solved only once. This methodology emphasizes two key principles: optimal substructure and overlapping subproblems. The optimal substructure states that optimizing original large-size problems requires the combination of optimal solutions of subproblems. Overlapping subproblems involves solving the same subproblems multiple times, but dynamic programming addresses this by storing solutions for future use. An excellent application of dynamic programming is in solving the Fibonacci sequence. By storing the solutions to smaller Fibonacci subproblems, the algorithm avoids redundant calculations, significantly enhancing efficiency. This approach contributes to a more optimal computation of Fibonacci numbers and showcases the effectiveness of dynamic programming in tackling problems with overlapping substructures.

e) **Divide-and-conquer:** Divide-and-conquer entails breaking down a complex problem into smaller, more manageable subproblems. Each subproblem is solved independently, and the solutions are combined to address the original problem. This approach often follows a recursive structure, systematically dividing a problem into smaller instances until base cases are reached. A notable application of the Divide-and-Conquer technique is observed in the merge sort algorithm. When sorting a list of elements, merge sort divides the overall sorting task into smaller, more manageable parts. These smaller parts are independently sorted, and their solutions are combined in a merging process. This method enhances sorting efficiency, showcasing the effectiveness of divide-and-conquer in dealing with complex problems through a recursive breakdown of tasks.

f) **NP-completeness:** It represents a class of decision problems for which no known polynomial-time algorithm exists. Problems falling under NP-completeness are deemed challenging, with solutions that may necessitate exponential time for discovery. These problems are considered computationally hard due to the absence of efficient algorithms to solve in polynomial time. A typical example of an NP-complete problem is the traveling salesman problem. In this problem, the objective is to determine the most efficient route that visits a set of cities exactly once and returns to the starting city. The inherent complexity of finding an optimal solution to this problem contributes to its classification as NP-complete, signifying the difficulty in achieving polynomial-time solutions.

g) **Randomized algorithms:** Randomized algorithms leverage randomness as a fundamental component in decision-making throughout their execution. The behavior of these algorithms incorporates a degree of unpredictability. A notable example is the randomized quicksort, where randomness is introduced in the pivot selection during the sorting process. This injection of randomness can lead to variations in algorithmic outcomes, providing certain advantages in specific scenarios and contributing to the versatility of randomized algorithms.

1.4 Organization of the Book

This primary aim of the book is to introduce readers to the design and analysis of algorithms, covering fundamental concepts and offering insights into effective algorithmic problem-solving. Throughout the book, the goal is to provide readers with a comprehensive understanding of algorithmic strategies for solving diverse computational problems. The organization of the book is structured as follows:

Unit 2: Initiates a comprehensive exploration of algorithmic efficiency principles. It establishes a robust framework for comparing algorithm performance, starting with asymptotic notations. The unit further examines average, worst, and best cases, revealing optimal and suboptimal algorithmic performance scenarios. Space complexity analysis is also covered, emphasizing the critical interplay between memory utilization and algorithmic efficiency. Empirical analysis and real-world case studies illustrate the practical utility of algorithmic efficiency.

Unit 3: Provides the advanced algorithmic concepts, focusing on sorting mechanisms, recurrence relations, and the maximum-subarray problem. Notable topics include the Heap sort algorithm, substitution method, recurrence tree method, and the Master theorem, providing powerful tools for analyzing and solving recurrence relations.

Unit 4: Explores fundamental graph algorithms and network flow techniques. The unit covers graph preliminaries, traversal algorithms (Breadth First and Depth First Search), complexities of shortest-path algorithms, Minimum Spanning Tree techniques, Topological Sorting, and Network Flow Algorithms.

Unit 5: Examines brute-force methodology, analyzing its characteristics, time and space complexity, and applications in various domains. Strategies to enhance brute-force algorithm efficiency and alternative approaches to reduce time and space complexities are discussed.

Unit 6: Delves into the principles of greedy algorithms, summarizing their attributes, time and space complexity, and widespread applications. The unit explores techniques to refine the performance of greedy algorithms, acknowledging their constraints and considering alternative algorithmic approaches.

Unit 7: Discusses dynamic programming, emphasizing its optimization techniques for solving complex problems. Specific problems such as the Knapsack problem and longest common subsequence are explored, addressing time and space complexity. Practical applications in combinatorial optimization and scheduling are highlighted.

Unit 8: Explores divide-and-conquer methodology, analyzing its characteristics, time and space complexity, and applications. Strategies for enhancing efficiency of divide-and-conquer algorithms, limitations, and alternative approaches are covered.

Unit 9: Explores the foundations of computational complexity, introducing fundamental concepts and delving into various computational problems. Concepts of P and NP problems and NP-Completeness are discussed and illustrated with specific examples like Independent Set, Clique, and Vertex Cover problems.

Unit 10: Explores fundamental algorithm design techniques, covering approaches like approximation algorithms, randomized algorithms, and their practical applications. The unit includes a detailed examination of vertex cover problems, an introduction to randomized algorithms, and a focus on the randomized version of quicksort.

UNIT SUMMARY

- This unit begins by discussing the fundamental necessity of algorithms, emphasizing their importance in problem-solving and efficiency.
- Time cmplexity: The time required for an algorithm to complete.
- Space complexity: The amount of memory an algorithm uses.
- Computation complexity: The overall computational cost of an algorithm.
- Approximation: Finding near-optimal solutions when exact solutions are impractical.
- Brute-force methodology: Solving problems through exhaustive search.
- Backtracking: Systematically searching for a solution by trying partial solutions and then abandoning them if they are not suitable.
- Greedy algorithms: Locally optimal choices with hope of finding a global optimum.
- Dynamic Programming: Breaking problems into simpler subproblems and storing their solutions to avoid redundant computations.
- NP-Completeness: Complexity of problems for that no efficient solutions are known.
- Randomized Algorithms: Utilizing randomization to simplify and speed up algorithms.

- In addition, the unit introduces the organization of the book, providing an overview of the upcoming units and offering readers a glimpse into the structured journey ahead.

MULTIPLE CHOICE QUESTIONS

1. What serves as the backdrop for exploring the concept of algorithms in the provided description?
   a. A journey from Delhi to Varanasi
   b. A road trip from Varanasi to Delhi
   c. A flight from Mumbai to Chennai
   d. A train journey from Kolkata to Bangalore

2. In the described scenario of finding the shortest route from Varanasi to Delhi, what is emphasized as paramount?
   a. Maximizing the number of waypoints
   b. Minimizing the travel distance
   c. Exploring multiple routes
   d. Maximizing the travel time

3. Which of the following is NOT mentioned as a drawback of manually calculating distances for each path in the scenario?
   a. Time-consuming process
   b. Subjectivity in decision-making
   c. Lack of robust error handling
   d. Difficulty in dealing with numerous points

4. What term is used to define a systematic approach that transcends manual calculations in the provided description?
   a. Computation complexity
   b. Algorithm
   c. Parallelization
   d. Scalability

5. What is the purpose of approximation algorithms mentioned in the description?
   a. To provide exact solutions to complex problems
   b. To find solutions within a reasonable computational timeframe
   c. To introduce randomness in decision-making
   d. To optimize algorithms for parallel processing

6. Which factor is NOT considered in critical algorithm design and selection in the provided description?
   a. Space complexity
   b. Approximation
   c. Failure probability
   d. Network latency

7. Which algorithm design technique systematically explores all possible solutions until the correct one is identified?
    a. Backtracking
    b. Greedy algorithms
    c. Dynamic programming
    d. Brute-force methodology

8. Which algorithm design technique involves breaking down a complex problem into smaller, more manageable subproblems?
    a. Divide-and-Conquer
    b. NP-Completeness
    c. Randomized algorithms
    d. Backtracking

9. Which algorithm design technique operates by making locally optimal choices at each step?
    a. Dynamic programming
    b. Brute-force methodology
    c. Greedy algorithms
    d. Divide-and-Conquer

10. Which algorithm design technique dissects a complex problem into simpler overlapping subproblems?
    a. Divide-and-Conquer
    b. NP-Completeness
    c. Dynamic programming
    d. Backtracking

11. Which class of decision problems is deemed challenging due to the absence of efficient algorithms to solve them in polynomial time?
    a. NP-Completeness
    b. Randomized algorithms
    c. Approximation
    d. Divide-and-Conquer

12. Which algorithm design technique introduces randomness as a fundamental component in decision-making?
    a. NP-Completeness
    b. Divide-and-Conquer
    c. Randomized algorithms
    d. Backtracking

13. What is emphasized as critical for an algorithm in the context of real-world scenarios where data inconsistencies or unexpected events are common?
    a. Time complexity
    b. Space complexity
    c. Robustness and error handling
    d. Scalability

14. What is the primary focus of time complexity in algorithm evaluation?
    a. Memory utilization
    b. Time utilization
    c. Space utilization
    d. Resource utilization

15. Which factor is emphasized as critical, especially for mobile devices with limited memory capacity?
    a. Time complexity
    b. Space complexity
    c. Computation complexity
    d. Failure probability

Solution of MCQ:

1	2	3	4	5	6	7	8	9	10	11	12	13	14	15
b	b	c	b	b	d	d	a	c	c	a	c	c	b	b

KNOW MORE

Online courses/materials/resources [Accessed May 2024]

- https://www.geeksforgeeks.org/fundamentals-of-algorithms/
- https://github.com/TheAlgorithms
- https://nptel.ac.in/courses/106105157
- https://www.programming4beginners.com/tutorial-beginners-algorithms

REFERENCES

[1] Thomas H. Cormen, Charles E. Leiserson, Ronald L. Rivest, and Clifford Stein. 2009. Introduction to Algorithms, Third Edition (3rd. ed.). The MIT Press.

[2] Brassard Gilles and Bratley Paul. 1996. Fundamentals of Algorithmics, Prentice Hall Englewood Cliffs.

[3] Goodrich, Michael T. and Tamassia, Roberto (2015), "18.1.2 The Christofides Approximation Algorithm", Algorithm Design and Applications, Wiley, pp. 513–514.

[4] ChatGPT (Nov 14 version) [Large language model]. https://chat.openai.com/chat, 2024.

2 Analysis of Algorithms

UNIT SPECIFICS

This unit covers the following aspects:

- *Introduction to algorithm analysis*
- *Insertion sort*
- *Asymptotic notations*
- *Analysis of best, average, and worst-cases*

In this unit, we describe a comprehensive exploration of fundamental principles that underlie algorithmic efficiency. The unit will commence by introducing asymptotic notations, providing a concise and powerful framework for comparing the performance of algorithms. Additionally, we go over the study of average, worst, and best cases, which shed light on situations when algorithms perform well or poorly. We also go over the space complexity analysis, highlighting the critical interaction between memory utilisation and algorithmic efficiency. Finally, we use empirical analysis and real-world case studies to demonstrate the usefulness of algorithmic efficiency. The link given in the QR code provides supplementary material of this unit.

RATIONALE

The rationale of this unit on the analysis of algorithms is to explore the fundamental principles governing the efficiency and effectiveness of various algorithmic solutions. It aims to equip learners with a comprehensive understanding of asymptotic notations, worst-case and average-case analyses, and the complexities associated with specific algorithms. By delving into space complexity and empirical analysis, this unit provides practical tools for evaluating algorithms in real-world scenarios. Furthermore, it emphasises the significance of algorithm analysis in making informed decisions for designing efficient software solutions. Through case studies and specialized topics, learners will gain insights into the broader applications of algorithmic techniques.

PRE-REQUISITES

Basic understanding of data structures and linear algebra

UNIT OUTCOMES

The unit will deliver the following outcomes:

U2-O1: Learning the concept of algorithm analysis

U2-O2: Understanding asymptotic notations

U2-O3: Learn to analyse the computational complexities of algorithms

U2-O4: Understanding space complexity and practical applications

Unit-2 Outcomes	EXPECTED MAPPING WITH COURSE OUTCOMES (1- Weak Correlation; 2- Medium correlation; 3- Strong Correlation)				
	CO-1	CO-2	CO-3	CO-4	CO-5
U2-O1	3	3	2	2	2
U2-O2	3	3	2	2	2
U2-O3	1	3	2	2	2
U2-O4	1	3	2	2	2

2.1 Introduction to Analysis of the Algorithm

Algorithms are the fundamental building blocks of computation, providing systematic, step-by-step instructions for solving problems. To design effective algorithms, it is essential to understand the key characteristics that define their behavior and applicability. Analyzing an algorithm employs the prediction of its resources requirement. These resources may encompass memory, communication bandwidth, or computer hardware, but most often, our primary concern is the *computational time*. By evaluating multiple candidate algorithms for a given problem, we aim to pinpoint the most efficient one. While there may be more than one viable option, this analysis eliminates several inferior algorithms [1-2]. Before discussing algorithm analysis, it is imperative to develop the implementation mechanism of the algorithm. This model should include a representation of the technology resources and their associated costs.

The computational model for this book will be a generic single-processor Random-Access Machine (RAM). In this case, instructions are carried out sequentially—without any concurrent operations—and algorithms are implemented as computer programs. Although a detailed specification of RAM instructions and their prices may be achieved, the process would be time-consuming and provide little useful information for creating and analyzing algorithms. As a result, we need to find a balance to prevent abusing the RAM model. Sorting may be completed in one step, for instance, if a RAM has a sorting command. This scenario is imaginary because real computers do not have specialized instructions.

We match the architecture of the computers with our computational model to ensure practicality. The instructions that are frequently seen in real computers are included in the RAM model. These instructions include data manipulation (load, store, copy), arithmetic operations (addition, subtraction, multiplication, division, *etc.*), and control flow (conditional and unconditional branching, subroutine calls, and returns). These instructions take the same amount of time to complete. We have integers and floating-point numbers (for real-number representation) as our data types. Precision might be crucial in some situations, although it is not always the most important factor. We also assume a maximum value for each data word. For example, while using input size N and assuming that integers requires $c.\, log\ N$ bits for storage in memory, where c is a constant greater than 1. This requirement ensures that each word can adequately index single entry, and c should be a constant to prevent arbitrary growth of word size. This restriction prevents the unrealistic scenario where one word could hold a massive amount of data.

The computers encompass implicitly mentioned instructions, and these implicit instructions fall into a gray area in the RAM. For example, let us consider the term a^b. Can you solve the expression in constant time? The answer is no, as its calculation involves various instructions when a and b are floating values. However, in specific contexts, exponentiation can be considered a constant-time execution. Several computers perform a "*shift left*" instruction, whereas shifts the integer bits by b positions in constant time. In various cases, shifting the one position to the left $\simeq$ multiplying by a. Consequently, shifting b positions $\simeq$multiplying by a^b. Thus, the computers evaluate a^b in a constant time, shifting the integer 1 by b , provided that b does not exceed the bits count in a word. While it aim to clear of such ambiguous areas in RAM, we treat the computation of a^b requires constant time when b is positive and suitably small. We do not try to emulate the memory hierarchy present in modern systems in model. This indicates that we do not simulate virtual memory or caches.

Examining a basic procedure in a RAM model is challenging. Probability, combinatorics, numerical aptitude, and the recognition of the key in computation are some of the necessary mathematical tools. We need a technique to distill behavior of an algorithm into concise, comprehensible formulas because its behavior could change based on any combination of inputs. Although we often select to examine a given algorithm using a single-machine model, there are still many ways we might display the results of our work. We want an easy-to-understand and apply approach that focuses on the essential aspects of resource competition by an algorithm and stays away from confusion.

2.2 Insertion Sort

Consider a simple illustration of the insertion sort algorithm, a sorting technique grounded in comparisons. This algorithm works well for sorting a limited set of elements. This is more similar to the way teachers often arrange the examination copies. It involves sorting a collection of exam copies based on their marks or other relevant criteria. The process is comparable to sorting a deck of cards. Initially, a stack of exam copies is arranged downhill on a table. You start with an empty pile. You pick it up one copy at a time and set it in the proper position among the ones you have already sorted. To find the correct position, you compare the selected copy with the copies already in your sorted pile, as illustrated in Figure 2.1. When doing this comparison, which is often done from right to left, ensure the copy is positioned correctly in relation to the sorting criterion (e.g., highest grade to lowest grade). You continue doing this until all of the exam copies have been reviewed. At the completion of this process, you obtain a stack of sorted exam copies. The top copies from the first unsorted stack on the table were originally the sorted copies you hold.

Insertion sort is a good choice for small collections. It is a simple algorithm that is easy to use. However, more complex sorting methods may be more efficient for large data sets. Insertion sort produces the final sorted array one item at a time by repeatedly choosing one element from the unsorted portion of array and inserting it into the sorted portion of the array at the proper location. The different insertion sort steps are as follows:

i) The sorting section begins at the index 1 , the second entry in the unsorted array.

ii) The current element and the previous one should be compared. Replace them if they are not in the correct sorting order.

iii) Once the element is in right place, move it back through the sorted section of array.

iv) Move to the next element (Index 2) and repeat the steps *ii* and *iii* until the entire array is sorted.

Figure 2.1: *Examination copies sorting (*source: AI tool Microsoft BIng).*

The insertion sort pseudocode is shown as a function called **InsertionSort** (array Arr) that considers $Arr[1:n]$ containing the array of size n to be sorted. Arr: $length$ indicates that there are n elements in Arr. This algorithm sorts in-place, rearranging them inside array Arr. After the procedure is finished, the sorted output sequence is stored in the input array Arr.

Insertion Sort (array *Arr*):

```
for i = 1 to Arr(2, len(Arr)):
    current_element = Arr[i]
    j = i − 1
    while j > 0 & current_element < Arr[j]
        Arr[j + 1] = Arr[j]
        j = j − 1
    Arr[j + 1] = current_element
```

Let us walk through the process of applying the insertion sort algorithm to the array $Arr = [8,2,4,9,3,6]$. We start with an empty sorted portion and the unsorted portion, *i.e.*, $Sorted = [\,], Unsorted = [8,2,4,9,3,6]$. We take the first element, which is 8, from the unsorted portion. Compare it with the elements in the sorted portion (which is currently empty). Since it is the smallest in the sorted list, it becomes the new sorted portion. The updated states: $Sorted = [8], Unsorted = [2,4,9,3,6]$. Take the next element (2) from the unsorted portion. Compare it with the elements in the sorted portion ([8]). 2 is smaller than 8, so we shift 8 to the right. Insert 2 at the correct position in the sorted portion. Updated states: $Sorted = [2,8], Unsorted = [4,9,3,6]$. Take the next element (4) from the unsorted portion. Compare it with the elements in the sorted portion ([2,8]). 4 is smaller than 8, so we shift 8 to the right. 4 is not smaller than 2, so no need to shift and updated states: $Sorted = [2,4,8], Unsorted = [9,3,6]$.

This process respects all the elements. The sorted portion now contains the sorted array, *Sorted*: [2,3,4,6,8,9]. The complete process of this example is shown in Figure 2.2.

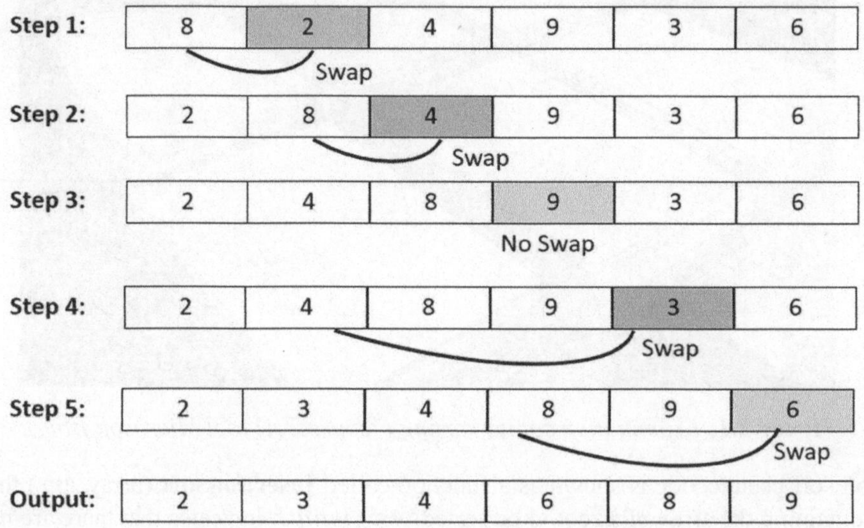

Figure 2.2: *Illustration of Insertion sort $Arr = [8,2,4,9,3,6]$. The indices of the array are $[1,2,3,4,5,6]$ for the respective rectangles and the values are shown within the rectangles. In each step, the key extracted from Arr[i] is held in the gray rectangle. Next, using the test in line, this key is compared against the element in the shaded rectangles to its left (line 6). Arc lines illustrate the movement of values one position right (line 7). Output: Exhibits the final sorted array, i.e., $Arr = [2,3,4,6,8,9]$.*

Figure 2.2 depicts the steps of this algorithm using $Arr = [8,2,4,9,3,6]$. The index i signifies the "current copy" being inserted. At the outset of each step within the for loop, indexed by i, the subarray comprising elements $Arr[1: i-1]$ represents the presently sorted array, while the remaining subarray $Arr[i: n]$ corresponds to the stack of copies still on the table. Essentially, in $Arr[1: i-1]$ the elements originally located in position 1 through i, now arranged in a sorted manner. We formally express these characteristics of $Arr[1: i-1]$ as a loop invariant [1]. At the start of every step in the for loop, the subarray $Arr[1: i-1]$ encompasses the elements initially found in $Arr[1: i-1]$, now organized in a sorted manner. The employment of loop invariants aids in comprehending the validity of an algorithm. It necessitates demonstrating three key conditions of loop invariant:

Condition 1 (Initialization)**:** This condition holds before the initial iteration of the loop.

Condition 2 (Maintenance)**:** If the condition is true before a loop iteration, it will persist before the subsequent iteration.

Condition 3 (Termination)**:** Upon the conclusion of the **for** loop, such invariant furnishes an important feature that aids in demonstrating the correctness of the algorithm.

The loop invariant is true before the loop iterates twice if the first two conditions are satisfied. It is important to note that, in addition to the loop invariant itself, we might choose to depend on known facts to verify its persistence prior to each iteration. This is similar to mathematical induction in that it relies on the establishment of a base condition followed by an inductive stage to demonstrate validity of a property. In this scenario, proving the invariant is valid prior to the 1st iteration is similar to base condition and it persists during subsequent iterations is similar to the inductive stage. It is crucial to remember that the third criterion is the foundation for proving correctness. Usually, we combine the condition leading to the end of the loop with the loop invariant. This termination condition is different from how mathematical induction is often applied, which involves continuing the inductive phase indefinitely. As soon as the loop breaks, we conclude the induction.

Now we have seen how the insertion sort operates, let us look at how these characteristics relate to the insertion sort algorithm. Let us utilise the example array $Arr[2,4,3,6,8,9]$ to apply the loop invariant to the Insertion sort algorithm.

Condition 1: We initiate insertion sort by demonstrating the validity of the loop invariant at onset of initial iteration, where $i = 2$. In this case, the subarray $Arr[1: i - 1]$ comprises only the element $Arr[1]$, which is essentially the original element in $Arr[1]$. Furthermore, it is evident that this subarray is inherently sorted, affirming the preservation of loop invariant preceding *initial iteration.*

Condition 2: Next, we address 2nd condition, where ∀ iterations *loop invariant should be maintained.* In simpler terms, the operations of the **for** loop involves shifting elements, and so forth, one position to the right, until it identifies the correct position for $Arr[i]$. Subsequently, it inserts the value of $Arr[i]$ at that position. The subarray now contains the elements ∈ $Arr[1: i - 1]$, following sorted order. The increment of i subsequent iteration of the loop ensures preservation of the loop invariant. While a more formal treatment of the 2nd condition stating and demonstrating the loop invariant of **while** loop, we do not opt to discuss such formalism. Instead, we incline with informal analysis to affirm that 2nd condition remains valid in conjunction with the outer loop.

Condition 3: Lastly, let us analyze what occurs upon the termination of the loop. The condition that leads to the termination of the for loop is that $j > A{:}\,length$ equals n. Since each iteration increments j by 1, it follows that $j = n + 1$ when the loop terminates. By substituting $n + 1$ for j in the context of the loop invariant, we affirm that the subarray $Arr[1: n]$ comprises the elements originally in $Arr[1: n]$, now arranged in a sorted order. Recognizing that the subarray $Arr[1: n]$ essentially represents the entire array, we can confidently conclude that the entire array is indeed sorted. Consequently, we establish the correctness of the algorithm. We utilize this technique of employing loop invariants to demonstrate correctness of algorithms not only in this unit but also in subsequent units.

Analyzing the insertion sort

The time duration to execute the insertion sort operation based-upon the input data: organising 1000 numbers takes more than 10. Further, depending on the initial degree of sorting of the two input sequences, insertion sort may have varying time requirements. Because the time complexity of algorithm usually grows in accordance with the input size; thus, runtime of a programme is typically described as a function of the size of the input.

The appropriate metric to determine the input relies on the given problem. The input items count, or size of array in the case of sorting, is the most logical measure in scenarios such as the computation of Fourier transforms. The efficient and accurate method to determine the size of an input for operations like multiplying two numbers, however, is to count the bits required to depict input in standard binary form. Using two distinct values rather than one to represent input size makes more sense in certain situations. For example, one can use the number of vertices and edges in a graph to calculate size of graph as an input to algorithm.

The length of time the algorithm takes to run on a given input depends on how many primitive operations or steps it must perform. To ensure machine independence for the time being, we define a step as follows: the time it takes to perform operation ∀ lines of the procedure are fixed. Even though one line may take longer to execute than another, we assume that the execution of the line always requires a constant time. This perspective aligns with the model and depicts the mechanism of running the pseudocode on the vast majority of real-world computers. Let us utilise a simple formula to generate a numerical estimate of the Insertion Sort running time in order to obtain a more precise and concise estimate. For every $j \in \{2,3,4 \cdots, n\}$, n is defined as $length\ of\ Arr$, we define $iter_j$ as the count of iterations and while loop test in 6th line undergoes $\forall\ j$ value. In contrast to the loop body, a for or while loop runs the test once more when it ends under normal circumstances—that is, as a result of the loop header test. It is considered that comments do not require any time investment because they do not represent executable sentences.

The running time of an algorithm, as shown in Table 2.1, is the sum of the running times for all statements executed and $ci(n)$ to the overall running time. A statement that requires ci steps to execute and is executed n times that contributes to this running time. To compute $T(n)$, the running time of Insertion sort on an input of n values, we sum the products of the cost and times columns, obtaining the expression as:

$$T(n) = c1(n) + c2(n-1) + c3(n-1) + c4\left(\sum_{j=2}^{n} iter_j\right)$$

$$+c5\left(\sum_{j=2}^{n} iter_j - 1\right) + c6\left(\sum_{j=2}^{n} iter_j - 1\right) + c7(n-1)$$

For a given input size, the runtime of an algorithm can vary as per the input. To illustrate, ley us consider the Insertion sort algorithm, where the **best-case scenario**, when array is sorted. In this case, $\forall\ j$ in the range of 2 to n, we observe that $A[i] > key$ in line 5 when i initially equals $j-1$. Consequently, $iter_j$ is equal to 1 for j ranging from 2 to n. It leads to best-case as follows: $T(n) = c1(n) + c2(n - 1) + c3(n-1) + c7(n-1)$.

Table 2.1: Step-by-step analysis of the insertion sort.

InsertionSort (array *Arr*)	**Cost**	**Times**
for i **in range** $n(2, len(Arr))$:	$c1$	n
$current\_element = Arr[i]$	$c2$	$n-1$
$j = i - 1$	$c3$	$n-1$
# Move elements ...current_element,	0	$n-1$
# one position ahead	0	$n-1$
while $j > 0$ *and* $current\_element < Arr[j]$:	$c4$	$\sum_{j=2}^{n} iter_j$
$Arr[j+1] = Arr[j]$	$c5$	$\sum_{j=2}^{n} iter_j - 1$
$j = j - 1$	$c6$	$\sum_{j=2}^{n} iter_j - 1$
$Arr[j+1] = current\_element$	$c7$	$n-1$

The formula for the running time is c times a constant x raised to the power of y, x & y are given by expenses in the statement ci. As such, it takes the form of a function of n as $(xn + y)$. Worst-case situation occurs if Arr is placed in descending sorted, or descending order. This means that every element in $Arr[j]$ must be compared to all the element sorted in subarray $Arr[1{:}j-1]$, resulting in $iter_j$ being equal to j for j in the range of 2 to n. Further, the following expression is obtained:

$$\sum_{j=2}^{n} iter_j = \frac{n(n+1)}{2} - 1$$

The worst case is:

$$T(n) = c1(n) + c2(n-1) + c3(n-1) + c4\left(\frac{n(n+1)}{2} - 1\right)$$
$$+c5\left(\frac{n(n-1)}{2}\right) + c6\left(\frac{n(n-1)}{2}\right) + c7(n-1),$$
$$T(n) = 0.5(c4 + c5 + c6)n^2 + 0.5(2(c1 + c2 + c3 + c7)$$
$$+(c4 - c5 - c6))n - (c2 + c3 + c4 + c7).$$

The worst case can be represented by quadratic function using n, denoted as $xn^2 + yn + z$, where x, y, and z are constants determined by the statement costs (ci). For an input, the execution of an algorithm is constant in situations. But interesting '*randomised*' algorithms that perform differently with a fixed input will appear in later chapters.

Worst and average-cases: We thoroughly examined both the worst-case scenario—where the input Arr in reverse order—and best-condition scenario—where Arr had already been sorted—in our examination of insertion sort. However, for most of this book, we will focus on determining the worst-case—*i.e.*, highest time an algorithm may take for a given size of input. We offer three strong arguments in favour of this viewpoint:

i. The worst-case running time of an algorithm acts as a higher bound on the amount of time it takes to process any given input. This information ensures that the algorithm never run longer than the given time. This removes the need to estimate the running for different input size.

ii. In some cases, the worst case for an algorithm is encountered rather frequently. For example, while looking up specific information in a database, the worst-case situation for the search algorithm frequently occurs when the information is missing from the database. There may be times when searching for missing data is necessary in some applications.

iii. The **average case** scenario often exhibits similar computational complexity to the worst-case scenario. For instance, if we were to randomly select n numbers and employ the insertion sort algorithm, we must determine the appropriate position in subarray $A[1{:}j-1]$ for adding an item in $A[j]$. On average, roughly $1/2$ of item in $A[1{:}j-1]$ will be $< A[j]$, while the other $1/2$ will be higher. Consequently, we tend to inspect approximately half of the subarray $A[1{:}j-1]$, leading to an average time complexity of $iter_j = j/2$. Therefore, the resultant average-case running time demonstrates a quadratic relationship with input.

We also focus on determining average execution time in certain situations. As a recurring theme, this book evaluates multiple algorithms using the probabilistic analysis technique. It is crucial to remember that average-case analysis has its limitations because it is not always clear what is an average input on a given circumstance. Sometimes we assume inputs have the same probability of appearing, regardless of their size. Even though this assumption might not always hold true in practice, there are situations in which we can utilize a randomised algorithm that contains random choices, to enable probabilistic analysis for providing an estimate of the running time.

2.3 Growth of Function and Asymptotic Analysis

Growth of Function refers to how quickly the value of function increases as its input (often denoted as n) becomes larger and larger. In the context of algorithms, this concept is important for analyzing and comparing the efficiency of different algorithms. There are several common classifications for the growth of functions, some are discussed as follows:

i. *Constant Time:* The runtime is constant, regardless of the size of the input. This means that the execution time does not depend on the size of the data it is processing.

ii. *$\log n$ (Logarithmic Time):* The runtime increases logarithmically with the size of the input. Algorithms with logarithmic time complexity are considered very efficient, especially as the input size grows.

iii. *n (Linear Time):* The runtime of the function grows linearly in the input size. This implies that the runtime will approximately double if the input size doubles.

iv. *$n \log n$ (Linearithmic Time):* Divide-and-conquer algorithms, such as many effective sorting algorithms (e.g., Merge Sort, Quick Sort), frequently exhibit this behaviour. Compared to linear growth, the runtime grows more slowly than quadratic growth.

v. *n^2 (Quadratic Time):* The runtime of function increases proportionally to the square of the input size. This is common in algorithms with nested loops.

vi. *n^k (Polynomial Time):* This represents a more general class of algorithms where the runtime grows as a power of the input size. When 'k' is larger, the algorithm is less efficient.

vii. *2^n (Exponential Time):* The runtime doubles with each additional element in the input. Algorithms with exponential time complexity are generally considered inefficient and impractical for large inputs.

viii. *2! (Factorial Time):* The runtime increases in direct proportion to the size of the input. This is extremely inefficient and is typically only used for minor inputs due to its rapid expansion.

We can determine how a function behaves as the input size increases by examining its growth. In other words, it makes it easier to choose the best option for a particular activity and enables us to make informed decisions about performance trade-offs. The behaviour of common functions on different input sizes is depicted in Table 2.2.

Table 2.2 : Rate of growth of common function over varying input sizes.

Input size (n)	**Common functions**						
	n	$\log n$	$n \log n$	n^2	$n^k (k = 5)$	2^n	$n!$
5	5	0.69	3.5	25	5^5	32	120
10	10	1	10	10^2	10^5	1024	3.6×10^6
100	100	2	20	10^4	10^{10}	1.26×10^{30}	9.3×10^{157}
1000	1000	3	30	10^6	10^{15}	1.07×10^{301}	-
10000	10000	4	20	10^8	10^{20}	-	-

2.4 Asymptotic Analysis

Asymptotic notation is a significant idea in computer science and algorithm analysis because it gives a mechanism to evaluate and compare the efficiency of algorithms in a way that is independent of the exact hardware or software platform on which they are implemented. It gives us a basic idea of how an algorithm performs as the size of the input increases and gives us information on how the algorithm will scale to larger datasets. The following considerations clarify the significance of the asymptotic notation:

i. **Platform independence:** The behaviour of algorithms as the input size gets closer to infinity is the main subject of asymptotic notation. In other words, it offers a high-level, cross-platform perspective on the effectiveness of an algorithm. It is an effective tool for theoretical study. It compares algorithms without getting exact details of specific hardware.

ii. **Simplicity and abstraction:** Asymptotic notation simplifies complex analyses by focusing on the dominant term(s) in time or space complexities of an algorithm. This abstraction helps us understand the fundamental efficiency characteristics of an algorithm without getting low-level implementation details.

iii. **Algorithm selection:** Comprehending the asymptotic performance of various algorithms can be crucial when selecting one to tackle a certain task. It enables us to determine with certainty which method is most likely to be effective given the magnitude of the challenge.

iv. **Predicting scalability:** Asymptotic notation helps us predict how an algorithm behaves with larger datasets. This is important in applications where performance at scale is a primary concern, such as in big data processing or large-scale simulations.

Let us describe the practical application of asymptotic notation. This involves applying mathematical notation to describe how the performance of algorithms changes as the **size of the input data increases**. By employing tools like **Big O notation (O)**, we can precisely characterize the upper bounds of an algorithm time complexity. This provides a valuable framework for assessing the scalability and efficiency of algorithms, enabling us to make informed decisions about their suitability for specific tasks. Additionally, asymptotic notation helps in identifying the most influential terms in complex algorithms, allowing us to focus on the key factors that determine their overall computational behavior. Let us describe the mechanism of using asymptotic notation:

i. **Analyzing time complexity:** When examining the time complexity of an algorithm, we concentrate on the way the running time increases in relation to the size of the input. Big O notation (O), which gives an upper bound on the worst-case temporal complexity.

ii. **Understanding space complexity:** Similar to time complexity, we can analyze an space complexity of algorithm, which refers to the amount of memory required by the algorithm as a function of the input size. Space complexity is also expressed using Big O notation.

iii. **Comparing algorithms:** Asymptotic notation allows us to compare algorithms and make informed decisions about which algorithm is better suited for a specific problem. For example, an algorithm with $O(n^2)$ time complexity is less efficient than one with $O(n)$ time complexity for large input sizes.

iv. **Identifying dominant terms:** In complex algorithms, there may be multiple terms contributing to the overall complexity. Asymptotic notation helps us identify the dominant term, which determines the overall behavior of the algorithm.

Asymptotic notation is a powerful tool for analyzing and comparing algorithms. It provides a framework for understanding their fundamental performance characteristics and helps guide the selection of algorithms for specific tasks. There are several commonly used asymptotic notations, including:

- **Big O notation (O):** This serves as an upper limit on an the time complexity of algorithm. The worst-case scenario for the amount of time an algorithm takes complete the execution is a function of input size. If the time complexity of an algorithm is $O(n)$, it means the running time grows linearly with the size of the input.
- **Omega notation (Ω):** This represents a lower bound on complexity of algorithms. The best-case scenario for the amount of time needed for an algorithm to complete the execution as a function of input size.
- **Theta notation (Θ):** This provides a tight bound on the complexity of an algorithm. It describes both the upper and lower bounds on the time complexity, indicating that the running time is bounded within a certain range.
- ***Little o notation (o):*** *This indicates a non-asymptotically tight upper bound. It describes* functions that grow strictly faster than a given function.
- **Little omega notation (ω):** This denotes a non-asymptotically tight lower bound. It describes functions that grow strictly slower than a given function.

These notations are employed in the analysis of algorithm performance characteristics and in the efficiency comparison of various algorithms. For example, an algorithm with a time complexity of $O(n^3)$ is considered less efficient than one with a time complexity of $O(n)$, because the latter grows more slowly with increasing input size.

2.4.1 Big O (O) Notation

Big O notation (simply "O notation") is a type of mathematical notation used in computer science to express the worst-case or upper bound on time complexity. It is a asymptotic notation of an algorithm, which is used to examine how well algorithms function as the size of their input increases. Big O notation represents the maximum amount of time (in terms of computational steps) that an algorithm takes to perform its task, assuming the worst-case scenario. It is used to express time complexity as a function of the input size. The "O" represents "order of," and it expresses how execution time varies with the size of its input. The characteristics of Big O notation are:

i. **Upper bound:** Big O notation gives an upper bound on the execution time of an algorithm. It ensures that the algorithm would not perform worse than the specified bound by representing the worst-case situation.

ii. **Simplification:** Big O notation simplifies the analysis of an algorithm time complexity by focusing on the most significant or dominant term(s) in the function, while ignoring constant factors and lower-order terms. This abstraction allows for a high-level assessment of efficiency.

iii. **General comparison:** The ability to compare algorithms using Big O notation facilitates the process of identifying the most efficient approach for a particular issue size. For high input sizes an algorithm with an $O(n)$ time complexity is typically more efficient than one with an $O(n^2)$ time complexity.

Big O notation is a fundamental tool in algorithm analysis and helps guide decisions in algorithm selection, allowing developers and engineers to choose the most efficient algorithms for specific tasks and understand how algorithms will perform as input sizes grow. In mathematical terms, Big O notation (often denoted as $O(g(n))$ is used to describe the **upper bound or worst-case** behavior of a function $f(n)$, when $n \to \infty$. Formally, we say $f(n)$ is $O(g(n))$ iff there exist positive constants c and n_0 such that:

$$0 \leq f(n) \leq cg(n), \quad \forall n \geq n_0.$$

This means that for larger n (beyond a certain threshold n_0), the function $f(n)$ is bounded above by a constant multiple of $g(n)$. In other words, $g(n)$ acts as an asymptotic upper bound of $f(n)$, as illustrated in Figure 2.3.

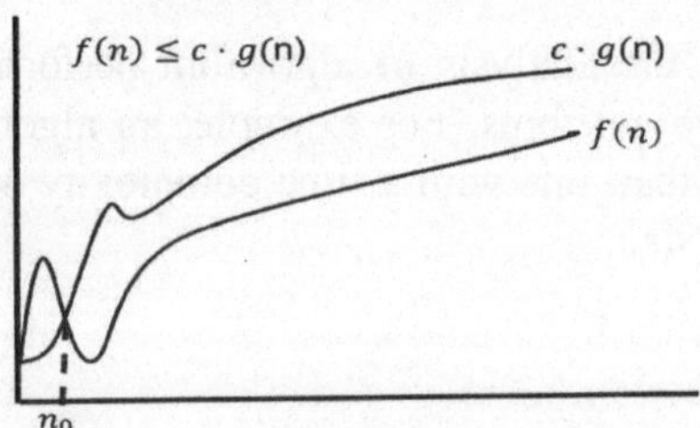

Figure 2.3: Big O notation provides an upper limit, bounded by c. We denote $f(n) = O(g(n))$ if $\exists n_0$ and c such that $\forall n \geq n_0$, the value of $f(n)$ always remains at or below $c.g(n)$.

The components of the the Big O notation are described as follows:

- **f(n):** The function whose time complexity we are analyzing.
- **g(n):** A reference function or upper bound that describes the growth rate of f(n) as n approaches infinity.
- **c:** A positive constant. It represents a scaling factor that ensures g(n) is an upper bound of $f(n)$ after a certain point.
- $\boldsymbol{n_0}$: The threshold value beyond which f(n) is bounded by $cg(n)$.

In simpler terms, **Big O** notation provides an upper limit for how fast a function grows, and it helps us understand the worst-case behavior of algorithms in terms of time complexity. For example, if we say $f(n)$ is $O(n^2)$, it means sufficiently large n, $f(n)$ will not grow faster than some constant times n^2. The actual growth rate of $f(n)$ may be slower than n^2, but it will not exceed quadratic growth.

A few common examples to illustrate Big O notation:

Example 1 [Constant time complexity (O(1))]:

In this case, no matter how large the input n is, the function always takes a constant amount of time to complete. The function is independent of the input size. Therefore, f(n) is O(1). We can say $f(n) \leq c \cdot 1, \forall n \geq n_0$ (where c = 5 and n_0 can be any positive integer).

Example 2 [Linear time complexity (O(n))]:

$$f(n) = 3n + 2$$

In this case, as n increases, time taken by the function increases linearly. The dominant term is n, so we say f(n) is O(n). We can deduce following: $f(n) \leq c \cdot n, \forall n \geq n_0$ (where c can be any positive constant and n_0 can be any positive integer).

Example 3 [Quadratic time complexity $(O(n^2))$]:

$$f(n) = 2n^2 + 3n + 1$$

As n increases, the time taken by the function increases quadratically. The dominant term is n^2, so we say $f(n) = O(n^2)$. We can say $f(n) \leq c \cdot n^2, \forall n \geq n_0$.

Example 4 [Logarithmic time complexity $(O(log\ n))$]:

$$f(n) = log_2(n)$$

In this case, the time of the function grows logarithmically for the input of size n. This often occurs in algorithms that divide the input in half at each step, such as binary search. We can say $f(n) \leq c \cdot log_2(n), \forall n \geq n_0$.

These examples demonstrate how Big O notation provides a concise way to express a growth rate of function in terms of the magnitude of its input. It enables us to compare several algorithms and determine how well they will function as the input data grows.

2.4.2 Omega (Ω) Notation

Omega notation (Ω) is another asymptotic notation that is closely connected to Big O notation and is used in computer science. As part of asymptotic notation, Ω notation describes the lower bound or best-case time complexity of an algorithm in a manner similar to Big O. By revealing the lowest time an algorithm will require in the best-case scenario as the size of the input rises, it enhances Big O. It is expressed as $f(n)$ in Ω notation: as $\Omega(g(n))$ if there exist positive constants c and n_0 (as shown in Figure 2.4) such that:

$$0 \leq c \cdot g(n) \leq f(n), \forall n \geq n_0$$

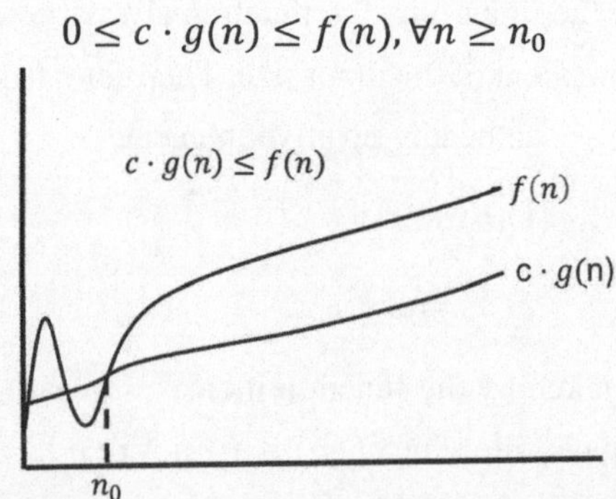

Figure 2.4: Asymptotic notation, denoted by Ω, establishes a lower bound for a function with respect to a constant factor. Specifically, we express $f(n) \geq \Omega(g(n))$ if there exist positive n_0 and c such that, $\forall n \geq n_0$, $f(n)$ consistently equals/exceeds $c \cdot g(n)$.

Ω notation, therefore, **focuses on the lower limits** of how efficiently an algorithm can perform. It answers the question: "*how well the algorithm can do in the best-case scenario?*" The key aspects of the Ω notation include:

i. **Best-case scenario:** Ω notation captures a best-case scenario for the lower bound of running time for an algorithm. It offers an assurance that the algorithm would not outperform the specified lower bound.

ii. **Simplification:** Similar to Big O Omega notation simplifies the analysis for the time complexity of an algorithm by emphasizing the most significant terms in the function, disregarding constant factors and lower-order terms. This abstraction allows for a high-level evaluation of efficiency in the best-case context.

iii. **General comparison:** Omega notation facilitates comparisons between algorithms, helping in the determination of which algorithm is more efficient in the best-case scenario for a given problem size. For example, an algorithm with a best-case time complexity of $\Omega(n^2)$ is more efficient than one with $\Omega(n^3)$ for large input sizes.

Together with Big O notation, omega notation helps in a thorough comprehension of the performance features of an algorithm. When combined, they offer a fair assessment that covers both worst- and best-case situations, assisting developers in selecting the optimum algorithm for a given task depending on its demands and input sizes. In computer science, it refers specifically to a mathematical term that is used to characterise the lower bound or best-case scenario for growth rate of a function, while analysing algorithms. This notation offers a means of expressing the growth rate of a function with an emphasis on the minimum growth rate as the input size approaches infinity.

The components of the the Ω notation are described as follows:

- $f(n)$: Represents the function describing the time complexity of an algorithm.
- $g(n)$: Represents a specific function that serves as a lower bound or best-case scenario for the growth rate of $f(n)$.
- c: A positive constant that signifies that $f(n)$ is at least as large as $f(n)$ up to a constant factor.
- n_0: A threshold value indicating that the relationship holds for all input sizes greater than or equal to n_0.
- In simpler terms, $\Omega(g(n))$ signifies that the time complexity of the algorithm represented by $f(n)$ grows at least as fast as $g(n)$, up to a constant factor.
- For example, if an algorithm has a time complexity of $\Omega(n)$, it implies that the performance is linear or better in the best-case scenario of an algorithm. The function $g(n)$ serves as a lower limit for the growth rate of $f(n)$.
- Ω notation is used in conjunction with Big O notation, which offers an upper bound. When combined, they provide a thorough grasp of how an algorithm performs as the size of the input rises.

Some examples of Ω notation are given as:

Example 5 [Constant time complexity ($O(1)$)]:

$$f(n) = 5 \; and \; g(n) = 1$$

$f(n)$ is $\Omega(g(n))$ because $f(n)$ is always greater than or equal to a positive constant multiple of $g(n)$. We can choose $c = 5$ and $n_0 = 1$.

Example 6 [Linear function]:

$$f(n) = 3n + 2 \; and \; g(n) = n$$

$f(n)$ is $\Omega(g(n))$ because for any constant c (e.g., $c = 1$), there is a value that n_0 (e.g., $n_0 = 2$), where $c \cdot g(n) \leq f(n), \forall n \geq n_0$.

Example 7 [Quadratic function]:

$$f(n) = 2n^2 + 3n + 1 \; and \; g(n) = n^2$$

$f(n)$ is $\Omega(g(n))$ because for any constant c (e.g., $c = 1$), there is a value that n_0 (e.g., $n_0 = 1$) such that $c \cdot g(n) \leq f(n), \forall n \geq n_0$.

Example 8 [Logarithmic function]:

$$f(n) = log_2 n + 3 \text{ and } g(n) = log_2 n$$

$f(n)$ is $\Omega(g(n))$ because for any constant c ($e.g., c = 1$), there is a value that n_0 ($e.g., n_0 = 1$) such that $c \cdot g(n) \leq f(n), \forall n \geq n_0$.

These examples demonstrate scenarios where $f(n)$ is at least as large as a positive constant multiple of $g(n)$, where n is sufficiently large. The key is to find appropriate constants c and n_0 that satisfy the definition of $\Omega(g(n))$.

2.4.3 Theta (Θ) Notation

Theta (Θ) notation, like Big O notation, is a component of the asymptotic notation that computer scientists use to evaluate how well algorithms work. Theta notation is more accurate than Big O in terms of providing an upper bound on the worst-case time complexity. It provides a narrow range where the performance of algorithm falls inside upper and lower constraint on the execution time. In the context of Θ notation following points can be given:

i. **Definition:** The time complexity of an algorithm is denoted as $\Theta(g(n))$ if there exist positive constants c_1, c_2 and n_0 such that $0 \leq c_1 g(n) \leq f(n) \leq c_2 g(n), \forall n \geq n_0$.

ii. **Upper bound and lower bound:** $\Theta(g(n))$ provides a dual bound by specifying that the time complexity of algorithm is at least $c_1 g(n)$ and at most $c_2 g(n)$ for sufficiently large input sizes.

iii. **Tight range:** The use of Θ notation shows that the time complexity of algorithm is accurately described by $g(n)$, and there is a tight range within which the actual running time of the algorithm fluctuates.

iv. **Simplifying analysis:** Similar to Big O notation, Θ concentrates on the most important or dominating term(s), notation makes the examination of time complexity for an algorithm easier. However, Θ goes by specifying upper and lower bounds.

To be more precise, notation offers both upper and lower bounds, whereas Big O notation just specifies an upper limitation on the running time. This makes notation especially helpful when describing the narrow range that the efficiency of algorithm falls inside since it enables a more detailed understanding of the performance characteristics. Another mathematical notation used in computer science to express the tight bound on a function growth rate is theta (Θ) notation. This notation is usually employed in the context of algorithm analysis. It offers a means of expressing the upper and lower bounds as well as a range of growth is bounded within boundries. $f(n) = \Theta(g(n))$ if there exist positive constants c_1, c_2, and n_0 such that $0 \leq c_1 g(n) \leq f(n) \leq c_2 g(n)$, $\forall n \geq n_0$, as shown in Figure 2.5.

This definition essentially states that $f(n)$ grows at the same rate as $g(n)$ within a constant factor for sufficiently large input sizes. The breakdown of Θ notation is defined as follows:

- $f(n)$: The function representing the time complexity of an algorithm.

- $g(n)$: Both upper and lower bounds on the growth rate are represented by the function.
- c_1, c_2: Positive constants.
- n_0: A threshold value, indicating that the relationship holds for all input sizes greater than or equal to n_0.

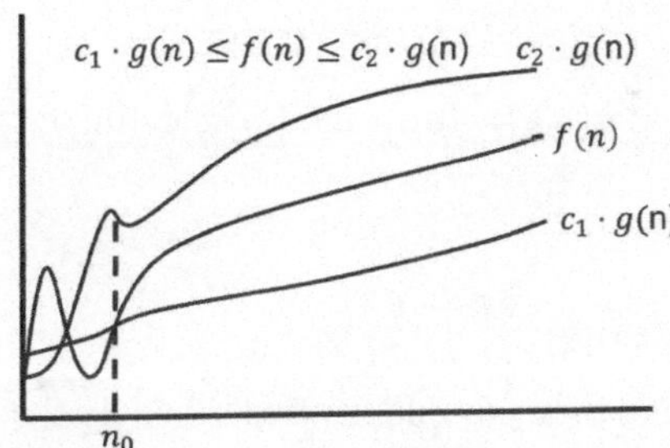

Figure 2.5: Θ notation places a function within constant factors. We express $f(n)$ as $\Theta(g(n))$ if there exist positive constants $n_0,\ c_1,\ and\ c_2$ such that $\forall n \geq n_0$, the function $f(n)$ consistently falls between $c_1 g(n)$ and $c_2 g(n)$.

In simpler terms, $\Theta(g(n))$ denotes time complexity is tightly bound by $g(n)$ for large enough input sizes, up to constant factors. It signifies that the performance of the algorithm matches the growth rate of $g(n)$ asymptotically. For example, if $\Theta(n)$ is the time complexity, it indicates that the growth rate of the algorithm is linear, where the real running time is exactly related to the input size, and that the upper and lower bounds are proportionate to n. Θ notation is useful for providing a precise characterization of an algorithm behavior, indicating a specific range for describing the efficiency. It complements both big O and Omega notations to offer a more comprehensive view for asymptotic performance of algorithm.

Let us consider a few more examples to illustrate Theta (Θ) notation.

Example 9 [Linear time complexity]:

Suppose we have an algorithm with the time complexity function:

$$f(n) = 4n + 2$$

In this case, we can choose $g(n) = n$ and $h(n) = n$. Now, Let us find constants c_1 and c_2 such that $c_1 n \leq 4n + 2 \leq c_2 n$. Choosing $c_1 = 1$ and $c_2 = 5$, we find $f(n) = \Theta(n)$.

Example 10 [Constant time complexity]:

Consider an algorithm with constant time complexity:

$$f(n) = 7$$

In this case, we can choose $g(n) = 1$ and $h(n) = 1$. The constants c_1 and c_2 are not critical since the function is constant. Therefore, $f(n) = \Theta(1)$.

Example 11 [Logarithmic time complexity]:

Logarithmic time complexity:

$$f(n) = 2\ log_2(n) + 3$$

We can choose $g(n) = log_2(n)$ and $h(n) = log_2(n)$. By selecting $c_1 = 1$ and $c_2 = 5$, we find that $f(n) = \Theta(log_2(n))$.

Example 12 [Quadratic time complexity]:

Suppose we have an algorithm with a time complexity described by the function:

$$f(n) = 3n^2 + 3n + 1$$

We want to express the complexity using Θ notation. We need to find functions $g(n)$ and $h(n)$ such that $c_1 g(n) \leq f(n) \leq c_2 h(n)$. For simplicity, let us consider the quadratic term $3n^2$ in our function. We can choose $g(n) = n^2$ and $h(n) = n^2$. We need to find positive constants c_1 and c_2 such that:

$$c_1 n^2 \leq 3n^2 + 2n + 1 \leq c_2 n^2$$

Let us choose $c_1 = 1$ and $c_2 = 5$. Now, we need to find a threshold n_0 such that the inequalities hold $\forall n \geq n_0$. For the lower bound $n^2 \leq 3n^2 + 2n + 1$. This is true $\forall n \geq 1$ because $n^2 \leq$ the given expression. For the upper bound $3n^2 + 2n + 1 \leq 5n^2$. This is true $\forall n \geq 1$ as well.

Whether linear, constant, or logarithmic, Theta notation helps describe the asymptotic behavior of the algorithm within a specific range as the input size increases.

Theorem 1 For any two functions $f(n)\ and\ g(n)$, the equality $f(n) = \Theta(g(n))$ holds iff $f(n) = O(g(n))$ and $f(n) = \Omega(g(n))$ [2].

Proof: The statement $f(n) = \Theta(g(n))$ is equivalent to stating that there exist positive constants $c_1, c_2, and\ n_0$ such that $\forall n \geq n_0,\ c_1 g(n) \leq f(n) \leq c_2 g(n)$.

Let us prove the equivalence:

- Direction (⇒): If $f(n) = \Theta(g(n))$, then there exist positive constants $c_1, c_2, and\ n_0$ such that $\forall n \geq n_0,\ c_1 g(n) \leq f(n) \leq c_2 g(n)$. This implies:

Big O Definition: $f(n) = O(g(n))$. $\exists\ \boldsymbol{c_1}$ and $\boldsymbol{n_1}$ such that $\forall n \geq n_1, f(n) \leq c_1 g(n)$.

Omega Definition: $f(n) = \Omega(g(n))$. $\exists + ve$ constants $\boldsymbol{c_2}$ and $\boldsymbol{n_2}$ such that $\forall n \geq n_2, c_2 g(n) \leq f(n)$.

- Direction ($\Leftarrow$): If $f(n) = O(g(n))$ and $(f(n) = \Omega(g(n))$, then there exist positive constants $\boldsymbol{C_1, C_2, n_1, and\ n_2}$ such that $\forall n \geq n_1 \forall n \geq n_1 and\ \forall n \geq n_2$:

Big O Definition: $f(n) \leq C_1 g(n), \forall\, n \geq n_1$

Omega Definition: $C_2 . g(n) \leq f(n), \forall\, n \leq n_2$

Now, let $n_0 = max(n_1, n_2)$ and $c_1 = C_2$ & $c_2 = C_1$. Then, $\forall n \geq n_0$: $C_1 g(n) \leq f(n) \leq C_2 g(n)$ This satisfies the definition of $f(n) = \Theta(g(n))$. Therefore, we prove $f(n) = \Theta(g(n))$ iff $f(n) = O(g(n))\ and\ f(n) = \Omega(g(n))$.

As an illustration of the application of this theorem, our proof demonstrating that $an^2 + bn + c \geq \Theta(n^2)$ for any constants $a, b, and\ c$, where $a > 0$, immediately implies that $an^2 + bn + c \geq \Theta(n^2)\ and\ an^2 + bn + c \geq O(n^2)$. Theorem 1 is more commonly employed to build asymptotically tight bounds from asymptotic upper and lower bounds, while this example shows how to generate asymptotic higher and lower bounds from asymptotically tight bounds. When we say that the unaltered execution time of an algorithm is Θ(g(n)), we are saying that for sufficiently big n, the running time on that input is at least a constant times g(n), regardless of the particular input selected for each n.

In essence, this gives a lower constraint on best-case execution time of an algorithm. For example, the best-case running time of insertion sort is $\Theta(n)$, indicating that the running time belongs to both $\Omega(n)$ and $O(n^2)$. These bounds are asymptotically as tight as possible, reflecting the range within which the efficiency of algorithm.

2.5 Asymptotic Notation: Equations and Inequalities

As demonstrated previously, asymptotic notation functions effectively in mathematical expressions. For instance, when presenting O-notation, it is expressed as $n \in O(n^2)$. Similarly, it is represented as formulas like $2n^2 + 3n + 1 = 2n^2 + g(n)$ where $g(n)$ is an unspecified function. When the right side of an equation (or inequality) has independent asymptotic notation, as in $n \in O(n^2)$, it signifies set membership: n is an element of $O(n^2)$.

On the other hand, when asymptotic notation is part of a formula, it represents an unnamed function. For example, the formula $2n^2 + 3n + 1 = 2n^2 + g(n)$ implies that $2n^2 + 3n + 1$ equals $2n^2 + f(n)$, where $f(n)$ is a function within the set represented by $g(n)$. In specific instance, we define $f(n)$ as $3n + 1$, confirming its inclusion in the set $g(n)$.

This kind of use of asymptotic notation simplifies and disintegrate equations by removing ambiguous information. For example, we used the recurrence to indicate the worst-case: $T(n) = 2T(n/2) + \Theta(n)$, detailed in next chapter. It is not necessary to explicitly state all lower-order terms when we are only interested in the asymptotic behaviour of $T(n)$. The phrase refers to an anonymous function that implicitly contains them. The more times asymptotic notation appears in an expression, the more anonymous functions there are in it. For instance, in the expression $\sum_{i=1}^{n} \quad O(i)$, the number of anonymous functions corresponds to the occurrences of the asymptotic notation $O(i)$. There exists only a singular anonymous function, denoted as function(i). Consequently, this expression differs from $O(1)$+ $O(2)$ +⋯ +$O(n)$, as it lacks a simple interpretation. In certain instances, asymptotic notation is positioned on the left side of an equation, expressed as $2n^2 + \Theta(n) = \Theta(n^2)$.

The following principle is applied when interpreting such equations: the equation is confirmed by a selection of anonymous functions on the right side, independent of anonymous functions selected on the left. Therefore, in our example, it signifies that for $f(n) \in \Theta(n)$, when some function $g(n)$ in $\Theta(n^2)$ such that $2n^2 + f(n) = g(n)$ holds $\forall$ n. To put it simply, the information on the right is more generalised than that on the left. These relationships can be chained together, as demonstrated by $2n^2 + 3n + 1 = 2n^2 + \Theta(n) = \Theta(n^2)$.

Each equation can be interpreted independently using the aforementioned rules. The first equation asserts that there exists some function $f(n) \epsilon \Theta(n)$ such that $2n^2 + 3n + 1 = 2n^2 + f(n) \;\; \forall n$. The second equation indicates that, for any function $g(n) \epsilon \Theta(n)$ (such as the $f(n)$ mentioned earlier), there exists some function $h(n) \epsilon \Theta(n^2)$ such that $2n^2 + gn = h(n)$ $\forall n$. It is noteworthy that this interpretation implies $2n^2 + 3n + 1 = \Theta(n^2)$, aligning with the intuitive result derived from chaining the equations.

2.6 Little o and Little ω Notations

Little o-notation signifies an upper bound, which does not possess asymptotic tightness. Formally defined as $o(g(n))$, it implies that, for any positive constant $c > 0$, there exists a constant $n_0 > 0$ such that $0 < f(n) < cg(n), \forall n \geq n_0$. This notation is employed when $f(n)$ is lesser relative to $g(n)$ when $n \to \infty$ [3]. Additionally, ω-notation, or **little-omega** is used to depict a bound which does not possess asymptotic tightness. For $\omega(g(n))$, it is defined as $\omega(g(n)) = f(n)$ for any positive constant $c > 0$, there exists a constant $n_0 > 0$ such that $0 < cg(n) < f(n)$ $\forall$ $n \geq n_0$. This notation is employed when $f(n)$ becomes very large in contrast with $g(n)$ as $n \to \infty$.

Asymptotic comparisons are subject to a variety of relational features that mimic those of real numbers. These include **transitivity, reflexivity, symmetry, and transpose symmetry**. The application of these properties in asymptotic notations allows us to draw relation between asymptotic function comparisons and real number comparisons, facilitating a clear understanding of their relationships.

Properties of asymptotic notations:

Transitivity:

$$f(n) = \Theta(g(n)) \;\&\; g(n) = \Theta(h(n)) \rightarrow f(n) = \Theta(h(n))$$

$$f(n) = O(g(n)) \;\&\; g(n) = O(h(n)), then\, f(n) = O(h(n))$$

$$f(n) = \Omega(g(n)) \;\&\; g(n) = \Omega(h(n)), it\ follows\ that\, f(n) = \Omega(h(n))$$

$$f(n) = o(g(n)) \;\&\; g(n) = o(h(n)), it\ implies\, f(n) = o(h(n))$$

$$f(n) = \omega(g(n)) \;\&\; g(n) = \omega(h(n)), it\ \ implies\, f(n) = \omega(h(n))$$

Reflexivity:

$$f(n) = \Theta(f(n))$$

$$f(n) = O(f(n))$$

Symmetry:

$$f(n) = \Theta(g(n))\ holds\ iff\ g(n) = \Theta(f(n))$$

Transpose symmetry:

$$f(n) \epsilon\, O(g(n))\ iff\ g(n)\ \epsilon\ \Omega(f(n))$$

$$f(n) \epsilon\, o(g(n))\ iff\ g(n)\ \epsilon\ \omega(f(n))$$

UNIT SUMMARY

- A simple sorting method called insertion sort creates the final sorted array one item at a time.
- Insertion Sort performs Iterative comparison and swapping, in-place sorting, stable sorting.
- Insertion Sort is suitable for small datasets or nearly sorted arrays.
- Algorithm analysis involves studying the efficiency and performance of algorithms.
- Time complexity, space complexity, big O, Omega, and Theta notations.
- Enables the comparison and selection of algorithms based on their efficiency.
- Mathematical symbols that represent how a function limits as its input size gets closer to infinity.
- Apart from Big $O(O)$, Omega (Ω), and Theta (Θ) notations, there are other significant notations Little $O(o)$, Little $Omega(\omega)$.
- Provides a high-level understanding of algorithm efficiency independent of hardware or implementation details.
- Different scenarios for algorithm performance analysis based on input characteristics.
- Best-case: Minimum possible time or space required.

- Average-case: Expected time or space over all possible inputs.
- Worst-case: Maximum time or space required.
- Significance: Helps in making informed decisions based on the nature of input data.
- Understanding insertion sort introduces fundamental sorting concepts, while algorithm analysis and asymptotic notations provide tools for evaluating and comparing algorithmic efficiency.
- Analyzing best, average, and worst-cases refines our understanding of algorithm behavior in various scenarios, guiding algorithm selection based on specific requirements.

MULTIPLE CHOICE QUESTIONS

1. What are algorithms?
   a. Random instructions
   b. Step-by-step instructions for problem-solving
   c. Artistic expressions
   d. Scientific formulas
2. Which of the following is NOT a resource evaluated in algorithm analysis?
   a. Memory
   b. Communication bandwidth
   c. Time
   d. None of the above
3. What is the computational model used in the described context?
   a. Multi-processor Random-Access Machine
   b. Single-processor Random-Access Machine
   c. Central Processing Unit
   d. Distributed Processing Unit
4. Which data types are assumed in the computational model?
   a. Only integers
   b. Only floating-point numbers
   c. Both integers and floating-point numbers
   d. Strings only

5. What is a key aspect of insertion sort?
    a. It is best for large data sets
    b. It is a complex algorithm
    c. It sorts elements based on comparisons
    d. It does not require comparisons
6. What is the primary concern when analyzing the time complexity of algorithm?
    a. Memory usage
    b. Time duration
    c. Input data count
    d. Output size
7. What is the metric commonly used to determine input size in sorting algorithms?
    a. Memory usage
    b. Time duration
    c. Input data count
    d. Output size
8. In the worst-case scenario, what function represents the execution time of the insertion sort algorithm?
    a. Linear
    b. Quadratic
    c. Logarithmic
    d. Exponential
9. What is the main advantage of analyzing the worst-case running time of algorithm?
    a. It provides an average running time
    b. It ensures the algorithm always runs fast
    c. It acts as a higher bound on the running time
    d. It guarantees the best-case scenario
10. What is a limitation of average-case analysis?
    a. It is not accurate
    b. It is not always clear what is an average input
    c. It is too complex
    d. It is not applicable to real-world scenarios

11. What does asymptotic notation provide in algorithm analysis?
    a. A mechanism to evaluate and compare algorithm efficiency
    b. A specific hardware platform for algorithm implementation
    c. A method to analyze real-time data
    d. A tool for debugging algorithms

12. Which notation is used to describe the upper bound on an algorithm time complexity?
    a. Omega (Ω)
    b. Theta (Θ)
    c. Little o (o)
    d. Big O (O)

13. What is the primary purpose of Little o notation?
    a. To describe the lower bound of an algorithm's time complexity
    b. To describe the upper bound of an algorithm's time complexity
    c. To provide a non-asymptotically tight upper bound
    d. To provide a non-asymptotically tight lower bound

14. Which notation provides both upper and lower bounds on an algorithm time complexity?
    a. Big O (O)
    b. Omega (Ω)
    c. Theta (Θ)
    d. Little o (o)

15. What is a key feature of Theta notation?
    a. It provides a lower bound on an algorithm time complexity
    b. It provides an upper bound on an algorithm time complexity
    c. It provides both upper and lower bounds on the time complexity of algorithm
    d. It provides a non-asymptotically tight upper bound

Solution of MCQ:

1	2	3	4	5	6	7	8	9	10	11	12	13	14	15
b	b	b	c	c	b	c	b	c	b	a	d	c	c	c

SHORT AND LONG ANSWER TYPE QUESTIONS

1 Revisit the InsertionSort procedure to arrange elements in nonincreasing order, as opposed to non-decreasing order.

2 Perform insertion sort on $A[31,45,91,21,47,58]$.

3 Elaborate on the concept of why the assertion, *the time complexity of algorithm A is at least* $O(n^2)$, lacks meaningful significance.

4 Briefly explain what insertion sort is and how it works.

5 Provide the complexity of insertion sort in all the cases.

6 When is insertion sort a suitable algorithm to use?

7 Why is algorithm analysis important in computer science?

8 Name two key metrics used in algorithm analysis and briefly describe each.

9 Explain why a low-level operation count might not always reflect the actual efficiency of an algorithm.

10 Define Big O notation and describe its purpose in algorithm analysis.

11 Explain the significance of Omega notation in the context of algorithmic complexity.

12 When is Theta notation used, and how does it differ from Big O and Omega notations?

13 Define the best, average, and worst-case scenarios in algorithm analysis.

14 Provide an example of an algorithm and explain when each of the three cases might occur.

15 Why is it important to consider all three cases when analyzing algorithmic efficiency?

16 Describe the step-by-step process of the insertion sort algorithm. Explain its advantages and limitations. Provide a comparative analysis of insertion sort with another sorting algorithm of your choice.

17 Explore the role of algorithm analysis in the design and evaluation of algorithms. Discuss how algorithm analysis contributes to making informed decisions about algorithm selection. Provide examples illustrating the importance of analyzing algorithms.

18 Compare and contrast Big O, Omega, and Theta notations. Discuss the scenarios in which each notation is most appropriately used. Provide examples of algorithms and express their time complexities using these notations. Discuss the implications of choosing one notation over another.

19 Discuss the concept of algorithmic complexity in the best, average, and worst-case scenarios. Explore real-world examples where each scenario is relevant. Provide insights into the trade-offs involved in optimizing an algorithm for a specific case and the challenges associated with making algorithms efficient across all scenarios.

20 Demonstrate that $\Theta(g(n))$ iff $O(g(n))$ and $\Omega(g(n))$.

KNOW MORE

Online courses/materials/resources [Accessed May 2024]

- https://www.geeksforgeeks.org/understanding-time-complexity-simple-examples/
- https://github.com/topics/time-complexity
- https://web.stanford.edu/class/archive/cs/cs106b/cs106b.1172/lectures/11-BigO
- https://onlinecourses.nptel.ac.in/noc24_cs05/preview
- https://www.simplilearn.com/tutorials/data-structure-tutorial

REFERENCES

[1] Furia, Carlo A., Bertrand Meyer, and Sergey Velder. "Loop invariants: Analysis, classification, and examples." *ACM Computing Surveys (CSUR)* 46, no. 3 (2014): 1-51.

[2] Levitin, Anany. *Introduction to design and analysis of algorithms, 2/E*. Pearson Education India, 2008. [Accessed October 2023]

[3] Goodrich, Michael T., and Roberto Tamassia. *Algorithm design and applications*. Vol. 363. Hoboken: Wiley, 2015. [Accessed October 2023]

3 Analysis of Recursive Algorithms

UNIT SPECIFICS

This unit covers the following aspects:

- *Recurrences*
- *Maximum-subarray problem*
- *Substitution, recurrence tree, and master theorem*
- *Heap sort*

In this unit, we discuss the into advanced algorithmic concepts, beginning with an in-depth study of sorting mechanisms, particularly emphasizing, efficient and versatile. Afterward, the discussion shifts towards analyzing algorithmic efficiency through recurrences, exploring the possibilities of solving recurrence relations and their applications in algorithms. The unit also unravel the maximum-subarray problem, a classic algorithmic challenge with implications for optimization. Moving on, we explore the Heap sort algorithm for sorting, revealing its potential approach for enhancing computational efficiency in sorting. The unit further describes the substitution method, recurrence tree method, and Master theorem, providing powerful tools for analyzing and solving recurrence relations. The link given in the QR code provides the supplementary material for this unit.

RATIONALE

The rationale of this unit on the analysis of algorithms is to describe the advanced principles governing the efficiency and effectiveness of various algorithmic solutions using recurrences. It aims to equip learners with a comprehensive understanding of existing recursive algorithms like heap sort and subarray with a discussion on the complexities associated with specific algorithms. Furthermore, it elaborates on the substitution method, recurrence tree method, and master theorem for analyzing and solving recurrence relations. Through case studies and specialized topics, learners gain insights into the broader applications of recursive algorithmic techniques.

PRE-REQUISITES

- *Basic knowledge of asymptotic analysis*
- *Basic knowledge of linear algebra, and sorting algorithms*
- *Knowledge about Data Structures*

UNIT OUTCOMES

The Unit provides the following outcome:

U3-O1: Learning recursive algorithms

U3-O2: Learn recurrences

U3-O3: Understanding Maximum-Subarray Problem

U3-O4: Understanding Substitution method, Recurrence Tree method, and Master Theorem for solving recurrence relations.

U3-O5: Understanding Heap sort

Unit-3 Outcomes	***EXPECTED MAPPING WITH COURSE OUTCOMES*** *(1- Weak Correlation; 2- Medium correlation; 3- Strong Correlation)*				
	CO-1	***CO-2***	***CO-3***	***CO-4***	***CO-5***
U3-O1	1	3	1	1	-
U3-O2	1	2	1	1	-
U3-O3	1	3	1	1	-
U3-O4	1	3	2	1	-
U3-O5	-	3	2	2	-

3.1 Recurrences

Recurrences denote mathematical expressions or equations that articulate the repetition of a function or sequence by referencing its prior values. These equations express a recursive relationship, defining the value of a function for a certain input in terms of its values for smaller inputs. These are often used to analyze the time complexity of recursive algorithms. The recurrences consist of the following key components:

i. Base case: A recurrence relation typically includes a base case, representing the starting point or condition where the recurrence stops. The solution for the base case is usually provided explicitly.

ii. Recursive case: The recurrence relation defines how to compute the value of the function for a given input based on the values of the function for smaller inputs. This is often expressed as a formula or equation involving the previous values of the function.

iii. Initial conditions: Along with the base case, initial conditions may be specified to determine the values of the function for small input sizes where the recurrence relation alone might not apply.

Exploring an example to deepen our comprehension of recurrence, we encounter the Fibonacci pattern, *i.e.,* the numerical sequence where an element is the sum of the previous twos. Representing the Fibonacci numbers through the recurrence relation $F(n) = F(n-1) + F(n-2)$ that initializes with $F(0) = 0$ & $F(1) = 1$, this relation highlights the nth Fibonacci sequence as the cumulative addition of its two predecessors. The base cases, $F(0)$ and $F(1)$, establish the foundational values for this recursive process.

3.1.1 Importance of Algorithm Analysis

Recurrence relations are fundamental components while studying the analysis of recursive methods. The time complexity of many recursive algorithms can be expressed through recurrence relations. Understanding and solving these recurrences helps in predicting and analyzing the efficiency of algorithms, providing insights into their behavior as the input size grows. The recurrences play a crucial role in modeling and analyzing the recursive behavior of functions and algorithms, providing a powerful tool for expressing and understanding repetitive patterns in mathematical and computational contexts. Let us see some examples of recurrences.

Example 1 (Factorial function): Consider the factorial function $n!$, defined as the product $\forall\ (+ve)\ integer\ upto\ n$. The relation for factorial is as follows:

$$n! = n \times (n-1)!$$

with the base case $0! = 1$. This recurrence relation expresses the factorial of n using the factorial of $(n-1)$. The solution to this recurrence is $n! = n \times (n-1)!$.

Example 2 (Linear recurrence): A linear recurrence is a mathematical relationship that defines a sequence, where each term is a linear combination of the preceding terms. Let a_n is the nth term in the sequence, the linear recurrence relation is given as

$$a_n = c \times a_{n-1} + d \times a_{n-2}$$

where a_0 and a_1 are initial values, and c and d are constants.

Example 3 (Binary search): The time complexity $T(n)$ of searching in a sorted array of size n using the searching in half of the array.

$$T(n) = T(\frac{n}{2}) + 1$$

The solution is $T(n) = O(log\ n)$, illustrating logarithmic time complexity of binary search [1].

Example 4 (Towers of hanoi): Towers of Hanoi problem with n disks is:

$$T(n) = 2T(n-1) + 1$$

With the base case $T(1) = 1$. This recurrence expresses the moves required to solve for n disks in terms of solving it for $n - 1$ disks twice and adding one additional move. The solution is $T(n) = 2^n - 1$ [2]. These examples illustrate the concept of recurrences in various contexts, showcasing how functions can be defined recursively in terms of their values on smaller inputs. Solving these recurrences helps analyze the time complexity of algorithms and understand the behavior of recursive functions.

3.1.2 Analyzing Recursive Algorithm

It involves determining its time complexity, space complexity, and solving recurrence relations. The step-by-step guide to performing a recursive algorithm analysis is as follows:

i) *Identify the recurrence relation:* First, identify the recursive structure and the relation describes how the problem is decomposed into smaller subproblems and how the solutions of these subproblems contribute to the overall solution.

ii) *Write down the recurrence relation:* Express the recurrence relation mathematically. For example, if $T(n)$ represents the complexity with input size n, the recurrence relation might look like $T(n) = aT\left(\frac{n}{b}\right) + f(n)$, where a is subproblems count, b is the factor of reducing the input into the subproblems, and $f(n)$ is the problem dividing and combining the results cost.

iii) *Solve the recurrence relation:* Solving the recurrence relation helps determine the complexity. There are several methods for solving recurrence relations, such as:

- Substitution method: Guessing followed by proving it using mathematical induction.

- Recurrence tree method: Drawing a tree to represent the recursive calls and summing up the costs.
- Master theorem: A specialized method for recurrence relations that fit a specific form.

iv) *Analyze time complexity:* After solving the recurrence relation, estimate the overall complexity of algorithm. It often involves Big O notation, and it expresses how the running time increases with size of input.

v) *Analyze space complexity:* This involves analyzing additional memory required for each recursive call, including function call overhead, parameter passing, and any auxiliary data structures used.

vi) *Identify base cases:* Ensure that the recursive algorithm has well-defined base cases. Base cases are essential for breaking the recursion and providing a simple solution for small inputs. They are important for correctness and efficiency.

vii) *Check for overlapping subproblems:* If the recursive algorithm exhibits overlapping subproblems, consider optimizing it using techniques such as memoization (caching previously computed results) or dynamic programming.

viii) *Consider tail recursion:* If applicable, consider whether the recursive calls are tail recursive. Tail recursion can often be optimized by compilers, leading to more efficient execution.

ix) *Test and validate:* Test the algorithm on various inputs to validate its correctness and assess its performance in practice. This step ensures that the theoretical analysis aligns with the real-world behavior of algorithm.

By following these steps, we can systematically analyze a recursive algorithm, understand its efficiency, and make informed decisions about its use in different scenarios. The method for solving the recurrence relation is detailed in the later part of the unit.

Master method: To utilize the master method, it is essential to commit to memorizing three distinct cases. However, once these cases are memorized, determining asymptotic bounds for numerous simple recurrences becomes a easier task. It determines run time of several divide-and-conquer procedures, such as those that deal with matrix multiplication and maximum-subarray problems. These principles are also extended to other divide-and-conquer algorithms discussed throughout this book. We may encounter recurrences expressed as inequalities, like $T(n) = 2T\left(\frac{n}{2}\right) + C.g(n)$. In cases where the recurrence provides upper bound over $T(n)$, it express its solution using Big O-notation $(O(g(n)))$ in-place of Theta $(\Theta(g(n)))$. Conversely, $T(n) = 2T\left(\frac{n}{2}\right) + C.g(n)$, signifying a lower bound, which uses Omega $(\Omega(g(n)))$.

Analyzing recurrences: in-depth technical considerations

In practical scenarios, challenges are often overlooked when formulating and solving recurrences. For instance, if we use merge sort (will discuss in unit 6) on an odd number of elements n, the resulting subproblems have sizes $floor(n/2)$ and $ceil(n/2)$. Neither of these sizes is precisely $n/2$, since $n/2$ is not an integer when n is odd. From a technical standpoint, the recurrence that represents the worst case of merge sort as:

$$T(n) = \begin{cases} \Theta(1) & \text{if } n = 1 \\ T(floor(n/2)) + T(ceil(n/2)) + \Theta(n) & \text{if } n > 1 \end{cases}.$$

The boundary conditions are an additional set of features that are frequently overlooked. Recurrences formed from algorithm running times often have constant run times, since the time for a constant-sized is $T(n) = \Theta(1)$ for smaller n. Therefore, we usually neglect boundary conditions in recurrences, considering $T(n)$ is constant lower value of n. We typically express recurrence in merge sort as $T(n) = 2T\left(\frac{n}{2}\right) + \Theta(n)$ without mentioning smaller n. This is because altering the value of $T(n)$ does affect the solution, but the change is usually < constant, preserving unchanged growth order.

In the formulation and solution of recurrences, details such as floors, ceilings, *etc.*, are eliminated frequently. We proceed with revisiting them later to determine their significance. While they often prove inconsequential, it is important to recognize situations where they do matter. Nevertheless, this unit discuss some of these details, highlighting the primer of the recurrence solution methods.

3.2 Maximum-Subarray Problem

Assume you are given a chance to invest in a chemical corporation. The stock price of corporation fluctuates, much like the erratic nature of the chemicals from the company. You are limited in how you can invest: you can only purchase one share at a time and sell it later, carrying out transactions after the daily trading session ends. You have the advantage of knowing the future stock price, which helps you overcome this limitation. It is obvious what the goal is: increase your benefits.

Figure 3.1 depicts a graphical representation of the price of the stock price for 17-days. When price begins on 100 rupees per share on day 0, you are free to buy it at any time. To maximize profit, the best strategy is to "buy low, sell high", meaning that you should purchase the stock at the lowest price then sell it at maximum price. That being said, it might not always be possible to accomplish this in the allotted time. As illustrated, lowest price is recorded after seven days that comes as greatest value recorded after 1st day. Figure 3.1 casts doubt on the notion that it is always sensible to maximise gain by purchasing at the lowest price. It shows that purchasing after day seven, when prices are lowest, does not always translate into the most profit. Finding the maximum and minimum prices, moving left from the highest price to find the lowest previous price and choosing the pair with the largest difference would be simple if this strategy is perfect.

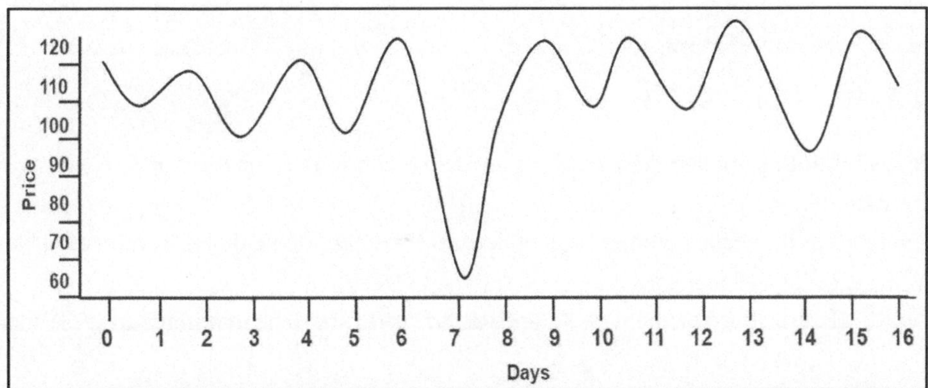

Figure 3.1: The horizontal axis represents each day, while the vertical axis displays prices. The bottom row provides the price change compared to the preceding day.

The Maximum-subarray problem is a classic algorithmic problem that involves finding the contiguous **subarray (of numbers)** within a one-dimensional array with the largest sum. This problem has applications in various fields, including finance, data analysis, and signal processing. Let us discuss a detailed explanation of the Maximum-Subarray problem.

Problem statement: The goal is to identify the contiguous subarray with the highest sum given an array of numbers.

Naive approach: A naive approach involves checking all possible subarrays and calculating their sums. The maximum sum subarray is then identified. However, this approach possesses a complexity of $O(n^3)$ because it uses three nested loops.

Efficient approach-Kadane's algorithm: Kadane's algorithm is a dynamic programming technique that optimizes the solution to $O(n)$ time complexity [3].

Kadane's algorithm steps:

1. *Initialization:* Initialize two variables, $currentSum$ and $maxSum$, on the first index of the array.

2. *Iterate through the array:*
   - Starting from the 2nd position, iterate through the array.
   - For each element perform
     $currentSum \leftarrow max\,\{current\ element, (current\ element\ +\ currentSum)\,\}$
   - Update $maxSum \leftarrow max\{currentSum, maxSum\}$.

3. *Result:* The *maxSum* at the end is the maximum sum of a contiguous subarray.

Example 5 (Kadane's algorithm):

Consider the array: $[-2,1,-3,4,-1,2,1,-5,4]$

- **Initialization:** Initialize $currentSum$ and $maxSum$ to the first element (-2).
- **Iteration:**
  - For the second element (1), update $currentSum$ to be the maximum of (1) and $(1+(-2))$, which is 1.
  - For the third element (-3), update $currentSum$ to be maximum of (-3) and $(-3+1)$, which is 1.
  - For the fourth element (4), update $currentSum$ to be the maximum of (4) and $(4+1)$, which is 5.
  - Continue this process for each element.
- **Result:** After the iteration, $maxSum$ is $\mathbf{6}$, which is the maximum sum of a contiguous subarray (subarray: $[4,-1,2,1]$).

The visualization of the algorithm in Figure 3.1 shows how it efficiently tracks the maximum sum as it iterates through the array, considering the local maximum at each step. The Maximum-subarray problem, addressed by Kadane's algorithm, is an efficient and widely used approach for finding the contiguous subarray with the maximum sum. It is a classic example of dynamic programming, providing a linear-time solution to a problem that could be solved naively in cubic time.

Pseudo-code of Kadane's algorithm

```
def max_subarray_sum(arr):
        current_sum = max_sum = arr[0]

        for num in arr[1:]:
          current_sum = max(num, current_sum + num)
          max_sum = max(max_sum, current_sum)

        return max_sum
```

3.3 Substitution Method

The substitution method is a technique for solving recurrence relations by guessing a solution and then proving its correctness through mathematical induction. This method is particularly useful for recurrences that have a specific pattern or structure. A step-by-step guide on how to apply the substitution method is discuss as follows:

Steps of the substitution method:

i. **Guess a solution:** Start by making an educated guess about the solution. The guess is based on observations of the recurrence relation or a pattern observed in similar problems. For example, if the recurrence relation involves a divide-and-conquer strategy, a guess might involve logarithmic terms.

ii. **Prove by induction:**
   - Base case: Prove that the guess holds for the base case(s) of the recurrence. This involves substituting the base case values into the guessed solution and verifying that they satisfy the recurrence. For example, if $T(1) = 1$, substitute $n = 1$ into guessed solution and ensure it equals $T(1)$.
   - Inductive step: Assume that the guess holds for some arbitrary k. This assumption is known as the inductive hypothesis.
   - Substitute $n = k$ into the recurrence relation with the guessed solution and prove that it implies the guess holds for $k = k + 1$.

iii. **Solve for constants:** If the guess involves undetermined constants, solve for them using the initial conditions or other information provided. This step may involve algebraic manipulation to determine the values of constants based on the known values of the recurrence.

iv. **Express the solution:** Once the correctness of the guess is established, express the solution. Include any estimated constants in the final expression.

Consider the recurrence relation $T(n) = 2T(n/2) + n, T(1) = 1$.

- Step 1: Guess a solution: $T(n) = n \log n + n$.
- Step 2: Prove by induction:
   - *Base Case:* Verify $T(1) = 1 \log 1 + 1 = 1$, which matches the base condition.
   - *Inductive Step:* Assume $T(k) = k \log k + k$. Prove for $k + 1$ by substituting this into the recurrence and showing that it implies the guess for $k + 1$.
- Step 3: Solve for constants: There are no additional constants introduced.
- Step 4: Express the solution: With the correctness established, solution is expressed as $T(n) = n \log n + n$.

Considerations and challenges: In the application of the substitution method, accurate predictions hinge on making an informed initial guess. This necessity is underscored by the reliance on intuition, experience, or the identification of recurring patterns. Moreover, the versatility of the substitution method is limited, as it may not be suitable for all types of recurrence relations. Certain recurrences may necessitate the utilization of alternative methods, such as the Master Theorem, tailored to specific forms of recurrences. Lastly, the complexity of the method escalates when dealing with complex recurrence relations, and the determination of constants may entail non-trivial algebraic manipulations.

The substitution method provides a structured approach to solving recurrences by guiding the process of guessing and proving the correctness of solutions. It is a powerful tool in the toolbox of techniques used for analyzing the time complexity of algorithms expressed through recurrence relations. The substitution method might not be suitable for all types of recurrences, and other methods like the Master Theorem may be more appropriate in some cases. The substitution method provides a systematic approach to solving recurrence relations by leveraging the power of mathematical induction to validate guessed solutions.

Let us consider another simple numerical example of a recurrence relation and solve it using the substitution method. Recurrence relation: $T(n) = 2T\left(\frac{n}{2}\right) + n$. The time complexity of an algorithm that splits the problem into two half-sized subproblems and completes n units of work at each level is represented by this recurrence relation. Let us solve this recurrence relation using the substitution method.

i. **Guess the form:** Assume that the solution has the form $T(n) = a \cdot n^b$. In this case, we are trying to find values for a and b .

ii. **Substitute and simplify:** Substitute the assumed solution into the recurrence relation and simplify.

$$a \cdot n^b = 2 \cdot a \cdot \left(\frac{n}{2}\right)^b + n$$

Upon simplification, we get:

$$a \cdot n^b = a \cdot n^b + n$$

iii. **Solve for unknowns:** Solve for the unknowns a and b . Cancel $a \cdot n^b$ from both sides: $0 = n$. This equation does not provide any information about a or b , but it suggests that our initial assumption was incorrect.

iv. **Adjust guess:** Since the initial guess $T(n) = a \cdot n^b$ does not work, we refine our guest. Let us try $T(n) = c \cdot n$, where c is a constant.

v. **Substitute and simplify:** Substitute the refined guess into the recurrence relation and simplify.

$$c \cdot n = 2 \cdot c \cdot \left(\frac{n}{2}\right) + n$$

$$\Rightarrow c \cdot n = c \cdot n + n$$

vi. **Solve for unknowns:** Solve for unknowns c. Cancel $c \cdot n$ from both sides $0 = n$. Similar to the previous attempt, this equation does not provide information about c.

The second attempt also did not yield a solution. In this case, the recurrence relation $T(n) = 2T\left(\frac{n}{2}\right) + n$ does not have a solution in the form $T(n) = a \cdot n^b$ or $T(n) = c \cdot n$ using the substitution method.

More advanced techniques, such as the iteration method or the Master theorem, may be necessary for solving this particular recurrence relation.

Determining the correct solutions to recurrences can be a challenging task. The art of making a **good guess relies on experience** and, at times, a touch of creativity. Experience plays a crucial role in guessing solutions. If a recurrence closely resembles one encountered previously, it is reasonable to make a similar guess. For instance, Let us examine the $T(n) = 2T\left(\frac{bn}{2} + 17 + n\right)$. Although the inclusion of 17 in argument of T on right might seem intentional; thus, this term is not expected to drastically impact the overall solution. For larger n , the disparity between $bn/2$ and $bn/2 + 17$ is relatively small, as both essentially divide n nearly evenly in half. By employing these heuristics and drawing on experiences, one can enhance their ability to make informed guesses, skill to solve recurrence relations.

Similarly, for solving $T(n) = O(n\ log\ n)$, alternate strategy is to define approximate upper and lower bounds, which will eventually reduce uncertainty. Because the term exists, we might first set a lower constraint of for the recurrence n, and a primer upper bound of $T(n) = O(n^2)$. Gracefully refining these bounds allows us to converge towards the accurate asymptotic solution $T(n) = \Theta(n\ log\ n)$. Genrally, despite correctly deducing an asymptotic bound for a recurrence solution, challenges may emerge during induction due to the inadequacy of the inductive assumption to establish the detailed bound. In such instances, adjusting the guess by subtracting a lower-order term often resolves the issue. For example, consider the recurrence $T(n) = T\left(\frac{n}{2}\right) + T\left(\frac{n}{2}\right) + 1$. Assuming $T(n) = O(n)$, we aim to demonstrate $T(n) \leq cn$ for a suitable constant c. Substituting our assumption into the recurrence, we obtain $T(n) = c \cdot \frac{n}{2} + c \cdot \frac{n}{2} + 1$, which does not directly imply $T(n) \leq cn\ if\ \exists\ c$. Adjusting the guess, perhaps to $T(n) = O(n^2)$, may yield a more appropriate result.

3.4 Recursion Tree Method

The recursion-tree method is a graphical technique for solving recurrences by representing the recursive calls as a tree. The method involves breaking down a recurrence relation into a tree structure, where each node denotes the cost of recursive call. The recursion-tree method is a technique used to solve recurrence relations, which describe the running time of algorithms in size of the input. This method visualizes the recurrence relation as a tree, where each level corresponds to a recursive call, and the nodes represent the work done at each level. We further provide multiple numerical examples to illustrate the recursion-tree method. The general steps for applying the recursion-tree method are discussed as follows:

i. **Express the recurrence relation:** Start with the given recurrence relation, which typically describes the time complexity in the input size. For example, a generic recurrence relation might be of the form $T(n) = aT\left(\frac{n}{b}\right) + f(n)$, where a is the recursive subproblems, b is the factor of problem size reduction, and $f(n)$ is the work done outside the recursive calls.

ii. **Visualize the recursion tree:** Construct a tree diagram where each level of the tree represents a recursive call, and the nodes represent the work done at each level. The root of the tree corresponds to the original problem, and each level corresponds to a recursive subdivision of the problem size.

iii. **Write down the work at each level:** Write down the work done at each level of the recursion tree. This includes both the work done within the recursive calls and the non-recursive work $f(n)$.

iv. **Sum up the work at each level:** Sum up the work done at each level to obtain a series or a recurrence relation. This step involves analyzing the work pattern at each level and expressing it mathematically.

v. **Solve or simplify the summation:** Solve the obtained series or recurrence relation to find a closed-form solution for the original recurrence relation. This may involve mathematical techniques such as solving a geometric series, applying known summation formulas, or other methods depending on the specific recurrence.

vi. **Analyze the solution:** Analyze the obtained solution in terms of big-O notation to express the overall time complexity of the algorithm.

Example 6: Consider the recurrence relation: $T(n) = 2T\left(\frac{n}{2}\right) + n$.

Recursion tree

1. Level 0: $T(n)$
   - Cost: n
   - Subproblems: $2T\left(\frac{n}{2}\right)$
2. Level 1: $2T\left(\frac{n}{2}\right)$
   - Cost: $\frac{n}{2} + \frac{n}{2} = n$
   - Subproblems: $4T\left(\frac{n}{4}\right)$
3. Level 2: $4T\left(\frac{n}{4}\right)$
   - Cost: $\frac{n}{4} + \frac{n}{4} + \frac{n}{4} + \frac{n}{4} = n$
   - Subproblems: $8T\left(\frac{n}{8}\right)$

   and so on.

Total cost: The total cost at each level is n, with $log_2 n$ levels. Thus, cost is $O(n\ log\ n)$.

Example 7: Consider the recurrence relation: $T(n) = T\left(\frac{n}{2}\right) + n^2$

Recursion tree:

1. Level 0: $T(n)$
   - Cost: n^2

- Subproblem: $T\left(\frac{n}{2}\right)$

2. Level 1: $T\left(\frac{n}{2}\right)$

- Cost: $\left(\frac{n}{2}\right)^2$

- Subproblem: $T\left(\frac{n}{4}\right)$

3. Level 2: $T\left(\frac{n}{4}\right)$

- Cost: $\left(\frac{n}{4}\right)^2$

- Subproblem: $T\left(\frac{n}{8}\right)$

and so on.

Total cost: The total cost at each level is n^2 with $log_2 n$ levels. Thus, cost is $O(n^2 log\ n)$.

These examples illustrate how the recursion-tree method helps to visualize the structure of recursive calls and how to determine the overall time complexity by analyzing levels and costs in different steps.

3.5 Master's Theorem

A mathematical method called the master's theorem, which is used to solve recurrence relations, which are frequently encountered in algorithm analysis. The master's theorem expresses the recurrence relation in a particular form, making it simple to calculate the time complexity of divide-and-conquer algorithms. The following generic form can be used to express recurrences, and this is where the master's theorem is especially useful:

$$T(n) = aT\left(\frac{n}{b}\right) + f(n)$$

where $T(n)$ is the time complexity of the algorithm, a is the number of subproblems in the recursion, b is the factor by which the input size is reduced in each subproblem, and $f(n)$ is the cost of partitioning and conquering the results (excluding recursive calls).

The master method provides a solution for the recurrence relation in terms of the function $f(n)$ and compares it with a specific form to determine the overall time complexity. The three cases of the master method are as follows:

- **Case 1** If $f(n)$ is $O(n^{log_b a-\epsilon})$ for some constant $\varepsilon > 0$: If this condition holds, then the time complexity is $T(n) = \Theta(n^{log_b a})$.
- **Case 2** If $f(n)$ is $\Theta(n^{log_b a})$: If this condition holds, then the time complexity is$T(n) = \Theta(n^{log_b a} log\ n)$.

- **Case 3** If $f(n)$ is $\Omega(n^{log_b a+\epsilon})$ for some constant $\varepsilon > 0$, and $af\left(\frac{n}{b}\right) \leq kf(n)$ for some constant $k < 1$ and sufficiently large n: If these conditions hold, then the time complexity: $T(n) = \Theta(f(n))$.

It simplifies the analysis of divide-and-conquer methods to provide a concise way to determine their time complexity based on the structure of the recurrence relation. It is a powerful tool for understanding and comparing the efficiency of algorithms that follow the divide-and-conquer mechanism. Let us go through a few numerical examples to demonstrate how the master's theorem is applied to solve recurrence relations.

Example 8: Consider the relation: $T(n) = 3T\left(\frac{n}{2}\right) + n^2$.

Here, $a = 3$ (number of subproblems), $b = 2$ (factor by which the input size is reduced), and $f(n) = n^2$ (cost excluding recursive calls). Now, we compare $f(n) = n^2$ with $n^{log_b a} = n^{log_2 3}$. $f(n) = n^2$ is $O(n^{log_2 3-\epsilon})$ for any $\epsilon > 0$, we are in **Case 1**. Therefore, the time complexity is $T(n) = \Theta(n^{log_2 3})$.

Example 9: Consider the recurrence relation: $T(n) = 2T\left(\frac{n}{2}\right) + n \log n$.

Here, $a = 2, b = 2$, and $f(n) = n \log n$. Compare $f(n) = n \log n$ with $n^{log_b a} = n^{log_2 2} = n$. Since $f(n) = n \log n$ is $\Theta(n^{log_2 2})$, we are in **Case 2**. Therefore, the time complexity is $T(n) = \Theta(n \log n \log n)$.

Example 10: Consider relation: $T(n) = 4T\left(\frac{n}{2}\right) + n^3$.

Here, $a = 4, b = 2$, and $f(n) = n^3$. Compare $f(n) = n^3$ with $n^{log_b a} = n^{log_2 4} = n^2$. Since $f(n) = n^3$ is $\Omega(n^{log_2 4+\epsilon})$ for any $\epsilon > 0$, and $af\left(\frac{n}{b}\right) = 4\left(\frac{n}{2}\right)^3 = \frac{1}{2}n^3 \leq kf(n)$ for $k = \frac{1}{2}$ and sufficiently large n , we are in **Case 3**. Thus, the time complexity is $T(n) = \Theta(n^3)$.

These examples illustrate how the master's theorem is utilized to different recurrence relations. The key is to identify the values of a, b, and $f(n)$, and compare $f(n)$ with the corresponding term $n^{log_b a}$ to determine the appropriate case for solving the recurrence.

Example 11: (Solving the recurrence relation of merge sort):

Applying the Master's theorem, we have $a = 2, b = 2,$ and $f(n) = n$. The recurrence relation falls into the second case of the Master Theorem.

$$T(n) = \Theta(n \ log \ n)$$

This means that the time complexity of Merge Sort (In Unit 6, we will discuss Merge Sort in detail) is $\Theta(n \ log \ n)$ in the worst, average, and best cases.

Example 12: Let us analyze the time complexity with a numerical example using the array [38, 27, 43, 3, 9, 82, 10].

1. **Divide (logarithmic):** Dividing the array into sublists until each sublist contains one element ($log_2 7 \approx 2.82 \Rightarrow 3$ levels of recursion).
2. **Conquer (constant):** Sorting each sublist containing one element.
3. **Combine (linear):** Merging the sorted sublists $O(n)$ for each level of recursion).

The overall time complexity is $O(n \ log \ n)$ for this example.

The efficiency of merge sort lies in its consistent and predictable time complexity of $O(n \ log \ n)$. This makes it suitable for sorting large datasets, and its divide-and-conquer strategy ensures a balanced and efficient approach to sorting. While Merge Sort incurs a higher space complexity due to the need for additional memory during merging, its time complexity makes it a popular choice for various applications.

3.6 Heap Sort

Heap Sort is a comparison-based sorting algorithm that uses a binary heap data structure to organize elements efficiently. Heap sort has a time complexity of $O(n \ \ log \ \ n)$ for the worst, average, and best cases, making it more efficient than some other quadratic sorting algorithms like bubble sort or insertion sort. The step-by-step explanation of Heap sort is discussed as follows:

1. Heap construction: It involves building a max heap of ascending order. This process commences from the last non-leaf node and proceeds upwards, applying heapification to each node. The goal is to guarantee that the value at each node >= values of its children. This step-by-step approach ensures that the largest element in the array ultimately becomes the root of the heap. Conversely, when constructing a min heap of descending order, the process ensures that each node possesses a value smaller than or equal to its children. This arrangement results in the smallest element being positioned at the root of the heap.

2. Sorting: Swap the root (maximum element for Max Heap) with the last element in the heap. Decrease the heap size (excluding the last element in its sorted position). Heapify the root to maintain the heap property. Repeat steps until the heap is empty.

Different from other sorting algorithms, heap sort covers the following advantages:

i. Efficiency: Heap Sort has a time complexity of $O(n \ log \ n)$ for worst, average, and best cases.

ii. In-place sorting: Heap Sort is an in-place sorting algorithm, meaning it uses a constant amount of additional memory space. This makes it suitable for scenarios where memory usage is a critical factor.

iii. *Stability:* Heap Sort is a stable sorting algorithm. Stable sorting means that the relative order of equal elements is maintained in the sorted output. This property can be important in certain applications.

iv. *Suitable for external sorting:* The efficient of algorithm use of memory makes it suitable for external sorting, where data is too large to fit into the main memory.

v. *No dependence on initial order:* Unlike some other sorting algorithms, Heap Sort does not depend on the initial order of elements. It consistently achieves $O(n \ log \ n)$ performance regardless of the input distribution.

In addition to the aforementioned advantages, heap sort has the following limitations

i. *Non-adaptive:* Heap sort is a non-adaptive sorting algorithm, meaning it does not take advantage of existing order information in the input data. It performs consistently regardless of the initial order, but this lack of adaptability can be a disadvantage in certain cases.

ii. *Not as cache-friendly:* The use of an implicit data structure (the heap) can lead to poor cache performance compared to algorithms that operate on contiguous memory locations. This may result in more cache misses, affecting overall performance.

iii. *Complexity and code length:* Implementing Heap Sort may require a larger amount of code compared to simpler sorting algorithms like Bubble Sort or Insertion Sort. The complex heapify procedure and the overall structure of the algorithm can make the code less simple.

iv. *Not ideal for small data sets:* Heap Sort might not be the best choice for small data sets or nearly sorted data. The overhead of building the heap initially could outweigh the benefits of its efficient sorting mechanism.

v. *Lack of parallelism:* Heap Sort does not naturally lend itself to parallel processing. While there are parallel versions, they may not achieve the same speedup as parallel versions of some other algorithms.

Heap sort is an in-place sorting algorithm with no additional space requirements. While it might not be as intuitive as some simpler algorithms, it is efficient and stable, making it a good choice for certain scenarios, especially when a stable sorting algorithm with $O(n \ log \ n)$ time complexity is needed.

Implementation details of heap sort: The *heapify procedure* is crucial in maintaining the heap property. For a given node at index i, its left child is at index $2i + 1$ and the right child is at index $2i + 2$, as shown in Figure 3.2. Compare the node with its left and right children, and swap with the larger (for *Max Heap*) or smaller (for *Min Heap*) child if necessary. Recursively apply heapify to the affected child until the heap property is restored.

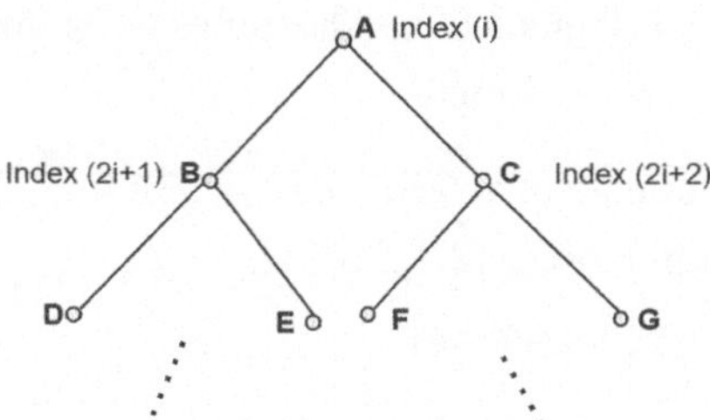

Figure 3.2: Index distribution of nodes in the heap of the tree starting from $A, B, C, D, E, F, \ldots$

The pseudo-code outlines two main procedures of Heap sort:

```
procedure heapify(arr, n, i)
  largest = i
  left_child  =  2 * i + 1
  right_child  =  2 * i + 2
  if left_child  <  n and arr[left_child] > arr[largest]
    largest = left_child

  if right_child  <  n and arr[right_child] > arr[largest]
    largest = right_child

  if largest ≠ i
    swap arr[i] with arr[largest]
    heapify(arr, n, largest)

procedure heap_sort(arr)
  n = length(arr)
  # Build max heap

  for i from n//2 − 1 to 0 step-1
    heapify(arr, n, i)

  # Perform sorting

  for i from n − 1 to 1 step-1
    swap arr[0] with arr[i]  # Swap root with last element
    heapify(arr, i, 0)  # Heapify root
```

1. heapify: This procedure is used to heapify a subtree rooted at a given index. It compares the root with its left and right children, and if necessary, swaps the root with the larger of its children. The procedure then recursively applies heapify to the affected child.

2. heap_sort: This is the main sorting procedure. It first builds a max heap from the input array by starting from the last non-leaf node and heapifying each node. After building the max heap, it repeatedly swaps the root (maximum) with the last element and heapifies to maintain the max heap property. This process is repeated until the entire array is sorted.

Example 13: Let us consider an example of an array $arr = [5,11,4,6,2]$, where we have to apply heap sort to obtain array sorted in ascending order [2,4,5,6,11].

a). Construct binary tree from $arr = [5,11,4,6,2]$:

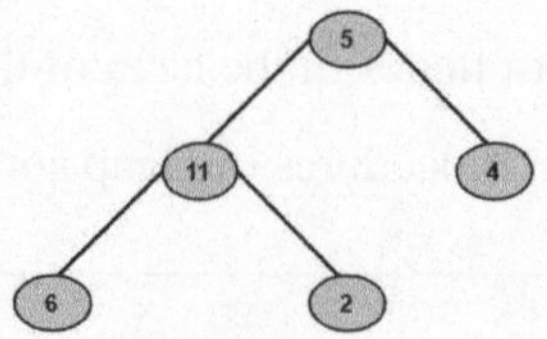

b). Determine heapify on the constructed binary tree

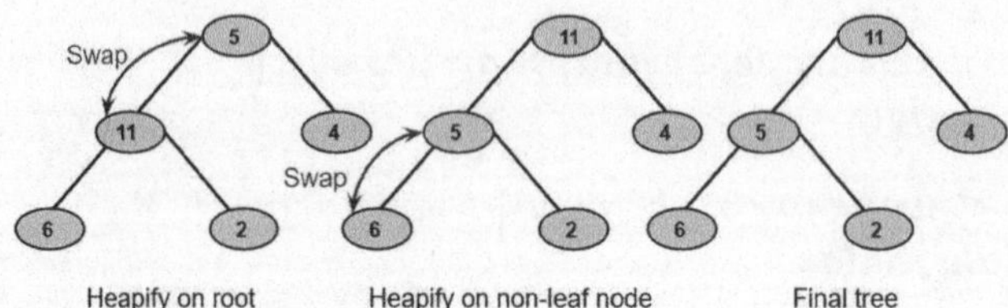

c). Eliminate maximum element and perform heapify

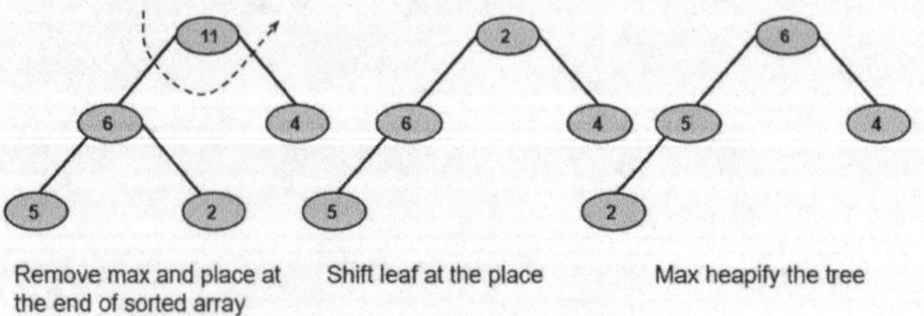

d). Remove the next maximum from root and perform heapify

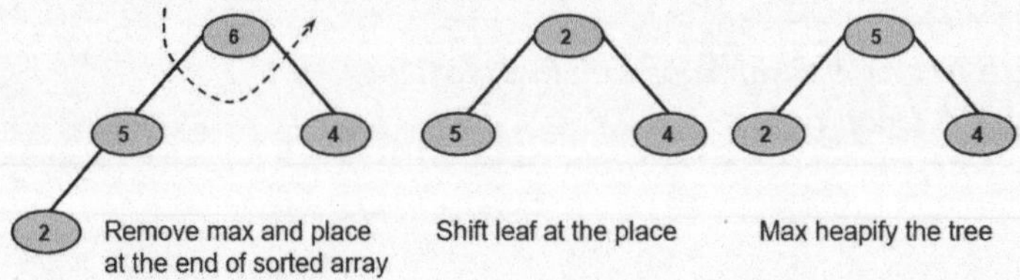

e). Remove the next maximum from root and perform heapify

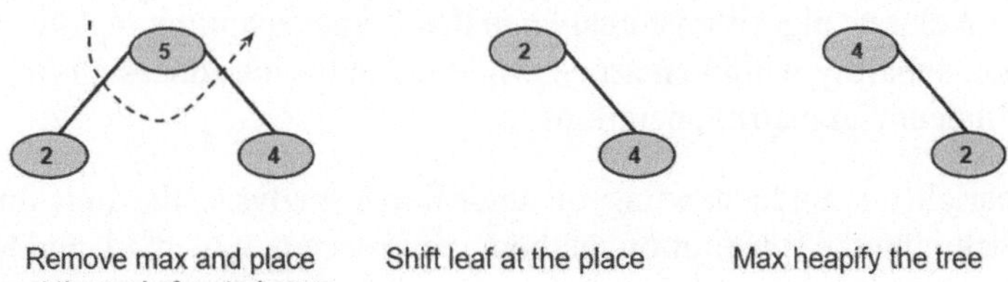

f). Remove the next maximum from root and perform heapify

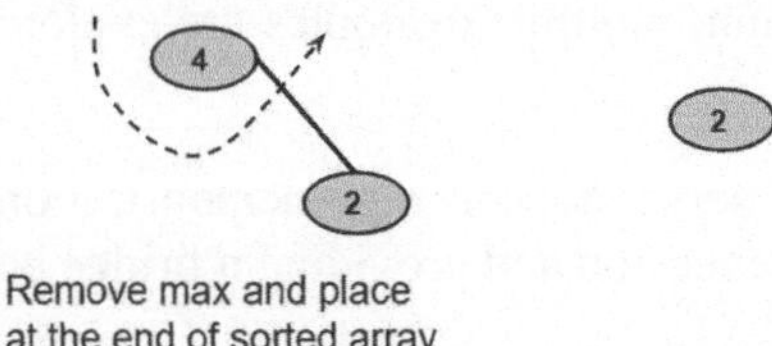

g). Finally sorted list is as follows: $arr = [2,4,5,6,11]$

Recurrence analysis of heap sort: Master's Theorem can be applied to analyze the recurrence relation of Heap sort. The recurrence relation for Heap sort is typically expressed as follows: $T(n) = 2T(n/2) + O(n)$, where $T(n)$ is the time complexity of the algorithm for a problem of size n. $2T(n/2)$ represents the time spent on recursively sorting the two halves of the array. $O(n)$ represents the time spent on heapifying the array. We can compare this recurrence relation with the standard form of the Master's Theorem: $T(n) = aT(n/b) + f(n)$. Heap Sort: $a = 2$ (two recursive calls in heapify), $b = 2$ (array divided into two halves), and $f(n) = O(n)$ (time spent on heapifying).

Let us find the value of c in n^c from $f(n)$: in this case $f(n) = O(n) = n^1$. Then, we compare $log_b a$ with c: $log_2 2 = 1$ (the exponent on n in $T(n) = 1$. In the case of Heap Sort: $c = 1$ and $log_b a = log_2 2 = 1$. Since $c = log_b a$, we fall in **case 2** of Master Theorem. Therefore, the time complexity of Heap Sort is: $T(n) = \Theta(n \log n)$.

UNIT SUMMARY

- This unit provides a comprehensive exploration of algorithmic efficiency by focusing on recurrences, the maximum-subarray problem, heap sort algorithm, and advanced methods for solving recurrence relations.
- The unit begins with an in-depth study of the recursive algorithms, an efficient sorting algorithm known for its versatility.
- Subsequently, it describes recurrences, uncovering their significance in analyzing the time complexity of algorithms.

- The unit extends its scope to encompass the Maximum-Subarray problem.
- The former is a classic algorithmic challenge that involves optimizing the identification of the maximum sum subarray within an array, while the latter introduces an important approach to enhancing efficiency in matrix operations.
- To further enrich our understanding of algorithmic analysis, the unit introduces advanced techniques including the substitution method, recurrence tree method, and Master's theorem.
- These methods provide powerful tools for solving and understanding recurrence relations, a crucial aspect of algorithmic efficiency analysis.
- Throughout the unit, multiple examples are explored to illustrate the practical application of these concepts.
- These examples serve as concrete demonstrations of the analytical methods discussed, enhancing comprehension and providing a bridge between theoretical understanding and real-world scenarios.
- By the end of the unit, learners is equipped with the knowledge and skills to tackle algorithmic efficiency challenges, understand the intricacies of recurrence relations, and apply advanced methods to analyze and optimize algorithms in various domains.

MULTIPLE CHOICE QUESTIONS

1. What are recurrences in the context of algorithms?
    a. Expressions that repeat same function
    b. Functions that generate random sequences
    c. Conditions that stop recursive functions
    d. Parameters that define algorithmic complexity
2. What are the key components of a recurrence relation?
    a. Base case, sub problems, constants
    b. Base case, recursive case, initial conditions
    c. Initial conditions, constant factors, solution
    d. Base case, decision trees, complexity analysis
3. Which mathematical technique is commonly used to solve recurrence relations by guessing a solution and proving it?
    a. Substitution method
    b. Recursion tree method
    c. Master theorem
    d. Divide-and-conquer method
4. What does the base case represent in a recurrence relation?
    a. Starting point or condition where the recurrence stops

   b. Condition for infinite recursion
   c. Maximum limit of the recursion depth
   d. Complexity factor for the algorithm

5. Which algorithm efficiently tracks the maximum sum of a contiguous subarray?
   a. Merge Sort
   b. Kadane's Algorithm
   c. Quick Sort
   d. Bubble Sort

6. What is the primary purpose of the substitution method in solving recurrences?
   a. To guess and verify the solution
   b. To construct recursion trees
   c. To identify overlapping subproblems
   d. To analyze time complexity

7. Which method involves representing recursive calls as a tree to solve recurrence relations?
   a. Substitution method
   b. Master theorem
   c. Recursion tree method
   d. Dynamic programming

8. Which case of the master method indicates that the time complexity is proportional to n log n?
   a. Case 1
   b. Case 2
   c. Case 3
   d. None of the above

9. What is the time complexity of Heap Sort?
   a. O(n^2)
   b. O(n log n)
   c. O(n)
   d. O(log n)

10. What is the primary advantage of Heap Sort over other sorting algorithms?
    a. Adaptive sorting
    b. Quadatic sorting
    c. In-place sorting
    d. Linear-time complexity

11. What technique is used to solve recurrence relations by breaking them down into a tree structure?
    a. Substitution method
    b. Master theorem
    c. Recursion tree method
    d. Dynamic programming

12. Which step is essential in applying the substitution method to solve recurrence relations?
    a. Guessing the solution
    b. Analyzing space complexity
    c. Constructing recursion trees
    d. Comparing runtimes of different algorithms

13. Which theorem provides a concise way to determine the time complexity of divide-and-conquer algorithms?
    a. Master theorem
    b. Substitution theorem
    c. Recursion theorem
    d. Dynamic programming theorem

14. Which algorithm uses a binary heap data structure to efficiently organize elements for sorting?
    a. Quick Sort
    b. Merge Sort
    c. Insertion Sort
    d. Heap Sort

15. What limitation of Heap Sort is mentioned in this chapter?
    a. Non-adaptivity
    b. Lack of stability
    c. High space complexity
    d. Dependency on initial order

Solution of MCQ:

1	2	3	4	5	6	7	8	9	10	11	12	13	14	15
a	b	a	a	b	a	c	b	b	c	c	a	a	d	a

SHORT AND LONG ANSWER TYPE QUESTIONS

1. Write pseudocode for binary search algorithm: provide pseudocode for the algorithm, outlining the complexity using Master's theorem?
2. Explain the basic principle behind Heap sort?
3. Provide a detailed explanation of the Heap Sort algorithm, including its steps, time complexity, and advantages?
4. What is the Maximum Subarray Problem? Define the "subarray" in the context of the Maximum Subarray Problem.
5. What is the objective of the Maximum Subarray problem? Explain the significance of the

"contiguous" condition in a subarray.

6. What is the time complexity of the brute-force approach for solving the Maximum Subarray Problem?
7. Describe the brute-force approach to solving the Maximum Subarray Problem. Provide an algorithmic overview?
8. Explain Kadane's algorithm for finding the Maximum Subarray. Include the key steps and discuss its time complexity?
9. Illustrate the divide-and-conquer approach for the Maximum Subarray problem. Provide a step-by-step explanation of the algorithm and analyze its time complexity?
10. Discuss the dynamic programming solution to the Maximum Subarray problem, outlining the recurrence relation and the main steps of the algorithm?
11. Examine the real-world applications of the Maximum Subarray Problem. How can the solution be applied in various domains, and what insights does it provide in those contexts?
12. Briefly explain the Substitution method in the context of solving recurrence relations?
13. What is the Recurrence tree method, how it aids in solving recurrence relations?
14. Summarize the Master's theorem and its application in algorithmic analysis.
15. Explain the step-by-step process of using heap sort on a given list of elements.
16. Describe the Recurrence Tree Method in detail, using an example to demonstrate how it is applied to analyze the time complexity of an algorithm.
17. Elaborate on the Master's theorem, its three cases, and provide examples illustrating each case. Explain when and how the Master's theorem is applied in algorithmic analysis.

KNOW MORE

Online courses/materials/resources [Accessed May 2024]

- https://github.com/topics/recurrence-relation
- https://www.geeksforgeeks.org/recurrence-relations-a-complete-guide/
- https://en.wikipedia.org/wiki/Recurrence_relation
- https://www.javatpoint.com/daa-recurrence-relation
- https://brilliant.org/wiki/recurrence-relations/
- https://archive.nptel.ac.in/courses/111/106/111106086/
- https://stanford-cs161.github.io/winter2023-bank/recurrence.pdf

REFERENCES

[1] Bentley, Jon Louis. "Multidimensional binary search trees used for associative searching." Communications of the ACM 18, no. 9 (1975): 509-517.

[2] Goel, Vinod, and Jordan Grafman. "Are the frontal lobes implicated in "planning" functions? Interpreting data from the Tower of Hanoi." Neuropsychologia 33, no. 5 (1995): 623-642.

[3] Takaoka, Tadao. "Efficient algorithms for the maximum subarray problem by distance matrix multiplication." Electronic Notes in Theoretical Computer Science 61 (2002): 191-200.

[4] Huss-Lederman, Steven, Elaine M. Jacobson, Jeremy R. Johnson, Anna Tsao, and Thomas Turnbull. "Strassen's algorithm for matrix multiplication: Modeling, analysis, and implementation." In Proceedings of Supercomputing, vol. 96, pp. 9-6. 1996.

4 Graph and Tree Algorithms

UNIT SPECIFICS

This unit covers the following aspects:

- *Preliminaries of graphs*
- *Depth first and breadth first search*
- *Shortest path algorithms, transitive closure*
- *Minimum spanning tree, topological sorting, network flow algorithm.*
- *Unit summary, short and long answer questions*

This unit provides an exploration of fundamental graph algorithms and network flow techniques. It begins by establishing the preliminaries of graphs, laying the foundation for a comprehensive understanding of their structures and properties. After that, the unit covers traversal algorithms, namely breadth first and depth first search. Afterwards, the time complexities of shortest path algorithm is described, providing insights on determining the most effective paths between nodes in a graph. We further investigate Minimum Spanning Tree techniques, which offer useful information for building the best tree structures in connected graphs. The unit also cover Topological Sorting, which provides a methodical means of organizing vertices in a directed acyclic network and is essential for a number of applications. In this unit, we will talk about network flow algorithms to wrap up our study. The link given in the QR code provides the supplementary material for this unit.

RATIONALE

The rationale for the unit on graph algorithms and network flow techniques lies in the foundational importance of these concepts in computer science and various practical applications. Graphs serve as versatile models to represent and analyze relationships among entities, and understanding algorithms related to graph traversal, connectivity, and optimization is fundamental in algorithmic design and analysis. Traversal algorithms are fundamental for exploring and navigating through graph structures efficiently. Depth First Search and Breadth First Search are essential techniques with diverse applications, including pathfinding, connected components identification, and cycle detection. Shortest path algorithms are pivotal for optimizing network routes, whether for transportation, communication, or resource allocation. Minimum Spanning Tree algorithms play a crucial role in network design and optimization. Topological sorting is indispensable in scenarios where dependencies need to be managed efficiently. It finds applications in task scheduling, project management, and optimizing parallel computations.

PRE-REQUISITES

Basic knowledge of data structures like linked lists, trees, and sorting algorithms.

UNIT OUTCOMES

The outcomes of the Unit are as follows:

U4-O1: Learning the concept of graph

U4-O2: Understanding depth first and breadth first search

U4-O3: Learn shortest path algorithms

U4-O4: Understanding minimum spanning tree algorithms

U4-O5: Understanding topological sorting and network flow algorithms.

Unit-4 Outcomes	***EXPECTED MAPPING WITH COURSE OUTCOMES*** *(1- Weak Correlation; 2- Medium correlation; 3- Strong Correlation)*				
	CO-1	***CO-2***	***CO-3***	***CO-4***	***CO-5***
U4-O1	*3*	*-*	*2*	*2*	*-*
U4-O2	*2*	*2*	*2*	*2*	*-*
U4-O3	*3*	*2*	*2*	*2*	*-*
U4-O4	*3*	*2*	*2*	*2*	*-*
U4-O5	*3*	*1*	*2*	*2*	*-*

4.1 Representation of Graphs

A graph is a collection of nodes (also known as vertices) and edges joining node pairs, is a basic data structure in computer science. Graphs are widely utilised in many applications, including computer networks, transportation systems, and social networks, to represent relationships between elements. Directed graphs, sometimes known as digraphs, and undirected graphs are the two primary categories of graphs. The primary elements and ideas of a graph data structure are as follows:

- *Node (Vertex):* A fundamental unit of a graph. Nodes represent entities, and they may contain additional information called attributes.
- *Edge:* A connection between two nodes that indicates a relationship between them. Edges may have a direction in directed graphs, pointing from one node to another, or they may be undirected, representing a two-way relationship.
- *Weight:* An optional value associated with an edge, indicating a numerical measure such as distance or cost. Graphs with weighted edges are called weighted graphs.
- *Adjacency:* The adjacency of an edge indicates whether it connects two nodes. When two nodes are connected by an edge, they are said to be neighbours.
- *Degree:* The degree of node is determined by the edges that link to it. Nodes may have an in-degree (number of incoming edges) and an out-degree (number of outgoing edges) in directed graphs.
- *Path:* A sequence of edges that connect nodes in a graph.
- *Cycle:* A path that forms a complete loop by beginning and ending at the same node.
- *Connected Graph:* A graph is connected iff there is a path between each pair of nodes.
- *Directed Acyclic Graph (DAG):* A directed graph with no cycles.

Graph Traversal Algorithms:

- *Depth-First Search (DFS):* Before turning around, travel as far as feasible along each branch.
- *Breadth-First Search (BFS):* Investigates every neighbor node at the current depth before going on to nodes at a subsequent depth level.

Applications:

a. Social network analysis
b. Routing algorithms in computer networks
c. Recommendation systems
d. Modelling dependencies in tasks

Various data structures can be used to represent graphs, and the choice of representation relies on the characteristics of the graph and the operations carried on it. A graph $G(V, E)$ is represented using one of two common methods: either as an adjacency matrix or as a set of adjacency lists. This option works for graphs that are directed or undirected. Adjacency-list representation should be used, especially for sparse graphs (where the square of the number of vertices ($|V|^2$) is much smaller than the number of edges ($|E|$). The effectiveness of this approach in managing sparse graph structures makes it the recommended solution. The majority of graph algorithms covered in this book are predicated on the idea that the input graph is given as an adjacency list. On the other hand, when working with dense graphs—where the edges count almost match to the square of vertices count—or when it is imperative to quickly ascertain whether an edge exists between two given vertices, an adjacency-matrix representation might be more appropriate. Each representation has benefits, and the selection is contingent upon the particular attributes and specifications of the given graph. The discussion on the two primary representations: the adjacency matrix and the adjacency list are as follows:

Adjacency list representation: The representation of a graph $G(V, E)$ using an adjacency list involves an array, denoted as Adj, consisting of $|V|$ lists, each corresponding to a vertex in V. Given a vertex $u \varepsilon V$, the list $Adj[u]$ have vertices v for which $\exists$ edge $(u, v) \varepsilon V$. As an alternative, it might hold references to these vertices. Similar to how we handle the edge set E, we utilize Adj as an attribute of G in pseudocode, $G.Adj[u]$. There is an array of lists used. The vertices in Adj determines its size. Here, benefits of using adjacency list representation are: efficient for sparse graphs and consumes less space as it only stores information. The disadvantages are not as efficient for dense graphs and checking the existence of an edge takes $O(V)$ time. In Figure 4.1(b), we can observe G in Figure 4.1(a) using an adjacency list. Similarly, Figure 4.1(c) illustrates the adjacency matrix corresponding to the directed G.

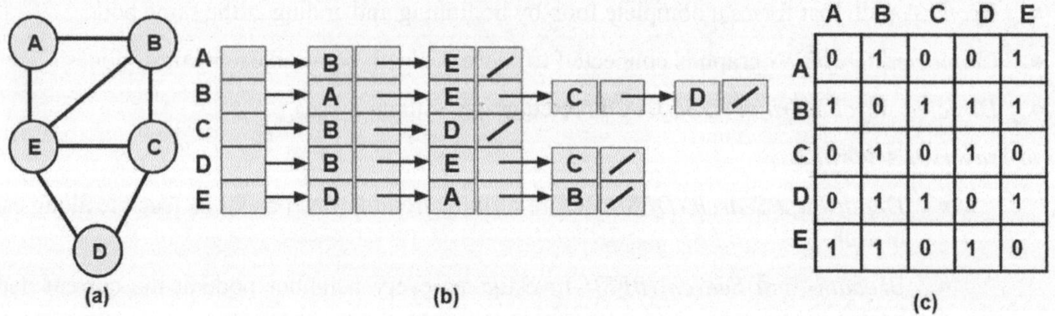

Figure 4.1: Adjacency list and adjacency matrix on undirected graph. (a) graph G, (b) adjacency-list of G, and (c) adjacency-matrix of G.

The length of every adjacency list in a directed graph is equal to the number of edges E. Since both u and v appear in the adjacency lists of each other given (u, v) is an undirected edge, the sum here for undirected graph is $2E$. One benefit of the adjacency-list is of handling both vertices and edges with $O(V + E)$ memory. This becomes simple for modification to accommodate weighted graphs having assigned weight to each edge. The adjacency list of vertex u contains $w(u, v)$. One potential drawback of adjacency-list is not offering a faster way to determine the presence of a given edge (u, v) than searching for v in $Adj[u]$. While an adjacency-matrix can expedite this process, it incurs a higher memory.

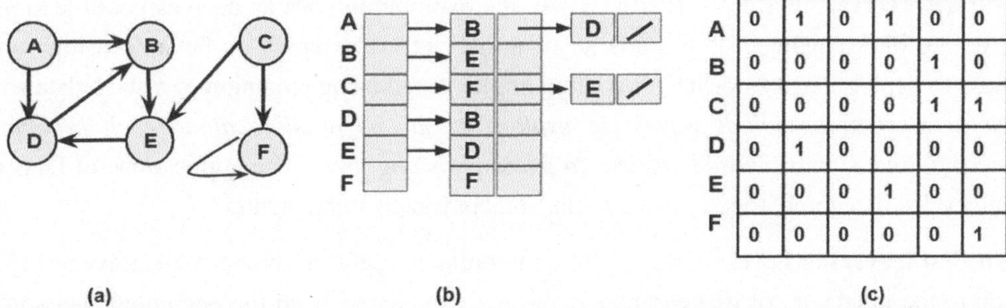

Figure 4.2: (a) a schematic showing a directed graph G with 6 vertices and 8 edges; (b) the adjacency-list of G; and (c) adjacency-matrix of G.

Adjacency matrix: An adjacency matrix is a two dimensional array of size $V \times V$, where V is the vertex count of G. The primary benefits of adjacency matrices are effectiveness for dense graphs with densities close to maximum. It also provide a clear indication of the presence of edges between vertices. However, it also possesses some disadvantages including being inefficient for sparse graphs (graphs with fewer edges) and consuming more space compared to the actual number of edges in sparse graphs.

Given an adjacency-matrix of $G = (V, E)$, V is assumed to be numbered $1,2,3,\ldots,|V|$. The adjacency-matrix G is a $V \times V$ matrix such that $A[i][j] = 1, if\ (i,j) \in E$, and and 0 otherwise. The adjacency matrices for directed & undirected G are shown Figures 4.1(a) and 4.2(a) are displayed in Figures 4.1(c) and 4.2(c), respectively. $O(V^2)$ memory is required for the adjacency matrix. Adjacency matrices are symmetrical for undirected graphs $A = A^T$, and in some cases, storing only the entries on and above the diagonal can reduce the memory needed to store G. Weighted graphs can be supported using adjacency-list and matrix, with weights saved appropriately. Adjacency matrices are simpler, hence they are preferred for short graphs, even if the adjacency-list form is at least as space-efficient as the adjacency-matrix representation. Because they only need one bit per entry, adjacency matrices are also useful for unweighted graphs.

4.2 Traversal Algorithms: Depth-First Search and Breadth-First Search

Graph traversal is a process of visiting and exploring the vertices of graph G. It involves moving from one vertex to another, following the edges, in a specific order until all vertices have been visited. Traversal is a fundamental operation in graphs and is employed for gathering information about the topology of the graphs. Graph traversal is a versatile concept that underlies many algorithms and applications, playing a crucial role in understanding and analyzing the relationships in a graph structure.

Depth-First Search (DFS) and Breadth-First Search (BFS) are two popular graph traversal techniques. These algorithms work on directed and undirected graphs alike. Depending on the needs of the challenge, depth-first or breadth-first approach should be chosen.

Depth-first traversal: In a depth-first traversal, the exploration goes as deep as possible along each branch before backtracking [1]. It starts at an initial vertex, explores as far as possible, and then backtracks to explore other branches. It is often implemented using recursion or a stack data structure. Process: *1) start at an initial vertex, 2) explore as far as possible along each branch before backtracking, and 3) mark visited vertices to avoid revisiting them.* The applications of DFS include detecting cycles in a graph, topological sorting, and connected components.

Breadth-first traversal: Level after level, the exploration happens in a breadth-first traverse [1]. Before going on to the neighbors of its neighbors, it visits every vertex from the beginning. This procedure keeps going until every vertex has been touched. It is usually implemented with a data structure called a queue. Process: 1) begin at a starting vertex, 2) queue the starting vertex, 3) dequeue a vertex, visit it, and queue its neighbors who have not been visited, and 4) continue until the queue is empty. Web crawling, connection testing, and shortest path discovery (unweighted graphs) are the uses of BFS.

Traversal purpose:

Connectivity analysis: It helps to determine whether a graph is connected or has isolated components.

- *Path finding:* It is useful for determining routes or paths that connect two vertices.
- *Cycle detection:* Traversal aids in identifying cycles within the graph.
- *Component identification:* Traversal helps to identify connected components in G.
- *Topological sorting:* For directed acyclic graphs, traversal is used to obtain a topological ordering.

Traversal in applications:

- *Network routing:* Used to find efficient routes in computer networks.
- *Web crawling:* Search engines use traversal to navigate and index web pages.
- *Maze solving:* Traversal is employed to find a path through a maze.
- *Game development:* In game environments, traversal is used for path finding and exploration.

Dijkstra's algorithm: In a weighted graph, Dijkstra's algorithm determines the shortest path between two vertices [2]. To quickly choose the vertex with the least tentative distance, it uses a priority queue. *Process:* when there are vertices that not yet visited, 1) set the distances to all of them to infinity, excluding the the source (distance = 0); and 2) choose the vertex that has the shortest tentative distance and update the distances of its unvisited neighbours. In weighted graphs, Dijkstra's algorithm is used to discover the shortest path.

Bellman-Ford algorithm: Bellman-Ford algorithm determines the shortest path between two vertices in a weighted graph, even if it contains negative weight edges [3]. It iteratively relaxes edges until the shortest paths are found. *Process:* 1) initialize distances to all vertices as infinity, except the source vertex (distance = 0), 2) relax all edges repeatedly, and 3) detect negative cycles if reachable from the source. Bellman-Ford algorithm application includes shortest path finding in weighted graphs with negative weights.

These traversal algorithms are important in various applications, including network routing, pathfinding, and connectivity analysis in computer science and real-world systems. This chapter will one-by-one discuss all the aforementioned algorithms in detail.

4.3 Breadth-First Search

Among the basic algorithms for graph exploration, Breadth-First Search (BFS) stands out as a model for many important graph algorithms. The ideas behind BFS serve as the basis for important algorithms like Dijkstra's single-source shortest-paths and Prim's minimum-spanning-tree algorithms.

Applying BFS on $G = (V, E)$ with a given source vertex s, it methodically explores all the edges of G to identify each vertex that can be reached from s. It creates a breadth-first tree rooted at s, which includes all accessible vertices by calculating the distance (route with least weight of edges) between each accessible vertex and s. The shortest path in G, a path with the fewest edges from s to v is equal to the simple path in the breadth-first tree for any vertex v reachable from s. The algorithm is capable of handling directed and undirected graphs, which is significant. The term breadth-first search refers to the process of gradually expanding the boundary between vertices that have been found and those that have not along the entire width of the frontier. In other words, it explores vertices at a distance $k + 1$ after uncovering all the vertices at a $dist(k, s)$.

To monitor progress, BFS assigns colors—white, gray/black—to each vertex. Initially, all vertices are white and may transition to gray or eventually black. A vertex becomes discovered during the search, signifying a change from its initial white state. While gray and black vertices both indicate discovery, the algorithm differentiates between them to ensure a breadth-first progression. In particular, a vertex v can be grey or black if an edge (u, v) exists in E and vertex u is black. This difference in color indicates the boundary between discovered and undiscovered vertices; grey vertices may contain some neighbouring white vertices, but all vertices adjacent to black are obtained. Building a breadth-first tree from the root, the source vertex s, is the first step in the breadth-first search process. When a white v found while reviewing adjacency list for a previously found vertex, edge (u, v) and vertex v are appended. In this case, u is considered as the parent of v or predecessor in breadth-first tree. v has a maximum one parent as it is only found once. In the breadth-first tree, ancestor and descendant relationships follow the standard definitions with regard to root s: if u is descendant of v and resides on the path that connects s to v, then v is a descendant of u.

BFS algorithm presented below assumes that $G = (V, E)$ is denoted via adjacency lists. Further, the attributes are associated with each vertex of G. The color $u \in V$ is preserved in $u{:}\,color$, and the predecessor of u in $u{:}\,predecessor$. If $u{:}\,predecessor \rightarrow NULL$ (e.g., if $u = s$ or u is nondiscoverable), then $u\!:\!predecessor \rightarrow NULL$. $u\!:d$ represents the distance s to vertex u. Additionally, algorithm utilizes a first-in, first-out queue Q to manage gray vertices. This pseudocode assumes G is denoted via adjacency lists and uses the colors WHITE, GRAY, and BLACK to denote the state of each vertex during the traversal. Adjustments may be needed based on specific implementation details and language conventions.

Procedure Breadth First Search (BFS)

BFS (G, s)**:**

1. Initialize all vertices in G:

    for each u in $G.V$:

    u:color = WHITE // *WHITE represents undiscovered*

    u:predecessor = NIL // *NIL indicates no predecessor*

    $d(u) = \infty$ // *Initialize distance to infinity*

2. Set the attributes for the source vertex s:

    s:color = GRAY // *GRAY represents the current frontier*

    s:predecessor = NIL

    $d(s) = 0$ // Distance from the source to itself is 0

3. Initialize the queue Q and enqueue the source vertex s:

    Q.enqueue(s)

4. while Q is not empty:

    a: Dequeue a vertex u from Q.

    b: for each v adjacent to u:

    If v color is WHITE: // v is undiscovered

    Set v: color to GRAY // Mark v as part of the frontier

    Set v: predecessor to u // Set u as the predecessor of v

    Set $v\!: d$ to $v\!: d + 1$ // Update distance from the source

    Enqueue v into Q // Add v to the queue

    c. Set u:color to BLACK // Mark u as fully explored

5. BFS traversal has completed.

Figure 4.3 illustrates the basic working principle of BFS using different color vertices as mentioned in the above procedure.

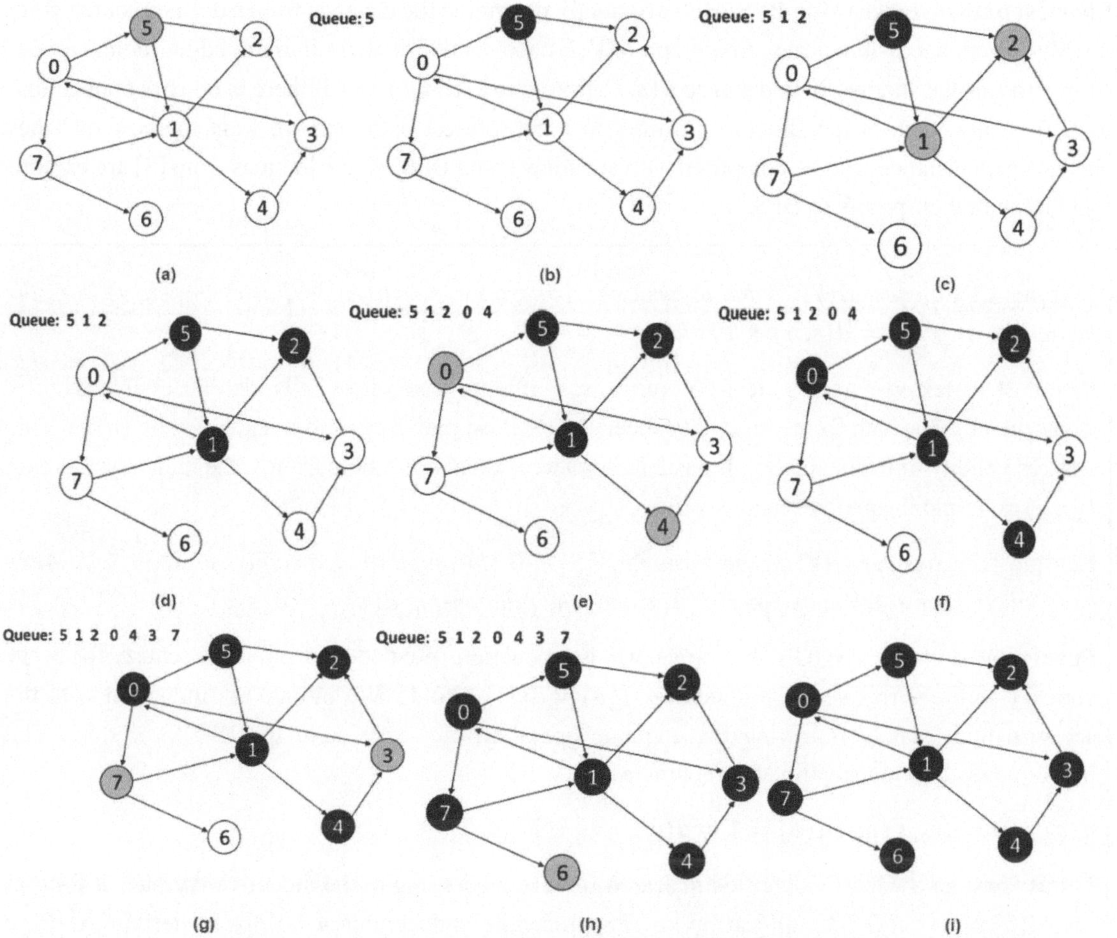

Figure 4.3: Executing BFS on a directed graph involves shading tree edges generated by the algorithm.

Analysis of BFS: Let us first tackle the relatively simpler issue of analysing the runtime of breadth-first search on a given input network $Q = (V, E)$ before diving into the presentation of various features related to it. By use of aggregate analysis, we find that breadth-first search guarantees that a vertex is never whitened following initialization. Every vertex will only be enqueued once and then dequeued once, according to the procedure's condition. The temporal complexity of both the enqueuing and dequeuing processes is $O(1)$. As a result, the total time spent on operations is $O(V)$. Every adjacency list is scanned a maximum of once by the method, which looks at adjacency list of each vertex only during the dequeue operation. The total scanning time of the adjacency lists is $O(E)$, where E is the addition of the lengths of all lists. Because of the $O(V)$ overhead related to initialization, the breadth-first search procedure total runtime complexity is $O(V + E)$. As a result, the breadth-first search takes a duration that is proportional to the adjacency-list of G.

Shortest path distance using BFS: BFS efficiently determine the distance from a defined source vertex $s \in V$ to every accessible vertex in a graph $G(V, E)$. Let us define the minimum edges along any path from s to t as the shortest-path distance $d(s, t)$ from s to t. $d(s, t) = 1$ if there is no path connecting s to t. We call a path of length $d(s, t)$ from s to t the shortest path, and we want to show that these shortest-path distances can be computed with accuracy using BFS. A few lemmas from [3] are explored together with their proofs of BFS.

Lemma 4.1 *Consider $G(V, E)$ and assume s is any arbitrary vertex in V. For every (u, v) in E, the inequality $d(s, v) <= d(s, u) + 1$ holds.*

Proof: If vertex u is accessible from vertex s, it implies that vertex v is also accessible from s. Consequently, the path from s to v not exceed the smallest path from s to u, extended by (u, v). This ensures validity of the inequality. In instances where u is not accessible from s, the indicator function $I(s, u) = 1$, and inequality remains valid. □

Lemma 4.2 *Consider $G(V, E)$, performing BFS on G starting with a specified source $s \in V$. After completion, each $v \in V$, computed $d(v)$ satisfy the relationship $d(v) <= d(s, v)$.*

Proof: Based on the ENQUEUE actions, we use induction. We deduce from this because, for every vertex v in the vertex set , the condition $d(v) = d(s, v)$ holds. We initiate the induction with the scenario immediately following the enqueue operation on vertex s in the BFS procedure. The inductive assumption is valid at this point, as

$d(s) = 0 = d(s, s)$ and $d(v) = 1 = d(s, v)\ \forall v \in V \backslash \{s\}$.

Let us consider a white v identified in search from u. According to the inductive premise, it follows that $d(u) = d(s, u)$. Such allocation in BFS procedure and Lemma 4.1 helps in deriving $d(v) = d(u) + 1 = d(s, u) + 1 = d(s, v)$. After the enqueue operation, v turns gray and enters a state where it will not be enqueued again due to the conditions specified in BFS procedure, applying to white vertices. Consequently, the value of d remains constant for v, maintaining inductive assumptions. To establish $d(v) = d(s, v)$, we need to provide a more detailed understanding of the queue Q operation during BFS. A subsequent lemma demonstrates that the queue always holds a maximum of two distinct d values at any given time.

Lemma 4.3 *Consider the scenario where BFS is being executed $G(V, E)$. Let us consider that queue Q is populated with vertices $v_1, v_2, \ldots, v_r$. v_1 represents the queue front, and v_r represents the rear. Then it can be observed that $d(v_r) <= d(v_1) + 1$ and $d(v_i) <= d(v_{i+1})\ \forall\ i = 1, 2, \cdots r - 1$.*

Proof: Using induction based on the quantity of queue operations, the proof is carried out. First, when the only elements in the queue are the vertices. The lemma holds with triviality. We want to show that the lemma is true on inductive step even after s has been both dequeued and enqueued.

Upon dequeuing 1, with 2 becoming the next front (or lemma holding if the queue becomes empty), we rely on hypothesis: $d(v_1) <= d(v_2)$. Consequently, you observe that $d(v_r) <= d(v_1) + 1 <= d(v_2) + 1$, and the other inequalities remain unchanged. Hence, the lemma persists with 2 as the new head.

To analyze the effects of enqueuing a vertex. When a vertex v is enqueued in the BFS procedure, it takes on v_{r+1}. Since the vertex u has already been eliminated from the queue Q at this point, the further front v_1 fulfills $d(v_1) <= d(u)$ according to the inductive hypothesis. Thus, we find that $d(v_{r+1}) = d(v) = d(u) + 1 <= d(v_1) + 1$, and inequalities remain unaffected. From hypothesis, we have $d(v_r) <= d(u) + 1$ and $d(v_r) <= d(u) + 1 = d(v) = d(v_{r+1})$ and remaining inequalities are unaffected. Thus, it holds if v is enqueued.

Breadth-First Tree: It is built by traversing a graph or a tree level by level. It is typically used in graph algorithms, and constructing a breadth-first tree starts on a selected root vertex and explores the graph or tree in a breadth-first manner.

Procedure Breadth-First Tree (BFT)

1. Initialization:
   a. Choose a starting vertex to serve as the root.
   b. Initialize an empty queue to keep track of vertices to be processed.
2. Enqueue the Root:

   Enqueue the root vertex into the queue.
3. Breadth-First Traversal:

   while $queue \neq empty$:

   i. A vertex at the front of the queue can be dequeued. In the breadth-first tree, this vertex is now the node.

   ii. Put all of the current nodes, unvisited neighbours on the queue.

   iii. To prevent going back to the dequeued vertex, mark it as visited.
4. Termination:

   When the queue is empty, meaning that all vertices that can be reached have been handled, stop.

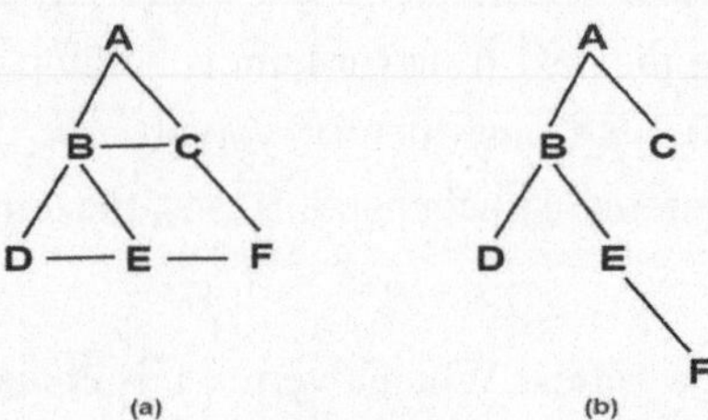

Figure 4.4: Illustration of the breadth-first tree using an undirected graph. a) considered undirected graph, and b) obtained breadth-first tree.

Let us illustrate the above procedure with an example using the undirected graph, as shown in Figure 4.4(a). Let us construct a breadth-first tree starting from vertex A:

- *Initialization:* a) start with the root vertex A and b) initialize an empty queue.
- *Enqueue the root:* enqueue A into the queue.
- *BFS Traversal:* dequeue A and enqueue its unvisited neighbours B and C.
    a. dequeue B and enqueue its unvisited neighbours D and E.
    b. dequeue C then enqueue its unvisited neighbour F.
    c. dequeue D then enqueue its unvisited neighbour E.
    d. dequeue E and enqueue its unvisited neighbour F.
- *Termination:* The breadth-first traversal is finished and the queue is empty.

The resulting breadth-first tree (with A as the root) is given in Figure 4.4(b). This tree represents the order of vertex discovery during the traversal, and the edges connect each vertex to its parent in the traversal.

4.4 Depth-First Search

The approach known as Depth-first Search (DFS) gets the term from its emphasis on diving deeper into the graph. Starting with the primarily identified vertex, which is unidentified, the procedure explores edges first. After all edges from this vertex have been thoroughly examined, the search goes back and examines edges from the vertex that disclosed the present one. Until all reachable vertices from the source are found, this iterative process is continued. DFS identifies the unexplored vertices as the next source and resumes the exploration. This process keeps going until all the vertices are marked visited. Unlike BFS, which creates a predecessor subgraph (resembles a tree), DFS creates a predecessor subgraph that has several trees in it, since the search may recommence from different sources. Thus, the predecessor of DFS subgraph is described as $G_D(V, E)$, E consists of edges (u, v) such that $v \in E$ and $u \neq nill$. A depth-first forest is constituted by multiple depth-first trees in the appearance of the depth-first predecessor subgraph.

Similar to BFS, DFS leverages vertex coloring to signify their states throughout the exploration. Initially, each vertex is white, transitioning to gray upon discovery, and ultimately turning black after completely examining its adjacency list. This coloring methodology ensures every vertex is encompassed by a precisely depth tree. DFS timestamps every vertex with two values: 1st timestamp (marks as d) marks the initial discovery, and 2nd timestamp (marks as f) signifies completion of the adjacency list examination. Providing important details about the structure of the graph, the subsequent content aids in comprehending the explanation of DFS behavior. In the DFS procedure outlined below, the identification of vertex u is documented in $u{:}\,d$ upon discovery and in $u{:}\,f$ upon completion. Such timestamps, falling within the integer range of 1 to 2 times the vertex count ($|V|$), to one discovery and other finishing events for each vertex. According to the following relation: $u{:}\,d < u{:}\,f$. For given u, state transitions as follows: it is WHITE $u{:}\,d$, GRAY between times $u{:}\,d$ & $u{:}\,f$, and BLACK further. Basic DFS algorithm is provided in the following method. The variable $time$ acts as a global timestamp on G, which can be either directed or undirected.

Procedure Depth First Search

```
DFS(G)
    1. for each u in G:V
           a. u:color ← WHITE
           b. u:π ← NULL
           c. t ← 0 // t = time
    2.     for each u in G:V
               if u:color==WHITE then DFS-VISIT(G, u)

DFS-VISIT(G, u)
    1. t ← t+1  // White vertex u has just been discovered
    2. u: d ← t and u:color ← GRAY
    3. for each v in G: Adj[u]
           if v:color == WHITE then v: π ← u and DFS-VISIT(G, v)
    4. u:color ← BLACK
    5. t ← t+1
    6. u: f ← t
```

The outcomes of DFS can be influenced by the sequence in which DFS examines vertices and the order in which DFS-VISIT traverses the neighbors. In real-world scenarios, these varied visiting orders typically do not pose significant issues, as we can generally apply any DFS result effectively, to obtain essentially equivalent outcomes. Determining the runtime of DFS involves analyzing the loops. These loops collectively consume a time of $\Theta(V)$, excluding the time required for executing DFS-VISIT. Employing aggregate analysis, it is noted that DFS-VISIT is invoked exactly once for each vertex $v \in V$, as the vertex u on which DFS-VISIT is applied must be white, and the initial action of DFS-VISIT is to mark vertex u as gray. Throughout the execution of DFS-VISIT(G, v), the loop iterates $|Adj[v]|$ number of times. For given,

$$\sum_{v \in V} |Adj[v]| = \Theta(E),$$

overall executing loop in DFS-VISIT demands the cost $= \Theta(E)$. Thus, runtime associated with DFS is expressed as $\Theta(V + E)$.

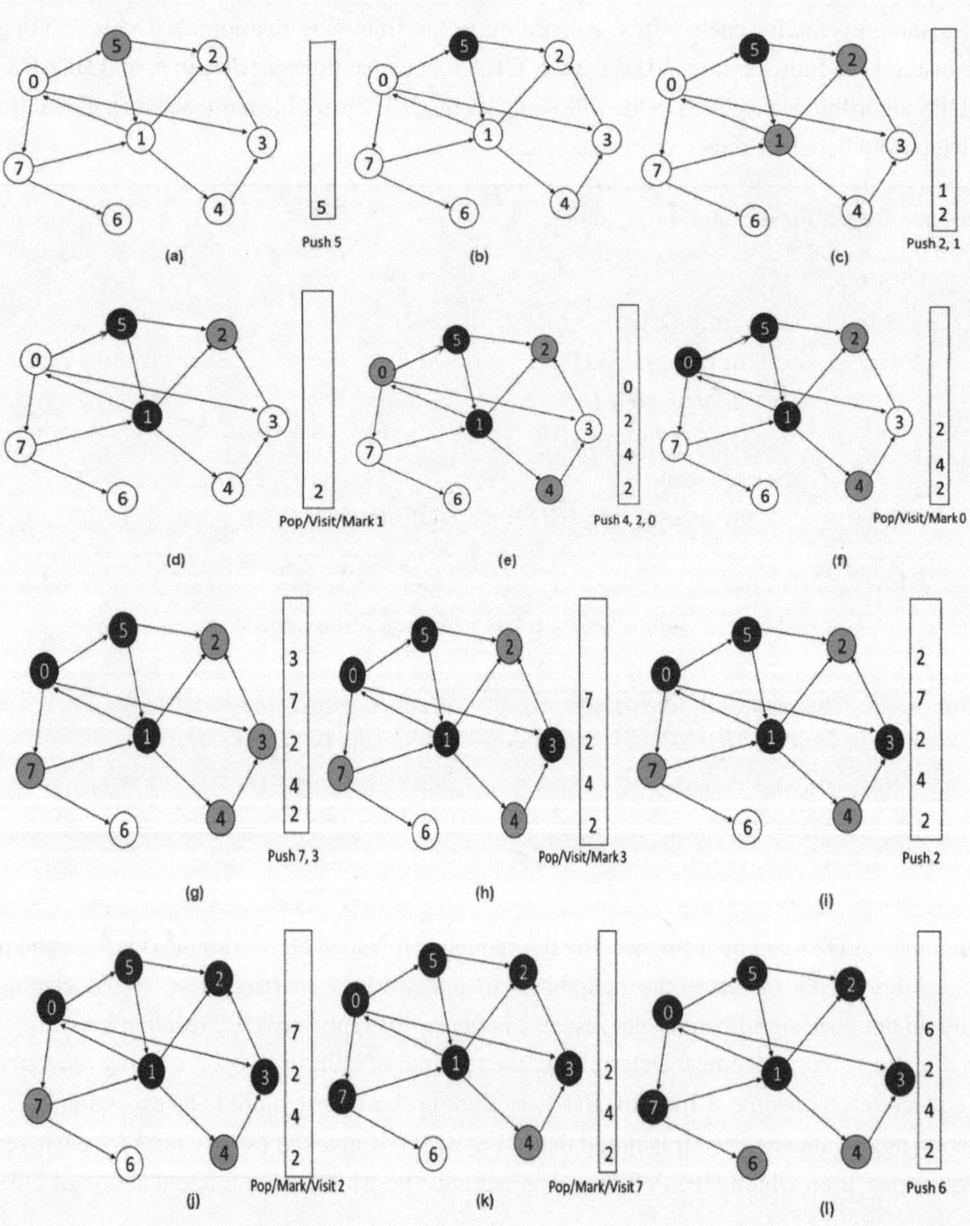

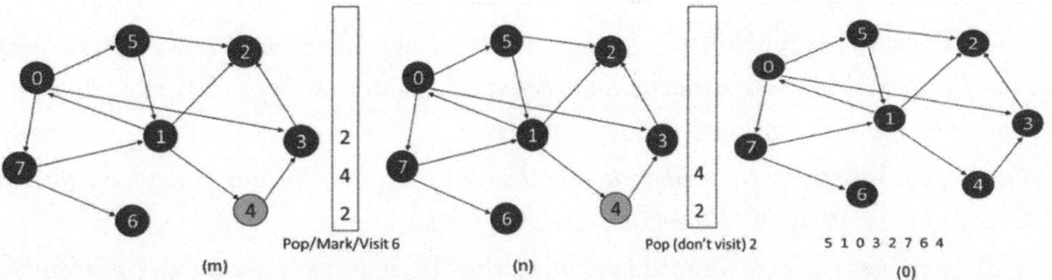

Figure 4.5: An illustration of DFS using given connected graphs, using the procedure of DFS from (a) to (o) to obtain traversal order: [5,1,0,3,2,7,6,4].

Example 4.1 (DFS)**:** Let us consider directed graphs Figure 4.5 (a), we have to perform DFS. Starting with the start node (5), we explore as far as possible along each directed edge before backtracking. Start at Node 5 and visit it 5. Explore outgoing edges from Node 5 and move to Node 1. Next, visit node 1 and explore the outgoing edges of node 1. Explore outgoing edges from node 1, move to node 0 and visit it. Explore the outgoing edges from node 0 and so on. further, explore outgoing edges from node 6, which have no outgoing edges and finally move to node 4 and visit node 4 with no outgoing edges. The resulting depth-first traversal sequence in the directed graph is [5,1,0,3,2,7,6,4]. This sequence represents the order in which nodes are visited.

Characteristics of depth-first search

i. *Predecessor subgraph:* DFS yields useful structured data for graphs. A fundamental observation is of the **predecessor subgraph** G_π forms a forest. This happens because the DFS-VISIT process the recursive calls are exactly mirrored in the organization of the depth trees. In other words, a vertex u is part of G_π if and only if the DFS-VISIT operation for u was invoked during the exploration of its adjacency list. Further, the relationship between vertices in the depth-first forest is well-defined. In the depth-first forest, a vertex v is specifically regarded as a descendant of vertex u if and only if v is found during the period when u is in the grey state, signalling the continuous investigation of its neighbouring vertices. This hierarchical structure within the forest encapsulates the temporal order of vertex contributes to a comprehensive understanding of the graph connectivity.

ii. *Parenthesis structure:* In graph algorithms, timestamps frequently have a parenthesis structure. When we use a left parenthesis to indicate that vertex u has been found. The order of discoveries and finishings creates a coherent phrase. The brackets in this instance are correctly nested and follow a systematic and ordered pattern.

Theorem 4.1 (Parenthesis Theorem): *In the context of any DFS conducted on a graph G with vertices V and edges E, whether directed/undirected (denoted as $G = (V, E)$), ∃ vertices u and θ, precisely one of the three conditions:*

1. *Within depth-first forest, neither u nor θ is a descendant of the other, and the intervals $[u{:}\,d, u{:}\,f]$ and $[\theta{:}\,d, \theta{:}\,f]$ are completely disjoint.*
2. *In a depth tree, u is a descendent of θ, and $[u{:}\,d, u{:}\,f]$ interval is completely lies in $[\theta{:}\,d, \theta{:}\,f]$.*
3. *The interval is entirely contained in the interval $[u{:}\,d, u{:}\,f]$, and in a depth-first tree, θ is a descendent.*

Proof:

Condition 1: Assume that there is some disjointness between the intervals in order to create a contradiction. This implies that there exists an overlap in time intervals, violating the depth-first search ordering. If u were a descendant of θ or vice versa, it would contradict the disjoint nature of the intervals. Thus, the statement holds true.

Condition 2: Consider the scenario where $[u{:}\,d, u{:}\,f]$ is not wholly contained within $[\theta{:}\,d, \theta{:}\,f]$. In this case, there would be an overlap, violating the DFS ordering. If u is not a descendant of θ, it contradicts the containment of interval. Thus, the statement is verified.

Condition 3: Similar to Condition 2, if $[\theta{:}\,d, \theta{:}\,f]$ is not wholly contained within $[u{:}\,d, u{:}\,f]$, an overlap occurs, violating DFS ordering. If θ is not a descendant of u, it contradicts the containment of the interval. Therefore, the statement holds true.

Edge categorization in DFS: An important characteristic of the DFS is its ability to categorize the edges of $G = (V, E)$. The classification of edges provides crucial insights into the nature of the graph. Four distinct types of edges can be defined based on the G_{DFS} generated using a depth-first search:

i. *Tree Edges:* The edges found in depth forest G_{DFS} are as follows. If studying edge (u, v) led to the discovery of vertex v, then edge (u, v) is a tree edge.

ii. *Back Edges:* In a depth-first tree, these are (u, v) edges that join u to v. Additionally included are self-loops, which can occur in directed graphs.

iii. *Forward Edges:* These are the non-tree edges (u, v) in the tree, which join a vertex u to a descendent v.

iv. *Cross Edges:* Every other edge is part of this group. They can join vertices inside the same depth-first tree, provided that one is not an ancestor of the other. As an alternative, they can connect the vertices of various depth-first trees.

Theorem 4.2: *In the context of a DFS in G, each edge in G is classified as a back edge.*

Proof: Consider an edge (u, v) in graph G, and assume that $u.d < v.d$. In this scenario, the search process must discover and complete the exploration of the edge before finishing the exploration of u

(while u is in the gray state). This is because it is part of $u's$ adjacency list. If, during the first exploration of edge (u, v), the direction is from u to v, then remains undiscovered (white) until that point. If it were already discovered, the search would have explored this edge earlier in the path that goes from v to u. As such, the pair (u, v) is categorised as a tree edge. But since u is still in the grey when the edge is first examined, (u, v) is regarded as a rearward edge if the search examines (u, v) in the direction of v to u.

4.5 Topological Sorting

Topological sorting is a linear ordering of the vertices of a Directed Acyclic Graph (DAG) [4] such that for every directed (u, v), vertex u comes prior to vertex v in the order. In simpler terms, it arranges the vertices in a way that all dependencies are satisfied, and there is an order in which the vertices can be processed. The topological sorting processes as follows:

i. *Select a source vertex:* Choose a vertex that has no incoming edges as the starting point. If there are multiple such vertices, any of them can be chosen.

ii. *Process the vertex:* Process the selected vertex and remove it from the graph, along with its outgoing edges. This step ensures that all the dependencies of the next vertices are satisfied.

iii. *Update in-degree:* Update the in-degree (number of incoming edges) of the remaining vertices, as some edges have been removed.

iv. *Repeat:* Repeat steps 1-3 until all vertices are processed.

If the graph has a cycle, it cannot have a topological ordering. Thus, topological sorting is only applicable to directed acyclic graphs. The algorithm can be implemented using DFS or BFS. The key is to systematically visit and process the vertices in a way that respects the partial order induced by the directed edges. A simplified procedure for topological sorting using DFS is as follows.

Procedure Topological Sort

```
TopologicalSort(Graph G):
    Initialize an empty stack to store the result
    Mark all vertices as not visited
    for each vertex in the graph:
       if the vertex is not visited then DFSUtil(vertex, visited, stack)
    return the contents of the stack in reverse order

DFSUtil(vertex, visited, stack):
    Mark the current vertex as visited
    for each adjacent vertex of the current vertex:
       if the adjacent vertex is not visited then
          DFSUtil(adjacent vertex, visited, stack)
    Push the current vertex onto the stack
```

This procedure ensures that the vertices are processed in the correct order, providing a topological sorting of the graph $\boldsymbol{G}$.

Example 4.2 (Topological Sorting)**:** Let us use a real-world example to illustrate topological sorting using DFS. Consider a course prerequisite scenario where courses have dependencies, and you need to find a valid order in which to take these courses. Suppose you have the following courses and their prerequisites:

Courses: 0,1,2,3,4,5 and *Prerequisites:* 1,0|2,1|3,2|4,2,3|5,4

It can be visualized as a directed graph, where each course is a vertex, and an edge (u, v) indicates that course u is a prerequisite for course v.

Graph: $0 \leftarrow 1 \leftarrow 2 \leftarrow 3 \leftarrow 4 \leftarrow 5$

In this case, the topological order could be [0,1,2,3,4,5], meaning you should take course 0 first, followed by course 1, and so on. In this example, we create a *Graph* class, add edges representing course prerequisites, and then use the *topological sort procedure* to find the order in which the courses should be taken. The output should be: [0,1,2,3,4,5]. This order satisfies the prerequisites, and you can take the courses in this sequence without violating any dependencies.

Lemma 4.3 *G is free from the cycles if and only if DFS has no back edges.*

Proof: We first assume the scenario where the DFS generates a back edge (u, v). In this case, v is considered as a previous node u in depth first. Thus, there exists a path from v to u in the graph G, and the back edge (u, v) forms a cycle. Further, let us consider the situation where G have a cycle c. We aim to demonstrate DFS of G that will result in a back edge. Let x be the initial vertex obtained in c, and let (u, v) be the prior edge in c. At time d, the vertices of c create a path of white from x to u. According to the **white-path theorem**, vertex u becomes a descendant of x. Hence, the edge (u, v) is identified as a back edge.

Theorem 4.3 *Topological sorting generates an ordered sequence for the given directed acyclic graph.*

Proof: Assume that DFS is executed on a given directed acyclic graph $G = (V, E)$ to compute finishing times for its vertices. It is enough to demonstrate that for any distinct pair of vertices $(u, v) \in E$, if there exists an edge from u to v in G, then $f(v) < f(u)$. Consider an arbitrary edge (u, v) explored by DFS in G. At the moment of exploring this edge, the vertex v cannot be in the gray state. If it were, v would be an ancestor of u, and (u, v) would be a back edge. Thus, v must be either white or black.

If v is white, it becomes a descendant of u, implying that $f(v) < f(u)$. On the other hand, if v is black, it has already been finished, meaning that $f(v)$ has been assigned. Since we are still exploring from u at this point, the timestamp $f(u)$ has yet to be assigned. Once it is assigned, $f(v) < f(u)$ will hold. Hence, for any edge (u, v) in the directed acyclic graph, it follows that $f(v) < f(u)$, thereby proving the validity of the theorem.

Strongly connected component: Consider directed graph G:

$$1 \rightarrow 2 \rightarrow 3 \rightarrow 1$$

$$4 \rightarrow 5 \rightarrow 4$$

$$6 \rightarrow 7$$

In G, there is a cycle $(1 \rightarrow 2 \rightarrow 3 \rightarrow 1)$, forming a strongly connected component. There is another cycle $(4 \rightarrow 5 \rightarrow 4)$, forming another strongly connected component. Vertices 6 and 7 do not form a cycle and are individual Strongly Connected Components (SSCs).

i. *First DFS (Topological Ordering):* a) perform a DFS traversal on the original graph, b) assign finishing times to vertices as they are processed, and c) this step creates a topological ordering of the vertices.

ii. *Reverse G:* reverse all edges of the original graph.

iii. *Second DFS (Identifying SCCs): a)* perform another DFS traversal on the reversed graph, b) DFS is started from the vertex with the highest finishing time obtained in step 1, and c) in the DFS forest, every tree stands for a highly connected component.

Application of topological sorting:

Decomposing a directed graph into its highly linked components is useful for a number of applications.

i. *Compiler optimization:* In the compiler design, identifying strongly connected components helps in optimizing code by understanding the interdependencies among different parts of the code.

ii. *Network analysis:* In network modeling, SCCs can represent clusters of closely connected nodes, providing insights into the structure and resilience of networks.

iii. *Graph algorithms:* Many graph algorithms determining connectivity, can be more efficiently applied within strongly connected components.

iv. *Distributed systems:* In distributed computing, SCC analysis can be used to identify components that operates independently, aiding in designing fault-tolerant systems.

By dividing a directed G In strongly connected components, we gain a deeper understanding of the underlying structure and connectivity patterns within the graph, facilitating various analytical and optimization tasks.

4.6 Minimum Spanning Tree

It is necessary for electronic circuit designs to create electrical equivalency between the pins of several components by connecting them. It is customary to connect a set of n pins using a configuration of $n - 1$ wires connecting 2 pins. Usually, the arrangement with the least quantity of wire used is selected. A linked, undirected graph $G = (V, E)$ is to visualise this wiring problem. V is the set of pins, E is the set of possible connections among the pin pairs, and each $(u, v) \in E$ has a weight $w(u, v)$ that represents the cost (wire required) to connect pins u and v. Finding an acyclic subset $T \subset E$, which joins every vertex while reducing the overall weight is the goal. $w(T) = \sum w(u, v): (u, v) \in T$.

Because T is acyclic and joins all of the vertices to form a tree, it spans the whole graph G and is referred to as a spanning tree. Determining T with the lowest total weight is known as the minimum-spanning-tree problem. Figure 4.6 displays a connected graph together with its corresponding MST.

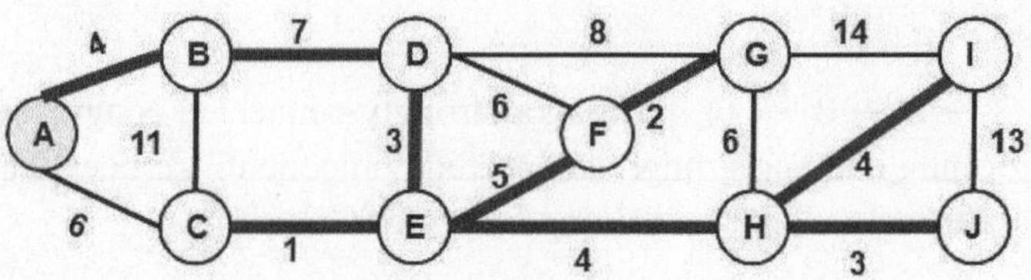

Figure 4.6: MST derived from G and weights associated with the edges are indicated. The edges constituting the MST are highlighted with shading.

MST is a key idea in optimisation and graph theory. A MST is a tree that spans every vertex in a linked, undirected graph with weighted edges while minimizing the total sum of edge weights. The characteristics of MST are as follows:

i. *Spanning Tree:* It is a tree containing all of the graph's vertices and the fewest amount of edges conceivable.

ii. *Acyclic:* The tree must be acyclic to avoid forming cycles.

iii. *Connected:* A path exists between any two vertices of the tree, and the tree must be connected.

Growing a minimum spanning tree: Consider a connected, undirected graph G represented as $G = (V, E)$ with a function $w: E \rightarrow R$. The objective of discovering a MST of G. We explore two algorithms that adopt a greedy approach to tackle this problem, differing in their application of this strategy. The generic method employed by these algorithms grows the MST incrementally. Throughout the process, a set of edges A is managed, and an important loop invariant is preserved: *A is guaranteed to be a subset of some MST.*

Edge (u, v) that does not break the invariant when added to A is found at every stage of the procedure. In other words, $A \cup (u, v)$ continues to be subset of MST. It may be precisely added to A without hampering the invariant, this kind of edge is known as a safe edge for A. This approach guarantees a methodical and secure growth of the least spanning tree, enabling the discovery of an ideal solution while upholding the greedy paradigm. Growing MST is a methodical procedure that builds a MST from a given linked graph. The objective is to construct a tree with the smallest possible total edge weight that spans all the vertices of the graph. The definition of the detailed description is as follows

i. *Initialization:* The first tree can be thought of as a trivial MST with one node, and it starts with an arbitrary vertex.

ii. *Selection of Edges:* Find the lowest edge with weight that joins a vertex inside the current tree to a vertex outside of it. It is advisable to include this edge in the MST.

iii. *Expansion:* To this extent MST append chosen edge and its corresponding vertex.

iv. *Repeat:* Find the lowest weighted edge connecting any vertex inside the current tree to a vertex outside the tree, then repeat the operation. To this extend MST, append the chosen edge and its corresponding vertex.

v. *Termination:* Continue until all vertices are MST and stop when the tree spans all vertices.

vi. *Result:* Final result is a MST, connecting all vertices with the least weight on edge.

The generic algorithm for finding a MST is given as follows.

```
GENERIC-MST(Graph G , Weight W)
  1. A ← Φ
  2. while A ≠ MST
              find (u, v) safe for A
                                          A ← A ∪ (u. v)
  3. return A
```

Explanation: Initialize A to represent the edges of MST. While the set A without forming spanning tree: a) find (u, v), safe for A and b) add (u, v) to A. Return the set A, which now represents a MST for the given graph G with weights W.

This generic algorithm outlines the process of iteratively selecting safe edges and adding them to the set A until a spanning tree is formed. Determining a safe edge may vary based on the algorithm used. We utilize the ***loop invariant*** of generic MST algorithm as:

Initialization: A inherently holds loop invariant.

Maintenance: It preserves invariant, exclusively combining safe edges.

Termination: MST includes every edge *i.e.,* added to A; thus, set A be an MST.

The challenge lies in identifying a safe edge. The invariant requires the existence of a spanning tree T, such that A is a proper subset of T. A must be a subset of T implies $(u, v) \in T$ where $(u, v) \notin T$ and (u, v) are safe for A.

A **cut** $(\boldsymbol{S}, \boldsymbol{V} - \boldsymbol{S})$ in an undirected graph $G = (V, E)$ forms a disjoint of the vertex set V. An edge $(u, v) \in E$ is said to cross the cut $(S, V - S)$ if one of its ends lies in S, and another point is in $\boldsymbol{V} - \boldsymbol{S}$. A cut does not cross any edge in set A if it respects that set of edges. If weight of edge is the lowest of all the edges that cross the cut, it is categorised as a light edge partition of the cut. It is important to remember the case of ties, where there could be more than one light edge spanning. If the weight is the lowest of all edges that satisfy a particular criteria, then that edge is said to be light.

Theorem 4.3: Let G be an undirected, connected graph with a real-valued weight function w defined on E. G can be represented as $G = (V, E)$. Allow $A \subset E$ to be a part of MST for G. If there is a light edge (u, v) that crosses a cut $(S, S - V) \in G$ that respects A, then the edge (u, v) is considered safe for A.

Proof: Let T be a MST of G, which includes the edges in A. Let $e = (u, v)$ be the lightest edge crossing the cut $(S, S - V)$. For any $B \subset E$, a **cut** (X, Y) respects B if no edge in B crosses the cut (X, Y). The edge is safe for a set of edges if adding it to the set does not create a cycle. We assume that the edge $e = (u, v)$ is safe for the set of edges A.

Proof by Contradiction: Assume that adding edge $e = (u, v)$ to the set A creates a cycle G. Since A is a subset of a MST, it is acyclic. Therefore, adding e to A forms a cycle that must include at least one edge not in A. Let f be the first such edge encountered along the cycle. Since e is the lightest edge crossing the cut and f is in the cycle, the weight of e must be less than or equal to the weight of f. Replace edge f with e in the MST T.

The resulting G is still connected, has no cycles, and includes all vertices, making it a spanning tree. The notion that T is a MST is contradicted by the fact that the total weight of the edges in the new tree is less than the total weight of T. Assuming edge $e = (u, v)$ to the set A creating a cycle leads to a contradiction. Therefore, edge e is safe for the set A.

Corollary 4.1: Consider a connected undirected graph $G = (V, E)$ having the weight function w defined on E that is real-valued. For G, let $C = (V_c, E_c)$ be a connected component (tree) in the forest $G_A = (V, A)$, and let A be a subset of E that is a part of some MST for G. If (u, v) is a edge connecting C to different component in G_A, then (u, v) is considered safe for A.

Proof: The cut $(V_c, V - V_c)$ respects A, and (u, v) is a light edge for this cut. Therefore, (u, v) is safe for A.

Further, we describe MST algorithms based on a generic method. Each algorithm employs a distinct rule to identify a safe edge for GENERIC-MST. Kruskal's algorithm operates on a set A, which is initially a forest containing all vertices of the given graph. The safe edge added to A is always the least-weight edge of the graph linking two distinct components. In contrast, the set A in Prim's algorithm consists of only a single tree. The safe edge introduced to A is always the least-weight edge that connects the tree to a vertex outside the tree.

4.7 Kruskal's Algorithm

A greedy approach called Kruskal's algorithm is used to determine the minimal spanning tree of an undirected, connected graph. The procedure involves selecting edges in ascending order of their weights while avoiding the formation of cycles. The simple steps are as follows:

- Initially, each vertex is treated as a separate component.
- Edges are sorted in ascending order by weight.
- Starting with the smallest edge, add it to MST unless create a cycle.
- Repeat until all vertices are connected.

Some examples to illustrate Kruskal's algorithm are discussed as follows.

Example 4.3: Consider a weighted undirected graph to G as shown in Figure 4.7 (a), we have to obtain MST using Kruskal's algorithm.

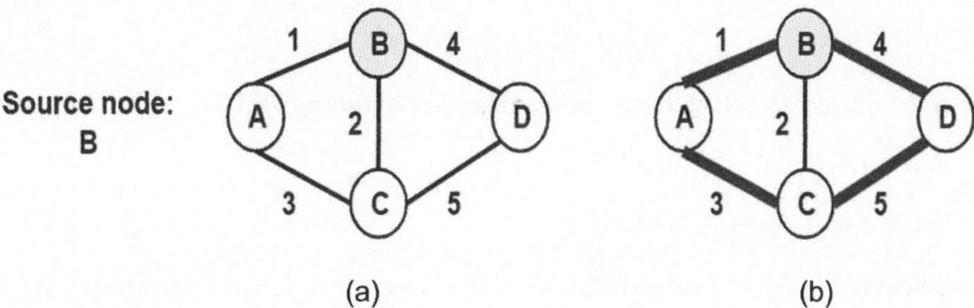

Figure 4.7: An example of a situation involving the Kruskal method. (a) Given a weighted undirected graph, and (b) after using Kruskal's approach, the minimal spanning tree.

Solution procedure:

i. *Sort edges by weight:* Sort the edges in ascending order by their weights:

$$[(B, A, 1), (B, C, 2), (A, C, 3), (B, D, 5), (C, D, 5)]$$

ii. *Initialize forest:* Start with each vertex in its own disjoint set: $\{B\}\{A\}\{C\}\{D\}$.

iii. *Select Edges:* Begin selecting edges in sorted order, avoiding cycles:

   a. Select $(B, A, 1) \rightarrow$ Add to MST.

   b. Select $(B, C, 2) \rightarrow$ Add to MST.

   c. Select $(A, C, 3) \rightarrow$ Forms a cycle, so skip.

   d. Select $(B, D, 4) \rightarrow$ Add to MST.

   e. Select $(C, D, 1) \rightarrow$ Add to MST.

The resultant MST is depicted in Figure 4.7(b).

Example 4.4: Consider a weighted undirected graph to G as shown in Figure 4.8 (a), we have to obtain the MST using Kruskal's algorithm.

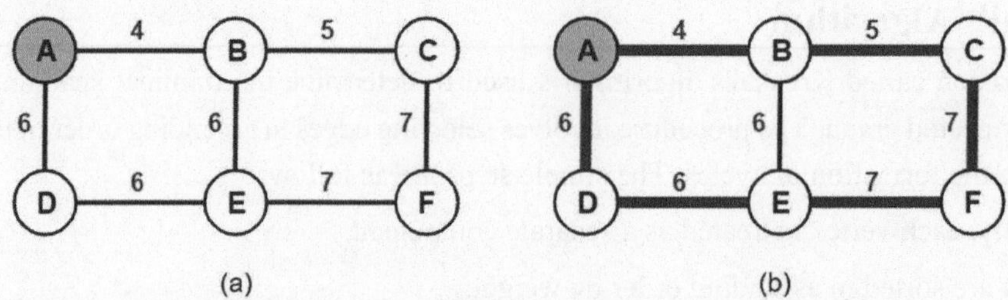

Figure 4.8: An illustration of Kruskal's algorithm scenario: (a) a weighted undirected graph; and (b) minimal spanning tree that is produced as a result of applying Kruskal's technique.

Solution procedure:

i. *Sort Edges by Weight:* Sort the edges in ascending order by their weights:

$$[(A,B,4),(B,C,5),(A,D,6),(B,E,6),(C,F,7),(D,E,6),(E,F,7)]$$

ii. *Initialize Forest:* Start with each vertex in its own set:

$$\{A\},\{B\},\{C\},\{D\},\{E\},\{F\}$$

iii. *Select Edges:* Begin selecting edges in sorted order, avoiding cycles:

a. Select $(A,B,4)$ → Add to MST.

b. Select $(A,D,6)$ → Add to MST.

c. Select $(B,C,5)$ → Add to MST.

d. Select $(D,E,6)$ → Add to MST.

e. Select $(E,F,7)$ → Add to MST.

The resultant minimum spanning tree is depicted in Figure 4.8(b).

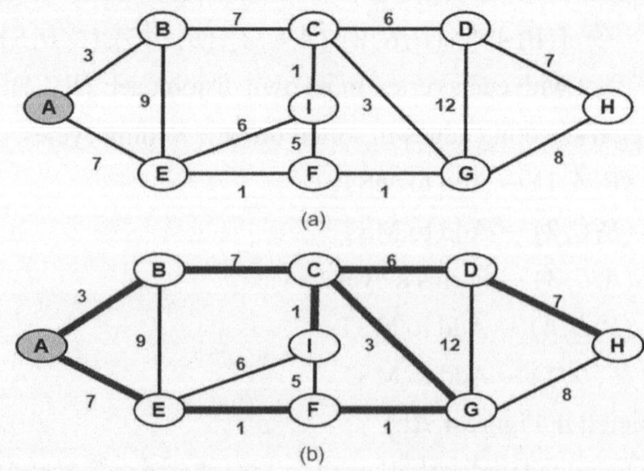

Figure 4.9: Application of Kruskal's algorithm on a weighted connected graph with nine nodes (a), showcasing the obtained MST (b).

Moreover, Figure 4.9(a) visually presents an additional illustrative scenario wherein Kruskal's algorithm is employed on a weighted connected graph comprising 9 nodes (denoted as $A, B, C, D, E, F, G, H, I$). The objective is to derive a MST, as shown in Figure 4.9(b). An algorithmic procedure for Kruskal's algorithm is discussed as follows:

Procedure of Kruskal's Algorithm

```
Input:  A connected and undirected G with n vertices and m edges.
Output: MST of G.
/*Arrange the edges of G as per weights in a non-decreasing sequence.*/
        edges = sort(G.edges, key = weight)
/*To keep track of the related parts, use a disjoint set data structure. */
        disjoint_set = make_set(V)
/*Create an empty set to represent the MST.*/
        minimum_spannin_tree   = set()
/*Iterate through the sorted edges*/
for edge in edges:
/*Determine whether adding an edge to the spanning tree would result in a cycle for each edge. Add
the edge to the spanning tree and combine the two sets if it connects two vertices in distinct sets.*/
        if find_set(edge.source) != find_set(edge.target):
          minimum_spannin_tree.add(edge)
          union(edge.source, edge.target)
/*Once all edges are processed, the set contains the edges of MST.*/
  return minimum_spannin_tree
```

```
/*Disjoint Set Operations Make Set*/
                    Symbols: v → Vertex, r → root
    function make_set(v):
        v.parent = vertex
        v.rank = 0
```

```
/*Find Set*/
function find_set(vertex):
        if v! = v.parent:
          v.parent = find_set(v.parent)
        return v.parent

/*Union*/
function union(v1, v2):
        r1 = find_set(v1)
        r2 = find_set(v2)
        if r1! = r2:
          if r1.rank < r2.rank:
            r1.parent = r2
          elif r1.rank > r2.rank:
            r2.parent = r1
          else:
            r2.parent = r1
            r1.rank+= 1
```

Time Complexity: The time complexity of $G = (V, E)$ is contingent while implementing. Initializing the set A takes $O(1)$ time, and the time to sort the edges is $O(E\ log\ E)$. Accounting for $|V|$ MAKE-SET operations, for loop executes $O(E)$ FIND-SET and UNION. Together with $|V|$ MAKE-SET operations, overall complexity is $O((V + E)\alpha(V))$ time, where α is inverse Ackermann function [5]. Since we assume that G is connected, and $|E|\ >=\ |V| - 1$, the disjoint-set operations take $O(E\alpha V)$ time. As $\alpha(|V|) = O(log\ V) = O(log\ E)$, run time of Kruskal's method can be expressed as $O(E\ log\ E)$. Recognizing that $|E| < |V|^2$, we can reformulate the running time as $O(E\ log\ V)$.

4.8 Prim's Algorithm

It is an example of universal MST technique, much like Kruskal's. Prim's algorithm functions similarly to Dijkstra's algorithm to obtain the shortest paths in a graph (discussed later in this chapter). It has an additional feature: the edges in set A are always part of a single tree. This tree, as shown in Figure 4.10, starts at an arbitrary root, P, and covers to includes all of vertices in V. Every time, the method connects A to an isolated vertex (having no incident edge from A), adding a lightweight edge. Specifically, this method only uses edges that are considered secure for A. As a result, after the algorithm runs, all of edges in A make up a MST. The strategy fits the greedy paradigm by iteratively adding edges that add the least amount of weight to the expanding tree.

For Prim's algorithm to work effectively, there must be a quick method of choosing an edge to add to tree that edges in A. The algorithm is described in the accompanying pseudocode. The inputs of the algorithm are root r of developing MST and the connected graph G. Vertices that are not yet part of the tree are handled during execution in a min-priority queue Q that is arranged according to a key attribute. The minimal weight of each edge from a vertex v to a tree vertex is represented by the property v:key for each vertex v; if no such connection exists, v:key is set to 1. The parent of the tree is indicated by the attribute v:parent. The set A from GENERIC-MST is implicitly supported by the method.

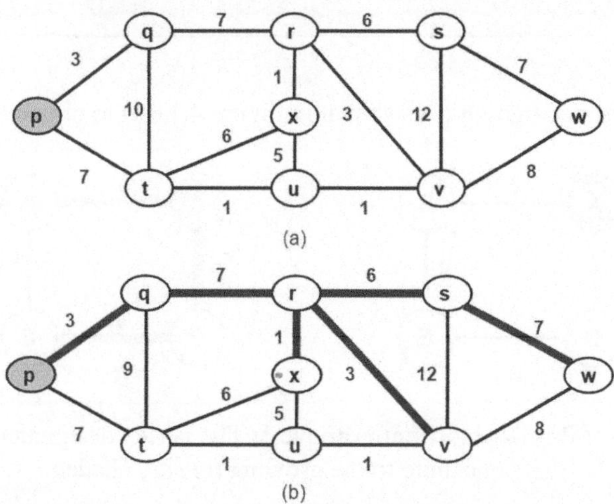

Figure 4.10: Illustration of Prim's algorithm. The vertex designated as the root is p. Edges that contribute to the growing tree are shaded, and vertices included in the tree are represented by black circles. Vertices of the tree define a cut in graph at each algorithmic step, and a light edge that crosses the cut is added to the tree. Initial graph is shown in (a), and the resulting MST with thick, shaded lines connecting the vertices is shown in (b).

The basic steps of the Prim's algorithm are described in the following steps.

i. Start with an arbitrary vertex and identify the MST.

ii. At every step, the minimum-weight edge from a vertex inside the MST to a vertex outside the MST needs to be added.

iii. Continue until the MST contains all of the vertices.

Procedure Prim's Algorithm (*T*):

Input: Graph G with vertices V and weighted edges E

1. Initialize an empty set T.
2. Choose starting vertex s from V and add to T.
3. Initialize a priority queue *(min-heap)* Q with all vertices in V, using their edge weights as keys.

4. while Q is not empty:
   a. Extract u with the minimum key value from Q.
   b. Add u to T.
   c. for each v adjacent to u:
      if $v \in Q$ and the weight of the edge $(u, v) <$ key:
         Update $v's$ key to the weight of (u, v).
         Set $v's$ predecessor to u.
5. return T as MST.

Example 4.5: Let us consider a graph G as shown in Figure 4.11(a) to obtain MST

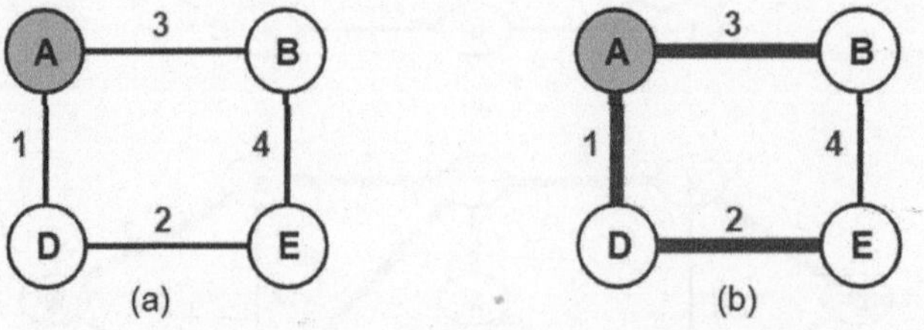

Figure 4.11 Illustration of Prim's algorithm example 1. The vertex designated as the root is A. Edges that contribute to the growing tree are shaded.

Solution procedure:

i. Start with a vertex A.
ii. Choose the minimum edge, AC (weight 1).
iii. Add C to the MST.
iv. The next minimum-weight edges are AB and CD. Choose AB.
v. Add B to the MST.
vi. The last minimum-weight edge is CD.
vii. Add D to the MST.

The resultant MST is shown in Figure 4.11 (b).

Example 4.6: Let us consider another graph G' as shown in Figure 4.12 (a).

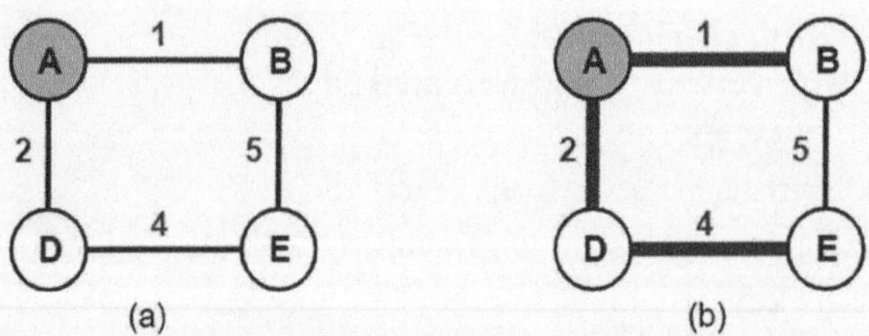

Figure 4.12 Illustration of Prim's algorithm example 2. Vertex A is designated as the root.

Solution procedure:

i. Start with an arbitrary vertex A.
ii. Choose the minimum-weight edge, which is AC.
iii. Add C to the MST.
iv. The next minimum edges are AB and CD. Choose AB.
v. Add B to the MST.
vi. The last minimum-weight edge is CD.
vii. Add D to the MST.

The resulting MST is given in Figure 4.12 (b).

Example 6: Let us consider third graph G'' as shown in Figure 4.13 (a) to use Prim's technique to get MST, as illustrated in Figure 4.13 (b).

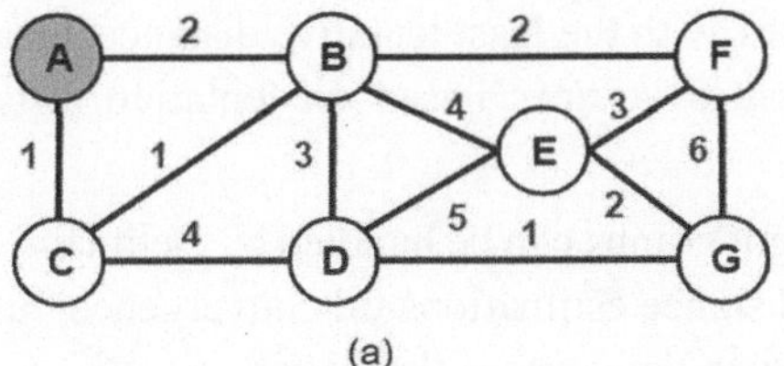

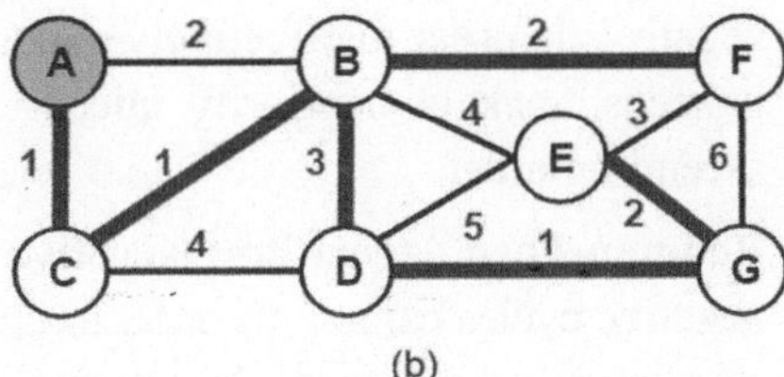

Figure 4.13 Illustration of Prim's algorithm example 3. The vertex designated as root is A. Edges that contribute to the growing tree are shaded.

These examples illustrate how Prim's algorithm systematically selects edges to construct the minimum spanning tree by connecting vertices with the minimum weights. Prim's algorithm's time complexity is $O(Elog\ V + Vlog\ V) = O(E\ log\ V)$, asymptotically equivalent to the Kruskal's algorithm procedure implemented in a specified language, refer [3] for more detail.

Applications of Kruskal's and Prim's algorithms

i. Network design and optimization.
ii. Circuit design to minimize the total wire length.
iii. Transportation and communication network planning.
iv. Cluster analysis and image segmentation in computer vision.

Second-best minimum spanning tree

Consider a connected, undirected graph G that has set V of vertices and set E of edges. The weight function of G is $w: E \rightarrow R$. It is presumed that all edge weights are distinct and that the number of edges $|E| = |V|$. Following is an introduction to the idea of a second-best MST: Let T_0 be the MST of G and let T be the set of spanning trees in G. A spanning tree G that has the weight of T, represented as $w(T)$, as the lowest value among all spanning trees in T that deviate from T_0—where T_0 is a MST—is considered the second-best MST.

4.9 Single-Source Shortest Paths

A well-known issue in graph theory and algorithms is Single-Source Shortest Paths (SSSP). In a weighted graph, the goal is to determine the shortest pathways between a single source vertex and every other vertex. Any measure related to navigating the edges can be represented by the weights on the edges, such as travel times or distances. The following defines SSSP problem at high level, lists some popular methods that are used to solve it:

Problem Definition: Finding the shortest paths and corresponding lengths from s to each other vertex in the graph $G = (V, E)$ with a weight function $w: E \to R$ and a source vertex $s \in V$ is given. The graph can be either directed or undirected.

The primary algorithms of the SSSP problems are 1) Dijkstra's Algorithm, 2) Bellman-Ford Algorithm, and 3) Floyd-Warshall Algorithm.

1. **Dijkstra's Algorithm:** Dijkstra algorithm works on graphs whose edge weights are non-negative. In order to effectively choose the vertex with the least tentative distance at each step, it keeps track of a priority queue. It investigates vertices based on tentative distances in ascending order.
2. **Bellman-Ford Algorithm:** Negative edge weight graphs can be handled by Bellman-Ford, but negative cycles cannot. In order to update the distance estimations till convergence, iteratively relaxing edges are used. Detects **negative cycles** in the graph if they exist.
3. **Floyd-Warshall Algorithm:** Floyd-Warshall is applicable to directed and undirected graphs with edge weights that are either positive or negative. It calculates all pairs of vertices shortest paths. To determine the shortest paths, it applies a dynamic programming technique.

Variants: In this chapter, our focus is directed towards addressing SSSP problem within context of a graph G represented as $G(V, E)$. Finding the shortest path from a specific source is the main goal vertices s, belonging to the vertex set V, to every other vertex v within the same set. The technique developed to solve the single-source problem can also be used to solve a number of related problems, such as the following variations:

1. *Single-Destination Shortest-Paths Problem:*
   a. *Objective:* Find the shortest path from every vertex in V to a vertex t.
   b. *Approach:* We can make this problem into a single-source by flipping the orientation of each edge in the graph.
2. *Single-Pair Shortest-Path Problem:*
   a. *Objective:* Discover the shortest path from a source vertex u to a target v.
   b. *Approach:* Solving the single-source problem with u as the source vertex inherently resolves the single-pair problem.
3. *All-Pairs Shortest-Paths Problem:*
   a. *Objective:* Determine the shortest path from every vertex u to every other vertex v in the graph.

b. *Approach:* Although running a single-source algorithm from every vertex can address this problem, there are more effective ways to do it.

This chapter explores the fundamentals of these related problems, providing insight into algorithms and approaches designed to handle the complexities of all-pairs and single-source shortest-paths challenges.

4.10 Dijkstra's Algorithm

A well-known method for determining the shortest paths between a single source vertex and every other vertex in a weighted network is Dijkstra's algorithm. This finds shortest pathways quickly by using a greedy approach on graphs with non-negative edge weights.

Overview:

i. *Initialization:* Initialize an array $dist[\,]$ to store the tentative distances from the source vertex to each vertex. Set all other distances to infinity and the source vertex to 0.
ii. *Priority Queue:* At each stage, choose the vertex with the least tentative distance as quickly as possible by using a priority queue.
iii. *Explore Neighbors:* If a shorter path is discovered, take into account all of a vertex neighbours and update their estimated distances.
iv. *Mark Visited*: To guarantee that every vertex is processed just once, mark the current vertex as visited.

Pseudo-code of Dijkstra algorithm:

```
function Dijkstra(G, s):
Initialize distance array dist[ ] to infinity for all vertices except s
  Set dist[s] = 0
  Initialize priority queue Q with all vertices and their tentative distances
  while Q is not empty:
    u =extractMin(Q) // Extract vertex with minimum distance from Q
    for each neighbor v to u:
      alt = dist[u] + weight(u, v) // Calculate tentative distance
      if alt < dist[v]
        dist[v] = alt
        decreaseKey(Q, v, alt) // Update priority queue
    return dist
```

Example 4.7: Consider the following weighted graph in Figure 4.14.

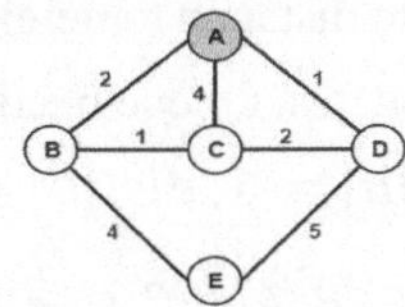

Figure 4.14 Illustration of Dijkastra's algorithm example 1. Vertex designated as source is *A*.

Let us find the shortest paths from vertex A using Dijkstra's algorithm:

i. Initialize : $dist[A] = 0, dist[B] = \infty, dist[C] = \infty, dist[D] = \infty, dist[E] = \infty$.

ii. Start with the priority queue containing all vertices and their tentative distances: $Q = (A,0),(B,\infty),(C,\infty),(D,\infty),(E,\infty)$.

iii. Iteratively select vertices from the priority queue, update distances, and mark them as visited.
   - *First iteration:* Select A, update distances to neighbors B, C and D. Queue becomes $Q = (B,2),(C,4),(D,1),(E,\infty)$.
   - *Second iteration*: Select D, update distance to neighbor E. Queue becomes $Q = (B,2),(C,3),(E,6)$.
   - *Third iteration:* Select B, no updates. Queue becomes $Q = (C,3),(E,6)$.
   - *Fourth iteration:* Select C, no updates. Queue becomes $Q = (E,6)$.
   - *Fifth iteration:* Select E, no updates. Queue becomes empty.
   - *Final:* $dist[A] = 0, dist[B] = 2, dist[C] = 3, dist[D] = 1, dist[E] = 6$.

iv. The shortest paths from A to other vertices are: $A \to B, B \to C, A \to D, D \to C, A \to D, D \to E$

Example 4.8: Let us examine an additional example to provide more insight into Dijkstra's approach. Examine the weighted graph that follows, which is displayed in Figure 4.15.

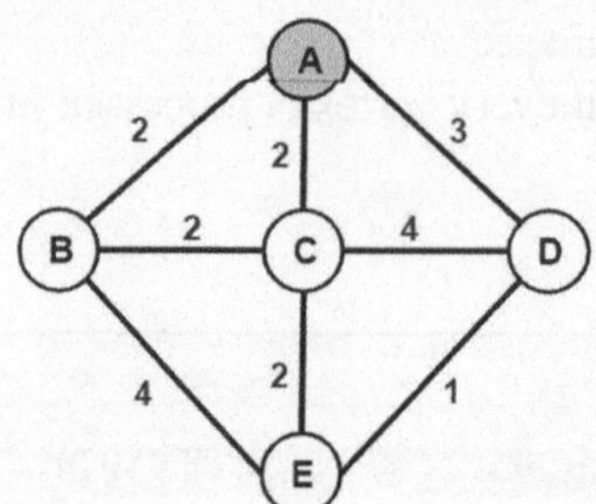

Figure 4.15 Illustration of Dijkastra's algorithm example 2. Vertex designated as source is A.

Let us find the shortest paths from vertex A using Dijkstra's algorithm:

i. *Initialization:* $dist[A] = 0, dist[B] = \infty, dist[C] = \infty, dist[D] = \infty, dist[E] = \infty$.
Queue: $Q = (A,0),(B,\infty),(C,\infty),(D,\infty),(E,\infty)$

ii. *Iterations:*

   a. *Iteration 1:* Select A, update distances to neighbors B, C and D. Queue becomes $Q = (B,1),(C,2)(D,3)(E,\infty)$.

   b. *Iteration 2:* Select B, update distance to neighbor E. Queue becomes $Q = (C,2)(D,3)(E,5)$

   c. *Iteration 3:* Select C, no updates. Queue becomes $Q = (D,3)(E,5)$.

   d. *Iteration 4:* Select D, update distance to neighbor E. Queue becomes $Q = (E,4)$.

   e. *Iteration 5:* Select E, no updates. Queue becomes empty.

iii. *Final Distances:* $dist[A] = 0, dist[B] = 1, dist[C] = 3, dist[D] = 3, dist[E] = 4$

So, the shortest paths from A are: $A \to C, A \to B, A \to C, C \to E, A \to D$

4.11 Bellman-Ford Algorithm

Bellman-Ford algorithm is based on dynamic programming, which can discover the shortest paths from a single source vertex to every other vertex in a weighted graph. Additionally, the technique finds negative cycles in the graph.

Bellman-Ford Algorithm:

1. *Initialization:* Put all other distances of vertices to ∞ and source distance to 0.

   Initialize an array $dist[\,]$ to store the tentative distances.
2. *Relax Edges:* Repeat the relaxation step $|V|-1$ times and $|V|$ is the count of vertices in the graph.
   a. **for** each (u,v) with weight w:
   b. **If** $dist[u]+w<dist[v]$**:**,

      update $dist[v]=dist[u]+w$.
3. *Negative Cycle Detection:* To look for negative cycles, do one more iteration. If any $dist[v\,]$ is updated, then a negative cycle is present.
4. *Result:* The shortest paths between the source vertex and every other vertex are shown by the final values in the $dist[\,]$ array.

```
Procedure BellmanFord
function BellmanFord(G, s):
  Initialize distance array dist[ ] to infinity for all vertices except s
  dist[s] = 0
  // Relax edges |V| − 1 times
  for i from 1 to |V| − 1:
    for each (u, v) in E:
      if dist[u] + weight(u, v) < dist[v]
        dist[v] = dist[u] + weight(u, v)
  for each (u, v) in E:
    if dist[u] + weight(u, v) < dist[v]:
      // Negative cycle detected
  return dist
```

Example: 4.15 Consider the following directed graph with weighted edges:

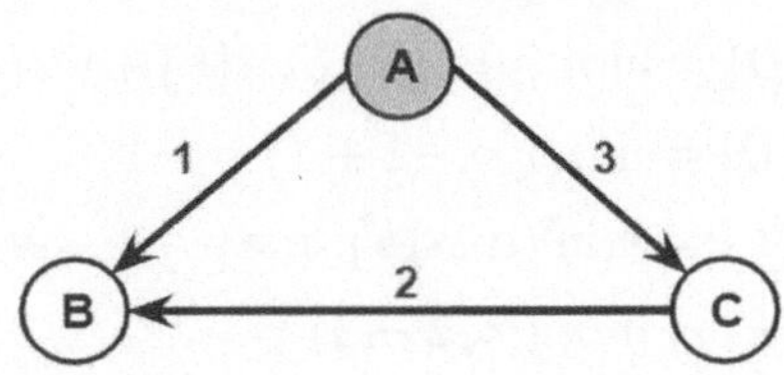

Applying the Bellman-Ford algorithm:

i. *Initialization:* $dist[A] = 0, dist[B] = \infty, dist[C] = \infty$,
ii. *Relaxation (Iteration 1):* Update $dist[B] = 1$ and $dist[C] = 3$.
iii. *Relaxation (Iteration 2):* No updates.
iv. *Relaxation (Iteration 3):* No updates.
v. *Result (*final distances): $dist[A] = 0, dist[B] = 1, dist[C] = 3$.

No negative cycles are detected in this example. The algorithm successfully finds the shortest paths from the source vertex *A* to all other vertices.

These algorithms play a crucial role in various applications, including network routing, GPS navigation, and optimization problems involving weighted graphs. Let us go through a Bellman-Ford algorithm example with a more complex graph and multiple iterations.

Example: 4.16 Consider the following directed graph with weighted edges:

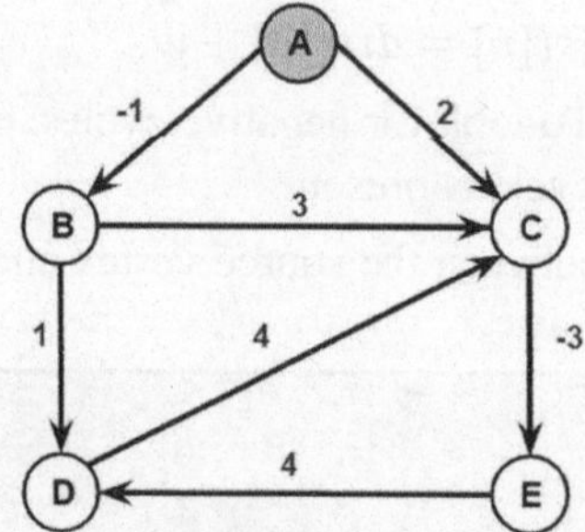

This graph has following edge weights: $A \rightarrow B$ with weight -1, $A \rightarrow C$ with weight 2, $B \rightarrow C$ with weight 3, $B \rightarrow D$ with weight 1, $C \rightarrow E$ with weight -3, $D \rightarrow C$ with weight 4, $E \rightarrow D$ with weight 4.

Now, Let us apply the Bellman-Ford algorithm step by step:

i. *Iteration 0 (Initialization):*

$dist[A] = 0, dist[B] = \infty, dist[C] = \infty, dist[D] = \infty, dist[E] = \infty$

ii. *Iteration 1:*

Relax edge $A \rightarrow B$: $dist[B] = min\ (dist[B], dist[A] + weight[A \rightarrow B])$

$$dist[B] = min\ (\infty, 0 - 1) = -1$$

Relax edge $A \rightarrow C$: $dist[C] = min\ (dist[C], dist[A] + weight[A \rightarrow C])$

$$dist[C] = min\ (\infty, 0 + 2) = 2$$

Relax edge $B \rightarrow C$: $dist[C] = min\ (dist[C], dist[B] + weight[B \rightarrow C])$

$$dist[C] = min\ (2, -1 + 3) = 2$$

Relax edge $B \rightarrow D$: $dist[D] = min\ (dist[D], dist[B] + weight[B \rightarrow D])$

$$dist[D] = min\ (\infty, -1 + 1) = -1$$

Relax edge $C \rightarrow E$: $dist[E] = min\ (dist[E], dist[C] + weight[C \rightarrow E])$

$$dist[E] = min\ (\infty, 2 - 3) = -1$$

iii. *Iteration 2:* No updates in this iteration.

iv. *Iteration 3:* No updates in this iteration.

v. Result: Final distances after three iterations are

$$dist[A] = 0, dist[B] = -1, dist[C] = 2\ , dist[D] = -1, dist[E] = -1$$

The shortest routes between vertex A and every other vertex in the graph is shown by this result. It should be noted that there are no negative cycles in the graph and that the Bellman-Ford algorithm can compute the shortest paths with success even when there are negative edge weights.

Example: 4.17 Let us discuss another example with a different graph for understanding Bellman-Ford algorithm.

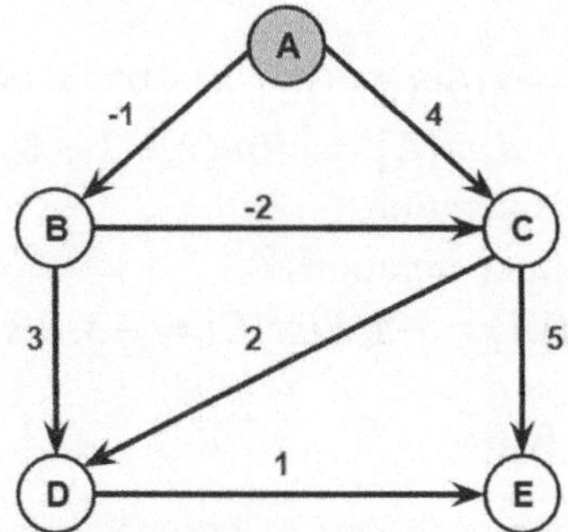

The above graph has the following edge weights: $A \longrightarrow B$ with weight -1, $A \longrightarrow C$ with weight 4, $B \longrightarrow C$ with weight -2, $B \longrightarrow D$ with weight 3, $C \longrightarrow E$ with weight 5, $D \longrightarrow E$ with weight $\mathbf{1}$, $C \longrightarrow D$ with weight 2.

Bellman-Ford Algorithm:

i. *Iteration 0 (Initialization):*

$$dist[A] = 0, dist[B] = \infty, dist[C] = \infty\ , dist[D] = \infty, dist[E] = \infty$$

ii. *Iteration 1:*

Relax edge $A \rightarrow B$:

$$dist[B] = min\ (dist[B], dist[A] + weight[A \rightarrow B])$$
$$dist[B] = min\ (\infty, 0 - 1) = -1$$

Relax edge $A \rightarrow C$:

$$dist[C] = min\ (dist[C], dist[A] + weight[A \rightarrow C])$$
$$dist[C] = min\ (\infty, 0 + 4) = 4$$

Relax edge $B \rightarrow C$:

$$dist[C] = min\ (dist[C], dist[B] + weight[B \rightarrow C])$$
$$dist[C] = min\ (4, -1 - 2) = -3$$

Relax edge $B \rightarrow D$:

$$dist[D] = min\ (dist[D], dist[B] + weight[B \rightarrow D])$$
$$dist[D] = min\ (\infty, -1 + 3) = 2$$

Relax edge $C \rightarrow E$:

$$dist[E] = min\ (dist[E], dist[C] + weight[C \rightarrow E])$$
$$dist[E] = min\ (\infty, -3 + 5) = 2$$

iii. *Iteration 2:*
Relax edge $A \rightarrow B$: No update.
Relax edge $A \rightarrow C$: No update.
Relax edge $B \rightarrow C$:

$$dist[D] = min\ (-3, -1 - 2) = -3$$

Relax edge $B \rightarrow D$:

$$dist[D] = min\ (dist[D], dist[B] + weight[B \rightarrow D])$$
$$dist[D] = min\ (2, -1 + 3) = 2$$

Relax edge $C \rightarrow E$:

$$dist[E] = min\ (dist[E], dist[C] + weight[C \rightarrow E])$$
$$dist[E] = min\ (2, -3 + 5) = 2$$

iv. *Iteration 3:* No updates in this iteration.

v. Result: Final distances after three iterations:

$$dist[A] = 0, dist[B] = -1, dist[C] = -3, dist[D] = 2. -dist[E] = 2$$

4.12 Floyd-Warshall Algorithm

Finding the shortest pathways between each pair of vertices in a weighted graph is the goal of this algorithm. The Warsahll algorithm computes the shortest pathways incrementally using a dynamic programming technique. It updates the shortest path matrix by treating every vertex as a possible intermediate vertex in the paths.

Algorithm Steps:

i. *Initialization:* Make a matrix D with the shortest distance between vertices i and j represented by $D[i][j]$. Set D to begin with a weight of ∞ if there is no edge and the weight of the edge from i to j if there is. Moreover, set $0\ \forall\ i$ for $D[i][i]$.

ii. *Iterative Update:* Iterate over all pairs of vertices, i and j, for each vertex k. Then, determine whether the path i to j via k is shorter than existing known path from i to j.

If $D[i][k] + D[k][j] < D[i][j]$, update $D[i][j]$ to $D[i][k] + D[k][j]$.

iii. *Final Result:* The matrix D holds the shortest distances between every pair of vertices when the iterations are finished.

Example: 4.18 Let us consider the following weighted graph:

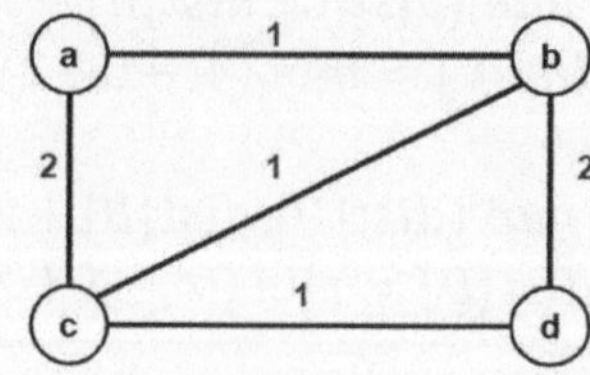

Edges: (a,b) with weight 1, (a,c) with weight 2, (b,c) with weight 1, (b,d) with weight 2, (c,d) with weight 1.

i. *Initialization:*

$$D = \begin{bmatrix} 0 & 1 & 2 & \infty \\ \infty & 0 & 1 & 2 \\ \infty & \infty & 0 & 1 \\ \infty & \infty & \infty & 0 \end{bmatrix}$$

ii. *Iteration:* $k = a$, no updates as D remains unchanged.

a. $k = b$, $D[c][a] + D[a][b] = 2 + 1 = 3$ is shorter than $D[c][b] = 1$, so $D[c][b]$ update to 3.

b. $D[c][d] + D[d][b] = 1 + 2 = 3$ is shorter than $D[c][b]$, update $D[c][b]$ to 3.

c. $D[a][c] + D[c][b] = 2 + 1 = 3$ is shorter than $D[a][b] = 1$, $D[a][b]$ to 3.

d. $k = c$, no updates as D remains unchanged.

e. $k = d$, $D[a][b] + D[b][d] = 3$ is shorter than $D[a][b] = \infty$, $D[a][d]$ to 3.

f. $D[c][b] + D[b][d] = 3$ is shorter than $D[c][d] = 1$, so update $D[c][d]$ to 3.

iii. *Final Result:*

$$D = \begin{bmatrix} 0 & 1 & 2 & 3 \\ \infty & 0 & 1 & 2 \\ \infty & \infty & 0 & 1 \\ \infty & \infty & \infty & 0 \end{bmatrix}$$

Shortest paths among each pair of vertices in provided graph are represented by matrix D.

Example: 4.19 Let us go through another example of Floyd-Warshall:

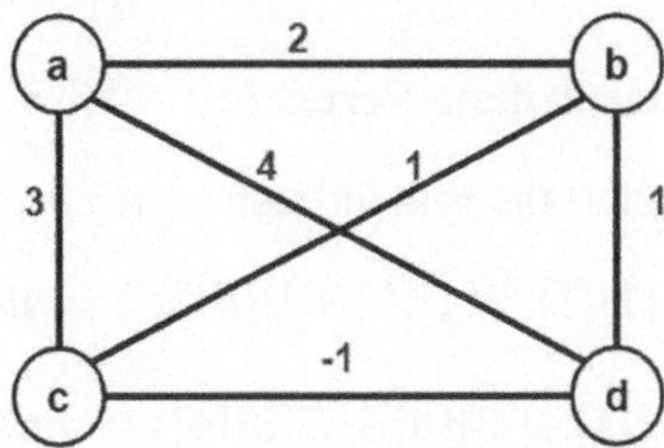

This graph has the following edge weights: $a \longrightarrow b$ with weight 2, $a \longrightarrow c$ with weight 3, $b \longrightarrow c$ with weight 1, $b \longrightarrow d$ with weight 1, $c \longrightarrow d$ with weight -1, and $d \longrightarrow a$ with weight 4.

Floyd-Warshall Algorithm:

Step 0 (Initialization): Initialize the distance matrix D as follows:

$$D = \begin{bmatrix} 0 & 2 & 3 & \infty \\ \infty & 0 & 1 & 1 \\ \infty & \infty & 0 & -1 \\ 4 & \infty & \infty & 0 \end{bmatrix}$$

$D[i][j]$ represents the distance from i to j.

∞ represents that there is no direct edge from i to j.

The diagonal elements $D[i][j]$ are set to 0.

Step 1: Update Distances using Intermediate Vertex a:

For each pair of vertices i and j, check if the path through vertex a is shorter:

$$D[2][3] = min(D[2][3], D[2][a] + D[a][3]) = min(1, \infty + 3) = 1$$

$$D[3][4] = min(D[3][4], D[3][a] + D[a][4]) = min(-1, \infty + 4) = -1$$

$$D[4][1] = min(D[4][1], D[4][a] + D[a][1]) = min(4, 4 + \infty) = 4$$

Update the distance matrix:

$$D = \begin{bmatrix} 0 & 2 & 3 & \infty \\ 4 & 0 & 1 & 1 \\ 5 & 7 & 0 & -1 \\ 4 & 6 & 7 & 0 \end{bmatrix}$$

Step 2: Update Distances using Intermediate Vertex b:

For each pair of vertices i and j, check if the path through vertex b is shorter:

$$D[1][3] = min(D[1][3], D[1][b] + D[b][3]) = min(3, 2 + 1) = 3$$

$$D[3][4] = min(D[3][4], D[3][b] + D[b][4]) = min(-1, 1 + 1) = -1$$

Update the distance matrix:

$$D = \begin{bmatrix} 0 & 2 & 3 & \infty \\ 3 & 0 & 1 & 1 \\ 5 & 7 & 0 & -1 \\ 4 & 6 & 7 & 0 \end{bmatrix}$$

Step 3: Update Distances using Intermediate Vertex c:

For each pair of vertices i and j, check if the path through vertex c is shorter:

$$D[1][4] = min\ (D[1][4], D[1][C] + D[C][4]) = min\ (3,3-1) = 2$$

Update the distance matrix:

$$D = \begin{bmatrix} 0 & 2 & 3 & 2 \\ 3 & 0 & 1 & 1 \\ 5 & 7 & 0 & -1 \\ 4 & 6 & 7 & 0 \end{bmatrix}$$

Result: The shortest paths between each vertex and every other vertex in the graph are represented as the final distances after three iterations:

$$D = \begin{bmatrix} 0 & 2 & 3 & 2 \\ 3 & 0 & 1 & 1 \\ 5 & 7 & 0 & -1 \\ 4 & 6 & 7 & 0 \end{bmatrix}$$

4.13 Transitive Closure

It is a fundamental concept that helps determine the reachability of vertices in the graph. It essentially answers the question: *Can you reach vertex j from vertex i?*

Transitive Closure: Explanation

i. *Definition:* The transitive closure of a directed graph G is represented by the matrix $TC[i][j]$, which is true when a directed path exists in the graph between vertices i and j and false otherwise.

ii. *Algorithm:* Matrix multiplication and dynamic programming are the foundations of the conventional approach used to calculate the transitive closure.

iii. *Steps:*

- Start with an adjacency matrix A representing the graph.
- Initialize the transitive closure matrix TC as a copy of the adjacency matrix A.
- For each intermediate vertex k, update $TC[i][j]$ to true if either $TC[i][j]$ is already *true* or both $TC[i][k]$ and $TC[k][j]$ are *true*.

Example: 4.20 Consider the following directed graph:

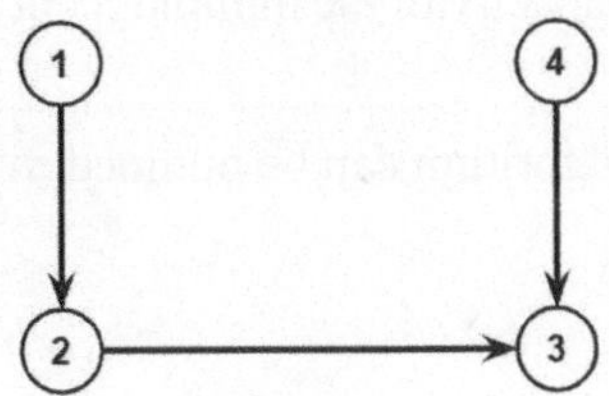

Adjacency matrix V For $K = 1$:   For $K = 2$:   For $K = 3$:

$$A = \begin{bmatrix} 0 & 1 & 1 & 0 \\ 0 & 0 & 0 & 1 \\ 0 & 0 & 0 & 1 \\ 0 & 0 & 0 & 0 \end{bmatrix} \quad A = \begin{bmatrix} 0 & 1 & 1 & 0 \\ 0 & 0 & 0 & 1 \\ 0 & 0 & 0 & 1 \\ 0 & 0 & 0 & 0 \end{bmatrix} \quad A = \begin{bmatrix} 0 & 1 & 1 & 1 \\ 0 & 0 & 0 & 1 \\ 0 & 0 & 0 & 1 \\ 0 & 0 & 0 & 0 \end{bmatrix} \quad A = \begin{bmatrix} 0 & 1 & 1 & 1 \\ 0 & 0 & 0 & 1 \\ 0 & 0 & 0 & 1 \\ 0 & 0 & 0 & 0 \end{bmatrix}$$

Initialize TC as V.

The final transitive closure matrix TC indicates the reachability between vertices in the graph.

Floyd-Warshall algorithm has an $O(V^3)$ time complexity when computing the transitive closure, where V is the number of vertices. Analysing the reachability characteristics of directed graphs is crucial, particularly in applications like network routing and programme analysis, where an understanding of the transitive closure is important.

4.14 Network Flow Algorithm - Ford-Fulkerson

The maximum flow in a network is determined by using network flow algorithms. It is a graph with a capacity for each edge to serve for the transmission of a specific quantity (flow). These algorithms are fundamental to many applications, including resource allocation, network design, and transportation planning. One of the most well-known network flow algorithms is the Ford-Fulkerson algorithm. Let us explore the key concepts and steps.

i. *Network representation:* A directed graph containing vertices, edges, and capacity is used to depict the network. Every edge has a capacity that represents the greatest amount of flow that it can support.

ii. *Residual graph:* It is an unused graph after the flow is dispatched. The residual graph G_f is utilised to monitor the remaining capacities on edges. Initially, G_f and the original graph G are identical.

iii. *Augmenting paths:* A path from source to sink in residual graph is called an augmenting path. The maximum flow that may be sent down a path is known as the bottleneck capacity.

iv. *Flow augmentation:* By using the bottleneck capacity, the method increases the flow along the augmenting path. Until there are no more enhancing pathways, this process is repeated.

v. *Termination:* When there are no more augmenting paths in the residual graph, the algorithm comes to an end.

vi. *Max-flow min-cut theorem:* The flow found by the algorithm is guaranteed to be the maximum possible flow in the network. Capacity of the minimum cut is equal to the value of the maximum flow.

vii. *Pseudocode:* Ford-Fulkerson algorithm can be outlined in pseudocode as follows:

```
FordFulkerson (G, s, t):
    Initialize flow ← 0
    while augmenting P ∈ G_f:
            Find bottleneck capacity along path P
            Flow along the route P
            Revise the residual diagram G_f
    return final flow
```

The complexity of the Ford-Fulkerson algorithm depends on how augmenting paths are chosen. In the worst case, where augmenting paths are poorly chosen, the algorithm may not terminate. However, with certain path selection strategies (*e.g Edmonds-Karp* algorithm using BFS). With V representing the number of vertices and E representing the number of edges, the algorithm is guaranteed to finish in $O(VE^2)$ time.

Example: 4.21 Consider a network where each edge has capacity, sinks t, and sources s. Using the Ford-Fulkerson algorithm, the objective is to determine the maximum flow from s to t. Until no more augmenting paths can be located, the algorithm keeps searching for augmenting paths and gradually increasing the flow.

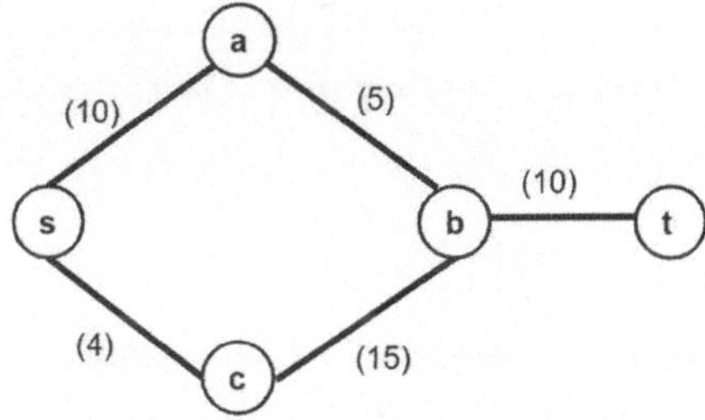

The numbers in parentheses represent the capacities of the edges. Until no more augmenting paths can be found, the algorithm would iteratively locate augmenting paths and update the flow. Understanding network flow algorithms is important for solving optimization problems in various domains: logistics, telecommunications, and computer networking.

UNIT SUMMARY

- The unit covers the foundational concepts of graph theory, providing a solid understanding of the basic elements and their relationships.
- Explores DFS and BFS as essential tools for navigating and analyzing graphs.
- Introduces graph-finding algorithms, which are essential for a number of applications, including network routing and transportation planning.

- Examines the concept of transitive closure, offering insights into the relationships and reachability in directed graphs.
- Covers algorithms to find the minimum spanning tree, an important structure with applications in network design and optimization.
- Discusses methods for arranging the vertices of a directed graph in a linear order, a key operation in scheduling and dependency resolution.
- Explores algorithms that optimize the flow of resources through a network, applicable in diverse scenarios such as transportation and communication networks.
- Includes short and long answer questions to assess comprehension and application of graph theory concepts.
- Emphasizes a holistic approach to understanding graphs, ensuring learners gain practical knowledge and problem-solving skills.
- Demonstrates the relevance of graph theory through real-world examples, fostering a connection between theoretical knowledge and practical applications.
- Equips learners with a solid foundation in graph theory, preparing them to tackle algorithmic challenges and problem-solving in various domains.

MULTIPLE CHOICE QUESTIONS

1. What is a fundamental unit of a graph?
   a. Edge
   b. Weight
   c. Node
   d. Degree
2. Which type of graph has no cycles?
   a. Directed Graph
   b. Undirected Graph
   c. Weighted Graph
   d. Directed Acyclic Graph DAG
3. What is the primary purpose of graph traversal algorithms?
   a. Sorting nodes alphabetically
   b. Identifying cycles in a graph
   c. Finding the shortest path in a graph
   d. Visiting and exploring vertices of a graph
4. Which representation of a graph is more space-efficient for sparse graphs?
   a. Adjacency Matrix

   b. Adjacency List
   c. Weighted Graph
   d. Directed Graph
5. What is the key characteristic of DFS?
   a. Explores every neighbor node at the current depth
   b. Processes vertices in ascending order of their weights
   c. Travels as far as possible along each branch
   d. Identifies cycles in a graph
6. Which application is BFS commonly used for?
   a. Detecting cycles in a graph
   b. Topological sorting
   c. Web crawling
   d. Finding strongly connected components
7. Which algorithm is used to find the shortest path between two vertices in a weighted graph?
   a. Depth-First Search (DFS)
   b. Breadth-First Search (BFS)
   c. Dijkstra's algorithm
   d. Bellman-Ford algorithm
8. Which type of edge connects vertices within the same depth-first tree but are not ancestors of each other?
   a. Tree Edge
   b. Back Edge
   c. Forward Edge
   d. Cross Edge
9. What is the primary goal of topological sorting?
   a. Finding cycles in a graph
   b. Identifying strongly connected components
   c. Determining routes or paths between vertices
   d. Providing a linear ordering of vertices in a directed acyclic graph
10. Which algorithm uses a greedy approach to find the MST of a graph?
    a. Depth-First Search
    b. Breadth-First Search
    c. Kruskal's algorithm
    d. Prim's algorithm
11. What is the key characteristic of the MST?
    a. It contains the maximum number of edges
    b. It forms a cycle
    c. It spans every vertex in the graph with the fewest edges

d. It is directed

12. Which algorithm is used to identify the strongly connected components in a directed graph?
    a. Kruskal's algorithm
    b. Dijkstra's algorithm
    c. Bellman-Ford algorithm
    d. Kosaraju's algorithm

13. What is the primary objective of topological sorting?
    a. Finding the shortest path in a graph
    b. Determining routes or paths between vertices
    c. Providing a linear ordering of vertices in a directed acyclic graph
    d. Identifying cycles in a graph

14. Which algorithm finds the shortest paths between a single source vertex and all other vertices in a graph with non-negative edge weights?
    a. Dijkstra's algorithm
    b. Bellman-Ford algorithm
    c. Floyd-Warshall algorithm
    d. Prim's algorithm

15. What type of graph does Dijkstra's algorithm work best on?
    a. Directed Acyclic Graph
    b. Weighted Graph
    c. Graph with negative edge weights
    d. Graph with non-negative edge weights

16. Which algorithm is used to find the shortest paths between all pairs of vertices in a graph?
    a. Dijkstra's algorithm
    b. Bellman-Ford algorithm
    c. Floyd-Warshall algorithm
    d. Prim's algorithm

17. What does Bellman-Ford algorithm detect in a graph while finding shortest path?
    a. Minimum Spanning Tree
    b. Shortest path
    c. Negative cycle
    d. Strongly connected components

18. Which of the following is NOT a property of a directed acyclic graph?
    a. Contains no cycles
    b. Can be linearly ordered
    c. Every vertex has a unique predecessor
    d. Every vertex has a unique successor

19. In a weighted graph, what does the weight of an edge typically represent?
    a. Distance between vertices
    b. Number of edges connected to a vertex
    c. Time complexity of a traversal algorithm
    d. Size of the graph
20. Which algorithm is typically used to solve the traveling salesman problem?
    a. Kruskal's algorithm
    b. Dijkstra's algorithm
    c. Floyd-Warshall algorithm
    d. Dynamic programming
21. Which of the following data structures is commonly used to implement priority queues in Dijkstra's algorithm?
    a. Stack
    b. Queue
    c. Heap
    d. Linked List
22. What is the time complexity of Dijkstra's algorithm when implemented with a priority queue?
    a. O(V)
    b. O(V^2)
    c. O(E log V)
    d. O(V + E)
23. Which of the following algorithms can handle negative edge weights?
    a. Dijkstra's algorithm
    b. Bellman-Ford algorithm
    c. Kruskal's algorithm
    d. Floyd-Warshall algorithm
24. What is the primary objective of Kruskal's algorithm?
    a. Finding the shortest path in a graph
    b. Identifying cycles in a graph
    c. Constructing a minimum spanning tree
    d. Topological sorting
25. Which of the following is a characteristic of the BFS algorithm?
    a. Uses a stack data structure
    b. Explores nodes at the deepest level first
    c. Determines the shortest path between two nodes
    d. Performs a depth-first traversal
26. What is the primary application of Dijkstra's algorithm?
    a. Topological sorting

b. Finding the shortest path in a graph
c. Detecting cycles in a graph
d. Constructing a minimum spanning tree

27. Which of the following algorithms has a higher time complexity for finding the shortest path in dense graphs?
    a. Dijkstra's algorithm
    b. Bellman-Ford algorithm
    c. Floyd-Warshall algorithm
    d. Prim's algorithm

28. Which of the following is NOT a step in Kruskal's algorithm?
    a. Sort all the edges in non-decreasing order of their weight
    b. Create a forest where each vertex is a separate component
    c. Add the edge with the highest weight to the minimum spanning tree
    d. Repeat steps until there is only one component

29. Which algorithm is used to find the shortest path between all pairs of vertices in a graph with negative edge weights?
    a. Dijkstra's algorithm
    b. Bellman-Ford algorithm
    c. Floyd-Warshall algorithm
    d. Prim's algorithm

30. What is the primary disadvantage of using an adjacency matrix to represent a graph?
    a. It requires less memory
    b. It is difficult to implement
    c. It is inefficient for sparse graphs
    d. It cannot represent weighted graphs

Solution of MCQ:

1	2	3	4	5	6	7	8	9	10	11	12	13	14	15
c	d	d	b	c	c	c	d	d	c	c	d	d	a	d
16	17	18	19	20	21	22	23	24	25	26	27	28	29	30
c	c	a	a	d	c	c	b	c	c	b	c	c	c	c

SHORT AND LONG ANSWER TYPE QUESTIONS

1 Let an edge in a connected graph G be of minimum weight (u, v). Prove that (u, v) is a part of at least one MST for G.

2 Prove an edge (u, v) is a light edge crossing a graph cut if in a MST.

3 Let L be the sorted edge weights of T, where T be the least spanning tree of graph G. Prove that the list L is the sorted list of edge weights for any other MST T' of G.

4 What are the key traversal algorithms of graphs?

5 Explain the significance of network flow algorithms in various real-world applications, providing an example scenario where it is applied?

6 Define and eloborate the traversal algorithms for DFS and BFS. Give an example graph where one approach could be more appropriate than the other, and highlight the use cases and limitations of each.

7 Discuss the role of topological sorting in scheduling and dependency resolution. Provide an example scenario where topological sorting is essential, and explain how it aids in solving the problem?

8 Explain the concept of transitive closure in graphs. Provide a real-world example where transitive closure can be applied and discuss the implications of computing the transitive closure in the given context.

9 Give an example of how to determine MST. Give an example of a situation where determining the MST is essential and discuss the practical significance.

10 Elaborate on the applications of shortest path algorithms in network routing. Discuss a specific routing problem and explain how a shortest path algorithm can be employed to obtain an optimal solution.

11 Discuss the concept of the Network Flow Algorithm and its applications in solving optimization problems. Provide an example and explain the steps involved in applying this algorithm to address the problem.

KNOW MORE

Online courses/materials/resources [Accessed May 2024]

- https://www.maths.ed.ac.uk/~v1ranick/papers/wilsongraph.pdf
- https://archive.nptel.ac.in/courses/111/106/111106050/
- https://www.cs.purdue.edu/homes/spa/courses/cs182/mod8.pdf
- https://www.coursera.org/learn/algorithms-on-graphs

- https://www.geeksforgeeks.org/graph-theory-tutorial/
- https://github.com/topics/graph-theory

REFERENCES

[1] Gillies, A. "Scott, DFS, Wilhelm von Humboldt and the Idea of a University (Book Review)." *The Modern Language Review* 55 (1960): 629.

[2] Agnarsson, Geir, and Raymond Greenlaw. *Graph theory: Modeling, applications, and algorithms*. Prentice-Hall, Inc., 2006.

[3] Sedgewick, Robert. *An introduction to the analysis of algorithms*. Pearson Education India, 2013.

[4] Kahn, Arthur B. "*Topological sorting of large networks.*" *Communications of the ACM* 5, no. 11 (1962): 558-562.

[5] Ackerman, Sharon H., and Alexander Tzagoloff. "*Function, structure, and biogenesis of mitochondrial ATP synthase.*" *Progress in nucleic acid research and molecular biology 80* (2005): 95-133.

5 Brute-Force Methodology

UNIT SPECIFICS

This unit covers the following aspects:

- *About brute-force methodology*
- *Characteristics of brute-force algorithms*
- *Design strategies of brute-force algorithms*
- *Applications in various domains*
- *Unit summary, short and long answer questions*

This unit covers brute-force methodology, which involves trying all the possible options to find a solution. It discusses the characteristics of brute-force algorithms, analyze their time and space complexity, and discover their applications in various domains such as text analysis, combinatorial optimization, and route optimization. Additionally, it covers strategies to enhance the efficiency and effectiveness of brute-force algorithms, while considering its limitations and discusses some alternative approaches to reduce time and space complexities. The link given in the QR code provides the supplementary material for this unit.

RATIONALE

The rationale of this unit with the design and analysis of algorithms is to introduce and explore the concept of brute-force methodology as a problem-solving technique. Its goal is to offer insight into the functioning, characteristics, and diverse applications of brute-force algorithms across various domains.

PRE-REQUISITES

- *Basic knowledge of data structure and complexity analysis*
- *Familiarity with algorithmic concepts, including sorting and searching algorithms*
- *Basic understanding of mathematical concepts, especially in relation to series and sequences*

UNIT OUTCOMES

The outcomes of the Unit are as follows:

U5-O1: Understand the concept of brute-force methodology

U5-O2: Identify characteristics of brute-force algorithms

U5-O3: Discuss design strategies of brute-force algorithms

U5-O4: Apply brute-force algorithms to various domains

Unit-5 Outcomes	***EXPECTED MAPPING WITH COURSE OUTCOMES*** *(1- Weak Correlation; 2- Medium correlation; 3- Strong Correlation)*				
	CO-1	***CO-2***	***CO-3***	***CO-4***	***CO-5***
U5-O1	-	1	3	3	-
U5-O2	-	1	3	3	-
U5-O3	-	1	3	3	-
U5-O4	1	1	3	3	-

5.1 Introduction to Brute-Force Methodology

Let us consider a simple example to illustrate the concept of brute-force methodology. Suppose you are searching for your laptop in your house, but you still cannot find it despite checking all the usual places like your desk, shelves, and bags. In this situation, you might try brute-force, searching every possible spot in your house to find the laptop. You start in one room and carefully look at every surface, open all the drawers, and check every corner to ensure you do not miss anything. If you do not find the laptop in that room, you move on to the next one and do the same thing. You search all possible hiding spots by going through each room and checking everywhere. If the laptop is in your house, this method guarantees that you will eventually find it. But it is important to note that brute-force methodology can take a lot of time and may not be the best choice if you have a big house or if the laptop could be somewhere outside. In those cases, it might be more helpful to think about where you last used it or ask others.

Similarly, the example of using brute-force methodology to crack a password. Suppose we have a lock with a four-digit combination. We have forgotten the combination and must try every possible one until we find the correct one. Using the brute-force methodology, we start with the first possible combination, which is 0000, and proceed to test each subsequent combination in sequential order: 0001,0002,0003, and so on, until we reach 9999. We continue this process until we find the correct combination to unlock. The brute-force methodology ensures that we exhaustively evaluate every possible combination. It leaves no possibility of overlooking the correct combination, guaranteeing that we will eventually find it, if it exists within the range of possibilities. However, it is important to note that brute-force methodology can be highly inefficient. In this example, we had to try 10000 combinations to find the correct one. If the number of possible combinations were larger, the time and computational resources required would increase exponentially.

Despite its inefficiency, brute-force methodology has a wider range of applications. It is commonly employed when there are no known shortcuts or more efficient algorithms available for solving a problem. It provides a reliable and simple approach that guarantees finding a solution if one exists within the problem space. It is worth noting that the effectiveness of brute-force methodology for cracking passwords depends on several factors, including password complexity, length, and the computational power available. In practice, additional security measures, such as account lockouts after multiple unsuccessful attempts or the use of more sophisticated encryption algorithms, are implemented to counter the brute-force attacks.

The brute-force methodology is employed to crack passwords by exhaustively trying every possible combination until the correct password is obtained. It guarantees success in finding the password if it exists within the search space. However, this approach can be highly time-consuming and inefficient, especially when dealing with complex and lengthy passwords. As the length and complexity of the password increase, the number of possible combinations grows exponentially, leading to a significant increase in the time and computational resources required for the exhaustive search. In practice, brute-force is often not the most efficient approach for cracking passwords, and other more advanced techniques, such as dictionary attacks, rainbow tables, or salting, are commonly used to enhance security and speed up the password recovery process.

5.2 Characteristics of Brute-Force Algorithms

This section discusses the fundamental characteristics of a brute-force algorithm, considering the previously discussed example of searching for a laptop within a house. Through a careful examination of this example, you can find valuable insights into the exhaustive nature of the algorithm, its simplicity, determinism, implications for time complexity, lack of assumptions, completeness, limitations in terms of scalability, and its role as a foundation for selecting alternative strategies. Let us describe the characteristics of brute-force algorithms based on the considered example:

i. **Exhaustive search:** Brute-force algorithms adopt a systematic approach by exploring all potential solutions to a problem. It rigorously considers every option within the solution space, leaving no potential solution unexplored. In the context of our example, the individual conducting the search for the laptop thoroughly examines every possible spot in the house. The search involves exploring each room and area, ensuring no location is skipped and all possibilities are investigated.

ii. **Simplicity and directness:** Brute-force algorithms are known for their simple and intuitive nature. They employ basic operations such as iteration, comparison, and the evaluation of all possibilities. Similarly, in our example, the search process is simple and direct. The individual conducts a systematic search by thoroughly examining each room, thoroughly inspecting every surface, opening drawers, and scrutinizing corners. This approach does not rely on complex algorithms or optimizations but focuses on exhaustively exploring all potential search space.

iii. **Time complexity:** Brute-force algorithms exhibit high time complexity due to the necessity of considering every possible solution. The time required generally increases exponentially with the problem size. In our example, brute-force is acknowledged to potentially consume substantial time, particularly when dealing with larger houses or when the laptop could be located outside. This emphasizes the inherent high time complexity associated with brute-force algorithms.

iv. **Deterministic:** Brute-force algorithms produce predictable and deterministic results. If a solution exists within the search space, the algorithm inevitably discovers it. The brute-force methodology assures that if the laptop is within the house, it is ultimately found. The individual conducting the search is confident that by thoroughly exploring every potential spot, the laptop is uncovered.

v. **No assumptions or special cases:** Brute-force algorithms do not rely on specific assumptions or exploit problem-specific characteristics. It uniformly considers all possibilities, irrespective of the particular problem instance. In our example, the individual refrains from making any assumptions about the location of the laptop. The individual carefully searches every room and thoroughly inspect all possible hiding spots, leaving no potential area unexplored.

vi. **Completeness:** Brute-force algorithms guarantee completeness by exhaustively searching the entire solution space. If a solution exists, the algorithm will determine it. By thoroughly examining every location within the house, the brute-force method ensures comprehensive coverage. If the laptop is present, the algorithm guarantees its eventual discovery.

vii. **Lack of optimization:** Brute-force algorithms often lack optimization techniques, as they focus on exhaustively considering all possibilities rather than implementing strategies to reduce the search space or enhance efficiency. The example highlights that brute-force may not be the most suitable choice for larger problem sizes or more expensive houses, implying the limitations of scalability and efficiency associated with brute-force algorithms.

viii. **Applicability:** Brute-force algorithms are applicable to a wide range of problems and serve as viable approaches when alternative methods are infeasible or when the problem size permits an exhaustive search. They are particularly effective for smaller problem instances where the exhaustive exploration can be conducted within reasonable time limits.

ix. **Limited scalability:** Brute-force algorithms may become impractical or inefficient for larger problem sizes due to their exponential time complexity. They are better suited for smaller problem instances. By exploring every possible location within the house, the brute-force method ensures completeness. However, as the problem size increases, the efficiency of brute-force algorithms diminishes, rendering them less viable for scalability.

x. **Baseline approach:** Brute-force algorithms serve as a baseline for evaluating and comparing the performance of alternative algorithms. They establish a reference point for assessing the effectiveness of more advanced techniques. In our example, alternative strategies such as retracing steps or seeking assistance from others are suggested, recognizing that brute-force serves as a foundational method, and more efficient approaches may be applicable depending on the specific problem circumstances.

5.3 Design Strategies of Brute-Force Algorithms

This section covers the design strategies of brute-force algorithms, which involve various techniques to enhance their efficiency and effectiveness. Some common strategies are discussed in terms of following points:

i. **Reducing the search space** is a crucial strategy to optimize the efficiency of brute-force algorithms. The process of reducing the search space involves several steps. First, it is important to analyze the problem and identify any constraints or characteristics that can be leveraged to narrow down the search space. In our example, this could include factors such as the size of the laptop, typical storage locations, or areas where it is unlikely to be found. By understanding these constraints, unnecessary areas can be excluded early on in the search, saving valuable computational resources. The next step is to eliminate unnecessary or invalid solutions as quickly as possible. By excluding areas or rooms that are irrelevant to the desired solution, unnecessary computations can be avoided, resulting in a more efficient search process. Finally, utilizing problem-specific knowledge becomes crucial. This involves leveraging personal understanding and familiarity with the laptop's typical usage patterns and storage habits. By taking advantage of this knowledge, portions of the solution space that are guaranteed not to contain the laptop can be eliminated, further narrowing down the search area. By following these steps and reducing the search space effectively, the brute-force algorithm can be optimized to focus efforts on the most likely areas where the desired solution is expected to be found.

ii. **Pruning techniques** play a critical role in enhancing the efficiency of a brute-force algorithm. By implementing these techniques, specific branches or subsets of the solution space that are known to be invalid or unpromising can be eliminated. This is achieved through early pruning, which allows for the exclusion of irrelevant parts of the search space from further exploration. By doing so, computational resources are conserved by avoiding unnecessary computations. For instance, when searching for a laptop in a house, excluding areas like the garage or root space can save time. Additionally, heuristics or evaluation functions can be utilized to guide the search process and prioritize more promising branches. By leveraging problem-specific knowledge or objective evaluation criteria, areas with a higher likelihood of containing the desired solution can be assigned greater importance. These pruning techniques ensure that the brute-force algorithm focuses its efforts on exploring the most fruitful and relevant areas, leading to a more efficient and effective search. Using problem-specific knowledge, such as focusing on the study room where the laptop is often used, improves efficiency.

iii. **Memoization** is a technique that can significantly enhance the efficiency of an algorithm, and it finds practical application when searching for a laptop in a house. By storing and reusing the results of expensive computations or intermediate solutions, redundant calculations can be avoided. In our example, let us consider the search process in different rooms of the house. With memoization, if you have already thoroughly searched the living room and found it empty, you can store this result. Subsequently, when revisiting the living room during the search, the memoized result can be retrieved, eliminating the need to repeat the search. This approach leads to significant time savings and boosts the overall efficiency of the algorithm. Memoization becomes especially valuable when the same computation is repeatedly required, enabling the algorithm to leverage precomputed results instead of performing redundant calculations. By employing memoization effectively, the search for the laptop becomes more efficient, reducing computation time and improving overall execution.

iv. **Parallelization** is a powerful strategy that enhances the performance of a brute-force algorithm. It is particularly useful when searching for a laptop in a house. By dividing the search space into independent tasks and distributing them across multiple processors or threads, parallelization allows for concurrent execution. For example, assigning different rooms to separate processors or threads enables simultaneous exploration. This approach optimizes efficiency by leveraging multiple computing resources and results in a significant speedup. It is especially beneficial for computationally intensive problems with large solution spaces. In our laptop search example, parallelization reduces the overall search time, leading to more efficient retrieval. Harnessing the potential of parallelization allows for a faster brute-force algorithm, making it an effective strategy for improving performance.

v. **Backtracking** is a valuable technique for efficient exploration of the search space in a brute-force algorithm, especially when searching for a laptop in a house. It involves maintaining a search state and undoing choices that lead to invalid solutions. By backtracking, the algorithm avoids unnecessary exploration of unfruitful branches and focuses on more promising options. In our laptop search example, backtracking allows the algorithm to backtrack from rooms that do not contain the laptop and explore other areas instead. By intelligently pruning unviable branches, backtracking reduces the search space and optimizes efficiency, leading to a faster and more efficient retrieval of the desired solution.

vi. **Optimizing a brute-force algorithm based on problem constraints** can significantly enhance its efficiency. By identifying specific constraints, you can modify the algorithm to prioritize them and adjust the search order accordingly. This approach guides the algorithm towards more promising solutions and reduces the overall search space. To optimize the algorithm, start by analyzing the problem and identifying relevant constraints, such as usual storage locations or areas with a higher likelihood of containing the desired solution. Based on their importance, adjust the search order or prioritize these constraints to expedite the search process. Additionally, fine-tune the algorithm's logic to effectively leverage these constraints. This may involve skipping iterations or excluding irrelevant parts of the search space, eliminating unnecessary exploration. By optimizing the brute-force algorithm using constraints, the search process becomes more efficient and targeted. For example, in the case of searching for a laptop, adjusting the search order to prioritize likely storage locations can expedite the retrieval process. By leveraging problem-specific constraints, the algorithm becomes more focused, reducing redundant computations and enabling faster and more efficient solution finding.

vii. **Considering the trade-offs between accuracy and computational efficiency** is crucial when designing a brute-force algorithm. Approximate or partial solutions may be acceptable in some cases, leading to significant speed improvements. Evaluate whether an approximate or partial solution would be sufficient for the problem at hand, especially in scenarios like optimization problems or large-scale computations. Assess the trade-off between accuracy and computational efficiency, as achieving high accuracy may come at the cost of extensive computational resources and time. By incorporating trade-offs with approximations, you can strike a balance between accuracy and efficiency. For instance, when searching for a laptop in a house, approximating the search by focusing on high-probability areas or using partial information can be considered. By exploring these trade-offs and accepting approximations when appropriate, you can enhance the efficiency of the brute-force algorithm, enabling faster computations and effective handling of larger problem sizes. Balancing accuracy and computational efficiency through approximations is a valuable strategy in brute-force algorithm design.

These strategies can be applied individually or in combination, depending on the specific problem and its characteristics. It is important to carefully analyze the problem, consider the trade-offs, and tailor the design strategies to optimize the brute-force algorithms.

5.4 Examples of Brute-Force Algorithms

Brute-force algorithms have wide-ranging applications across various domains. This section discusses three specific applications: String Matching, Subset Generation, and the Traveling Salesman Problem (TSP). We explore the corresponding algorithms for each of these applications, analyze their time complexity, and assess their space complexity.

5.4.1 Use Cases

Despite the simplicity of brute-force algorithms and potential inefficiency for large problem sizes, it finds applications in various real-world scenarios. Some important use cases are:

i. **String matching:** Brute-force algorithms are commonly employed for pattern matching and searching within strings. Applications include text editors performing find and replace operations, search engines indexing and searching through documents, and DNA sequence analysis for genetic pattern matching.

ii. **Cryptanalysis:** Brute-force algorithms are used in cryptanalysis to crack encrypted codes or passwords by systematically trying all possible combinations. While computationally expensive, brute-force can be effective when the key space is small or when combined with optimizations like parallel processing or pruning.

iii. **Combinatorial optimization:** Brute-force algorithms can be used as a baseline approach for solving combinatorial optimization problems. By exhaustively trying all possible solutions, they can provide an exact solution, although they may be impractical for large problem sizes.

iv. **Chess and game playing:** Brute-force algorithms are used to evaluate and search through the game tree in chess and other games. This allows computers to analyze all possible moves and outcomes, leading to optimal gameplay strategies.

v. **Image and video processing:** Brute Force algorithms can be used for template matching in image and video processing tasks. These algorithms can identify matching patterns or objects by comparing the template with different locations in an image or video sequence.

5.4.2 String Matching

The string matching problem involves finding occurrences of a given pattern within a larger text or string. The objective is to identify all positions or indices where the pattern appears in the text. The string-matching problem is fundamental in many applications that involve searching for specific patterns or sequences within large bodies of text or data. By efficiently solving this problem, various tasks such as information retrieval, data analysis, and pattern recognition can be performed effectively. The goal is to efficiently determine the starting positions of all matches of the pattern within the text.

Several algorithms are available to solve this problem, each with its trade-offs regarding time complexity and space requirements. Brute-force string matching is one of the most simple algorithms for solving this problem. It involves systematically comparing the pattern with each possible substring of the text to identify matches.

Brute-force string matching algorithm description: The algorithm compares the pattern with each possible text substring, starting from the leftmost position. It moves the pattern one character at a time and checks for a match at each position. If a match is found, it continues comparing subsequent characters. If a mismatch occurs, it moves to the next possible position in the text and restarts the comparison. The process continues until either a match is found or the end of the text is reached. The BRUTE-FORCE-STRING-MATCHING algorithm assumes that text represents the given text string and pattern represents the pattern to search. It works first by calculating the text lengths and pattern denoted as n and m, respectively. Then, it iterates through the text from index 0 to $n - m$, considering each possible starting position for the pattern. Inside the loop, a pointer j is initialized to 0 to keep track of the current position in the pattern. It enters a while loop that continues as long as j is less than m and the characters at $text[i + j]$ and $pattern[j]$ match. If a match is found, j is incremented by 1 for each subsequent character match. If j becomes equal to m, it indicates that the entire pattern has been found in the text starting from the position i. In such a case, the algorithm returns the starting index i. However, if the loop completes without finding a match, the function returns -1, indicating that the pattern does not exist.

```
BRUTE-FORCE-STRING-MATCHING(text, pattern)
    n = length(text)
    m = length(pattern)
    for i from 0 to n − m
        j = 0
        while j < m and text[i + j] == pattern[j]
            j = j + 1
        if j == m
            return i
    return -1
```

Example 1: Consider the inputs for BRUTE-FORCE-STRING-MATCHING algorithm as follows: the text is "IIT(BHU) Varanasi" and the pattern is "BHU". Initialize the variables: set n as 17 (the length of the text) and m as 3 (the length of the pattern). The algorithm begins by iterating through the text from index 0 to 1. During each iteration, it compares the characters of the pattern with the corresponding characters in the text. In the first iteration, the algorithm compares B (pattern[0]) with I (text[0]), but they do not match. It then proceeds to the next iteration. This process continues until the $5th$ iteration, where the B (pattern[0]) matches the B (text[4]) in the text. In this case, the algorithm finds a complete match, and it returns the starting index of the match, which is 4. This indicates that the pattern "BHU" is present in the text starting at index 4. The algorithm further continues till $(n = 17) - (m = 3)$ iterations to obtain other occurrences of BHU in the text. By systematically comparing each character of the pattern with the corresponding characters in the text, the Brute Force string matching algorithm enables the identification of pattern occurrences within the text. Figure 5.1 portrays the steps of the algorithm by visualizing the movement of the pattern over the text. It illustrates that the algorithm systematically compares each character of the pattern with the corresponding characters in the text, moving from left to right.

Time and space complexity analysis: The brute-force string matching algorithm has a time complexity of $O((n - m + 1) \times m)$ and this bound is tight in the worst case. For instance, let us consider the scenario where the text string consists of n times a characters (a string of n $a's$) and the pattern is a followed by m times a characters. In this case, for each of the $(n - m + 1)$ possible values of the shift

s, the algorithm needs to compare each character of the pattern with the corresponding character in the text, which requires m comparisons. Therefore, the worst-case running time of the algorithm is $O((n - m + 1) \times m)$, which simplifies to $O(n \times m)$. In particular, if we assume that the pattern length m is equal to half the length of the text $m = (n/2)$, the worst-case running time becomes $O(n^2)$. This occurs because, for each possible shift, the algorithm needs to compare m characters, resulting in a quadratic time complexity.

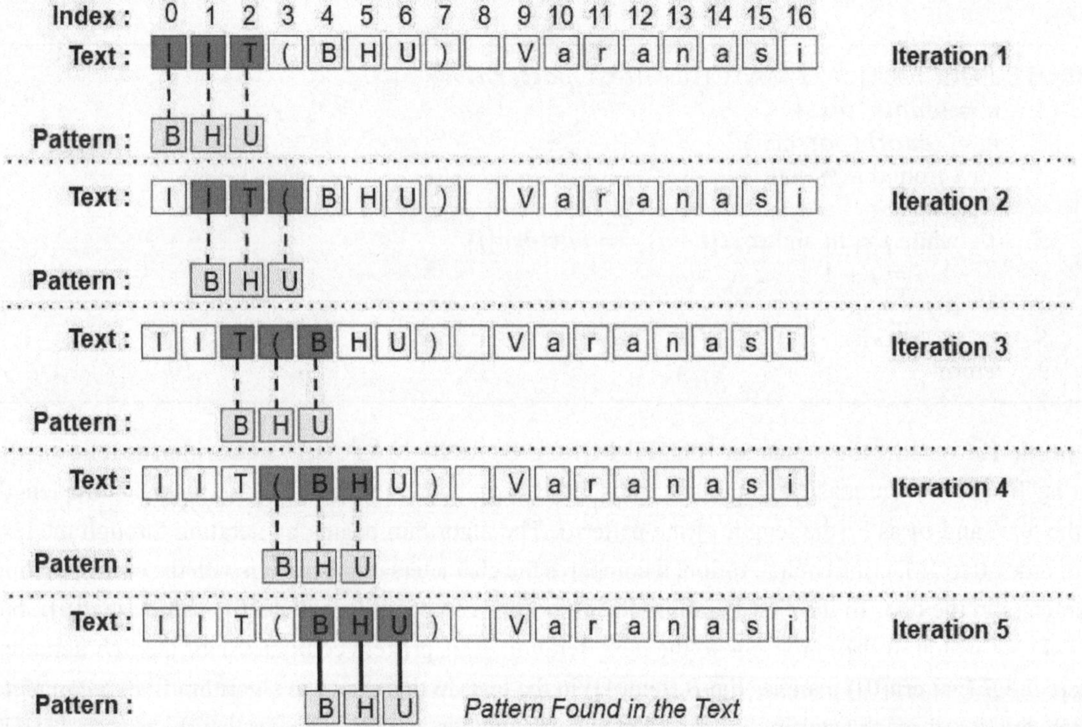

Figure 5.1: An illustration of pattern matching algorithm Using Brute-force method. Given **Text:** IIT(BHU) Varanasi and **Pattern:** BHU requires five iterations to detect the pattern. Here "- - - -" lines indicate there is character mismatch and "—" lines indicate the matched characters.

Space complexity of the brute-force string matching algorithm is $O(1)$, which means that it uses a constant amount of additional space regardless of the input size. The algorithm does not require any additional data structures or memory allocation, and it performs its operations in-place. Specifically, the brute-force algorithm does not require any preprocessing, and its running time directly corresponds to its matching time. While it is a simple and simple approach for string matching, its time complexity can be relatively high for larger problem sizes. Other more efficient algorithms, such as Knuth-Morris-Pratt (KMP) or Boyer-Moore, provide better time complexities by utilizing additional preprocessing steps [1].

5.4.3 Subset Generation Problem

The Subset generation problem involves generating all possible subsets of a given set. It aims to find all combinations of elements within the set, including the empty set and the set itself. This problem is widely applicable in various domains, such as combinatorial optimization, data analysis, and algorithmic problem-solving. By solving the subset generation problem, we can explore various combinations and variations of elements within a set, enabling us to analyze and derive insights from data. The algorithm efficiently generates all possible subsets, providing a foundation to analyze or problem-solving tasks.

Brute-force subset generation is one of the simplest approaches to solve this problem. The algorithm exhaustively explores all possible combinations of elements within the set. It iterates through each element and includes or excludes it in each subset, creating a binary decision for each element. By systematically evaluating these decisions, all possible subsets are generated. Although the Brute-force subset generation algorithm guarantees the generation of all subsets, it may not be efficient for large sets due to its exponential time complexity. As the size of the set increases, the number of subsets grows exponentially, resulting in high computational requirements. Therefore, for larger sets, more advanced optimization techniques, such as backtracking or dynamic programming, can be employed to reduce redundant computations and improve efficiency [2].

Theorem: The number of subsets that can be generated from a set of size n using the Brute-force subset generation algorithm is equal to 2^n.

Proof: The proof is by mathematical induction on the set of size n.

- *Base Case:* For $n = 0$, the set is empty, and there is only one subset, which is the empty set {} and promising.
- *Inductive Hypothesis:* Assume that for a set of size k (where $k \geq 0$), the number of subsets generated by the algorithm is 2^k.
- *Inductive Step:* Consider a set of size $k + 1$. We want to show that the number of subsets generated by the algorithm for this set is $2^{(k+1)}$. For a set of size $k + 1$, each element can either be included or excluded in a subset, *i.e.*, it can either be in the subset or not in the subset. Since there are $k + 1$ elements in the set, the total number of subsets is the product of these choices, which is $2 \times 2 \times \ldots \times 2(k + 1)$, or $2^{(k+1)}$. Thus, the number of subsets generated by the algorithm for a set of size $k + 1$ is $2^{(k+1)}$. By the principle of mathematical induction, the theorem holds true for all non-negative integers n.

This completes the proof by mathematical induction that the number of subsets that can be generated from a set of size n using the algorithm is equal to .

Brute-force subset generation algorithm description: The brute-force subset generation algorithm generates all possible subsets of a given set by systematically considering inclusion or exclusion of each element. Given a set of size n, the algorithm aims to create all possible combinations of subsets, including the empty set and the set itself. The process starts by initializing an empty list to store the subsets. To generate all possible subsets of a given set using $BRUTE\_FORCE\_SUBSET\_GENERATION$ algorithm, it follows the following steps. First, it initializes an empty list called subsets to hold the subsets that are generated. Then, it determines the size of the given set as n. Next, we iterate from 0 to $(2^n - 1)$ to represent all possible binary strings of length n. Each binary string corresponds to a subset, where each bit indicates the inclusion or exclusion of the corresponding element in the set. Within each iteration, it creates a new empty list called subset to construct the current subset. It iterates from 0 to n to consider each element of the set, and for each element, it checks if the jth bit of the binary representation i is set. If the jth bit is set, it means that the element is included in the current subset, so it adds the jth element of the set to the subset. After considering all elements, it adds the subset to the subsets list, representing one of the possible combinations of elements in the set. It repeats steps 4 to 8 for all binary strings from 0 to $(2^n - 1)$, generating all possible subsets of the given set. Finally, we return the subsets list as the final result, containing all the unique subsets of the original set, ranging from the empty set to the complete set itself.

```
BRUTE_FORCE_SUBSET_GENERATION(set)
1. subsets = []
2. n = size of set
3. for i from 0 to (2^n − 1)
4.     subsets = []
5.     for j from 0 to n
6.       if i bit j is set
7.          add set[j] to subset
8.     add subset to subsets
9. return subsets
```

Example 2: Consider the $BRUTE\_FORCE\_SUBSET\_GENERATION$ algorithm with the set "VARANASI". To generate all possible subsets of the set "VARANASI" using the Brute-force subset generation algorithm, we start by initializing an empty list called $subsets$ to store the subsets we'll generate. The set "VARANASI" contains eight elements, so we determine the size of the set, which is $n = 8$. The algorithm iterates from 0 to $(2^8 - 1) = 255$, representing all possible binary strings of length $8(00000000\ to\ 11111111)$. For each iteration, we create a new empty list called $subset$ to construct the current subset. We iterate from 0 to 8 to consider each element of the set ("V", "A", "R", "A", "N", "A", "S", "I"). During each iteration, we check if the jth bit of the binary representation i is set to 1. If the jth bit is set (equals **1**), it means the element at index j is included in the current $subset$. Thus, we add the corresponding element of the set to the $subset$ list. After considering all elements, we add the $subset$ list to the $subsets$ list, representing one of the possible combinations of elements in the set "VARANASI". We repeat steps 4 to 8 for all binary strings from 0 to 255, generating all possible $subsets$ of the set "VARANASI". Finally, we return the $subsets$ list as the final result, which contains all unique subsets of the original set, ranging from the empty set to the complete set itself.

Time and space complexity analysis: The time complexity of the brute-force subset generation algorithm depends on the number of subsets that need to be generated. For a given set of size n, there are 2^n possible subsets. The algorithm uses two nested loops to generate all possible binary strings of length n, representing each subset. The outer loop runs from 0 to $2^n - 1$, and the inner loop iterates n times for each iteration of the outer loop. The time complexity of the algorithm is $O(2^n \times n)$, where 2^n represents the number of subsets, and n represents the number of elements in the set. The space complexity of the brute-force subset generation algorithm is determined by the storage required for storing the $subsets$. The algorithm initializes an empty list called $subsets$ to hold the generated subsets. For a given set of size n, the number of subsets is 2^n. Each subset may contain up to n elements, and the maximum number of subsets is 2^n. Therefore, the space complexity of the algorithm is $O(2^n \times n)$, considering the storage required for all subsets.

5.4.4 Traveling Salesman Problem

Brute-force Traveling Salesman Problem (TSP) is a classic optimization problem in computer science and operations research. In this problem, a salesman is given a list of cities and the distances between each pair of cities. The objective is to find the shortest possible route that visits each city exactly once and returns to the starting city, forming a closed loop. While the Brute-Force TSP algorithm guarantees finding the optimal solution, it becomes impractical for large instances of the TSP due to its exponential time complexity. For smaller instances or cases where exact solutions are necessary, this algorithm can be effectively utilized. However, for larger instances, more efficient heuristic or approximation algorithms are commonly employed to find near-optimal solutions in reasonable time.

Brute-force traveling salesman problem algorithm description: The algorithm to solve Brute-force traveling salesman problem is a simple approach to finding the optimal route for the TSP. It starts by taking a list of cities and the distances between each pair of cities as input. The algorithm initializes a variable $shortest\_distance$ to store the length of the shortest route found so far, setting it to a very large value initially. Next, it generates all possible permutations of the cities, considering all the different orders in which the cities can be visited, using backtracking or recursive techniques. For each permutation of cities, the algorithm calculates the total distance of the route by summing the distances between consecutive cities in the permutation. To find the optimal route, the algorithm continuously compares the total distance of each permutation with the current $shortest\_distance$. If the total distance of the current permutation is smaller than $shortest\_distance$, the algorithm updates $shortest\_distance$ with the new smaller value. Alongside this process, the algorithm keeps track of the order of cities that resulted in the current $shortest\_distance$, representing the optimal route. The algorithm repeats the process of finding permutations and calculating distances for all possible combinations of cities. Once all permutations are explored, the algorithm will have found the shortest route and its corresponding distance. The shortest route and its total distance are then returned as the output. Let the *gen_permutations* function generates all permutations of the input cities list, and the *dist_between* function should calculate the distance between two cities.

```
BRUTE_FORCE _TRAVELING_ SALESMAN(cities)
shortest_distance = ∞
optimal_route = [ ]
all_permutations = gen_permutations (cities)
for each permutation in all_permutations
    total_distance = 0
    for i from 0 to len(permutation) − 2
        total_distance+= dist_between(permutation[i], permutation[i + 1])
total_distance + = dist_between(permutation[len(permutation) − 1]
                                         ,permutation[0])
    if total_distance < shortest_distance
        shortest_distance = total_distance
        optimal_route = permutation
return shortest_distance, optimal_route;
```

Example 3: Consider a student who has admission interviews at IIT Delhi, IIT (BHU) Varanasi, IIT Bombay, IIT Kanpur, and IIT Madras. The student needs to travel to the following cities: Delhi, Varanasi, Bombay, Kanpur, and Madras. To find the shortest possible route for traveling to all these cities and returning to the starting point, the student decides to use the brute-force traveling salesman algorithm. Let us assume the distances between these cities as given in Table 5.1.

Table 5.1: Distances between the considered cities in the given example.

	Delhi	Varanasi	Bombay	Kanpur	Madras
Delhi	0	8	14	4.5	19
Varanasi	8	0	12	9	18
Bombay	14	12	0	13	12
Kanpur	4.5	9	13	0	19
Madras	19	18	12	19	0

- Initialize a variable $shortest\_distance$ to store the length of the shortest route found so far. Set it to a very large value initially and set $optimal\_route$=[ ] (**Steps** $1, 2$)
- Generate all possible permutations of the cities. For the cities {Delhi, Varanasi, Bombay, Kanpur, Madras}, there are a total of $5! = 120$ permutations. (**Step** 3)
- For each permutation of cities, calculate the total distance of the route by summing the distances between consecutive cities in the permutation. For example, for the permutation Delhi → Varanasi → Kanpur → Bombay → Madras → Delhi, the total distance is $8 + 9 + 13 + 12 + 19 = 61$. Compare the total distance of each permutation with the current $shortest\_distance$. (**Steps** $4 - 8$)
- If the total distance of the current permutation is smaller than $shortest\_distance$, update $shortest\_distance$ with the new smaller value. (**Steps** $9 - 11$)
- During the process of finding permutations and calculating distances, keep track of the order of cities that resulted in the current $shortest\_distance$. This order represents the optimal route. Continue calculating distances and updating $shortest\_distance$ for all possible permutations of cities. (Repeat **Steps** $4 - 11$)
- Once all permutations are explored, the algorithm has found the shortest route and its corresponding distance. Return the shortest route and its total distance as the output of the algorithm. (**Step** 12)

For the distances between the cities {Delhi, Varanasi, Kanpur, Bombay, Madras}, the algorithm outputs the shortest route and its total distance, which represents the optimal path for the student to attend the admission interviews at all the IITs efficiently.

Time and space complexity analysis: Brute-force TSP algorithm utilizes an exhaustive approach by exploring all possible permutations of cities to discover the optimal route. With n cities, the algorithm generates $n!$ permutations. For each permutation, the algorithm calculates the total distance by summing the distances between consecutive cities. Thus, the overall time complexity of the algorithm is $O(n! \times n)$. Regarding space complexity, the algorithm requires storage for the distance matrix, with a size of $n \times n$, representing distances between each pair of cities. Additionally, it generates and stores all $n!$ permutations of cities. Overall, the space complexity of the algorithm is $O(n^2 + n \times n!)$, where the permutations list mainly dominates the space requirements.

UNIT SUMMARY

- Brute-force methodology is a technique that involves trying every possible option to solve a problem.
- Brute-force guarantees a solution if it exists within the problem space but can be inefficient for large search spaces.
- The characteristics which collectively define the nature and behavior of Brute-force algorithms are exhaustive search, simplicity and directness, time complexity, deterministic, no assumptions or special cases, completeness, lack of optimization, applicability, limited scalability, and baseline approach
- Design strategies for enhancing the efficiency and effectiveness of brute-force algorithms involve techniques such as reducing the search space, utilizing pruning, memoization, parallelization, backtracking, optimizing based on problem constraints, and considering trade-offs between accuracy and computational efficiency.
- The string matching problem involves finding pattern occurrences in a larger text, with brute-force string matching being a simple but relatively time-consuming algorithm. Other more efficient algorithms, like KMP or Boyer-Moore, use preprocessing to achieve better time complexities for larger problem sizes.
- The subset generation problem involves finding all possible combinations of elements in a set, with brute-force subset generation being a simple approach but with exponential time complexity for larger sets. More advanced optimization techniques like backtracking or dynamic programming can improve efficiency.
- The brute-force TSP is a classic optimization problem seeking the shortest route visiting all cities once and returning to the starting city, but its exponential time complexity makes it impractical for large instances; heuristic or approximation algorithms are more suitable for such cases.

MULTIPLE CHOICE QUESTIONS

1. What is the primary characteristic of a brute-force algorithm?
   a. Optimization techniques
   b. Assumption-based approach
   c. Exhaustive search
   d. Heuristic evaluation
2. In the example of searching for a laptop, what is the significance of *"brute force"*?
   a. Searching only in specific areas
   b. Skipping some potential hiding spots

   c. Searching exhaustively in every possible spot
   d. Asking others for assistance

3. What does the brute-force methodology ensure in cracking passwords?
   a. High efficiency
   b. Time optimization
   c. Exhaustive evaluation of every possible combination
   d. Avoiding account lockouts

4. What is a drawback of brute-force algorithms mentioned in the text?
   a. High scalability
   b. Low computational resources
   c. Lack of effectiveness in problem-solving
   d. Exponential time complexity

5. Which characteristic ensures that brute-force algorithms produce predictable results?
   a. Time complexity
   b. Determinism
   c. Optimization
   d. Scalability

6. What makes brute-force algorithms applicable to a wide range of problems?
   a. Problem-specific assumptions
   b. Lack of completeness
   c. Uniform consideration of all possibilities
   d. Limited scalability

7. How does backtracking contribute to the efficiency of brute-force algorithms?
   a. It eliminates irrelevant parts of the search space
   b. It reduces the time complexity
   c. It prioritizes high-probability areas
   d. It avoids unnecessary exploration of unfruitful branches

8. What role does memoization play in improving the efficiency of brute-force algorithms?
   a. It speeds up the computation by storing intermediate results
   b. It reduces the number of iterations
   c. It eliminates irrelevant possibilities
   d. It increases the scalability

9. In which problem-solving scenario is parallelization a valuable strategy?
   a. Small-scale computations
   b. Large problem sizes
   c. Sequential exploration
   d. Irrelevant branches

10. What is the primary benefit of reducing the search space in brute-force algorithms?
   a. Faster convergence
   b. Lower memory usage

c. Avoiding irrelevant computations
d. Improved scalability

11. What is the primary objective of the brute-force subset generation algorithm?
    a. Maximizing the number of subsets
    b. Prioritizing specific elements in the set
    c. Generating all possible combinations of elements
    d. Eliminating redundant computations

12. Which problem-solving domain extensively uses string matching with brute-force algorithms?
    a. Image processing
    b. Cryptanalysis
    c. Combinatorial optimization
    d. Chess and game playing

13. What is a common characteristic of problems suitable for brute-force algorithms?
    a. Large problem sizes
    b. High efficiency requirements
    c. Known shortcuts or optimizations
    d. Limited scalability

14. In the traveling salesman problem, what is the primary goal of the brute-force algorithm?
    a. Maximizing the number of cities visited
    b. Minimizing the distance traveled
    c. Parallel exploration of routes
    d. Prioritizing specific cities

15. What is a limitation of brute-force algorithms in the context of the traveling salesman problem?
    a. Inability to find the optimal solution
    b. Exponential time complexity
    c. Lack of scalability
    d. Requirement of special cases

Solution of MCQ:

1	2	3	4	5	6	7	8	9	10	11	12	13	14	15
c	c	c	d	b	c	d	a	b	c	c	b	c	b	b

SHORT AND LONG ANSWER TYPE QUESTIONS

1. What does brute-force guarantee in terms of solutions?
2. What are some design strategies to enhance the efficiency of brute-force algorithms?
3. What is the brute-force TSP, and why is it impractical for large instances?
4. Describe the subset generation problem and the challenges with brute-force subset generation.
5. Describe the brute-force algorithm for solving a sudoku puzzle. What are the advantages and disadvantages of using this approach?
6. Describe the brute-force algorithm for generating all permutations of a given set of elements. How does it handle the challenges of combinatorial explosion for larger input sizes?
7. How does the Brute-Force algorithm apply to finding the maximum subarray sum in a given array? Discuss its time complexity and potential optimizations to handle large input arrays.
8. In what situations would you recommend considering alternative approaches over brute force, and why?
9. What are some common techniques used to optimize or enhance the performance of a brute force algorithm?
10. Can you provide an example of a problem or scenario where a brute force methodology would be the most suitable solution?
11. What are the advantages of using a brute force methodology in certain scenarios?

KNOW MORE

Online courses/materials/resources: [Accessed May 2024]

- https://github.com/topics/brute-force?o=asc&s=forks
- https://www.geeksforgeeks.org/brute-force-approach-and-its-pros-and-cons/
- https://www.coursera.org/learn/algorithms-part2

REFERENCES

[1] Fau, Alwin, Mesran Mesran, and Guidio Leonarde Ginting. "Analisa Perbandingan Boyer Moore Dan Knuth Morris Pratt Dalam Pencarian Judul Buku Menerapkan Metode Perbandingan Eksponensial." Jurnal TIMES 6, no. 1 (2017): 12-22.

[2] Johnston, Leigh A., and Vikram Krishnamurthy. "Performance analysis of a dynamic programming track before detect algorithm." IEEE Transactions on Aerospace and electronic systems 38, no. 1 (2002): 228-242.

6 Greedy Algorithms

UNIT SPECIFICS

This unit covers the following aspects:

- *About Greedy algorithms*
- *Characteristics of Greedy algorithms*
- *Design strategies of Greedy algorithms*
- *Applications in various domains*
- *Unit summary, short and long answer questions*

This unit will delve into the principles of greedy algorithms, which focus on making locally optimal choices at each step to find a solution. We will dissect the key attributes of greedy algorithms, scrutinize their time and space complexity, and unearth their widespread applications in fields ranging from scheduling and spanning trees to optimization problems in computer networking and game theory. Furthermore, we will explore techniques to refine the performance and efficacy of greedy algorithms, all while acknowledging their constraints and exploring alternative algorithmic approaches. The link provided in the QR code offers supplementary material for this unit.

RATIONALE

The rationale of delving into the realm of algorithms lies in acquainting oneself with the potent paradigm of Greedy algorithms. This unit endeavors to elucidate and scrutinize the concept of greedy algorithms as an impressive problem-solving approach. It endeavors to provide insight into greedy algorithms' inner workings, elucidating their defining attributes, and shedding light on their versatile applications across diverse domains.

PRE-REQUISITES

- *Familiarity with algorithmic concepts, such as sorting and searching.*
- *Basic mathematical knowledge, especially in relation to series and sequences.*

UNIT OUTCOMES

The outcomes of the Unit are as follows:

U6-O1: Understand the concept of Greedy algorithms

U6-O2: Identify characteristics of Greedy algorithms

U6-O3: Discuss design strategies of Greedy algorithms

U6-O4: Perform data compression using Greedy algorithms

Unit-6 Outcomes	EXPECTED MAPPING WITH COURSE OUTCOMES (1- Weak Correlation; 2- Medium correlation; 3- Strong Correlation)				
	CO-1	CO-2	CO-3	CO-4	CO-5
U6-O1	-	1	3	3	-
U6-O2	-	1	3	3	-
U6-O3	-	1	3	3	-
U6-O4	1	1	3	3	-

6.1 Introduction to Greedy Algorithms

In the previous units, we delved into the Brute-Force methodology for problem-solving. The methodology involves systematically trying out all possible solutions and then selecting the best one based on predefined criteria or objective functions. We explored various applications of the Brute-Force algorithms, such as String Matching, Subset Generation, and the Traveling Salesman Problem, highlighting its simple nature and systematic methodology. The Brute-force algorithm guarantees to find the optimal solution since it leaves no possibility unexplored. However, it comes at the cost of computation. As the size of the problem's search space increases, the number of possible combinations grows exponentially, rendering the Brute-Force impractical and inefficient for problems with a large number of elements.

To address the inefficiencies of the Brute-Force algorithms, alternative methods and algorithms have been developed. Greedy algorithms are a problem-solving approach that aims to be efficient by making the best choices at each step, even if it does not guarantee the absolute best solution. The idea is to hope that these good choices will add up and lead us to a great solution in the end. It is like taking one step at a time, always picking the option that seems best at the current moment, without worrying too much about what might happen later. Greedy algorithms focus on the present moment and the best immediate benefit. While they may not always find the perfect answer, they often get very close and save a lot of time compared to the slower Brute-Force algorithms. So, they are really useful when you need quick solutions to problems with lots of possibilities.

Let us consider a simple example to illustrate the concept of Greedy algorithms. Suppose you are a student, and your activity is to select the periods in which you can attend the maximum number of subjects without overlapping. You have a list of subjects, each with its start and finish times. Your goal is to maximize the number of subjects you can attend by selecting non-overlapping time periods. In this example, the starting and finishing times of subjects are as follows:

$\boldsymbol{Subject\ A}$: Start Time - $9:00\ am$, Finish Time - $10:30\ am$

$\boldsymbol{Subject\ B}$: Start Time - $10:00\ am$, Finish Time - $11:30\ am$

$\boldsymbol{Subject\ C}$: Start Time - $11:00\ am$, Finish Time - $12:30\ pm$

$\boldsymbol{Subject\ D}$: Start Time - $11:30\ am$, Finish Time - $01:30\ pm$

To solve this problem using the Greedy approach, you can sort the subjects in ascending order based on their finish times. Then, you can iteratively select the subject with the earliest finish time, making sure it does not overlap with any previously selected subject. The Greedy steps are as follows: Select $\boldsymbol{subject\ A}$ (Finish Time: $10:30\ am$) and Select $\boldsymbol{subject\ C}$ (Starting Time: $11:00\ am$). The result of the Greedy approach is selected $\boldsymbol{subjects\ \{A, C\}}$. By using the Greedy approach, you can attend the maximum number of subjects without overlapping, which, in this case, is $\boldsymbol{2\ subjects}$ ($\boldsymbol{A}$ and $\boldsymbol{C}$). This approach helps you efficiently schedule your study time and ensures that you can cover as many subjects as possible during your available time slots. Let, $\boldsymbol{subjects}$ is a list of objects representing the subjects, each with attributes $\boldsymbol{start\_time}$ and $\boldsymbol{finish\_time}$. The algorithm selects non-overlapping subjects by iterating through the sorted list of subjects and adding each subject to the $\boldsymbol{selected_subjects}$list only if it does not overlap with the finish time of the previously selected subject. The final $\boldsymbol{selected\_subjects}$ list will contain the maximum number of subjects that can be attended without overlapping. The pseudocode for the Greedy approach to select the maximum number of subjects without overlapping is shown as follows:

$GREEDY\_SELECT\_MAXIMUM\_SUBJECTS(subjects, start\_time, finish\_time)$

1. $sorted\_subjects =$ sort the $subjects$ in ascending order based on $finish\_time$
2. $selected\_subjects = [\,]$
3. **for** each $subject \in sorted\_subjects$
4.   **If** $selected\_subjects$ is empty **or** $subjects.finish\_time \leq subjects.start\_time$
5.   Add the current $subject$ to $selected\_subjects$
6. **return** $selected\_subjects$

6.2 Characteristics of Greedy Algorithms

In this section, we explore the important features of greedy algorithms by relating them to the context of searching for subjects. Greedy algorithms stand out as a particular algorithmic paradigm celebrated for their simplicity and efficiency. They exhibit distinct traits that render them well-suited for specific problem types:

i. **Greedy choice property:** Greedy algorithms employ a strategy of making the best possible decision at each stage, with the expectation that these choices will collectively lead to the best overall solution. In the scenario of subject selection, this translates to picking the subject with the earliest finish time at each step, ensuring the maximum number of attended subjects without any overlaps. In our example, following the greedy choice property, we first select $\boldsymbol{subject\ A}$ (Finish Time: $10{:}30\ am$) due to its earliest finish time. Subsequently, we choose $\boldsymbol{subject\ C}$ (Finish Time: $12{:}30\ pm$) as it has the next earliest finish time among the remaining subjects. Consequently, the Greedy algorithm results in selecting two $\boldsymbol{subjects}$: $\boldsymbol{A\ and\ C}$.

ii. **Suboptimal decisions:** Suboptimal decisions are one of the main limitations of greedy algorithms. While they make locally optimal choices at each step, these choices may not always lead to the globally optimal solution. In the subject selection example, the Greedy algorithm selects $\boldsymbol{subject\ A}$ (Finish Time: $10{:}30\ am$) first, as it has the earliest finish time. However, this decision prevents you from attending $\boldsymbol{subject\ D}$ (Start Time: $11{:}30\ am$), which has a later start time and conflicts with $\boldsymbol{subject\ B}$ (Finish Time: $11{:}30\ am$). Consequently, you miss out on the opportunity to attend $\boldsymbol{subject\ D}$ and can only select ($\boldsymbol{A}$ and $\boldsymbol{C}$) subjects using the greedy approach. In contrast, the Brute-Force methodology exhaustively explores all possible combinations of subjects to find the optimal solution. In this case, it would consider the option of attending $subject\ D$ and avoiding the conflict with $subject\ B$. This exhaustive evaluation might lead to a different and potentially better solution, but it comes at the cost of significantly higher time complexity for larger sets of subjects.

iii. **Simplicity:** Simplicity is a prominent characteristic of greedy algorithms. They are often simple to implement and understand, making them accessible to a wide range of users. For instance, in the subject selection example using a greedy algorithm, the process is relatively easy to implement. You sort the subjects based on their finish times, iterate through the sorted list, and at each step, select the subject with the earliest finish time that doesn't overlap with the previously selected subjects.

iv. **Efficiency:** Efficiency is a key characteristic of greedy algorithms, primarily in terms of time complexity. These algorithms typically evaluate only a limited set of choices at each step, which leads to faster computation compared to exhaustive approaches like the Brute-Force methodology. In the subject selection example, the Greedy algorithm efficiently sorts the subjects based on their finish times once and then iterates through the sorted list to make selections. On the other hand, the Brute-Force methodology involves exploring all possible combinations of subjects, which results in a significantly higher time complexity, often exponential in nature, particularly for larger sets of subjects.

v. **Lack of backtracking:** Once a decision is made at each step in the Greedy algorithm, it is not reconsidered or undone in subsequent steps. This can lead to suboptimal solutions in some cases. In the context of subject selection, the greedy algorithm selects the subject with the earliest finish time at each step without considering the potential consequences of that choice on future selections. For example, if the greedy algorithm selects $subject\ A$ (Finish Time: $10{:}30\ am$) as the first subject, it cannot backtrack and choose a different subject later, even if that would lead to a better overall schedule. In contrast, algorithms that involve backtracking, such as the Brute-Force approach, can explore different paths and undo previous decisions to find the optimal solution. Backtracking allows for more thorough exploration of the solution space but comes with a trade-off in terms of time complexity.

vi. **Not suitable for all problems:** Greedy algorithms, while simple and efficient in many cases, may not always produce the correct or optimal solution for complex problems. In subject selection, the greedy approach prioritizes locally optimal choices by picking subjects with the earliest finish times. However, this can lead to suboptimal schedules when there are overlapping time intervals or additional constraints to consider. For instance, in the subject selection example, the greedy algorithm might struggle with subjects having strict prerequisites or dependencies, resulting in conflicts or lower-quality schedules. On the other hand, Brute-force algorithms offer a more exhaustive approach that does not rely on specific assumptions or exploit problem-specific characteristics. They systematically explore all possibilities, considering every potential solution regardless of the problem's unique instance. This comprehensive evaluation can lead to a more accurate and optimal solution, especially in situations where the greedy algorithm falls short due to its limited local focus.

vii. **Heuristic approach:** A heuristic approach involves using approximate methods or rules of thumb to find solutions to problems. In greedy algorithms, this often means choosing the locally optimal choice at each step. While this can lead to efficient solutions, it may not always guarantee the globally optimal solution. Heuristic approaches are valuable for quickly solving large and complex problems, but they may not always provide the optimal outcome. Fine-tuning or exploring alternative methods may be necessary for better results. For example, in subject selection, choosing subjects with the earliest finish time may allow you to attend the maximum number of subjects without overlaps. However, it may not always result in the best overall schedule, as other factors like subject importance or prerequisites might be overlooked.

viii. **Iterative approach:** An iterative approach in the context of greedy algorithms involves performing a sequence of steps repeatedly until a desired outcome is achieved. For instance, in subject selection, the algorithm starts by choosing the subject with the earliest finish time. Then, in each subsequent iteration, it selects the next subject based on heuristic criteria, such as the next earliest finish time subject that doesn't conflict with previously chosen subjects. The iterative nature of greedy algorithms allows them to build solutions step by step, making local decisions at each stage. However, it is important to note that this approach may not guarantee the globally optimal solution since each choice is made locally without considering future implications. Nonetheless, the iterative approach is fundamental to greedy algorithms, enabling them to efficiently construct solutions by incrementally making choices until the desired outcome is reached.

ix. **Independence of subproblems:** The independence of subproblems is a crucial characteristic of greedy algorithms, especially in subject selection. Each choice is made solely based on the current state of the schedule, without considering the future impact on other subjects. This simplifies decision-making and makes the algorithm efficient. However, it may lead to suboptimal solutions as strategic choices may be missed. Overall, when subproblems are independent and local optimal choices align with the global optimal solution, greedy algorithms can be effective and efficient for various problems.

6.3 Design Strategies of Greedy Algorithms

Design strategies of greedy algorithms involve various techniques and approaches to enhance their efficiency and effectiveness in solving optimization problems. Some common design strategies include:

i. **Define the problem:** The first crucial step in designing a greedy algorithm is gaining a clear understanding of the problem statement and the specific objective to be achieved. This involves identifying the key elements of the problem, such as input data, constraints, and the desired output. For the subject selection scenario, the objective is to maximize the number of attended subjects without overlapping. With a list of subjects and their start and finish times, the goal is to select a set of non-overlapping subjects, enabling the coverage of as many subjects as possible during available time slots. The ultimate aim is to create an optimal schedule for efficient studying and attending the maximum number of subjects.

ii. **Identify greedy choice property:** The second step involves determining the property or criteria that enable us to make locally optimal choices at each step of the algorithm. This choice property is crucial for the success of the greedy algorithm. In the subject selection example, the greedy choice property is to select the subject with the earliest finish time at each step. By doing so, we ensure that we attend as many subjects as possible without overlapping, maximizing the number of subjects covered within the available time slots. The locally optimal choice of selecting the subject with the earliest finish time contributes to the overall objective of attending the maximum number of subjects without conflicts.

iii. **Sort or arrange data:** The third step is to sort or arrange the data based on specific criteria if the problem involves a set of elements or options. Sorting the data can help us identify the best choices efficiently and simplify the decision-making process. In the subject selection example, we can sort the subjects in ascending order based on their finish times. By doing so, we can easily identify the subject with the earliest finish time at each step, which aligns with the greedy choice property. Sorting the data enables us to quickly access the most suitable subjects and streamline the selection process, contributing to the overall efficiency of the greedy algorithm.

iv. **Develop a greedy strategy:** The fourth step involves devising a strategy to make decisions at each step of the algorithm, based on the greedy choice property and the sorted data (if applicable). The goal is to select choices that are locally optimal and contribute to the overall objective. In the subject selection example, the strategy is to choose the subject with the earliest finish time at each step, ensuring that the selected subjects do not overlap and allow you to attend the maximum number of subjects.

v. **Iterate and build solution:** The fifth step is to begin the iterative process of building the solution step by step. In each iteration, the algorithm selects the locally optimal choice according to the greedy strategy. The selected choices are added to the solution, and the process continues until the desired schedule is complete. The algorithm considers any constraints or limitations while making choices to ensure a feasible and efficient schedule.

vi. **Check for optimality:** The final step is to check the solution to see if it meets the desired objective and satisfies any specified constraints. It is essential to verify if the locally optimal choices made in each iteration indeed lead to a globally optimal solution. While the greedy algorithm provides a practical and efficient approach to solve certain problems, it is crucial to assess whether the resulting solution is optimal for the given problem instance. In some cases, the greedy algorithm may yield suboptimal solutions due to its locally focused nature. Thus, it is essential to review the solution and consider other algorithms or optimization techniques if a more optimal result is required.

By incorporating these design strategies, developers can construct efficient greedy algorithms that provide practical and viable solutions for various optimization problems. However, the effectiveness of these strategies depends on the nature of the specific problem being tackled. It is worth noting that while greedy algorithms can yield locally optimal solutions, achieving a globally optimal solution may not always be guaranteed. Hence, it is essential to carefully analyze the problem's unique characteristics and constraints when utilizing greedy algorithms.

6.4 Knapsack Problem

The Knapsack problem is a well-known and extensively studied combinatorial optimization challenge. It serves as a fundamental example in computer science and algorithm courses, demonstrating a wide array of optimization techniques. Its simplicity and practical relevance have led to its popularity in research and academic exploration.

Let us consider an illustrative scenario of flight check-in before delving into the Knapsack problem. Congratulations on cracking the entrance exam and securing a seat in your allocated institute! As you prepare for the exciting journey to your new academic destination, you face a challenge - the airline imposes a fixed luggage weight allowance for each passenger. As you gather your belongings, you have a diverse list of items to take from home, each holding its weight and significance to you. These items encompass essentials like clothes and study materials, personal belongings, sentimental treasures, and even cherished luxury items. Your objective is to carefully select a combination of items to pack for your flight, ensuring that the total weight of your luggage adheres to the airline's restrictions. Simultaneously, you strive to maximize the overall importance or value of the items you carry, optimizing your journey experience. In this scenario, you encounter a situation analogous to the Knapsack problem. The Knapsack problem mirrors your awkward situation, where you are presented with a set of items, each characterized by a weight and a value, and you must thoughtfully choose the items to include in your luggage to maximize their overall importance while abiding by the airline's weight constraint.

6.4.1 Introduction to Knapsack Problem

The statement of the Knapsack problem is as follows. Given a set of items, each with a weight and a value, and a knapsack with a maximum weight capacity, the goal is to determine the most valuable combination of items to include in the knapsack without exceeding its weight capacity. Formally, the Knapsack problem can be defined as: Given the following inputs - the number of items, an array containing the weight of each item, an array containing the value of each item, and the maximum weight capacity of the knapsack - the goal is to maximize the total value of the selected items while ensuring that their combined weight does not exceed the maximum weight capacity of the knapsack.

There are several variations of the Knapsack problem, each with its unique characteristics and additional constraints. Some common variations include:

i. 0/1 ***Knapsack problem***, also known as the binary problem, represents the standard version of the challenge. In this variant, items can only be included entirely (0) or excluded (1), making it impossible to take fractional parts of an item. The problem finds relevance in the context of resource allocation in project management. Its application involves allocating limited resources, such as time, budget, or manpower, to maximize project efficiency and outcomes.

ii. ***Fractional Knapsack problem*** is a variation of the Knapsack problem where items can be taken in fractional quantities, enabling partial selections. This variant finds significant application in various domains, especially in finance. Investors use it to decide how to allocate their funds among various financial assets to achieve an optimal balance between risk and reward. In the context of finance, each item represents a financial asset, such as stocks, bonds, or commodities, with a specific weight (quantity) and value (return or profit potential). The objective is to maximize the total value (return) of the portfolio while considering the risk associated with each asset for purchasing.

iii. ***Multiple Knapsack problem*** is a variation of the Knapsack problem that deals with multiple knapsacks, each having its capacity constraint. This problem can be approached through binary knapsack and fractional knapsack. The main application is to efficiently pack items into several containers, where each container has its weight capacity constraint, with the aim of minimizing transportation costs and maximizing space utilization.

iv. ***Unbounded and bounded Knapsack problems*** are two variations of the Knapsack problem, each with distinct characteristics. The Unbounded Knapsack problem allows an unlimited number of copies of each item, while the Bounded Knapsack problem restricts the number of copies available for each item.

6.4.2 Fractional Knapsack Problem Using Greedy Algorithm

We consider a scenario where we have a knapsack and n items. Each item i has a positive weight $W[i]$ and a positive value $V[i]$, where $i = 1,2,\dots,n$. The objective of the Knapsack problem is to maximize the total value of the items included in the knapsack while ensuring that the weight constraint is not violated. To tackle this, we can use the fractional Knapsack problem, which allows items to be fragmented, permitting us to carry only a fraction $X[i]$ of item i, where $0 \leq X[i] \leq 1$. Symbolically, the problem can be formulated as follows:

$$maximize \sum_{i=1}^{n} (X[i] \times V[i])$$

$$subject\ to \sum_{i=1}^{n} (X[i] \times W[i]) \leq W$$

$$where\ 0 < V[i], 0 < W[i], and\ 0 \leq X[i] \leq 1\ for\ 1 \leq i \leq n.$$

The constraints on $V[i]$ and $W[i]$ define the specific instance of the problem, while the constraints on $X[i]$ are related to the solution. To solve the problem, we will utilize a greedy algorithm. This approach treats the different items as candidates, and the solution is represented by a vector $(X[1],\dots,X[n])$, denoting the fraction of each item to include in the knapsack. The solution must satisfy the given constraints, and the objective function should maximize the total value of the selected items within the knapsack. To design an effective greedy algorithm, our general strategy is to select each item in a suitable order, incorporating as much of the chosen item into the knapsack as possible, and halting the process when the knapsack reaches its weight capacity. The procedure for fractional Knapsack problem using greedy search is summarized as follows:

FRACTION_KNAPSACK_PROBLEM $(V[i], W[i], W)$

1. Begin with an empty knapsack.
2. Select objects in a predetermined order.
3. **for** each selected object i
    a. Determine the fraction $X[i]$ of object i to include in the knapsack, ensuring that $X[i] \times W[i]$ does not exceed the remaining capacity of the knapsack.
    b. Add the fraction $X[i]$ of object i to the knapsack.
    c. Update the remaining capacity of the knapsack $W = W - X[i] \times W[i]$.
    d. Update the total value of the load: $total\_value = total\_value + X[i] \times V[i]$
4. Stop when the knapsack is full or when all objects have been considered.

By applying this algorithm and defining the appropriate order for selecting items, we aim to find an optimal solution that maximizes the value of the items within the knapsack while respecting the weight constraint. To demonstrate this, let us consider a numerical example as shown in Table 6.1 below:

Table 6.1: Items and their properties (Weight, Value, and fractional value).

Item	Weight ($W[i]$)	Value ($V[i]$)	Fractional Value ($V[i]/W[i]$)
1	4	20	5
2	3	18	6
3	2	14	7
4	5	30	6

In this example, we have four items ($n = 4$), each with a positive weight $W[i]$ and positive value $V[i]$. The knapsack has a weight capacity W not exceeding 10. Now, let us explore three different ways of arranging the items in an order to determine the optimal solution. The different ways are the arranging the items in ascending order of weight ($W[i]$), descending order of value ($V[i]$), and descending order of the fractional value $V[i]/W[i]$. The example illustrates that arranging the selected items in descending order of the fractional value $V[i]/W[i]$ provides the highest value of the solution, which is 62. This arrangement allows us to maximize the total value of the items included in the knapsack while ensuring that the weight constraint (total weight $\leq$ 10) is met.

Theorem (Fraction Knapsack Algorithm): When items are chosen in the order of decreasing $V[i]/W[i]$ (value-weight ratio), the knapsack algorithm yields an optimal solution.

Proof: Proof techniques are systematic approaches or strategies employed to establish the truth or accuracy of a statement, theorem, or proposition. In this section, we will explore two distinct proof techniques to demonstrate the validity of the fraction Knapsack theorem.

a) Proof by contradiction for the Knapsack algorithm: It involves assuming the opposite of the theorem's claim and then showing that this assumption leads to a logical contradiction. By demonstrating that the contrary assumption is false, we can affirm the truth of the original theorem. Let $S1$ and $S2$ denote the solutions when items are chosen in the order of decreasing value-weight ratio and another selection order of items, respectively. The total value of solutions $S1$ and $S2$ is denoted as $V[1]$ and $V[2]$, respectively. Suppose we assume that the knapsack algorithm fails to provide an optimal solution in $S1$, thus, we have $V[2] > V[1]$. Since $S1$ and $S2$ are different solutions, chosen at least one item differently. Let $S1$ select item A, and $S2$ select item B. As $S1$ selects A instead of B, we have:$V[i]/W[i](A) \geq V[i]/W[i](B)$. Next, considering that $V[2] > V[1]$ and based on the previous inequality, we get:$(X[i](B) \times V[i](B))/W[i](B)) > (X[i](A) \times V[i](A))/W[i](A))$. As we know that the following expression $V[i](A)/W[i](A) \geq V[i](B)/W[i](B)$, thus$(X[i](B) \times V[i](B))/W[i](B)) - (X[i](A) \times V[i](A))/W[i](A)) > 0$. Here $X[i]$ represents the fraction of items included in the selection. Since $S1$ selects items as $V[i]/W[i]$ ratio, we have: $(X[i](A)/W[i](A)) \geq (X[i](B)/W[i](B))$. However, the previous inequality

$(X[i](B)/W[i](B)) \times V[i](B) - X[i](A)/W[i](A)) \times V[i](A) > 0$ contradicts this assumption. Therefore, our initial assumption that the knapsack algorithm does not yield an optimal solution when items are selected in the order of decreasing $V[i]/W[i]$ is false. Hence, we conclude that the knapsack algorithm indeed yields an optimal solution when items are chosen in the order of decreasing $V[i]/W[i]$ ratio.

b) Proof by greedy exchange property for the Knapsack algorithm: The greedy exchange property is a useful proof technique to demonstrate the optimality of a greedy algorithm. To apply this technique, we assume that the greedy solution (selecting items in the order of decreasing $V[i]/W[i]$ ratio) is not optimal. Let us suppose there exists an optimal solution that differs from the greedy solution. Let us consider the first point where the two solutions differ. At this point, the greedy solution includes item A, while the optimal solution includes item B. Since the greedy solution selects items in order of decreasing $V[i]/W[i]$ratio, we have $V[i]/W[i](A) \geq V[i]/W[i](B)$. Further, considering the total value of the two solutions at this point: 1) total value of the greedy solution $\sum_{i=1}^{n} \quad (X[i] \times V[i])$ (where $X[i]$ represents the fraction of items included in the greedy solution) and 2) total value of the optimal solution $\sum_{i=1}^{n} \quad (Y[i] \times V[i])$(where $Y[i]$ represents the fraction of items included in the optimal solution). Let us perform a swap between items A and B. After this swap, the total value of the greedy solution becomes total of the greedy solution $\sum_{i=1}^{n} \quad (X[i] \times V[i]) - X[i](A) \times V[i](A) + Y[i](B) \times V[i](B)$. Since $V[i]/W[i](A) \geq V[i]/W[i](B)$; thus, we have $V[i](A)/W[i](A) - V[i](B)/W[i](B) \geq 0$.

Time and space complexity analysis: Fractional Knapsack algorithm using greedy is a popular approach for solving the knapsack problem when items can be divided into fractions. The most time-consuming step in the greedy algorithm is the sorting of items based on their value-weight ratios. Sorting typically takes $O(n \log n)$ time, where n is the number of items in the input. After sorting, the algorithm goes through each item to calculate the fraction to be included in the knapsack. This loop iterates over all n items, performing constant-time operations for each item. Therefore, the loop takes $O(n)$ time. The overall time complexity of the fractional Knapsack algorithm using greedy is dominated by the sorting step, which is $O(n \log n)$. The space complexity of the fractional Knapsack algorithm is determined by the data structures used in the algorithm. The input data consists of the weights and values of n items, which are typically stored in arrays. Therefore, the space complexity for storing input data is $O(n)$. The sorting operation may be in-place or require an additional array for temporary storage. Assuming a typical implementation, the sorting space complexity is $O(n)$ since we need to store the value-weight ratios and their corresponding items. The algorithm uses a few additional variables like the total value of the knapsack, the remaining capacity, and the fraction of each item included. These variables require constant space, and hence the additional space complexity is $O(1)$. The overall space complexity of the fractional Knapsack algorithm is $O(n)$ due to the input data and sorting. The additional space required by the algorithm is constant and does not grow with the input size.

6.5 Data Compression Using Greedy Algorithm

Data compression serves as a foundational technique within the realms of computer science and information theory, aiming to curtail the dimensions of data files while upholding their intrinsic informational essence. Its significance resounds profoundly in enabling efficient storage, seamless transmission, and effective manipulation of digital data. The compression process entails the representation of data in a more condensed configuration, leading to a reduction in its spatial footprint, thereby optimizing storage capacities and economizing on transmission bandwidth.

Before we proceed further, let us delve into an illustration involving the coding of words. Imagine a scenario where we are presented with a data file containing 60000 characters that need to be stored. This particular file encompasses five distinct characters, each characterized by the corresponding frequencies: Characters a through e with frequencies of $12000, 10000, 13000, 20000$, and 5000 occurrences respectively. Our main objective is to establish a binary code for each of these characters. In this code, the representation of each character is expressed as a binary string or codeword. The fundamental aim is to devise a binary encoding strategy that minimizes the total number of bits required to represent the entirety of the data file, ultimately achieving optimal compression.

Fixed and variable length code: In a fixed-length code, each codeword maintains a uniform length. Conversely, in a variable-length code, codewords have varying lengths. To illustrate, let us explore examples of both fixed and variable length codes for the given scenario, as shown in Table 6.2. For the fixed-length code, it requires 300000 bits to encode the entire file. This is because each character, regardless of its frequency, is assigned the same number of bits. In contrast, the variable-length code employs a different strategy. By assigning shorter codes to more frequent characters and longer codes to less frequent ones, it can achieve significant space savings. The required bits in variable-length code is$(12 \times 1 + 10 \times 3 + 13 \times 3 + 20 \times 3 + 5 \times 4) \times 1000$ bits. This is notably less than the space required by the fixed-length code.

Table 6.2: Frequency of characters, fixed length and variable length codes.

Characters	a	b	c	d	e
Frequency in '000 s	12	10	13	20	5
Fixed-length code	000	001	010	011	100
Variable-length code	0	101	100	111	1101

This example highlights the advantage of using a variable-length code in scenarios where characters have varying frequencies. By adapting the code lengths to the character frequencies, the variable-length code achieves a substantial reduction in required space compared to the fixed-length code. This demonstrates the efficiency and effectiveness of variable-length coding in achieving optimal compression.

Prefix Code: A code is referred to as a prefix (free) code when each of its codewords is constructed in such a way that no codeword serves as a prefix to another codeword within the same code. In other words, *there exists no codeword that is a leading subset of another codeword in the same coding system.* The significance of the prefix (free) property lies in its capacity to ensure unambiguous decoding. Since no codeword is a prefix of another, the process of decode the encoded message remains unambiguous. This property prevents any potential confusion during decoding, as there is no possibility of misinterpreting the sequence of codewords. Suppose we have a set of characters $\{A, B, C, D\}$ and we want to create a binary code for each character. A code is considered a prefix code if no codeword is a prefix of another codeword. Let us consider two coding schemes to understand this concept:

Coding Scheme 1 (Not Prefix Code): $A{:}\,0\;\; B{:}\,01\;\; C{:}\,10\;\; D{:}\,011$

Coding Scheme 2 (Prefix Code): $A{:}\,0\;\; B{:}\,10\;\; C{:}\,110\;\; D{:}\,1110$

In Coding Scheme 1, the codeword for $A(0)$ is a prefix of the codeword for $B(01)$ and $D(011)$. This violates the prefix (free) property, making this coding scheme not a prefix code. In Coding Scheme 2, no codeword is a prefix of another codeword. For instance, $A(0)$ is not a prefix of any other codeword, and the same applies to other characters. This coding scheme satisfies the prefix (free) property and is therefore a prefix code. The prefix (free) property ensures that the decoding process remains unambiguous and reliable, as each codeword has a unique starting point. This property is particularly important in various data encoding applications to prevent confusion during decoding and maintain the integrity of the original information.

Lossless and lossy coding: Broadly categorized, data compression assumes two principal forms: lossless and lossy. In the landscape of lossless compression, data can be encoded and subsequently decoded with exact resemblance to the original, unaltered data. This is achieved through the identification and efficient encoding of patterns, repetitions, or redundancies within the data. Contrarily, lossy compression, while significantly reducing data size, is characterized by the intentional omission of certain details that are ostensibly indiscernible to human perception. To further illustrate the practical application of these compression techniques, let us delve into a scenario where both text messages and high-resolution images coexist, and discern how lossless and lossy compression methods can be adeptly employed. Consider the context of preparing an interactive multimedia presentation for an academic term project. This presentation encapsulates textual content, high-resolution images, and potentially audio clips. A dual focus on aesthetic appeal and efficient sharing drives the selection of compression strategies. In the pursuit of text compression, the application of lossless techniques proves particularly prudent. Textual data often harbors patterns, recurring phrases, and whitespace that lend themselves to efficient compression without compromising content integrity. By judiciously applying lossless compression methodologies, the file size of textual content within the presentation can be significantly reduced. Consequently, the resultant presentation file becomes more wieldy for storage, expediting sharing endeavors. Simultaneously, the images embedded within the presentation demand attention. High-resolution images frequently entail considerable file sizes due to intricate details. In this facet, the utilization of lossy compression comes to the fore. This approach scrutinizes the images, intelligently discarding less noticeable minutiae while preserving the overarching visual quality. The outcome is a diminished file size that remains acceptably visually appealing, aligning with the constraints of bandwidth and storage.

6.5.1 Huffman Coding Overview

The optimum source coding problem, also known as the optimal variable-length source coding problem, is a fundamental concept in information theory. It deals with the task of designing an efficient variable-length code to represent a set of symbols with their associated probabilities or frequencies. The goal is to minimize the average code length while ensuring that the resulting code is uniquely decodable, *i.e.*, each code word can be unambiguously decoded without confusion. In this problem, the objective is to find the best way to encode symbols based on their probabilities in order to achieve optimal compression. The mathematical definition of the problem is defined as follows:

Problem: Given a set of alphabet $A = \{a_1, a_2, \dots, a_n\}$ with frequency distribution $f(a_i)$, find a binary prefix code C for A that minimizes the number of bits, as represented by $B(C) = \sum_{i=1}^{n} f(a_i) \times L(c(a_i))$. This encoding is necessary for a message with a total of $\sum_{i=1}^{n} f(a_i)$characters, where $c(a_i)$ denotes the codeword for encoding a_i, and $L(c(a_i)$ is the length of the codeword $c(a_i)$.

Huffman coding is a widely used variable-length prefix coding algorithm used for data compression and file encoding. Named after its creator David A. Huffman, it is designed to efficiently represent characters or symbols in a way that minimizes the total number of bits required to encode a message. Huffman coding is particularly effective for compressing text files and data with varying symbol frequencies. The code that it produces is called a Huffman code. The key Concepts of Huffman Coding are as follows:

i) **Variable-Length Codes:** One of the defining features of Huffman coding is its ability to assign variable-length codes to symbols. Unlike fixed-length codes where every symbol is represented using the same number of bits, Huffman codes allocate shorter codes to frequently occurring symbols and longer codes to those that appear less often. This adaptive approach optimizes the overall code length, resulting in improved compression efficiency. High-frequency symbols, benefiting from shorter codes, contribute significantly to compression gains.

ii) **Prefix Property:** Huffman coding guarantees the absence of code prefixes among its encodings. This prefix property ensures that no code sequence can be mistaken for another during decoding. As a consequence, the decoding process remains unambiguous and simple. This property is vital for the effectiveness of Huffman coding, allowing efficient retrieval of the data from the encoded form.

iii) **Frequency-Based Encoding:** The foundation of Huffman coding lies in leveraging the frequency distribution of symbols within the input data. By assigning shorter codes to high-frequency symbols and longer codes to low-frequency ones, the algorithm exploits the inherent redundancy in the data. This frequency-based encoding translates to more efficient data representation. The constructed Huffman tree positions frequently occurring symbols closer to the root, facilitating quicker traversal during both encoding and decoding.

iv) **Optimal Encoding Tree:** The Huffman tree construction process aims to create an optimal tree that minimizes the average code length. This optimization entails placing symbols with higher frequencies closer to the root, resulting in shorter codes. The tree structure evolves through a process of merging nodes, with the most frequent symbols eventually residing at shallower levels. The efficiency of this construction strategy in compressed data sizes that approach the entropy of the source data.

v) **Entropy and Information Theory:** Huffman coding finds its roots in information theory, specifically the concept of entropy. Entropy characterizes the average minimum number of bits required to encode symbols in a given data source with known probabilities. Huffman coding often approaches the entropy of the source, indicating a level of compression where further reduction is not feasible without losing information. This relationship with entropy solidifies the algorithm's status as an optimal encoding method.

6.5.2 Huffman Coding Algorithm

Consider a scenario where we are tasked with encoding a set of characters using the Huffman Coding Algorithm. We are given a dataset containing characters and their respective frequencies. Each character has an associated positive frequency denoted as $f[i]$, where i ranges from 1 to the total number of characters. The objective of the Huffman Coding Algorithm is to create an optimal variable-length prefix code for these characters, with the intention of minimizing the average code length. This involves constructing a binary tree, where characters with higher frequencies are assigned shorter codewords, ensuring efficient compression.

The Huffman Coding algorithm begins by calculating the frequency of each character in the *data*. Subsequently, a priority queue (*min* heap) is created, containing nodes associated with each character and their respective frequencies. These nodes are arranged in ascending order based on their frequencies. As the algorithm progresses, the priority queue is utilized to repeatedly select nodes with the lowest frequencies. These nodes are then removed, and a new internal node is generated, featuring the selected nodes as its children. The frequency of the internal node is set as the sum of the frequencies of its children, and the node is re-inserted into the priority queue. The constructed Huffman tree is then traversed, and binary codes are assigned to each character. Specifically, 0 is assigned to the left child of each node, while 1 is assigned to the right child. The paths followed from the root to the leaf nodes of characters define their respective Huffman codes. Finally, the characters in the original dataset are substituted with their corresponding Huffman codes, yielding encoded data characterized by its compactness. Notably, frequently occurring characters are assigned shorter codes, contributing to efficient data compression, while less frequent characters receive longer codes. The algorithm culminates in the effective reduction of data size while retaining its essential information. The algorithm can be summarized as follows:

```
HUFFMAN_CODING(data)
1.  frequencies = CalculateFrequencies(data)   // Calculate character frequencies
2.  queue = PriorityQueue()  Create a priority queue
    for each character in frequencies:
       queue.insert(Node(character, frequencies[character])
3.  while queue.size()> 1                        // Build the Huffman Tree
       node1 = queue.removeMin()
       node2 = queue.removeMin()
       combinedFrequency = node1.frequency + node2.frequency
       internalNode = Node(null, combinedFrequency)
       internalNode.left=node1
       internalNode.right=node2
       queue.insert(internalNode)
4.  huffmanTree = queue.removeMin()                //Assign Huffman codes
    huffmanCodes = {}
    AssignCodes(huffmanTree, '', huffmanCodes)
5.  encodedData = ''                               //Encode the data
    for each character in data:
       encodedData += huffmanCodes[character]
6.  return encodedData, huffmanTree
```

```
AssignCodes(node, currentCode, huffmanCodes):
  if node is a leaf node:
    huffmanCodes[node.character] = currentCode
  else:
    AssignCodes(node.left, currentCode+'0', huffmanCodes)
    AssignCodes(node.right, currentCode+'1', huffmanCodes)
```

Example: To grasp the essence of the Huffman Coding Algorithm, let us delve into an illustrative example utilizing input data represented by the alphabet and its associated frequency distribution: Let $D = \{a\ b\ a\ c\ d\ a\ c\ f\ e\ d\ a\}$ be the data with frequency. These character frequencies hold a pivotal role in the construction of the Huffman Tree, a cornerstone that facilitates the generation of optimal Huffman codes for every character embedded within the input data. The process begins with **Step** 1, where the character frequencies are enumerated as follows $\{a{:}\,4, b{:}\,1, c{:}\,2, d{:}\,2, e{:}\,1, f{:}\,1\}$. In **Step** 2, a priority queue, represented as a min heap, is formed, housing nodes reflecting character-frequency pairs. The queue arrangement is depicted as follows $[node(b,1), node(e,1), node\ (f,1), node(c,2), node(d,2), node\ (a,4)]$. **Step** 3 involves the construction of the Huffman Tree, an intricate structure that embodies the hierarchical relationships between characters and their frequencies. This tree's visualization is illustrated in Figure 6.1. Moving to **Step** 4 Huffman codes are assigned to each character, representing a pivotal part of the compression process. The assigned Huffman codes are as follows: $\{b{:}\,000, e{:}\,001, f{:}\,010, c{:}\,11, d{:}\,10, a{:}\,01\}$. Finally, **Step** 5 concludes the process with the generation of encoded data. Thw compressed data embodies the optimized Huffman codes, ensuring efficient data storage and transmission.

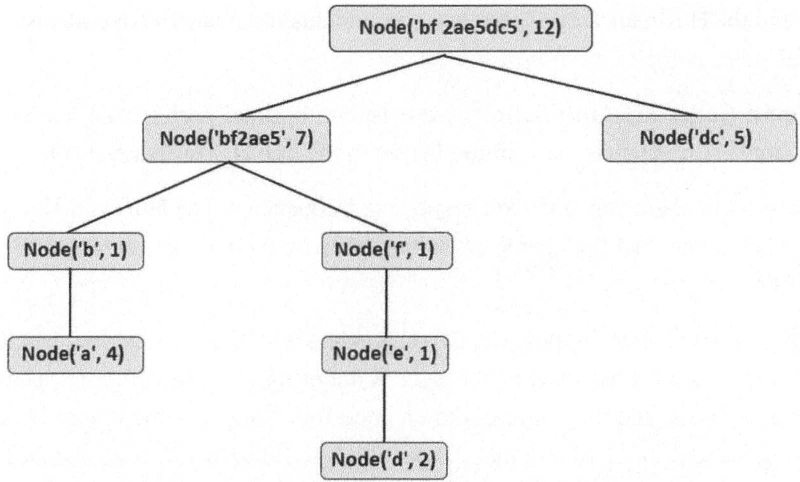

Figure 6.1: Tree Visualization of the Huffman Tree.

Time and Space Complexity Analysis: The Huffman Coding Algorithm's time and space complexity analysis is essential to understand its efficiency in terms of execution time and memory usage.The time complexity analysis of the Huffman Coding Algorithm involves assessing each step's computational demands. Initially, calculating the character frequencies necessitates traversing the input data, contributing to a time complexity of $O(n)$, where n signifies the data length. Subsequently, the creation of the Priority Queue (Min Heap) involves inserting n nodes, each of which requires $O(\log n)$ time for insertion in a min heap. Consequently, the cumulative time complexity for building the priority queue becomes $O(n \log n)$. Moving on to constructing the Huffman Tree, the process entails $n-1$ iterations, wherein two nodes are removed and a new node is inserted in each step. This procedure leads to an overall time complexity of $O(n \log n)$. Assigning Huffman codes, based on each character's depth in the tree, results in a time complexity of $O(n)$, considering that the total depth is bounded by $O(\log n)$. The encoding of the data, executed character by character, adds to a time complexity of $O(n)$, where n denotes the data's length. In summation, while the steps contribute to the overall time complexity, the primary determinant is the construction of the Huffman Tree, ultimately yielding a total time complexity of $O(n \log n)$.

The analysis of the space complexity of the Huffman Coding Algorithm entails evaluating the memory requirements of various data structures. Firstly, the Priority Queue is considered, with a space complexity of $O(n)$ since it can accommodate a maximum of n nodes. The Huffman Tree, encompassing n leaf nodes, also contributes $O(n)$ to the space complexity. The storage of Huffman Codes incurs $O(n)$ space, as each character's code needs to be stored. Additionally, the space required for Encoded Data is $O(n)$, as the encoded output may be of similar length to the original input. In summary, the space complexity of the Huffman Coding Algorithm is primarily influenced by the space requirements of the Priority Queue and the Huffman Tree. These two components dominate the overall space consumption, leading to a final space complexity of $O(n)$.

Lemma (Huffman Codes are Optimal): There exists an optimal prefix code tree in which the two letters with the smallest frequencies are sibling leaves in the tree at lowest level [1].

Proof: Consider a set of characters and their respective frequencies. The Huffman algorithm constructs a binary tree in such a way that the characters with higher frequencies are closer to the root, reducing the overall encoding length.

a) *Proof by contradiction:* Suppose the two characters with the smallest frequencies in the set are not siblings at the lowest level of the tree. Without loss of generality, let us assume they are labeled as A and B, and they have common ancestors P and Q at the lowest level, respectively. Swapping A and B in the tree to make them siblings at the lowest level would not increase the total length of the encoding. In fact, it might even reduce it since P and Q may have higher frequencies and be placed higher in the tree. This contradicts the assumption that the original tree was optimal.

b) If the two characters with the smallest frequencies are already siblings at the lowest level, then we have a tree that satisfies the lemma, as shown in Figure 6.1

Combining the two cases, we can conclude that there exists an optimal prefix code tree in which the two characters with the smallest frequencies are sibling leaves at the lowest level. This lemma is crucial in understanding the structure of optimal prefix code trees and is a key property exploited in the Huffman coding algorithm. It ensures that the algorithm can consistently find an optimal solution for any given set of character frequencies.

Lemma: An essential property of any optimal prefix code tree is its "fullness," wherein each internal node of the tree is equipped with exactly two children [2].

Proof: We aim to demonstrate that in an optimal prefix code tree, every internal node has exactly two children. To do so, we will employ a proof by contradiction. Assume, for the sake of contradiction, that there exists an optimal prefix code tree in which at least one internal node has fewer than two children. Let T be such an optimal prefix code tree, and let N be the internal node with fewer than two children. This implies that N must have either one or zero children.

Case 1 when N has one children: In this scenario, N is not at the deepest level of the tree, as there is at least one leaf node further down the tree. Since N is not at the deepest level, it can be replaced by its child without altering the total depth or the number of bits required for encoding. This contradicts the assumption that T was an optimal prefix code tree, as we found a tree T that requires fewer bits for encoding.

Case 2 when N has no children *(i.e., it is a leaf node):* If N is a leaf node, it must represent a character with a non-zero frequency in the source alphabet. However, if N is a leaf node, it cannot be a part of an optimal prefix code tree because it would not contribute to the encoding of any other character. We could remove N and replace it with its parent node, resulting in a smaller tree that still encodes all characters in the source alphabet. This again contradicts the assumption that T was an optimal prefix code tree.

Since both cases lead to contradictions, our initial assumption that there exists an optimal prefix code tree with an internal node having fewer than two children must be incorrect. Therefore, we conclude that in any optimal prefix code tree, every internal node has exactly two children, proving the lemma.

Theorem: The algorithm devised by Huffman yields an optimal prefix code tree [3].

Proof: To prove this theorem, we'll demonstrate that the Huffman algorithm generates a prefix code tree that is both optimal and satisfies the prefix property.

1. Optimality: The Huffman algorithm constructs the prefix code tree in a manner that minimizes the total number of bits required to encode a given set of characters based on their frequencies. This is achieved by repeatedly combining the two nodes with the lowest frequencies into a new node, and assigning the sum of their frequencies as the frequency of the new node.

Claim 1: At each step of the algorithm, the combined node with the lowest frequency is selected for merging.

Proof of Claim 1: Suppose, for contradiction, that at some step, the algorithm combines a node A with frequency $f(A)$ and a node B with frequency $f(B)$, where $f(B) < f(A)$. Since this combination is chosen, it implies that $f(B) \leq f(C)$ for any other node C in the tree. However, if we were to combine B with any other node instead of A, the resulting tree would have a higher total frequency, contradicting the optimality of the Huffman algorithm.

Therefore, at each step, the algorithm selects the nodes with the lowest frequencies for combination, ensuring that it constructs an optimal prefix code tree.

2. Prefix Property: The algorithm maintains the prefix property because it always combines the nodes with the lowest frequencies. As a result, no code for one character is a prefix of the code for another character.

Claim 2: The prefix property is preserved throughout construction of the tree.

Proof of Claim 2: Suppose, for contradiction, that at some step, the algorithm combines two nodes X and Y where the code for X is a prefix of the code for Y. This implies that $f(X) \leq f(Y)$, since X had a lower frequency than Y and was chosen for the combination. However, combining X and Y in this manner would have resulted in a tree with a higher total frequency, contradicting the optimality of the Huffman algorithm. Thus, the prefix property is maintained throughout.

Since the algorithm consistently selects nodes with the lowest frequencies for combination and maintains the prefix property, the resulting tree is both optimal and satisfies the prefix property. This completes the proof, demonstrating that the algorithm devised by Huffman yields an optimal prefix code tree.

UNIT SUMMARY

- Greedy algorithm is a problem-solving approach that focuses on making the locally optimal choice at each step with the hope of finding a global optimum.
- It is characterized by its myopic decision-making, choosing the best immediate option without considering the broader consequences. Greedy algorithms are generally efficient and suitable for a wide range of problems.
- Greedy algorithms make decisions based on what seems best at the current step, aiming for a locally optimal solution.

- Unlike techniques like backtracking, which explore multiple options, greedy algorithms do not revisit or revise their choices.
- Greedy algorithms are often simple and efficient, making them suitable for problems with large input spaces.
- Greedy algorithms do not rely on specific assumptions or special cases. The choice at each step depends solely on the current state.
- While not guaranteed to find the absolute optimum, greedy algorithms often provide very good approximations.
- Greedy algorithms may not be the best choice for problems where the locally optimal choice at each step doesn't lead to a globally optimal solution.
- It is helpful in activity selection problems, determining the maximum number of activities that can be performed by a single person, assuming they can only work on one activity at a time.
- Fractional Knapsack is a well-known application of the Greedy algorithm. The target is to optimize the selection of items to maximize the total value within a knapsack's weight capacity.
- Huffman Coding is another popular example of a Greedy algorithm. The goal is to construct a variable-length prefix encoding for efficient data compression.
- In summary, greedy algorithms provide a powerful and efficient approach to solving a wide range of optimization problems.
- They are particularly useful in scenarios where locally optimal choices lead to globally optimal solutions. However, careful consideration is needed to ensure that the greedy approach is applicable and leads to the desired outcome.

MULTIPLE CHOICE QUESTIONS

1. What are algorithms?
    a. Random instructions
    b. Step-by-step instructions for problem-solving
    c. Artistic expressions
    d. Scientific formulas
2. Which of the following is NOT a resource evaluated in algorithm analysis?
    a. Memory

b. Computation

c. Time

d. None of the above

3. Which algorithmic paradigm is celebrated for its simplicity and efficiency?

   a. Dynamic Programming

   b. Greedy Algorithm

   c. Divide and Conquer

   d. Backtracking

4. What is one of the main limitations of greedy algorithms?

   a. They guarantee globally optimal solutions

   b. They exhibit suboptimal decisions

   c. They are computationally expensive

   d. They always lead to the best possible outcome

5. What does a heuristic approach in greedy algorithms involve?

   a. Choosing globally optimal choices at each step

   b. Making random selections at each step

   c. Choosing the locally optimal choice at each step

   d. Avoiding making decisions at each step

6. Which design strategy enhances the efficiency and effectiveness of greedy algorithms?

   a. Backtracking

   b. Dynamic Programming

   c. Randomization

   d. Fine-tuning the heuristic approach

7. Suppose you have coins of denominations 1, 3 and 4. You use a greedy algorithm, in which you choose the largest denomination coin which is not greater than the remaining sum. For which of the following sums, will the algorithm produce an optimal answer?

   a. 100

   b. 10

   c. 6

   d. 14

8. What is the goal of the Knapsack problem?
    a. To minimize the weight of items in the knapsack
    b. To maximize the number of items in the knapsack
    c. To determine the most valuable combination of items to include in the knapsack without exceeding its weight capacity
    d. To distribute items evenly among multiple knapsacks
9. Which variant of the Knapsack problem allows fractional parts of items to be taken?
    a. 0/1 Knapsack Problem
    b. Fractional Knapsack Problem
    c. Continuous Knapsack Problem
    d. Complete Knapsack Problem
10. In what context does the Knapsack problem find relevance?
    a. Sorting algorithms
    b. Searching algorithms
    c. Resource Allocation in Project Management
    d. String matching algorithms
11. What is the goal of Huffman Coding?
    a. To maximize the compression ratio
    b. To minimize the compression ratio
    c. To reduce the number of bits required to represent data
    d. To increase the size of the compressed file
12. Another name of the fractional knapsack is?
    a. Non-continuous knapsack problem
    b. Divisible knapsack problem
    c. 0/1 knapsack problem
    d. Continuous Knapsack Problem
13. Which type of Knapsack problem allows items to be included entirely or excluded entirely?
    a. Continuous Knapsack Problem

b. 0/1 Knapsack Problem

c. Fractional Knapsack Problem

d. Unbounded Knapsack Problem

14. What approach does Huffman Coding algorithm use to compress data?

    a. Divide and Conquer

    b. Dynamic Programming

    c. Greedy Algorithm

    d. Backtracking

15. What makes the Greedy algorithm in the subject selection example suboptimal?

    a. It guarantees the globally optimal solution

    b. It considers all possible combinations of subjects

    c. It makes locally optimal choices at each step

    d. It avoids conflicts between subjects

16. Which methodology exhaustively explores all possible combinations of subjects to find the optimal solution?

    a. Greedy algorithm

    b. Brute-Force methodology

    c. Heuristic approach

    d. Dynamic Programming

Solution of MCQ:

1	2	3	4	5	6	7	8	9	10	11	12	13	14	15	16
b	d	b	b	c	d	a	c	b	c	c	d	b	c	c	b

SHORT AND LONG ANSWER TYPE QUESTIONS

1 What defines the decision-making process in Greedy algorithms?

2 How does Greedy algorithm differ from backtracking in terms of revisiting choices?

3. What are the characteristics that make Greedy algorithms suitable for problems with large input spaces?
4. In what scenarios might Greedy algorithms not lead to a globally optimal solution?
5. Provide an example of a problem where the Greedy algorithm is particularly effective.
6. Explain the objective of the Fractional Knapsack problem and how the Greedy algorithm helps in solving it.
7. What is the goal of Huffman Coding, and how does the Greedy algorithm play a crucial role in achieving it?
8. How do Greedy algorithms provide approximate solutions to optimization problems?
9. What are some of the limitations of Greedy algorithms in certain problem-solving scenarios?
10. What is the fundamental principle behind Greedy algorithms, and how does it guide decision-making in problem-solving?
11. Explain the distinction between locally optimal and globally optimal solutions in the context of Greedy algorithms. Provide an example to illustrate this concept.
12. Discuss the key characteristics of Greedy algorithms that make them a suitable choice for a wide range of problem-solving scenarios. Provide specific examples to support your explanation.
13. How do Greedy algorithms differ from techniques like backtracking in terms of their decision-making process and revisiting of choices? Provide an example problem to highlight this distinction.
14. Provide a detailed explanation of the Fractional Knapsack problem and how the Greedy algorithm is applied to optimize item selection within the knapsack's weight capacity. Discuss the advantages and limitations of this approach.

KNOW MORE

Online courses/materials/resources [Accessed May 2024]

- https://www.geeksforgeeks.org
- https://www.hackerearth.com/practice/algorithms/greedy
- https://www.javatpoint.com/greedy-algorithms
- https://www.programiz.com/dsa/greedy-algorithm

- https://web.stanford.edu/class/archive/cs/cs161/cs161.1166/lectures/lecture14.pdf
- https://www.coursera.org/learn/algorithms-greedy
- https://github.com/topics/greedy-algorithms

REFERENCES

[1] Pigeon, Steven. "Huffman coding." *Lossless Compression Handbook (2003): 79-100.* [Accessed: October-2023]

[2] Feder, Meir. "A note on the competitive optimality of the Huffman code." *IEEE Transactions on Information Theory* 38, no. 2 (1992): 436-439.

[3] Moffat, Alistair. "Huffman coding." *ACM Computing Surveys (CSUR)* 52, no. 4 (2019): 1-35.

7 Dynamic Programming

UNIT SPECIFICS

This unit covers the following aspects:

- *Introduction to Dynamic programming*
- *Characteristics and Design Strategies of Dynamic programming technique*
- *Knapsack problem*
- *Chained Matrix multiplication*
- *Longest common subsequence*
- *Weight interval scheduling*

This unit will discuss the principles of Dynamic Programming, an optimization technique that focuses on breaking down complex problems into simpler overlapping subproblems. It will provide an introduction to Dynamic Programming, elucidate the key characteristics of this technique, and explore various design strategies employed in its application. The unit will further examine specific problems, including the Knapsack Problem, Chained Matrix Multiplication, Longest Common Subsequence, and Weight Interval Scheduling, illustrating how Dynamic Programming can be effectively utilized to solve these challenges. Throughout the exploration, the module will address the time and space complexity of Dynamic Programming solutions, highlighting their efficiency. The unit will also touch upon the limitations of Dynamic Programming and explore alternative approaches in problem-solving. The link given in the QR code provides this unit is supplementary material.

RATIONALE

The rationale of this unit with the design and analysis of algorithms is designed to familiarize you with the concept of dynamic programming as a problem-solving technique. The objective is to explore the complexities of dynamic programming, explain how it functions, its distinctive features, and its diverse applications across various domains.

PRE-REQUISITES

- *Understanding of basic data structures, including arrays, linked lists, and trees.*
- *Familiarity with algorithmic concepts, such as sorting, searching, and recursion.*
- *Basic knowledge of mathematical principles, particularly in relation to sequences and optimization.*

UNIT OUTCOMES

The outcomes of the Unit are as follows:

U7-O1: Understand the concept of dynamic programming and characteristics

U7-O2: Elaborate design strategies of dynamic programming technique

U7-O3: Discusses knapsack problem and chained matrix multiplication

U7-O4: Explains longest common subsequence and weight interval scheduling

Unit-7 Outcomes	EXPECTED MAPPING WITH COURSE OUTCOMES (1- Weak Correlation; 2- Medium correlation; 3- Strong Correlation)				
	CO-1	CO-2	CO-3	CO-4	CO-5
U7-O1	-	1	3	3	-
U7-O2	-	2	3	3	1
U7-O3	-	2	3	3	-
U7-O4	1	2	3	3	-

7.1 Introduction to Dynamic Programming

In the previous unit, our focus turned to the Greedy approach within the realm of problem-solving. The Greedy approach is centered on selecting the most advantageous option at each step, *considering the immediate context, with the ultimate goal of revealing a solution of optimal value across the entire problem.* Within this context, we examined diverse applications of the Greedy approach, including instances like Huffman coding and interval scheduling, which highlighted its inherent simplicity and methodical procedure. However, while the Greedy approach can often yield results that are reasonably close to the optimum, it is crucial to acknowledge its limitations. In certain scenarios, due to its localized decision-making, the Greedy approach might overlook complex relationships and broader patterns that could potentially lead to better solutions. Despite these limitations, it remains a valuable tool in *problem-solving*, particularly in situations where a quick and pragmatic solution is important.

To mitigate the limitations of the Greedy approach, innovative methodologies and algorithms have emerged. Among these, dynamic programming techniques play a pivotal role. Dynamic programming involves a systematic and methodical approach to problem-solving that aims to optimize outcomes through the breakdown of complex problems into smaller, more manageable subproblems. The key concept behind dynamic programming is the efficient reuse of previously computed solutions to avoid redundant calculations and expedite the overall problem-solving process.

The underlying idea is to leverage the knowledge gained from solving subproblems and store these solutions in a way that allows for their efficient retrieval when needed. By doing so, dynamic programming minimizes computation time and effort, making it especially adept at addressing problems with overlapping substructures. This technique hinges on the hope that the accumulated knowledge and optimal solutions derived from solving smaller subproblems will contribute to the attainment of a superior solution for the overall problem. In essence, dynamic programming embodies a strategic trade-off between memory utilization and computational efficiency, tackling complex optimization challenges.

Let us discuss a simple example that can help in comprehending dynamic programming better: the Fibonacci sequence. The Fibonacci sequence operates as a sequence of interconnected numbers. The generation of each subsequent number results from the addition of the two preceding numbers. The sequence initiates with 0 and 1. Thereafter, each newly generated number is the sum of the previous two numbers $(0,1,1,2,3,5,8,13,\ldots)$. However, it is imperative to approach the generation of the Fibonacci sequence using a modicum of caution when employing rudimentary methods. Such methodologies are inclined to consume considerable time, ultimately culminating in a deceleration of the process due to the recurrent nature of calculations. This repetitiveness is engendered by the persistent reiteration of the same calculations. For a clearer perspective, here's the pseudocode representing the recursive approach for generating Fibonacci numbers is shown as $FIBONACCI\_NUMBER\_GENERATE(n)$ for n number.

```
FIBONACCI_NUMBER_GENERATE(n)
    if n ≤ 1
        return n
    else
        return FIBONACCI_NUMBER_GENERATE(n − 1)
                + FIBONACCI_NUMBER_GENERATE(n − 2)
```

In the context of time complexity analysis, the recursive approach for generating Fibonacci numbers is notably exponential. The time complexity can be approximated as $O(2^n)$, signifying an exponential increase in the number of operations as the input value n grows. This is primarily due to the numerous overlapping subproblems that lead to redundant calculations, resulting in a significant inefficiency for larger values of n.

Dynamic programming intervenes to counteract the computational slowdown, ultimately expediting the entire process. It is important to note that dynamic programming is more of a methodology than a specific algorithm. The term *programming* in this context has historical origins and predates the modern concept of computer programming. Dynamic programming provides a structured approach to problem-solving, aiding in efficiently solving complex problems by breaking them down into smaller subproblems and systematically storing solutions to avoid redundant computations.

To apply dynamic programming to address this challenge, commence by breaking down the task of determining Fibonacci numbers into smaller, manageable subproblems. For instance, consider the calculation of the Fibonacci number at position n. This can be achieved by summing the Fibonacci numbers at positions $n-1$ and $n-2$. Initiate this process with the foundational scenarios, represented by the base cases $F(0) = 0$ and $F(1) = 1$ for Fibonacci. As progress is made, construct solutions for more extensive scenarios by leveraging the outcomes of their smaller counterparts. To illustrate, to compute $F(2)$, the summation of $F(1)$ and $F(0)$ is performed, and likewise for $F(3)$, $F(2)$ and $F(1)$ are summed, and so forth. The mechanism of the approach lies in deriving optimal solutions for larger positions based on the solutions obtained from smaller ones. For instance, the Fibonacci number $F(5)$ can be deduced by adding the results of $F(4)$ and $F(3)$. To circumvent redundant recalculations, it is prudent to retain the solutions of subproblems. By storing the computed values of $F(0), F(1), F(2)$ and so forth, the ability to efficiently calculate large Fibonacci numbers is facilitated, without necessitating repetitive computations. The pseudocode representing the dynamic programming technique for generating Fibonacci numbers is shown as $FIBONACCI\_NUMBER\_GENERATE(n)$ for n numbers.

```
FIBONACCI_NUMBER_GENERATE(n)
    if n ≤ 1
        return n
    Let fib[ ] be an array of size n + 1
    fib[0] = 0
    fib[1] = 1
```

```
6.  for i from 2 to n
7.      fib[i] = fib[i − 1] + fib[i − 2]
8.  return fib[n]
```

In the realm of time complexity analysis, the dynamic programming approach for generating Fibonacci numbers presents a remarkably more efficient scenario. The time complexity of this method is notably linear, characterized as $O(n)$. This signifies a linear growth in the number of operations as the input value n increases. The dynamic programming approach meticulously sidesteps the redundancy inherent in the recursive approach. By systematically storing the results of previously computed subproblems, it obviates the need for recalculations, thereby greatly enhancing efficiency. This strategic optimization ensures that the time complexity remains linear, allowing for swift and proficient computation of Fibonacci numbers even for larger values of n.

7.2 Characteristics of Dynamic Programming Technique

The dynamic programming technique stands apart from the previously discussed brute-force and greedy approaches, offering a distinctive set of characteristics that enhance its efficiency in addressing intricate computational problems. This section explores the characteristics of the dynamic programming technique with the example of Fibonacci sequence:

- **Overlapping subproblems:** In continuation with Fibonacci sequence, dynamic programming operates by subdividing the task of computing Fibonacci numbers into smaller subproblems. Primarily, these subproblems often interconnect and share common computations. For instance, when calculating $F(5)$, both $F(4)$ and $F(3)$ need to be evaluated, and $F(4)$ in turn requires $F(3)$ and $F(2)$. Dynamic programming leverages this interdependence by storing previously computed results, eliminating the need to repeatedly solve the same subproblems. This prevents redundant calculations and enhances efficiency.
- **Optimal substructure:** Fibonacci sequence inherently exhibits an optimal substructure. The optimal solution for any given Fibonacci number relies on the optimal solutions of smaller Fibonacci numbers. For instance, the optimal solution for $F(5)$ can be constructed using the solutions for $F(4)$ and $F(3)$. Dynamic programming takes advantage of this property, enabling the construction of the optimal solution by building upon smaller subproblems.
- **Memoization and tabulation:** Dynamic programming technique employs two main strategies: *memoization* and *tabulation*. In the case of the Fibonacci sequence, memoization involves storing intermediate results to accelerate subsequent calculations. Tabulation, on the other hand, entails constructing a table or array to iteratively compute solutions. Both approaches contribute to efficiency and reduced time complexity.
- **Bottom-up approach:** To optimize the computation of Fibonacci numbers, dynamic programming employs a bottom-up approach. Starting with the base cases $F(0)$ and $F(1)$. The technique systematically calculates subsequent Fibonacci numbers in ascending order. This approach ensures that each Fibonacci number is computed only once, eliminating redundancy.

- **Time and space trade-off:** Dynamic programming involves a trade-off between memory utilization and computation time. In the context of the Fibonacci sequence, while storing intermediate results accelerates computations, it does consume additional memory. This trade-off is especially valuable when seeking to enhance time efficiency.
- **Complexity reduction:** Dynamic programming dramatically reduces the time complexity of solving the Fibonacci sequence. As we have seen in the above discussion, the naive recursive approach has exponential time complexity ($O(2^n)$), while Dynamic programming transforms it to linear time complexity ($O(n)$) by avoiding duplicate calculations.
- **Problem generalization:** While the Fibonacci sequence serves as a simple example, the principles of dynamic programming extend to solving diverse and complex problems. The technique's adaptability is not limited to Fibonacci numbers but can be applied to a range of optimization, alignment, and traversal problems.

7.3 Design Strategies of Dynamic Programming Technique

Design strategies of dynamic programming techniques involve approaches to enhance their efficiency and effectiveness in solving optimization problems. This section explores the strategies of the dynamic programming technique with the example of Fibonacci sequence:

- **Break down the problem into smaller, manageable subproblems:** The initial step in employing the dynamic programming technique is to divide the problem into smaller, more manageable subproblems. Analyze these subproblems to determine if they can be solved independently, which is a foundational concept of dynamic programming. For the problem of generating Fibonacci numbers, this strategy involves breaking down the task into smaller subproblems. For instance, to generate $F(5)$, we can observe that it relies on the calculations of $F(4)$ and $F(3)$. This breakdown allows us to solve the subproblems ($F(4)$ and $F(3)$) independently and then utilize their solutions to compute the final result for $F(5)$.
- **Formulate recurrence relations:** In dynamic programming, it is essential to establish recurrence relations that describe how the solution to a larger problem depends on the solutions of its smaller subproblems. These relations define the interdependency between the current problem state and its subproblem states, guiding the approach to solving the problem. Express the relationship between Fibonacci numbers using recurrence relations. For example, $F(n) = F(n-1) + F(n-2)$. This relation defines how the current Fibonacci number depends on its two preceding numbers.
- **Bottom-up approach:** Begin by solving the smallest subproblems and build up to the main problem iteratively. Use an array or table to store solutions for subproblems to avoid recomputation. Begin by solving the smallest subproblems, $F(0)$ and $F(1)$. Utilize an array or table to store solutions for subproblems, iterating from $F(2)$ up to $F(n)$. This approach prevents redundant calculations.
- **Memoization:** A fundamental concept in dynamic programming is to store solutions of subproblems in memory as they are computed. This storage enables efficient access to already

solved subproblems and prevents the need for redundant calculations. The use of memory to store computed results is a crucial aspect of dynamic programming. This memory serves as a repository for solutions, which can be accessed later when needed, avoiding the computational overhead of recalculating them. Store computed Fibonacci numbers in memory as they are calculated. When calculating $F(n)$, check if $F(n-1)$ and $F(n-2)$ are already stored, and retrieve them to calculate $F(n)$.

- **Tabulation:** Create a table or array to store solutions for subproblems in a systematic order. Use an iterative approach to fill in the table, ensuring that each subproblem is solved only once. Create a table or array to store solutions for Fibonacci numbers. Calculate and fill in the table iteratively, starting with $F(0)$ and $F(1)$, and proceeding to $F(2)$, $F(3)$, and so on.
- **Identify and solve base cases:** In dynamic programming, it is important to identify and address the base cases of a problem separately. Base cases represent the simplest instances of the problem and serve as the foundational starting points for the dynamic programming process. These are the simplest instances that serve as the starting point for the dynamic programming approach. Solve the base cases directly: $F(0) = 0$ and $F(1) = 1$. These serve as the initial values required for the dynamic programming calculations.
- **State representation:** Dynamic programming involves defining the state of the problem, which encompasses the variables or parameters that uniquely identify the current instance of the problem. This state representative serves as a guide for structuring the solution approach. The state representation for the Fibonacci sequence involves the current position n for which the Fibonacci number needs to be calculated. This state guides the calculation process.
- **Testing and validation:** Begin with small instances of the problem and validate that your dynamic programming solution produces the expected results. Debug any issues that arise. Begin with small values of n (*e.g.*, $n = 5$) and validate that your dynamic programming solution produces the correct Fibonacci numbers. Debug any discrepancies.

These strategies are flexible and can be adapted to different types of problems. Employing these strategies effectively will help you design efficient and optimized solutions using the Dynamic Programming technique. However, the effectiveness of these strategies depends on the nature of the specific problem being tackled.

7.4 Knapsack Problem

Unit 6 has offered an in-depth exploration of the knapsack problem, with a specific focus on the Fractional Knapsack Problem. This problem variation introduces an intriguing twist—the items at hand are divisible, allowing for the selection of fractional portions to maximize the collective value. The importance of solving this challenge lies in deploying a well-known greedy algorithm. This algorithm operates by employing a key criterion: ***the value-to-weight ratio of the items***. By prioritizing items with higher value-to-weight ratios, the greedy algorithm strives to optimize the total value while staying within the *knapsack's capacity*. This strategic approach is grounded in the belief that favoring items with superior value in relation to their weight will culminate in an optimal solution. The Fractional

Knapsack Problem ingenious underscores how a seemingly simple yet intelligent methodology can be harnessed to proficiently handle scenarios involving divisible items. This empowers us to efficiently leverage available resources. However, it is imperative to note that this approach comes with an inherent trade-off. The computational effort required to navigate through the extensive spectrum of potential combinations grows exponentially with the item count. Specifically, this computational complexity escalates in line with $O(2^n)$, illustrating the inherent challenges in exhaustively assessing all possible item selections.

In this section, we discuss an alternative modification of the knapsack problem, recognized as the ***0-1 Knapsack Problem.*** Here, the task entails efficiently filling a knapsack to attain the highest achievable cumulative value. *The scenario encompasses a set of items, each characterized by its weight and corresponding value*. A critical constraint is that the collective weight of the chosen items must not surpass a fixed limit. Hence, this variation requires a strategic assessment that considers both the weights and values of items. The aim is to curate a selection of items that collectively optimize the total value while adhering to the specified weight constraint. This intricate interplay between weights and values forms the core of *0-1 Knapsack Problem*, paving the way for dynamic and systematic decision-making to achieve the best possible outcome.

0-1 Knapsack problem

In this scenario, we introduce a new perspective and assume that the objects at hand cannot be divided into smaller fragments; rather, they are taken as complete entities. You are faced with a decision: either include a whole object or leave it behind entirely, fractional choices are no longer possible. For each object, indexed from 1 to n, with positive weights w_i and positive values v_i, we encounter a knapsack with a maximum weight capacity W. Our objective remains consistent: efficiently fill the knapsack to maximize the total value of the enclosed objects, all while staying within the capacity limit. We introduce a binary variable x_i that takes the value 0 if we choose not to include object i, and 1 if we decide to include it. The new problem is formulated as follows:

$$maximize \sum_{i=1}^{n} v_i \times x_i$$

$$subject\ to \sum_{i=1}^{n} w_i \times x_i \le W,$$

$$x_i \in \{0,1\}, for\ 1 \le i \le n$$

Here, v_i and w_i are positive values representing the value and weight of object i, respectively. The decision variable x_i is constrained to be either 0 or 1, indicating whether the object is included or not.

Solution of 0/1 Knapsack problem

To address this problem using dynamic programming, we construct a table denoted as $V[L \ldots n][0 \ldots W]$, where each row corresponds to an available object, and each column represents a weight value ranging from 0 to W. In this table, $V[i][j]$ holds the maximum value of the objects that can be carried, considering the weight constraint j and incorporating only objects indexed from 1 to i $(1 \leq i \leq n)$. Consequently, the solution for this problem instance can be extracted from $V[n][W]$. This setup closely resonates with the problem of making change, demonstrating the application of the principle of optimality. We can populate the table either row by row or column by column. In the general context, $V[i][j]$ is determined by selecting the larger value (since the goal is value maximization) between $V[i-1][j]$ and $V[i-1][j-w_i]+v_i$. The former choice signifies excluding object i from the load, while the latter corresponds to including object i. The inclusion of object i boosts the total value of the load by v_i and reduces the available capacity by its weight w_i. Incorporating these insights, we populate the entries in the table according to the general rule as follows:$V[i][j] = max(V[i-1][j], V[i-1][j-w_i]+v_i)$.

To handle entries that fall out of bounds, we define $V[0][j]$ as 0 when $j > 0$, and for $j < 0$, we set $V[i][j]$ to be -∞ (negative infinity) $\forall i$. This algorithm follows closely the pattern of the function algorithm, albeit tailored to the context of the knapsack problem. The algorithm can be summarized as follows:

```
0/1 KNAPSACK_PROBLEM (V[i],W[i],W)
  1. Initialize a 2D array V[n + 1][W + 1] with all elements initially set to 0.
  2. for w = 0 to W
         V[0][w] = 0
  3. for i = 1 to n
         V[i][0] = 0
  4. for i = 1 to n
         for w = 0 to W
             if w_i ≤ W
                 V[i][w] = max(V[i − 1][w], V[i − 1][w − w_i] + v_i)
             else:
                 V[i][w] = V[i − 1][w]
  5. return V[n][W]
```

This algorithm constructs a table V to store the maximum values that can be achieved for different subproblems. It iterates through each item and weight combination, considering whether the current item's weight can fit within the available capacity w. The value at $V[i][w]$ is updated based on the maximum value between excluding the current item and including it. The final result is stored in $V[n][W]$, representing the maximum value that can be obtained with the given items and weight capacity.

Next, to determine the actual items that make up the optimal knapsack solution, the information required is already available within table V. The maximal value of items that can be placed in the knapsack is denoted as $V[n][W]$. To extract the specific items that compose the optimal solution, the following procedure can be followed:

FIND_KNAPSACK_ITEM(V)

1. Initialize $i = n$
2. $k = W$ // *Current weight constraint*
3. **for** $j = n\ to\ 1$ // Iterating through the table V
4. **if** $B[i, k] \neq B[i-1, k]$ **then** // Item i is in the knapsack
   Mark item i as included in the knapsack
   $i = i - 1, k = k - w_i$ // Reduce the remaining weight
5. **else** // Item i is not in the knapsack
   $i = i - 1$
6. **return** $V[n][W]$

By navigating through table V and making comparisons, this procedure identifies the items that should be included in the optimal knapsack solution. This approach leverages the calculated values in the table to determine the specific items that lead to the maximal value within the given weight constraint.

Example of 0/1 Knapsack problem: Let us apply our algorithm to a specific dataset consisting of four elements. We are given that the total number of elements is $n = 4$, and the maximum weight capacity of the knapsack is $W = 5$. Each element is represented by a pair (w, v), where w corresponds to the weight of the element, and v represents its value. The dataset includes the following elements: $(2,3), (3,4), (4,5), and\ (5,6)$. Our aim is to determine the combination of elements that should be included in the knapsack to maximize its total value while staying within the weight capacity constraint. By following the algorithmic steps for dynamic programming, we can compute the optimal value achieved and consequently make informed decisions about the selection of elements to achieve the highest overall value for the given weight constraint. In Step 1 of the process, we create a two-dimensional array labeled $V[5][6]$, where the rows correspond to different weights from 0 to 5, and the columns correspond to different elements from 0 to 4. In the initial state, the entire array is initialized to 0, which is visually represented in Table $1(a)$. Specifically, when examining the cell $V[1][1]$, the value is set to 0 due to the condition that the weight of the first item, $w[1]$, is greater than the current weight constraint, denoted as w. Since $2 > 1$, the value of $V[1][1] = V[0][1]$, leading to the value of 0, as illustrated in Table $1(b)$. Continuing onward to the cell $V[1][2]$, we encounter a situation where $w[2]$(which is 2) is less than or equal to the current weight constraint w (which is 2). This allows us to calculate the value for this cell by adding the value of the first item, $v[1]$ (which is 3), to the value of $V[0][0]$ ($V[1][2] = v[1] + V[0][0]$), resulting in a value of 3, as depicted in Table $1(c)$. This sequence of evaluations showcases how the dynamic programming approach fills in the array step by step based on the specified conditions and calculations.

Table 1 outlines the process of utilizing the FIND_KNAPSACK-ITEM(V) algorithm to determine the actual items to be included in the knapsack. The process begins with $V[4][5]$, where it compares $V[4][5]$ with $V[3][5]$. Since they are equal, it proceeds to $V[3][5]$, as illustrated in Table 1. In a similar manner, $V[3][5]$ is compared with $V[2][5]$, and they are found to be equal, leading to a movement to $V[2][5]$, as shown in Table 1(g)-(h). However, the situation changes with $V[2][5]$, which is not equal to $V[1][5]$. Thus, the algorithm shifts the selection of items to $V[1][2]$, indicated by the decrement of i and reduction of k by $w[2]$, as depicted in Table 1[(i). This process showcases how the algorithm progressively traces back through the table to identify the items that should be included in the knapsack based on their contributions to the optimal solution. The final selected items that form the optimal solution for the knapsack problem based on the given data are items 1 and 2. These correspond to the elements (2,3) and (3,4) with weights and values (2,3) and (3,4),respectively.

Table 7. 1: Illustration of the Knapsack algorithm example.

i\W	0	1	2	3	4	5
0	0	0	0	0	0	0
1	0					
2	0					
3	0					
4	0					

(a)

i\W	0	1	2	3	4	5
0	0	0	0	0	0	0
1	0	0				
2	0					
3	0					
4	0					

(b)

i\W	0	1	2	3	4	5
0	0	0	0	0	0	0
1	0	0	3			
2	0					
3	0					
4	0					

(c)

i\W	0	1	2	3	4	5
0	0	0	0	0	0	0
1	0	0	3	3	3	3
2	0	0	3	4		
3	0					
4	0					

(d)

i\W	0	1	2	3	4	5
0	0	0	0	0	0	0
1	0	0	3	3	3	3
2	0	0	3	4	4	7
3	0	0	3	4	5	7
4	0	0	3	4	5	

(e)

i\W	0	1	2	3	4	5
0	0	0	0	0	0	0
1	0	0	3	3	3	3
2	0	0	3	4	4	7
3	0	0	3	4	5	7
4	0	0	3	4	5	7

(f)

i\W	0	1	2	3	4	5
0	0	0	0	0	0	0
1	0	0	3	3	3	3
2	0	0	3	4	4	7
3	0	0	3	4	5	7
4	0	0	3	4	5	7

(g)

i\W	0	1	2	3	4	5
0	0	0	0	0	0	0
1	0	0	3	3	3	3
2	0	0	3	4	4	7
3	0	0	3	4	5	7
4	0	0	3	4	5	7

(h)

i\W	0	1	2	3	4	5
0	0	0	0	0	0	0
1	0	0	3	3	3	3
2	0	0	3	4	4	7
3	0	0	3	4	5	7
4	0	0	3	4	5	7

(i)

i\W	0	1	2	3	4	5
0	0	0	0	0	0	0
1	0	0	3	3	3	3
2	0	0	3	4	4	7
3	0	0	3	4	5	7
4	0	0	3	4	5	7

(j)

i\W	0	1	2	3	4	5
0	0	0	0	0	0	0
1	0	0	3	3	3	3
2	0	0	3	4	4	7
3	0	0	3	4	5	7
4	0	0	3	4	5	7

(k)

Time and Space Complexity Analysis: The time complexity of the algorithm is determined by the nested loops used to populate the $2D$ table V of size $(n+1) \times (W+1)$, where n is the number of items and W is the maximum weight capacity of the knapsack. The outer loop iterates through each item (i) and the inner loop iterates through each weight (w). Within the loops, constant time operations are performed (comparisons, additions, and assignments). So, the time complexity can be expressed as $O(nW)$. *The space complexity is primarily governed by the* $2D$ *table* V *that is used to store the* maximum values of packed items for different weight constraints and different items. The size of the table is $(n+1) \times (W+1)$. Thus, the space complexity can be expressed as $O(nW)$.

7.5 Chained Matrix Multiplication

The Chain Matrix Multiplication (CMM) problem involves finding the optimal sequence for performing matrix multiplications within a series of matrices. This particular problem holds significance in various domains such as compiler design for code optimization and query optimization in databases. Although we are dealing with a restricted scenario, the insights gained from this problem shed light on the fundamental dynamic programming concepts. Imagine we want to multiply a series of matrices $A1, A2, \ldots, An$. It is important to note that matrix multiplication is associative but not commutative. This means we can choose how to parenthesize the multiplication, but we cannot change the order of the matrices. The dimension restrictions during multiplication also play a crucial role. When multiplying a $p \times q$ matrix A with a $q \times r$ matrix B, the result is a $p \times r$ matrix C. Each entry of C is computed as the sum of the product of corresponding elements from matrices A and B.

Let us discuss the Chain Matrix Multiplication problem with an example. Consider matrices $A1$ with dimensions 6×4, $A2$ with dimensions 4×5, and $A3$ with dimensions 5×3. This example underscores how the sequence of matrix multiplications can substantially influence the overall computational complexity of the operation. Matrix multiplication is not only about carrying out the mathematical operation itself but also about making strategic decisions on how to arrange the multiplications to minimize the computational workload. In this case, two parenthesization options, $((A1A2)A3)$ and $(A1(A2A3))$, offer distinct operation counts and underscore the importance of finding the optimal multiplication sequence. For the first parenthesization, $((A1A2)A3)$, the sequence of operations involves multiplying $A1$ with $A2$ first, resulting in a matrix that is then multiplied by $A3$. Each of these multiplications comes with its own set of operations based on the dimensions of the matrices involved. The second parenthesization, $(A1(A2A3))$, involves multiplying $A2$ with $A3$ initially, followed by the multiplication of $A1$ with the result. Again, this sequence introduces its own set of operations based on matrix dimensions.

Next, let us calculate the required number of operations for different parenthesization options. For $((A1A2)A3)$, the sequence starts by multiplying matrices $A1$ and $A2$. $A1$ is a 6×4 matrix, and $A2$ is a 4×5 matrix as shown in Figure 7.1. The multiplication results in a 6×5 matrix. The total number of scalar multiplications required for this step is $(6 \times 4 \times 5) = 120$. Moving forward, we multiply the obtained 6×5 matrix with matrix $A3$. $A3$ is a 5×3 matrix, and the multiplication yields a 6×3 matrix. The total number of scalar multiplications needed here is $(6 \times 5 \times 3) = 90$. Therefore, for the $((A1A2)A3)$ sequence, the combined total number of operations is $120 + 90 = 210$. Similarly, for the $(A1(A2A3))$ sequence, we begin by multiplying matrices $A2$ and $A3$. $A2$ is a 4×5 matrix, and $A3$ is a 5×3 matrix. The multiplication results in a 3 matrix. The total number of scalar multiplications required for this step is $(4 \times 5 \times 3) = 60$. Next, we multiply the obtained 4×3 matrix with matrix $A1$. $A1$ is a 6×4 matrix, and the multiplication yields a 6×3 matrix. The total number of scalar multiplications needed here is $(6 \times 4 \times 3) = 72$. Thus, for the $(A1(A2A3))$ sequence, the combined total number of operations is $60 + 72 = 132$. Thus, based on this example, it is clear that the parenthesization $(A1(A2A3))$ requires fewer operations (132) compared to $((A1A2)A3)$ which required (210) operations.

The key insight here is that different parenthesizations can lead to different numbers of operations, which in turn affects the computational efficiency. The CMM problem seeks to determine the most optimal sequence of matrix multiplications that results in the minimum number of operations. By exploring different parenthesization options and calculating the associated operation counts, we can strategically choose the sequence that minimizes computational complexity and maximizes efficiency. In this problem, the goal is not to actually perform the multiplications, but to identify the sequence that yields the most efficient outcome. This illustrates the dynamic programming approach, where we analyze the problem's substructure and overlapping subproblems to find an optimal solution by considering all possible combinations. Ultimately, this problem exemplifies how a seemingly simple task—matrix multiplication—can be intricately optimized through strategic decision-making in choosing the multiplication sequence.

Solution of CMM problem using dynamic programming

We initiate the CMM process with a sequence of matrices $A1, \ldots, An$, each having dimensions $p0, \ldots, pn$, where Ai is of dimension $pi - 1 \times pi$. The CMM is tasked with determining the optimal order of multiplication to minimize the total number of operations. It is crucial to note that the CMM itself does not execute the multiplications; rather, it identifies the most efficient sequence for performing them and calculates the overall number of operations.

Consider Ak as the matrix where we have the option to divide the chain of matrices $A1,\ldots,An$ as shown in Figure 7.2. At this stage, the operation involves multiplying two matrices: $A1,\ldots,An = A1,\ldots Ak \times A(k+1),\ldots An, \forall k \in 1 \leq k \leq n-1$. The key challenge is identifying the optimal location to split the chain, denoted by k, and determining the appropriate parenthesization for each of the subsequences $A1,\ldots,Ak$ and $A(k+1),\ldots,An$. To tackle these challenges, we delve into formulating the optimal cost of multiplication in a recursive manner.

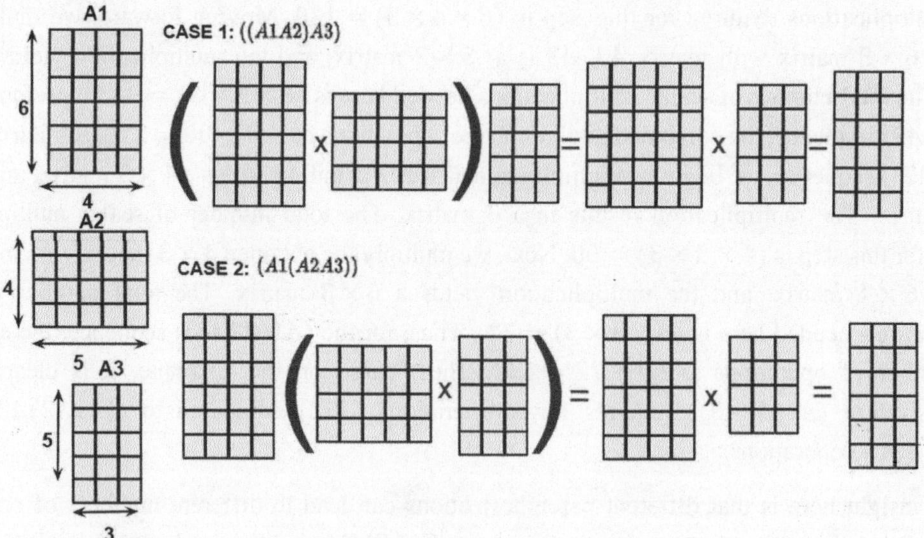

Figure 7.1: Illustration of CMM using three matrices $A1$, $A2$, and $A3$.

Let $m(i,j)$ denote the minimum number of multiplications required to compute $Ai,\ldots,Aj$, where $1 \leq i \leq j \leq n$. The ultimate goal is to find the total cost of multiplying all the matrices, represented by computing the entire chain $Ai,\ldots,An$, given by $m(1,n)$. The foundational observation is that if $i == j$, the sequence comprises only one matrix, resulting in a cost of 0 as no multiplication is necessary; thus, $m(i,i) = 0$. In the case where i is less than j, signifying the product $Ai,\ldots,Aj$, it can be split into two groups: $A1,\ldots Ak \times A(k+1),\ldots Aj$, considering each k where $i \leq k < j$.

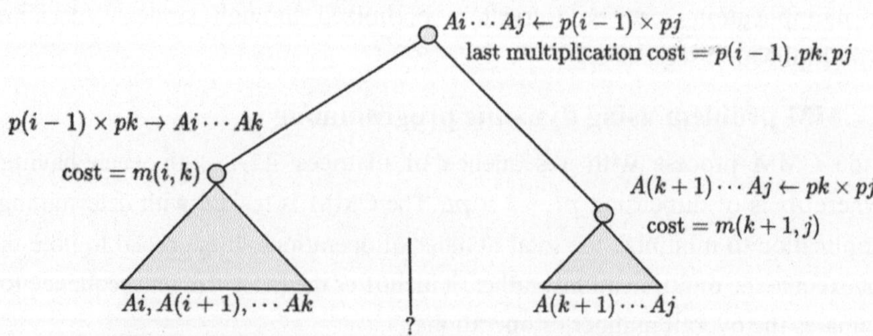

Figure 7.2 Illustration of dynamic programming decision.

The optimal times to compute $A1,\ldots,Ak$ and $A(k+1),\ldots,Aj$ are, by definition, $m(i,k)$ and $m(k+1,j)$, respectively. Assuming inductively that we can compute these values, and noting that each involves a strictly smaller number of matrices, there is no possibility of circularity. As $A1,\ldots,Ak$ is a $p(i-1) \times pk$ matrix, and $A(k+1),\ldots,Aj$ is a $pk \times pj$ matrix, the time to multiply them is $p(i-1) \times pk \times pj$. It leads to the formulation of recursive rule for $m[i,j]$.

$$m[i,j] = 0$$
$$m[i,j] = min_{i \le k < j}(m[i,k] + m[k+1,j] + p(i-1) \times pk \times pj), \forall i < j$$

After devising the recursive formula, determining the CMM becomes a simple process. However, employing a direct recursive implementation of this formula may lead to high inefficiency and result in exponential-time complexity. Thus, there arises a necessity to explore a more efficient procedure for computing the length and constructing the CMM.

The procedure for estimating the CMM using dynamic programming involves taking an input sequence p as $p = p0, p1, p2, \ldots, pn$ representing matrix dimensions, accompanied by n. For $i = 1,2,\ldots,n$ matrix Ai has dimensions $p(i-1) \times pi$. The algorithm utilizes an auxiliary table $m[1{:}n, 1{:}n]$ to store the costs $m[i,j]$ and another auxiliary table $s[1{:}n-1, 2{:}n]$ to record the index k that achieved the optimal cost in computing $m[i,j]$. The s table assists in constructing an optimal solution. The algorithm $CMM\_FIND(p,n)$ outlines the steps for creating the tables m and s. The process involves filling the values in the m table from shorter matrix chains to longer ones. $CMM\_FIND(p,n)$ uses four variables: the length of the subchain, the starting index of the subchain, the ending index of the subchain, and the breaking point.

Let L represent the length of the subchain being multiplied. We consider an example with four matrics $A1, A2, A3,$ and. The case $L = 1$ is simple as there is only one matrix, such as $A1, A2, A3,$ and $A4$ individually. For $L = 2$, the possible sub chains include $A1A2$, $A2A3$, and $A3A4$. Similarly, for $L = 3$ and $L = 4$, the sub chains consist of $A1A2A3$, $A2A3A4$, and $A1A2A3A4$, respectively. In general, the length of the subchain is denoted as $L = j - i + 1$, where $1 \le i \le j \le n$. The case $L = 1$ is trivial, resulting in $m[i,i] = 0$, indicating that there is only one matrix, and no multiplication is needed. For our example with matrices $A1$ to $A4$, when $L = 2$, the possible values for i are 1 ,2, and 3 (representing $A1A2$, $A2A3$, and $A3A4$). Similarly, for $L = 3$, i can be 1 or 2 (representing $A1A2A3$ and $A2A3A4$), and for $L = 4$, i is 1 (representing $A1A2A3A4$). In general, i ranges from 1 to $n - L + 1$. Next, the algorithm determines the ending index of the subchain j. In our example, when $L = 2$, the possible j values are 2, 3, and 4 (representing $A1A2$, $A2A3$, and $A3A4$). Similarly, for $L = 3$, j can be 3 or 4 (representing $A1A2A3$ and $A2A3A4$), and for $L = 4$, j is 4 (representing $A1A2A3A4$). In general, j is determined by $i + L - 1$. Finally, the algorithm finds the inner loop k (break point). For instance, when $L = 2$, i is 1 and j is 2 (representing $A1A2$), then possible break points k include $1(A1 \times A2)$. Similarly, for $A2A3$ and $A3A4$, k can be 2 and 3. When $L = 3$, $i = 1$, and $j = 3$ (representing $A1A2A3$), then possible break points k include $1(A1 \times A2A3)$ and $2(A1A2 \times A3)$. Similarly, for $A2A3A4$, k can be

$2(A2 \times A3A4)$ and $3(A2A3 \times A4)$. In general, k ranges from i to $j-1$. After determining the variables $L, i, j,$ and k, the $CMM\_FIND(p, n)$ algorithm utilizes the recursive rule formulation.

```
CMM_FIND(p, n)
  1. Initialize m[1:n, 1:n] and s[1:n − 1,1:n]  tables
  2. for i = 0 to n
             m[i, i] = 0
  3. for L = 2 to n
         for i = 1 to n − L + 1
               j = i + L − 1
               m[i, j] = ∞
  4.           for  k = i to j − 1
                     cost = m[i, k] + m[k + 1, j] + p(i − 1)p(k)p(j)
  5.                 if (cost < m[i, j])
  6.                     m[i, j] = cost
  7.                     s[i, j] = k
  8. return m, s
```

Table m and table s provide the necessary information to identify the CMM. In dynamic programming, a bottom-up approach is employed to retrieve the CMM of p and n. $CMM\_PRINT(i, j)$ algorithm illustrates an optimal parenthesization of matrix chain products.

```
CMM_PRINT(i, j)
  1. if i == j
  2.      print Ai
  3. else
  4.      print "("
  5.      k = s[i, j]
  6.      X = CMM_PRINT(i, k)
  7.      Y = CMM_PRINT(k + 1, j)
  8.      print ")"
```

Let us continue the above example and apply the algorithm to find CMM. The tables, as shown in Figure 7.3, undergo rotation, aligning the main diagonal in a horizontal orientation. The m table exclusively utilize the main diagonal and upper triangle, whereas the s table utilizes only the upper triangle. The minimum order of scalar multiplications required to multiply the 6 matrices is denoted as $m[1,6] = 15125$, amounting to 15125 entries excluding those involving tangent as shown in Figure 7.3. When computing, pairs with the same color are considered.

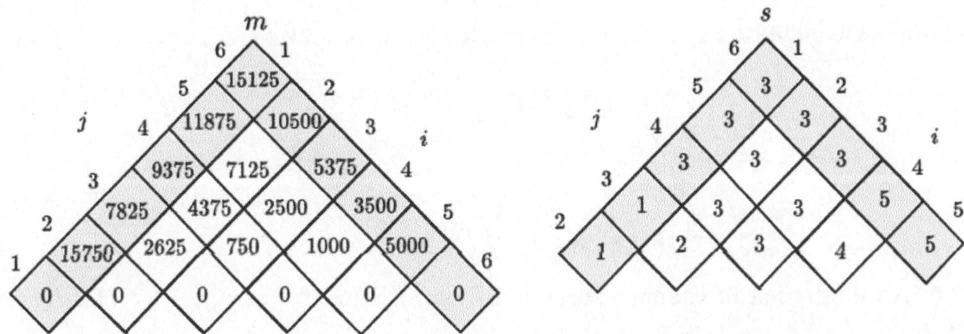

Figure 7.3: An illustration of Matrix-Chain-Order for m and s tables for $n = 6$.

$$m[2,5] = \min \begin{cases} m[2,2] + m[3,5] + p1.p2.p3 = 0 + 2500 + 36.15.20 = 13000 \\ m[2,3] + m[4,6] + p1.p3.p5 = 2625 + 1000 + 35.5.20 = 7125 \\ m[2,4] + m[5,5] + p1.p4.p5 = 4375 + 0 + 35.10.20 = 11375 \end{cases}$$

$$m[2,5] = 7125$$

Time and Space Complexity Analysis: The procedure CMM_FIND is utilized to extract the actual multiplication sequence. Its time complexity is $O(n^3)$ due to the presence of three nested loops, with each capable of iterating at most n times.

7.6 Longest Common Subsequence

In the field of algorithm design, a crucial focus area revolves around the development of algorithms that manipulate character strings. The capacity to identify patterns and resemblances within strings holds great importance in a wide array of applications, ranging from the analysis of documents to the complexities of computational biology. An oft-used measure for gauging the similarity between two strings entails the examination of the lengths of their Longest Common Subsequence (LCS). Within this section, we explore an efficient approach for determining the longest common subsequence between two strings through the application of dynamic programming.

Introduction to LCS: We begin by considering a subsequence of a given sequence, particularly character strings treated as sequences of characters. Given two sequences, $X = \{x1, x2, \ldots, xm\}$ and $Z = \{z1, z2, \ldots, zk\}$, we declare that Z is a subsequence of X if there exists a strictly increasing sequence $< i1, i2, \ldots, ik >$ $(1 \leq i1 < i2 < \ldots < ik \leq n)$ such that $Z =< xi1, xi2, \ldots, xik >$. For instance, if we take $X = IITBHU$ and $Z = IITU$, then Z is indeed a subsequence of X.

Now, let us delve into the concept of finding the LCS between two sequences. To illustrate this, consider two strings, $X = IITBHU$ and $Y = IITKANPUR$. The longest common subsequence of X and Y is $Z = IITU$, as depicted in Figure 7.4.

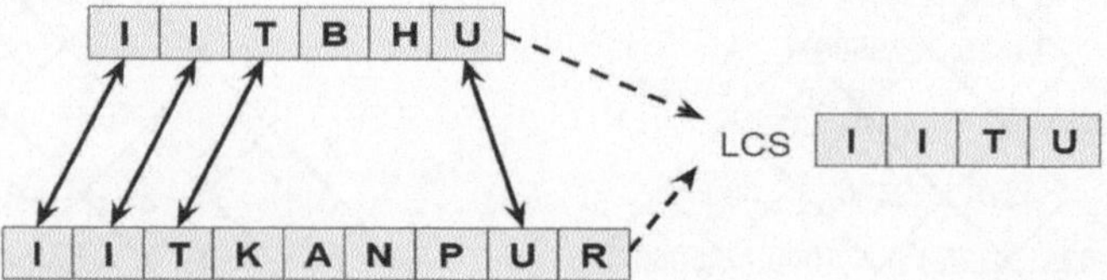

Figure 7.4: An illustration of example scenario of the LCS for two strings $X = IITBHU$ and $Y = IITKANPUR$.

In this context, the LCS represents the sequence of characters that is shared by both strings X and Y, allowing for character deletions while preserving the original order of characters. It is worth noting that there can be multiple subsequences in X and Y. For example, if $X = IITBHU$ and $Y = IITGUWAHATI$ there are two possible subsequences, namely $Z = IITH$ and $IITU$ However, the LCS refers to the longest subsequence among all the possible common subsequences. The simple brute-force approach to this problem involves systematically generating all conceivable subsequences from X and then searching for corresponding matches in Y. This method proves exceedingly inefficient due to the exponential proliferation of potential subsequences. In the rest of this section, we will discuss how to solve LCS problems using dynamic programming.

Solution of LCS problem using dynamic programming

We commence our discussion on finding the LCS using dynamic programming by building the foundation with recursive solutions. This entails computing the lengths of subsequences and employing memoization to ascertain the LCS. In the LCS problem, the input consists of sequences, denoted as $X = \{x1, x2, x3, \ldots, xm\}$ and $Y = \{y1, y2, y3, \ldots, yn\}$ and the objective is to identify a maximum-length common subsequence of X and Y. The length of this common subsequence of Xi and Yj is represented as $LEN(i, j)$. For instance, consider the example where $X6 = IITBHU$ and $Y9 = IITKANPUR$. Their LCS is $Z = IITU$ so $LEN(6,9) = 4$. To initiate our exploration, we formulate a recursive approach for computing $LCS(i, j)$. The recursive formula takes into account three distinct cases:

Case 1: If either sequence is empty, then the longest common subsequence is also empty. Thus, we set $LCS(i,0)$ and $LCS(0,j)$ equal to 0.

Case 2: We focus on the last characters of X and Y. If the last characters match, *i.e.*, $xm = yn$, we include the last character (xm or yn) in the LCS. In this scenario, we find the overall LCS by (i) removing the last character (xm or yn) from both X and Y, (ii) determining the LCS of $Xi - 1$ and $Yj - 1$, and (iii) appending the last character (xm or yn) to the end of the LCS. Consequently, the length of the final LCS is the length of $LEN(Xi - 1, Yj - 1) + 1$. This can be expressed in recursive formulas as follows: $if(xi == yj)\ then\ LEN(i,j) = LEN(i-1,j-1) + 1$.

Figure 7.5 illustrates **Case 2**, where the last characters match. For example, let $Xi = IITBHU$ and $Yj = IITJAMMU$. Since both end with U, it becomes evident that the LCS must also end with U.

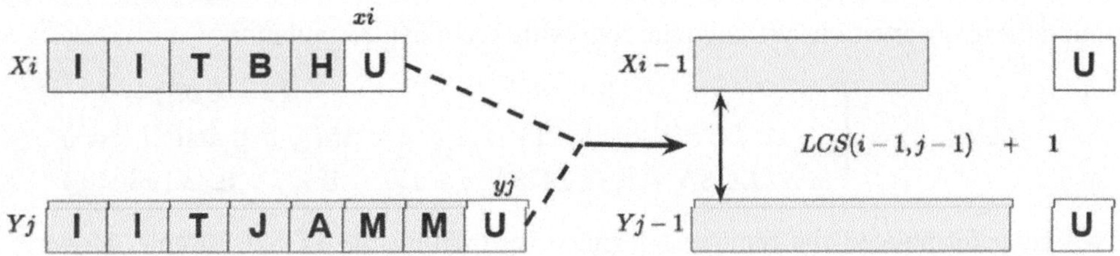

Figure 7.5: An illustration of LCS for two strings whose last characters are equal.

Case 3: When the last characters of X and Y do not match, meaning $xm \neq yn$. We need to make a choice. In this situation, either xi is not a part of the LCS, or yj is not a part of the LCS, and it is even possible that neither of them is included in the LCS. Instead of making a *smart* choice, dynamic programming explores all possibilities and selects the best one. If we decide not to include xi in the LCS, then the LCS of Xi and Yj is the same as the LCS of $Xi - 1$ and Yj, which can be represented as $LEN(i-1,j)$. Similarly, if we exclude yj from the LCS, we can deduce that the LCS of Xi and Yj is the LCS of Xi and $Yj - 1$, denoted as $LEN(i,j-1)$. We calculate both options and choose the one that yields the longer LCS. This can be expressed in recursive formulas as follows: $if(xi \neq yj)\ then\ LEN(i,j) = max(LEN(i-1,j), LEN(i,j-1))$.

Figure 7.6 illustrates **Case 3**, where the last characters do not match. For example, consider $Xi = IITBHU$ and $Yj = IITKANPUR$. Since the last characters of X and Y are U and R, and they do not match, in this case, the LCS can either include U, R, or none of these two characters.

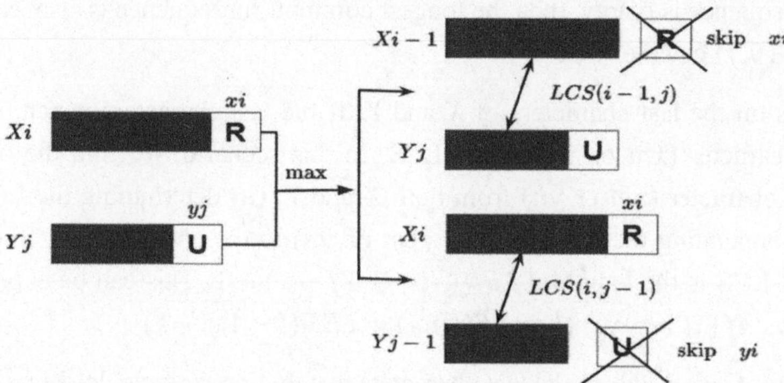

Figure 7.6: Illustration of Case 3 for LCS in dynamic programming, where last characters do not match.

Combining these observations we have the following recursive formulation:

$$LCS(i,j) = \begin{cases} 0 & \textbf{if } i = 0 \textbf{ or } j = 0, \\ LCS(i-1, j-1) + 1 & \textbf{if } i, j > 0 \textbf{ and } xi == yj, \\ \max\{LCS(i-1, j), LCS(i, j-1)\} & \textbf{if } i, j > 0 \textbf{ and } xi \neq yj. \end{cases}$$

Once we have formulated the recursive formula, estimating the LCS is simple. However, a direct recursive implementation of this formula can be highly inefficient and result in exponential-time complexity. Therefore, we need to discuss a procedure for computing the length and constructing the LCS efficiently.

The procedure for estimating the LCS using dynamic programming takes two sequences as inputs, along with their respective lengths m and n. A table $C[i,j]$ is created to compute the length, and another table $B[1{:}m, 1{:}n]$ is maintained to aid in constructing the optimal solution. Intuitively, $B[i,j]$ points to the table entry that corresponds to the optimal subproblem solution chosen when computing $C[i,j]$. Table $C[i,j]$ can be computed as discussed for the recursive formula. Case 1 of the recursive formula is reflected in $C[1{:}m, 0]$ and $C[0,1{:}n]$, both of which are set to 0. Subsequently, if $xi = yj$ (as shown in Case 2 of the recursive formula), then $C[i,j]$ is updated to $C[i-1, j-1] + 1$, signifying that when characters in X and Y are the same, they can contribute to the LCS. The table entry $B[i,j]$contains the symbol $\nwarrow$ because $C[i,j]$ is computed based on $C[i-1, j-1]$. Finally, if $C[i-1,j] > C[i, j-1]$, then $C[i,j]$ is set to $C[i-1,j]$, and conversely, if $C[i-1,j] \leq C[i,j-1]$, then $C[i,j]$ is set to $C[i,j-1]$. In this case, the table entry $B[i,j]$ bears the symbols $\uparrow$ and $\leftarrow$ to indicate that $C[i,j]$ is determined by $C[i-1,j]$ and $C[i,j-1]$. The algorithm $LCS\_LEN(X, Y, m, n)$ summarizes the steps to create the tables $C[i,j]$ and $B[i,j]$.

```
LCS_LEN(X, Y, m, n)
Initialize C[0:m, 0:n] and B[1:m, 1:n] tables
for i = 0 to m
    C[i, 0] = 0
for j = 0 to n
    C[0, j] = 0
for i = 1 to m
    for j = 1 to n
        if xi == yj
            C[i, j] = C[i − 1, j − 1] + 1 and B[i, j] = ↖
        else if C[i − 1, j] > C[i, j − 1]
            C[i, j] = C[i − 1, j] + 1 and B[i, j] = ↑
        else
            C[i, j] = C[i, j − 1] + 1 and B[i, j] = ←
return C and B tables
```

Table C and Table B provide the necessary information to identify the LCS. Extracting the specific characters that form the LCS in the optimal solution involves the following procedure: In dynamic programming, a bottom-up approach is employed to retrieve the LCS of X and Y, with X having a length of m and Y having a length of n. Initiate the process at $B[m, n]$ and navigate through the table by following the symbols. ↑ and ← symbols indicate that the characters of X and Y at this position are not the same. The arrow ↖signifies that both characters are the same and should be included in the LCS. As this approach is bottom-up, it yields reversed LCS, necessitating the traversal from the end to the beginning of LCS. The recursive procedure *LCS_PRINT* outlines the steps for printing the LCS.

```
LCS_PRINT(B, X, m, n)
if m = 0 or n = 0
    exit
if B[m, n] = ↖
    print X[m]
    LCS_PRINT(B, X, m − 1, n − 1)
elseif
    LCS_PRINT(B, X, m − 1, n)
else
    LCS_PRINT(B, X, m, n − 1)
return X
```

Example of LCS problem: Let us apply algorithms to find the LCS of sequences $X = IITBHU$ and $Y = IITGUWAHATI$. The C and B tables are computed by the LCS_LEN algorithm, with the lengths of X and Y being $m = 6$ and $n = 6$. The inputs for LCS_LEN are $X, Y, m = 6, and\ n = 11$. Using lines $2 - 5$, the values of $C[0:6, 0:11]$ are initialized to 0, as shown in Figure 7.7(a). Since the algorithm is row-major, we start from the first row, fill all column values, and then move to the second row until the end of the rows of C. Figure 7.7(a) also illustrates the procedure for filling $C[3,3]$. Here, we observe that $i = j = 3$, and $X[3] = Y[3] = T$. Thus, according to line 9, we have $C[3,3] = C[2,2] + 1 = 3$. Similarly, we fill all other entries of Table C in Figure 7.7(b). The value of $B[3,3]$ is filled using line 9 in Figure 7.7(c). Finally, using lines $8 - 13$, Table B is filled, as shown in Figure 7.7(d).

For printing the LCS, we use the LCS_PRINT algorithm. Starting from the bottom of Table $B(m = 6\ and\ n = 11)$, we follow the arrow symbols, moving up for ↑, left for ←, and jumping diagonally for ↖. Following line 5 of LCS_PRINT, we print the LCS in reverse order whenever ↖ is found. For example, $B[5,8]$ has ↖, and we save it as the last element of the LCS. Next, we find ↖ in $B[3,3], B[2,2]$, and $B[1,1]$, and therefore, $LCS = IITH$.

		Y	1	2	3	4	5	6	7	8	9	10	11
			I	I	T	G	U	W	A	H	A	T	I
X		0	0	0	0	0	0	0	0	0	0	0	0
1	I	0	1	1	1	1	1	1	1	1	1	1	1
2	I	0	1	2	2	2	2	2	2	2	2	2	2
3	T	0	1	2	**3**								
4	B	0											
5	H	0											
6	U	0											

X[3]=Y=[3]='T'
C[3,3]=C[2,2]+1=3

(a) Illustration of filling $C[3,3]$.

		Y	1	2	3	4	5	6	7	8	9	10	11
			I	I	T	G	U	W	A	H	A	T	I
X		0	0	0	0	0	0	0	0	0	0	0	0
1	I	0	1	1	1	1	1	1	1	1	1	1	1
2	I	0	1	2	2	2	2	2	2	2	2	2	2
3	T	0	1	2	3	3	3	3	3	3	3	3	3
4	B	0	1	2	3	3	3	3	3	3	3	3	3
5	H	0	1	2	3	3	3	3	3	4	4	4	4
6	U	0	1	2	3	3	4	4	4	4	4	4	4

(b) Table C using LCN_LEN.

		Y	1	2	3	4	5	6	7	8	9	10	11
			I	I	T	G	U	W	A	H	A	T	I
X		0	0	0	0	0	0	0	0	0	0	0	0
1	I	0	1↖	1↖	1←	1←	1←	1←	1←	1←	1←	1←	1↖
2	I	0	1↖	2↖	2←	2←	2←	2←	2←	2←	2←	2←	2↖
3	T	0	1↑	2↑	**3**↖								
4	B	0											
5	H	0											
6	U	0											

X[3]=Y=[3]='T'
B[3,3]="↖"

(c) Illustration of filling $B[3,3]$.

		Y	1 I	2 I	3 T	4 G	5 U	6 W	7 A	8 H	9 A	10 T	11 I
X		0	0	0	0	0	0	0	0	0	0	0	0
1	I	0	1↖	1↖	1←	1←	1←	1←	1←	1←	1←	1←	1↖
2	I	0	1↖	2↖	2←	2←	2←	2←	2←	2←	2←	2←	2↖
3	T	0	1↑	2↑	3↖	3←	3←	3←	3←	3←	3←	3↖	3←
4	B	0	1↑	2↑	3↑	3↑	3↑	3↑	3↑	3↑	3↑	3↑	3↑
5	H	0	1↑	2↑	3↑	3↑	3↑	3↑	3↑	4↖	4←	4←	4←
6	U	0	1↑	2↑	3↑	3↑	4↖	4←	4←	4↑	4↑	4↑	4↑

(d) Table B using LCN_LEN.

		Y	1 I	2 I	3 T	4 G	5 U	6 W	7 A	8 H	9 A	10 T	11 I
X		0	0	0	0	0	0	0	0	0	0	0	0
1	I	0	↖	↖	←	←	←	←	←	←	←	←	↖
2	I	0	↖	↖	←	←	←	←	←	←	←	←	↖
3	T	0	↑	↑	↖	←	←	←	←	←	←	↖	←
4	B	0	↑	↑	↑	↑	↑	↑	↑	↑	↑	↑	↑
5	H	0	↑	↑	↑	↑	↑	↑	↑	↖	←	←	←
6	U	0	↑	↑	↑	↑	↖	←	←	↑	↑	↑	↑

(e) Illustration of computing LCS using LCS_PRINT algorithm

Figure 7.7: An illustration of computing LCS using dynamic programming.

Time and Space Complexity Analysis: The LCS_LEN procedure has a time complexity of $O(mn)$ because each table entry can be computed in $O(1)$ time. On the other hand, the LCS_PRINT procedure takes $O(m + n)$ time, as it decrements at least one of i and j in each recursive call. Consequently, the overall time complexity for the entire procedure of computing the LCS is $O(mn)$. The space complexity is primarily governed by Tables C and B that are used to store the values and symbols. The size of the table is $(m + 1)(n + 1)$. Thus, the space complexity can be expressed as $O(mn)$.

7.7 Weight Interval Scheduling

The Interval Scheduling Problem stands as a fundamental optimization challenge within computer science and scheduling theory. Its primary aim is to identify the maximum count of non-overlapping intervals from a given set. Each interval is linked to a specific task, defined by both a start time and an end time. The non-overlapping criterion dictates that the commencement of the subsequent task must occur after the completion of the preceding one. Let S be a set of n activity requests, each expressed as an interval $[si, fi]$ denoting a start time si and a finish time fi.

The objective is to construct a schedule that accommodates the greatest possible number of tasks without any overlapping intervals. In a scheduling scenario, tasks may be unweighted or weighted. Unweighted task scheduling typically assumes a unit weight for all tasks. Conversely, weighted interval scheduling introduces the concept of a numeric weight or value associated with each request. For a task i, denoted by $[si, fi, vi]$, vi represents the weight of the task. The goal of weighted interval scheduling is to identify a set of non-overlapping requests such that the sum of their values is maximized. The unweighted version can be viewed as a special case where all weights are equal to 1.

Figure 7.8 illustrates an example scenario of a class timetable, where tasks correspond to periods with unequal intervals. The starting and finishing times of each period are independent. Part (a) depicts the unweighted tasks scenario, where all periods are considered equally important for a student. The scheduling problem's objective in this case is to cover the maximum number of periods. Part (b) assigns weightage to each period, and the goal is to cover the maximum weightage. Therefore, both the unweighted interval scheduling and weighted interval scheduling problems are distinct and significant. While a greedy approach suffices for the unweighted problem, no known greedy solution exists for the weighted version. In this context, we will demonstrate a method based on dynamic programming.

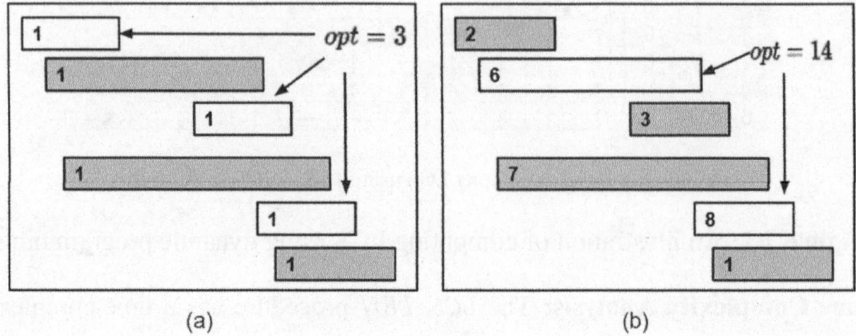

Figure 7.8: An illustration of weighted and unweighted interval scheduling.

Solution of weight interval scheduling using dynamic programming: We begin the solution process for the Weighted Interval Scheduling (WIS) problem using dynamic programming. As discussed earlier in the context of various problems, dynamic programming initially provides a recursive solution, computing the optimal cost of solutions, and constructing the optimal solution.

The dynamic programming approach commences by sorting all tasks in non-decreasing order of finish time, denoted as $f1 \leq \cdots \leq fn$. Subsequently, attention is focused on the last task, fn, in the sorted list, according to finishing time. At this juncture, it remains uncertain whether task fn is part of the optimal scheduling. If it is, then fn is included in the optimal solution, and all requests with intervals overlapping this task must be eliminated. Conversely, if fn is not part of the optimal solution, it is disregarded, and attention shifts to the task $f(n-1)$. The process repeats recursively, computing the optimum solution for the first $n-1$ requests. However, a critical challenge emerges in determining the optimal solution, as the inclusion or exclusion of the fn task depends on it. To address this, dynamic programming calculates the cost of both scenarios recursively, considering the option to either select or reject fn. The final decision is made by choosing the better of the two alternatives.

To initiate the problem-solving process, tasks are sorted based on their finish times, with each task indexed as j from 1 to n. If $j = 0$, there is no action required. We define the values of $p(j)$ and $opt(j)$. The term $p(j)$ represents the largest integer such that $f_b(j) < s_j$, indicating the task index just before the finishing of task j. Figure 7.9 illustrates the values of $p(j)$ for j ranging from 1 to 6. Next, we define $opt(j)$, which signifies the maximum achievable value when considering tasks $\{1, \cdots, j\}$ (assuming tasks are given in order of finish time). This value represents the sum of all selected tasks.

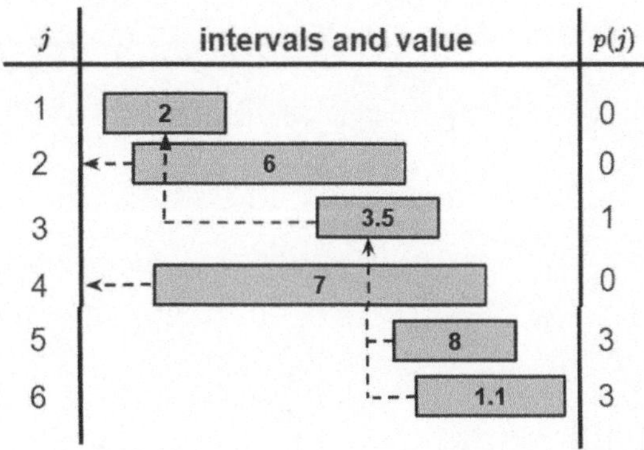

Figure 7.9: An illustration of weight interval scheduling input and p-value.

To calculate $opt(j)$, we consider various cases. Firstly, we address the base case where $j = 0$, signifying that no task is considered. In this case, the value of $opt(j)$ holds no significance, and thus, $opt(0) = 0$. To compute $opt(j)$ for an arbitrary j, where $1 \leq j \leq n$. It is essential to consider whether j is included or not in the optimal schedule. If j is not included in the schedule, we should optimize with the remaining $j - 1$ requests. The optimal schedule utilizes the previous values, *i.e.*, $opt(j) = opt(j-1)$. When the request j is part of the optimal schedule, we add the gain v_j to $opt(j)$. However, considering task j in the scheduler also implies that we can only consider tasks that finished earlier. Therefore, we have $opt(j) = v_j + opt(p(j))$. We employ the dynamic programming principle, trying all feasible options and selecting the best. Here, two options are present, leading to the recursive rule: $opt(j) = max\{opt(j-1), v_j + opt(p(j))\}$.

After formulating the recursive formula, calculating the WIS is a simple process. However, a direct recursive implementation of this formula can be highly inefficient, leading to exponential-time complexity. Therefore, it is essential to discuss an efficient procedure for computing the length and constructing the WIS.

The procedure for estimating the WIS using dynamic programming takes the gain v_j and $p_j$as input. A one-dimensional array $M[0:n]$ is created to compute the total gain, and another array $T[1:n]$ is maintained to aid in constructing the optimal solution. The computation of table $M[j]$ follows the discussed recursive formula. **Case 1** of the recursive formula is reflected in $M[0]$, which is set to 0.

Subsequently, it calculates $N = M[j-1]$ and $C = v[j] + M[p[j]]$ for $1 \leq j \leq n$. If $N > C$ (as shown in **Case 2** of the recursive formula), it indicates that not considering task j provides a better solution. Therefore, the gain remains unchanged, and $M[j] = N = M[j-1]$, with $T[j]$ equal to $j - 1$. Otherwise, the task j is considered, and the new total gain $M[j]$ is the sum of the gain $v[j]$and the previous gain $M[p[j]]$. Here, $T[j]$ is set to $p[j]$, indicating the previously scheduled tasks. The algorithm $WIS\_COMP(V, P)$ summarizes the steps to create the tables $M[j]$ and $T[j]$, where $V = \{v1, v2, \cdots, vn\}$ and $P = \{p1, p2, \cdots, pn\}$.

```
WIS_COMP(V, P)
Initialize M[0: n]
M[0] = 0
for j = 1 to m
    N = M[j - 1]
    C = v[j] + M[p[j]]
    if (N > C)
        M[j] = N
        T[j] = j - 1
    else
        M[j] = C
        T[j] = p[j]
return M[0: n], T[1: n]
```

The WIS_PRINT algorithm is designed to generate and display the optimal schedule based on the information stored in the tables T and P, along with the total number of tasks represented by n. Beginning with the last task, the algorithm iteratively traverses through the tasks, checking whether each task should be included in the optimal schedule. If the task is part of the optimal solution, it is prepended to the schedule list. If not, the algorithm backtracks to the predecessor of the current task and continues the traversal. This process continues until the starting point of the schedule is reached. The final schedule, constructed during this traversal, is then returned as the output of the algorithm. The WIS_PRINTalgorithm thus plays a crucial role in extracting and presenting the optimal schedule determined by the Weighted Interval Scheduling problem [3].

```
WIS_PRINT(T,P,n)
j = n                     //starting from last
S[]                       // empty list
while (j > 0)
    if (T[j] = p[j])      // take request j
        prepend j to the front of the sched.
else
    j = T[j]              // continue with j's predecessor
return sched              // return the final schedule
```

Example of LCS problem: Figure 7.10 depicts the LCS problem example, where it demonstrates the input interval and corresponding p values, followed by all the steps involved in the constriction of table and processor values. Further, Figure 7.11 illustrates the final schedule.

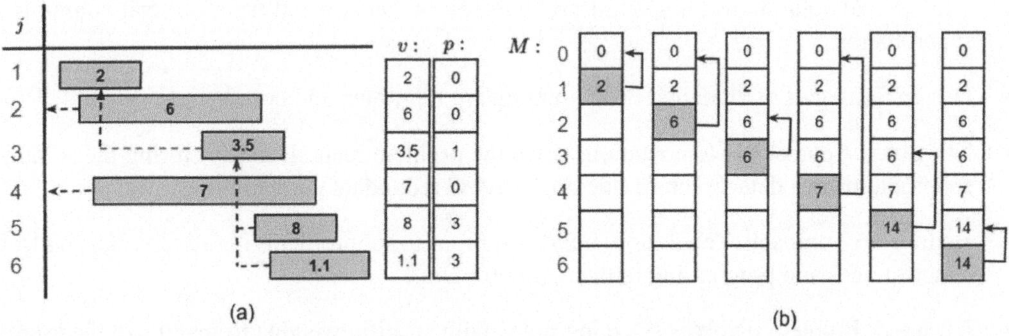

Figure 7.10: (a) Provide the input intervals and corresponding p values and (b) illustrate the step-by-step bottom-up construction of the table and processor values.

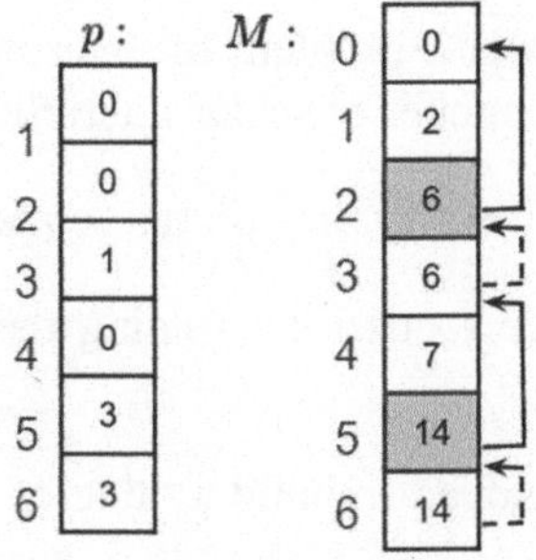

Figure 7.11: An illustration of predecessor links to compute the final schedule.

Time and Space Complexity Analysis: The overall time complexity of the combined WIS_COMP and WIS_PRINTalgorithms is $O(n)$, where n represents the total number of tasks. The *WIS_COMP* algorithm contributes $O(n + m)$ due to the m-times iteration, while *WIS_PRINT* has an $O(n)$ time complexity. Since m is typically propo rtional to n in scheduling problems, the combined efficiency remains $O(n)$. This linear time complexity underscores the algorithm's effectiveness in solving the Weighted Interval Scheduling problem, particularly in scenarios with a significant number of tasks.

UNIT SUMMARY

- Dynamic Programming is a technique in computer science that involves solving complex problems by breaking them down into smaller, overlapping subproblems.
- *It emphasizes reusing solutions to subproblems to optimize overall problem-solving.*
- Dynamic Programming identifies and solves subproblems that recur multiple times within the problem.
- The optimal solution to the overall problem can be constructed from optimal solutions to its subproblems.
- Design Strategies of Dynamic Programming are top-down and bottom up.
- Top-down Approach (Memoization) solve the problem recursively by storing the solutions to subproblems in a data structure (memo) to avoid redundant computations.
- Bottom-up Approach (Tabulation) builds solutions to subproblems iteratively, starting from the simplest ones and progressing to the main problem.
- Knapsack Problem involves selecting items with specific weights to maximize the total value within a limited capacity.
- Dynamic Programming can be applied to efficiently find the optimal combination of items.
- Chained Matrix Multiplication is a problem of determining the optimal parenthesization of matrices to minimize the total number of scalar multiplications.
- Dynamic Programming helps identify the optimal sequence of matrix multiplications.
- Longest Common Subsequence focuses on finding the longest subsequence shared by two sequences.
- Dynamic Programming is employed to build a table of solutions for subproblems, leading to the optimal solution.

- Weight Interval Scheduling involves optimizing the scheduling of weighted tasks within a given time interval.
- Dynamic Programming is applied to efficiently determine the optimal arrangement of tasks to maximize total weight.
- This unit provides a comprehensive exploration of Dynamic Programming, covering its fundamental characteristics, design strategies, and practical applications through the detailed examination of specific problems such as Knapsack, Chained Matrix Multiplication, Longest Common Subsequence, and Weight Interval Scheduling.

MULTIPLE CHOICE QUESTIONS

1. What is the primary focus of dynamic programming?
   a. Maximizing computational complexity
   b. Minimizing computational efficiency
   c. Optimizing outcomes through the breakdown of complex problems
   d. Reducing the number of subproblems

2. What is the time complexity of the recursive approach for generating Fibonacci numbers?
   a. O(n)
   b. O(2^n)
   c. O(log n)
   d. O(n^2)

3. What is the primary goal of dynamic programming?
   a. Maximizing computation time
   b. Minimizing memory utilization
   c. Efficiently solving problems by storing solutions to avoid redundant computations
   d. Avoiding the breakdown of complex problems into smaller subproblems

4. Which technique is employed to efficiently fill a knapsack to achieve the highest possible cumulative value?
   a. Fractional Knapsack Problem
   b. Greedy Algorithm
   c. Dynamic Programming
   d. Brute Force

5. What is the main objective of the 0-1 Knapsack Problem?
   a. Maximizing the number of items selected
   b. Minimizing the weight of items selected
   c. Minimizing the total value of items selected
   d. Maximizing the total value of items selected while adhering to a weight constraint

6. Which strategy involves breaking down the problem into smaller, more manageable subproblems?
   a. Tabulation
   b. Memoization
   c. Divide and Conquer
   d. State representation

7. What does LCS stand for in dynamic programming?
   a. Least Common Subsequence
   b. Longest Continuous Subsequence
   c. Largest Common Sequence
   d. Longest Common Subsequence

8. What is the primary focus of the Chain Matrix Multiplication problem?
   a. Minimizing the number of matrix multiplications
   b. Maximizing the number of matrix multiplications
   c. Ensuring commutativity in matrix multiplications
   d. None of the above

9. What is the purpose of the Weighted Interval Scheduling problem?
   a. To maximize the total number of tasks scheduled
   b. To minimize the total weight of tasks scheduled
   c. To maximize the total value of tasks scheduled
   d. To minimize the total time taken for scheduling

10. Which of the following is NOT a characteristic of dynamic programming?
    a. Memoization, which involves storing the results of expensive function calls and reusing them.
    b. Breaking a problem into smaller overlapping subproblems.
    c. Solving problems in a sequential manner.
    d. Dynamic programming can be used for problems where the solution has an optimal substructure.

11. Which problem variation introduces an intriguing twist by allowing the selection of fractional portions of items?
    a. Knapsack Problem
    b. 0-1 Knapsack Problem
    c. Fractional Knapsack Problem
    d. Dynamic Knapsack Problem

12. What is the time complexity of the dynamic programming approach for generating Fibonacci numbers?
    a. O(n)
    b. O(log n)
    c. O(n^2)
    d. O(2^n)

13. Which characteristic sets dynamic programming apart from brute-force and greedy approaches?
    a. Its reliance on randomness
    b. Its focus on maximizing computational complexity
    c. Its efficient reuse of previously computed solutions
    d. Its preference for localized decision-making

14. What does the Weighted Interval Scheduling problem seek to determine?
    a. The maximum number of overlapping intervals
    b. The minimum number of non-overlapping intervals
    c. The maximum sum of values of non-overlapping intervals
    d. The minimum sum of values of overlapping intervals

15. What is the main difference between the Greedy approach and dynamic programming?
    a. Greedy approach focuses on maximizing computational complexity, while dynamic programming focuses on minimizing it.
    b. Greedy approach relies on randomness, while dynamic programming does not.
    c. Greedy approach may overlook broader patterns, while dynamic programming systematically stores solutions to avoid redundant computations.
    d. Greedy approach involves breaking down problems into smaller subproblems, while dynamic programming does not.

Solution of MCQ:

1	2	3	4	5	6	7	8	9	10	11	12	13	14	15
c	b	c	c	d	c	d	a	c	c	c	a	c	c	c

SHORT AND LONG ANSWER TYPE QUESTIONS

1. Define Dynamic Programming. What are the key characteristics of Dynamic Programming?
2. Explain the top-down approach in Dynamic Programming.
3. How does Dynamic Programming address the issue of overlapping subproblems?
4. Provide an example of a problem where Dynamic Programming is commonly applied.
5. Discuss the fundamental characteristics of Dynamic Programming and how they contribute to problem-solving efficiency. Provide examples to illustrate each characteristic.

1.6 Compare and contrast the top-down (memoization) and bottom-up (tabulation) approaches in Dynamic Programming. When would you choose one over the other, and why?

1.7 Explore the application of Dynamic Programming in solving the Knapsack Problem. Explain the problem statement, the role of Dynamic Programming, and how it optimally selects items within a limited capacity.

1.8 Examine the Longest Common Subsequence problem and its solution using Dynamic Programming. Discuss the steps involved in building a table of solutions for subproblems and how it leads to the determination of the longest shared subsequence between two sequences.

1.9 Analyze the Weight Interval Scheduling problem and how Dynamic Programming can be employed to optimize task scheduling within a given time interval. Discuss the advantages and limitations of using Dynamic Programming in this context.

KNOW MORE

Online courses/materials/resources [Accessed May 2024]

- https://web.stanford.edu/class/cs97si/04-dynamic-programming.pdf
- https://github.com/topics/dynamic-programming-algorithm
- https://www.geeksforgeeks.org/dynamic-programming/
- https://www.coursera.org/learn/dynamic-programming-greedy-algorithms
- https://nptel.ac.in/courses/106106131
- https://www.spiceworks.com/tech/devops/articles/what-is-dynamic-programming/
- https://www.javatpoint.com/dynamic-programming

REFERENCES

[1] Lew, Art, and Holger Mauch. Dynamic programming: A computational tool. Vol. 38. Springer, 2006.

[2] Apostolico, Alberto, and Concettina Guerra. "The longest common subsequence problem revisited." Algorithmica 2 (1987): 315-336.

[3] OpenAI. (2023). ChatGPT (Mar 14 version) [Large language model]. https://chat.openai.com/chat

8 Divide-and-Conquer

UNIT SPECIFICS

This unit covers the following aspects:

- *About Divide-and-Conquer*
- *Characteristics of Divide-and-Conquer*
- *Design strategies of Divide-and-Conquer*
- *Applications in various domains*
- *Organization of the book*

This unit will explore divide-and-conquer methodology, which involves trying all the possible options to find a solution. It will delve into the characteristics of divide-and-conquer algorithms, analyze their time and space complexity, and discover their applications in various domains such as text analysis, combinatorial optimization, and route optimization. Additionally, it covers strategies to enhance the efficiency and effectiveness of divide-and-conquer algorithms, while considering their limitations and alternative approaches. The link given in the QR code provides this unit is supplementary material.

RATIONALE

The rationale of this unit with the design and analysis of algorithms is to introduce and explore the concept of divide-and-conquer methodology as a problem-solving technique. Its goal is to offer insight into the functioning, characteristics, and diverse applications of divide-and-conquer algorithms across various domains.

PRE-REQUISITES

Basic knowledge of data structure and complexity analysis

UNIT OUTCOMES

The outcomes of the Unit are as follows:

U8-O1: Understand the concept of divide-and-conquer

U8-O2: Identify characteristics of divide-and-conquer

U8-O3: Discuss design strategies of divide-and-conquer

U8-O4: Apply divide-and-conquer to various domains

Unit-8 Outcomes	***EXPECTED MAPPING WITH COURSE OUTCOMES*** *(1- Weak Correlation; 2- Medium correlation; 3- Strong Correlation)*				
	CO-1	***CO-2***	***CO-3***	***CO-4***	***CO-5***
U8-O1	-	*1*	*3*	*3*	-
U8-O2	-	*1*	*3*	*3*	-
U8-O3	-	*1*	*3*	*3*	-
U8-O4	*1*	*1*	*3*	*3*	-

8.1 Introduction to Divide-and-Conquer Methodology

Let us explore the concept of the divide-and-conquer methodology through a practical example. Imagine you have two large-size numbers, X and Y, and you intend to multiply them to yield the product, Z. The traditional multiplication method, often known as long multiplication, is employed. This approach initiates by aligning X and Y from their rightmost digits, typically the ones place. Subsequently, each digit in the one's place of X is multiplied by every digit in Y, and these results are meticulously recorded below the line, ensuring alignment with the corresponding digit in Y. Following this, the partial products are summed, with consideration given to carrying digits when necessary. Should there be additional digits in X to the left of the processed portion, the algorithm shifts X to the left, aligning it with the next digit in Y. This process of multiplication and summation continues until all digits in Y have been processed. The end result is the product Z. For X and Y, both being n-digit numbers, this classical multiplication method exhibits a time complexity of $O(n^2)$, making it less efficient for very large numbers due to the substantial number of multiplications and additions involved.

Let us tackle the multiplication of large integers using the divide-and-conquer approach. This methodology is a potent technique for addressing intricate problems by deconstructing them into more manageable subproblems. To employ the divide-and-conquer method for enhancing multiplication efficiency, we initiate the process by breaking down the two substantial numbers, X and Y, into smaller sub-numbers. This entails dividing X and Y into two equal-sized sub numbers, $x1, x0, y1, and\ y0$. In cases where X and Y have an odd number of digits, you can add leading zeros to ensure an even digit count. Subsequently, we embark on the recursive computation of three essential products: $P1 = x1 \times y1, P2 = x0 \times y0$, and $P3 = (x1 + x0) \times (y1 + y0)$. To conclude, the ultimate product, Z, is determined as: $Z = P1 \times 10^n + (P3 - P1 - P2) \times 10^{n/2} + P2$. Let us examine a rectangular field with a length (X) measuring 12 units and a width (Y) of 34 units. Our objective is to determine the area of this rectangular field. Employing the divide-and-conquer method, we can express X as the product of $x1$ and $x0$, where $x0$ is 2 and $x1$ is 1, and likewise, Y is represented as the product of $y1$ and $y0$, with $y0$ being 4 and $y1$ being 3. We can calculate the sub areas as follows: $P2 = 2 \times 4 = 8, P1 = 1 \times 3 = 3$, and $P3 = (2 + 1) \times (4 + 3) = 21$. With the number of digits (n) equal to 2, we compute the final area, Z, as $Z = P1 \times 10^2 + (P3 - P1 - P2) \times 10^1 + P2 = 3 \times 100 + 10 \times 10 + 8 = 408$. Therefore, the area of the rectangular field is 408 square units. This approach significantly reduces the number of required multiplications by dissecting the numbers into smaller components and implementing recursive calls. With each iteration, it effectively diminishes the problem's size by a factor of 2.

```
DC_MULTIPLICATION(X,Y)
    Input : Number X and
    Output : Multiplication of X and Y as Z, i.e., Z = X × Y.
      1. if len(str(X)) == 1 or len(str(Y)) == 1
```

```
2.      return X × Y
3.  else
            n = max(len(str(X)), len(str(Y)))//2    # Find the middle index
            Xl, Xr = divmod(X, 10 ** n)
            Yl, Yr = divmod(Y, 10 ** n)
            P1 = DC_MULTIPLICATION(Xl, Yl)
            P2 = DC_MULTIPLICATION(Xr, Yr)
            P3 = DC_MULTIPLICATION(Xl + Xr, Yl + Yr)
            Z = P1 × 10^(2n) + (P3 − P1 − P2) × 10^n + P2
4.  return Z
```

The $DC\_MULTIPLICATION(X, Y)$ algorithm initially divides the numbers into smaller subproblems, each with roughly half the number of digits, resulting in a factor of 2 in each division. The recursive calls occur in a tree-like structure with a depth of $log(n)$, where n is the number of digits in the input numbers. At each level of the recursion, three multiplications $(P1, P2, P3)$ are computed, each of which has a time complexity of $O(n)$. Combining these factors, the overall time complexity is $O(n^{log(3)})$, which is more efficient than the $O(n^2)$ time complexity of traditional long multiplication, especially for large input numbers. This makes divide-and-conquer multiplication a more efficient choice for large number multiplication.

8.2 Characteristics of Divide-and-Conquer Algorithms

Designing divide-and-conquer algorithms effectively is crucial for optimizing their performance. Let us explore the design strategies using the multiplication of large numbers as an illustrative example:

i. **Divide:** Divide the problem into smaller, more manageable subproblems. In the multiplication example, the large numbers X and Y are split into smaller sub numbers, such as $x1, x0, y1$, and $y0$, each with roughly half the number of digits. This division simplifies the problem and prepares it for further processing.

ii. **Conquer:** Solve the subproblems independently. In the multiplication example, we recursively calculate products $(P1, P2, P3)$ for the sub numbers ($x1, x0, y1, y0$) separately. Solving these subproblems involves independent multiplication operations.

iii. **Combine:** Merge the solutions of the subproblems to derive the solution of the original problem. In multiplication, we combine results of subproblems $(P1, P2, P3)$ to calculate the final product Z using a specific formula that incorporates these subresults.

iv. **Recursion**: Divide-and-conquer algorithms typically involve recursion. The algorithm repeatedly applies the divide, conquer, and combine steps to progressively reduce the problem size. Each level of recursion addresses a smaller subproblem, and the base case terminates the recursion when the problem becomes simple enough to solve directly.

v. **Optimization**: Divide-and-conquer algorithms often aim to optimize performance by reducing the number of redundant operations. In the multiplication example, dividing the numbers into smaller sub numbers reduces the number of multiplications and leads to more efficient computation.

vi. **Efficiency**: Divide-and-conquer algorithms are known for their efficiency, particularly when dealing with large problem instances. They exploit the inherent structure of the problem to streamline the solution process and minimize redundant work.

vii. **Complexity**: The time complexity of divide-and-conquer algorithms is often expressed in terms of the recurrence relation that characterizes the number of operations required at each level of recursion. Analyzing the time complexity helps assess the efficiency and scalability of the algorithm.

Divide-and-conquer algorithms exhibit a set of key characteristics that enable them to efficiently address complex problems by breaking them down into smaller, solvable subproblems. These characteristics are leveraged in a wide range of computational tasks to enhance performance and optimize problem-solving strategies.

8.3 Design Strategies of Divide-and-Conquer Algorithms

Design strategies of divide-and-conquer algorithms involve various techniques to enhance their efficiency and effectiveness. Some common strategies are discussed as follows:

- **Base Case Identification:** Start by identifying the base case for the problem. In the case of multiplying large numbers, it could be when the numbers have a small enough digit count to calculate the product directly using elementary multiplication.

- **Problem Division:** Divide the problem into smaller, more manageable subproblems. In large number multiplication, divide both input numbers into equal-sized halves $(x1, x0, y1, y0)$, ensuring they have an even number of digits.

- **Recursive Approach:** Implement a recursive approach where you calculate the products of the subproblems, namely $P1(x1 \times y1), P2(x0 \times y0)$, and $P3((x1 + x0) \times (y1 + y0))$.

- **Combine Solutions:** Combine the results of the subproblems to derive the final solution. In the multiplication example, you'd use a combination formula to calculate Z based on $P1$, $P2$, and $P3$.

- **Optimize Intermediate Results:** Consider optimizing intermediate results to avoid redundant computations. Cache or memoization techniques can be used to store and reuse subproblem solutions, reducing the number of repeated multiplications.

- **Parallelization:** Explore the possibility of parallelizing the algorithm. Large number multiplication lends itself well to parallel computing, as subproblems can be computed simultaneously on multiple processors or threads.

- **Efficient Data Structures:** Choose efficient data structures for storing and manipulating data during the divide-and-conquer process. This ensures that lookups, insertions, and deletions are performed optimally.
- **Recursion Depth Analysis:** Analyze the depth of recursion. Depending on the problem, you may need to tune the algorithm to reduce recursion depth by, for example, modifying the division strategy or using a more efficient algorithm for small input sizes.
- **Algorithm Variants:** Be open to algorithm variants that might better suit the problem at hand. Different divide-and-conquer approaches or hybrid algorithms may provide better performance for specific inputs.
- **Pruning Subproblems:** Implement techniques to prune the exploration of certain subproblems when it is clear that exploring them is unnecessary. This can save both time and computational resources.

By applying these design strategies, you can develop highly efficient divide-and-conquer algorithms, as exemplified by large number multiplication. These strategies enhance performance, reduce computational overhead, and ensure that the algorithm scales effectively with the size of the problem.

8.4 Examples of Divide-and-Conquer Algorithms

Divide-and-Conquer Algorithms have wide-ranging applications across various domains. In this section, we will delve into three specific applications: *Merge sort, Binary search, Matrix multiplication, Finding the median, and Closest pair problem*. For each of these applications, we will explore the corresponding algorithms, analyze their time complexity, and assess their space complexity.

8.4.1 Merge Sort

The sorting problem serves as a foundational challenge, fundamental to numerous fields and real-world situations. It finds relevance in diverse domains, extending from computer science and data analysis to everyday tasks. The primary goal is to effectively organize a collection of items, ensuring they follow a specific order. To tackle this challenge, a variety of algorithms have been devised, each presenting unique advantages and trade-offs concerning the time and space they require. Among these sorting algorithms, merge sort distinguishes itself as an exceptionally clear and efficient solution.

Merge sort algorithm description: Merge sort follows a divide-and-conquer approach to find a specific target element within the dataset by iteratively splitting the search range in half. Before delving into the Merge Sort algorithm, it is essential to understand the Merge function, which is used to merge and create a sorted array by combining two sorted arrays. The Merge function takes two sorted arrays of size $n/2$, denoted as Upper (U) and Lower (L), as input. It initializes a new array C to store the merged result, with a size of $2n$ since it is merging two $n/2$ sized arrays. The Merge function operates by maintaining two pointers, a and b, initially set to 1 for U and L arrays, respectively. These pointers facilitate the traversal of arrays U and L. It employs a loop to iterate through the elements of the merged array C. In each iteration, it compares the elements at $U[a]$ and $L[b]$. The smaller of the two elements is selected and placed in $C[i]$. If the element from U is smaller, pointer a is incremented. If the element from L is smaller, pointer b is incremented. This process continues until all elements from both U and L are merged into C. The merged array C is then returned. Now, let us delve into the primary Merge Sort (MS) algorithm. It takes an array A as input, which you intend to sort. If the array's size, denoted as $\boldsymbol{n}$, is already 1 (indicating it is a single element or empty), there is no need for further sorting, and the array can be returned as is. However, if the array size is larger than 1, the sorting process commences. The algorithm begins by creating two new arrays, U and L, each of size $n/2$. These arrays are used to divide the original array into two halves. The MS function is then recursively called on the first half of the array, $A[1 \cdots n/2]$, and the result is stored in the U. Similarly, the MS function is invoked on the second half of the array, $A[n/2+1 \cdots n]$, and the result is stored in L. Finally, the two sorted halves, U and L, are merged using the Merge function, as previously discussed, and the merged array is returned as the sorted result. Below is the pseudocode for the $MERGE\_SORT()$ algorithm.

```
MERGE_SORT(A: array[1 ··· n])
    if n = 1
        return A
    New U: array[1:n/2]= MERGE_SORT(A[1 ··· n/2])
    New L: array[1:n/2]= MERGE_SORT(A[n/2 + 1 ··· n])
    return MERGE(U, L)

MERGE(U, L: array[1 ··· n])
    New C: array[1 ··· 2n]
    a = 1
    b = 1
    for i = 1 to 2n
        C[i] = min{U[a], L[b]}
        if U[a] is smaller, increment a; else, increment b
    return C
```

Example: Let us consider an example to understand the Merge Sort algorithm. We will take the input as a list of Indian currency notes, which are initially unordered, *i.e.,* $A[2,1,20,50,5,10,100,2000,500]$. Our objective is to sort them in ascending order, resulting in $A[1,2,5,10,20,50,100,500,2000]$, as shown in Figure 8.1. At the beginning, the input array represents these currency notes, but they are not in any specific order. The Merge Sort algorithm starts by dividing the array into smaller halves until you have sub-arrays of size 1. We begin by splitting the initial array in half, creating two sub-arrays: $U[2,1,20,50,5]$ and $L[10,100,2000,500]$. We then apply the Merge Sort algorithm recursively to each of these sub-arrays. For example, the sub-array $U[2,1,20,50,5]$ is further split into [2,1] and [20,50,5]. We apply Merge Sort to each of these sub-arrays and continue this process until they are reduced to sub-arrays of size 1. The same process is applied to sub-array $L[10,100,2000,500]$, which is split into [10,100] and [2000,500]. When we reach the base case of sub-arrays with only one element, we begin merging them back together in sorted order using the Merge function. For instance, the first pair [2] and [1] is merged into [1,2]. The next pair [20] and [50] is merged into [5,20,50]. The pair [1,2] and [5,20,50] is merged into [1,2,5,20,50]. We continue merging the other pairs until we have [1,2,5,20,50] and [10,100,500,2000] in sorted order. Finally, we merge the two sorted sub-arrays [1,2,5,20,50] and [10,100,500,2000] to obtain a fully sorted array representing Indian currency notes. After this process, the Indian currency notes will be sorted in ascending order: [1,2,5,10,20,50,100,500,2000].

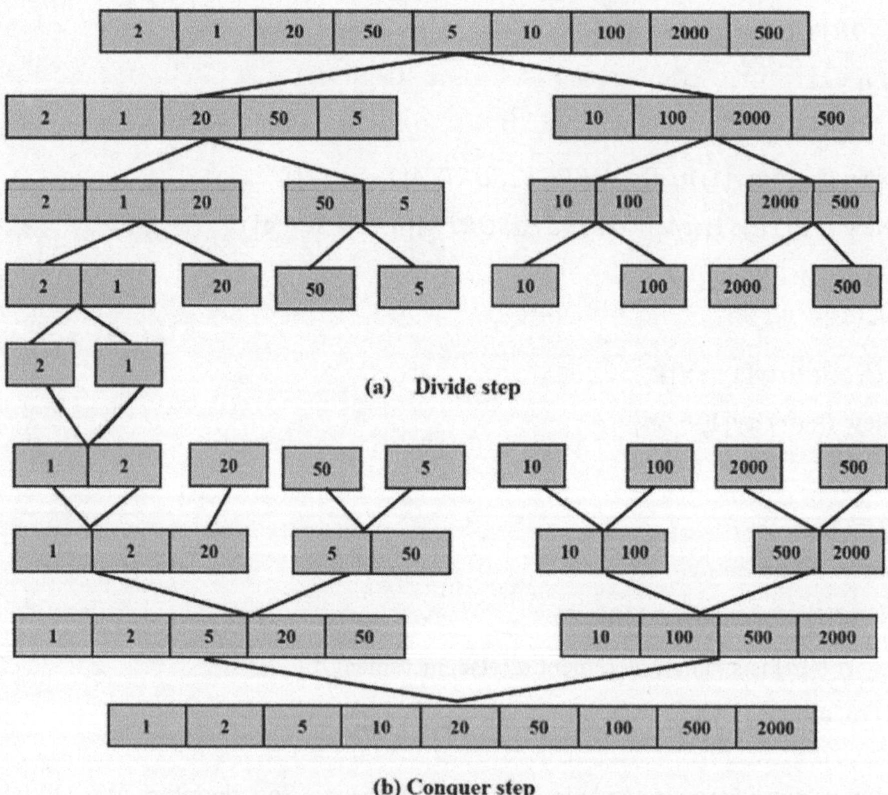

Figure 8.1: An illustrative example of Merge sort using divide and conquer stages.

Time and space complexity analysis: Merge sort is an algorithm that systematically divides the elements to be sorted in half and continually refines the possibilities. The recurrence relation for the Merge Sort algorithm can be expressed as follows: $T(n) = 2T(n/2) + O(1)$. In this relation, $T(n)$ represents the time required to sort an array of size n. The relation signifies that to sort an array of size n, the algorithm divides it into two equal-sized subarrays (each of size $n/2$) and recursively sorts them.

Here, It is often difficult to solve recurrences involving floors and ceilings and therefore we are assuming equal subarrays and not considering floors and ceilings in recurrence relation. The term represents the time taken to merge the two sorted subarrays back into a single sorted array. To solve this recurrence relation, we can apply the Master Theorem, a general framework for analyzing divide-and-conquer algorithms. In the context of merge sort, the values of a and b in Master Theorem's typical form $T(n) = aT(n/b) + cn$ are 2 and 2, respectively. Utilizing **Case 3** of the Master Theorem, we can conclude that merge sort has a time complexity of $O(n\ log_2\ n)$. It reflects the fact that Merge Sort consistently divides the problem into smaller subproblems until it reaches subarrays of size 1 and then merge them back together efficiently. This also implies that the time required for merge sort increases logarithmically with the dataset's size, making it an efficient algorithm for sorting data structures.

Merge Sort is a divide and conquer algorithm that creates temporary arrays for splitting and merging subarrays. During the splitting phase, the algorithm creates additional space to store the divided subarrays. In the merging phase, temporary space is also required to combine the sorted subarrays into a single sorted array. The space used for merging is typically proportional to the size of the input data ($i.e.,$ the n elements being sorted). In the worst-case scenario, the algorithm may require additional space for temporary storage. This space complexity of $O(n)$ means that the algorithm uses extra space that is directly proportional to the size of the input array. In terms of space efficiency, it is important to consider if your system can afford the additional memory required for the sorting process, especially when dealing with large datasets.

8.4.2 Binary Search

The searching problem is a fundamental and ubiquitous computational task that revolves around locating a specific element within a given large collection or set of elements. This problem appears in various domains and applications, ranging from computer science and data analysis to everyday life scenarios. The core objective is to efficiently determine whether the desired element exists in the dataset and, if so, to identify its position or other relevant information. There are several algorithms available to solve this problem, each with its own trade-offs in terms of time complexity and space requirements. Among these algorithms, binary search stands out as one of the most simple and efficient solutions.

Binary search algorithm description: Binary search is a highly efficient search algorithm frequently used with sorted data structures like arrays or lists. It relies on a divide-and-conquer approach to pinpoint a specific target element within the dataset by repetitively dividing the search range in half. To grasp the concept, think of binary search as seeking a particular dish in a lengthy restaurant menu. Picture a menu filled with dishes listed in order, where the first item is Chapati, the second is paneer butter masala, and so on. Your goal is to locate a specific dish, say Biryani, without knowing its exact position. Rather than painstakingly checking each item one by one, binary search offers a smarter method to find your desired dish. Here is how it works: Let all items in manu and searching item are called as element arr and $target$, respectively. You start with the left end of the menu (the first item) and the right end (the last item). You look at the middle item. Such left and right ends are called $left\_pointer$ and $right\_pointer$, respectively. Initialize $left\_pointer$ to 0, indicating the start of the menu, and to $length(arr) - 1$, representing the end of the menu. As long as $left\_pointer$ is less than or equal to $right\_pointer$, repeat the following steps. Calculate $mid\_pointer$ as the middle point between $left\_pointer$ and $right\_pointer$. This is like flipping to the center of the menu. Check if the dish at $arr[mid\_pointer]$ is your desired$target$. If it is, you have found your dish, and you return $mid\_pointer$ which is the menu item number for the Biryani. If $arr[mid\_pointer]$ is less than your $target$ it means the Biryani would be on the right side of the menu, so update $left\_pointer$ to $mid\_pointer + 1$. This narrows down your search to the right half of the menu. If $arr[mid\_pointer]$ is greater than your $target$ it implies the Biryani is on the left side of the menu, so update $right\_pointer$ to $mid\_pointer - 1$ Now, you are focusing on the left half of the menu. Continue these steps until $left\_pointer$ exceeds $right\_pointer$ at which point you have searched the entire menu, and the dish ($target$) is not found. In this case, return -1 to indicate that the Biryani, unfortunately, is not on the menu. This binary search algorithm effectively locates your desired dish, saving you the trouble of examining each item one by one, much like a clever way to find your favorite meal in a restaurant. The following $BINARY\_SEARCH(element\ arr, search\ target)$ algorithm illustrates the steps of searching the items.

$BINARY\_SEARCH(element\ sorted\ arr, search\ target)$

1. $left\_pointer = 0$
2. $right\_pointer = length(arr) - 1$
3. **while** $left\_pointer \le right\_pointer$
4. $\quad mid\_pointer = (left\_pointer + right\_pointer)/2$
5. $\quad$ **if** $arr[mid\_pointer] == target$
6. $\qquad$ **return** $mid\_pointer$
7. $\quad$ **if** $arr[mid\_pointer] < target$

   $\qquad left\_pointer = mid\_pointer + 1$
8. $\quad$ **if** $arr[mid\_pointer] > target$

   $\qquad right\_pointer = mid\_pointer - 1$
9. **return** -1

Example: Consider the inputs for $BINARY\_SEARCH$ algorithm as the elements in the arr represent Indian currency notes (as shown in Figure 8.2), which would look like $10,20,50,100,200,500,2000$ and the search $target$ is to check whether the Indian currency includes a 20 rupee note or not. Here is how the binary search algorithm operates for this specific case: Initialize the $left_pointer$to 0, pointing to the first element (10 in this case), and the $right\_pointer$ to the last index in the array, which is $length(arr) - 1$ (pointing to 2000). The $length(arr)$ is 7 in this case. The algorithm enters a loop that continues as long as $left\_pointer$ is less than or equal to $right\_pointer$. This loop is where the magic happens. Inside the loop, the algorithm calculates the $mid\_pointer$ by averaging the $left\_pointer$ and $right\_pointer$. In this case, it starts with $(0 + 6)/2$, which is 3. So, it checks the element at index 3, which corresponds to 100. The algorithm compares the value at the $mid\_pointer(100)$ with the $target(20)$. Since 100 is greater than 20, it realizes that the 20-rupee note can not be on the right side of 100. Thus, it updates the $right\_pointer$ to $mid\_pointer - 1$, which becomes 2. The algorithm then recalculates $mid\_pointer$ as $(0 + 2)/2$, which is 1. It checks the element at index 1, which is 20. Now, it compares 20 (the element at the $mid\_pointer$) with the $target$ value, which is also 20. A match is found. Since a match is found, the algorithm returns the $mid\_pointer$, which is 1, indicating that the 20-rupee note is present in the Indian currency. The algorithm terminates, having successfully found the target, and the result is 1, indicating that the 20-rupee note is present. This is how binary search works in this example. It quickly identifies whether a 20-rupee note is among the Indian currency denominations by repeatedly dividing the search range in half until it finds the target or determines not there.

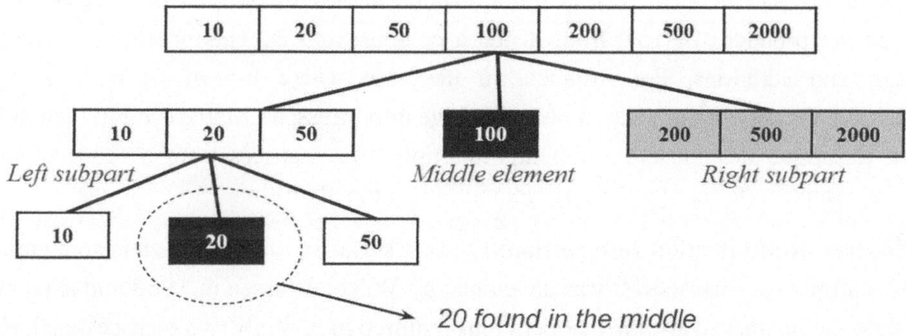

Figure 8.2: An illustrative example of Binary search using divide and conquer stages.

Time and space complexity analysis: Binary search operates by iteratively dividing the search range in half, progressively narrowing down the possibilities at each step. We can denote the time taken for a dataset of size n as $T(n)$, where $T(n/2)$ accounts for the time spent searching within one half of the dataset, and $O(1)$ represents the constant time required for comparisons and calculations. This can be expressed using recurrence relation: $T(n) = T(n/2) + O(1)$.

To solve this recurrence relation, we can apply the Master Theorem, a general framework for analyzing divide-and-conquer algorithms. In the Master Theorem, the recurrence relation is typically in the form $T(n) = aT(n/b) + c$. In the case of binary search, the values of a and b are 1 and 2, respectively. By utilizing Case 2 of the Master Theorem, we can conclude that binary search has a time complexity of $O(log_2 n)$. This means that the time required for binary search grows logarithmically with the size of the dataset, making it an efficient algorithm for searching in sorted data structures. The space complexity of the binary search algorithm is $O(1)$, which means it uses a constant amount of additional memory space regardless of the size of the input dataset. This is because binary search typically doesn't require any data structures or memory allocations that depend on the size of the dataset. It operates by making comparisons and maintaining a few pointers or variables to keep track of the search range, but the amount of memory required for these operations remains constant.

Real-World applications and use cases: The binary search algorithm is a fundamental and efficient technique used in various real-world applications and use cases. For example, it uses file systems, spell checkers, game development, information retrieval, genetics and bioinformatics, network routing, e-commerce and stock market, media libraries, geographical and spatial data, airline reservation system, *etc.*

8.4.3 Matrix Multiplication

Matrix multiplication is a fundamental operation in linear algebra with wide-ranging applications in fields like physics, engineering, computer graphics, and data analysis. Given two matrices, $A(n \times m)$ and $B(m \times p)$, the result is a new matrix, $C(n \times p)$, where A has n rows and m columns, and B has m rows and p columns. The standard matrix multiplication algorithm computes each element of C by performing the dot product of a row from A and a column from B. This process involves multiple multiplications and additions. For instance, in the case where $n = m = p = 2$, a total of 8 multiplications are needed. In this section, we will delve into Strassen's Matrix Multiplication, which is an advanced technique designed to efficiently multiply two matrices with a reduced number of multiplications compared to the standard matrix multiplication algorithm.

Strassen's Matrix Multiplication Description: Strassen's Matrix Multiplication is an algorithm used to efficiently multiply two matrices. It was developed by Volker Strassen in 1963 and is known for its ability to reduce the number of arithmetic operations required to multiply two matrices, making it more efficient than the traditional matrix multiplication algorithm, especially for large matrices. The basic idea behind Strassen's algorithm is to divide the two input matrices into smaller submatrices, perform a limited number of recursive multiplications, and then combine the results to obtain the final product. This approach reduces the number of multiplications from 8 (as required in the standard algorithm) to just 7, although at the expense of additional addition and subtraction operations. This trade-off is beneficial for large matrices because multiplication is usually more time-consuming than addition or subtraction. Strassen's Matrix Multiplication is used to multiply two input matrices, A and B, each of size $n \times n$, where n is a power of 2. The algorithm begins by dividing both matrices into four equal-sized submatrices, i.e., $A = \begin{bmatrix} A11 & A12 \\ A21 & A22 \end{bmatrix}$ and $B = \begin{bmatrix} B11 & B12 \\ B21 & B22 \end{bmatrix}$. The algorithm proceeds to compute seven intermediate products, labeled as ***P*1** to ***P*7**, using these submatrices in a recursive manner. These intermediate products are then used to calculate the four quadrants of the resulting matrix C, where

$C = \begin{bmatrix} C11 & C12 \\ C21 & C22 \end{bmatrix}$. Finally, the algorithm combines these four quadrants to obtain the final product matrix C. The pseudocode for Strassen's Matrix Multiplication illustrates the complete steps of the algorithm, including the calculation of $P1$ to $P7$ and the determination of $C11$ to $C22$. This algorithm is particularly useful for efficiently multiplying matrices and reduces the number of required multiplications compared to standard matrix multiplication techniques.

$STRASSEN\_MATRIX\_MULTIPLY(A, B)$

1. #Split A and B of size $n \times n$, where n is a power of 2
   $A = \begin{bmatrix} A11 & A12 \\ A21 & A22 \end{bmatrix}$ and $B = \begin{bmatrix} B11 & B12 \\ B21 & B22 \end{bmatrix}$
2. # Calculate seven products recursively using these submatrices
   $P1 = A11 \times (B12 - B22)$
   $P2 = (A11 + A12) \times B22$
   $P3 = (A21 + A22) \times B11$
   $P4 = A22 \times (B21 - B11)$
   $P5 = (A11 + A22) \times (B11 - B22)$
   $P6 = (A12 - A22) \times (B21 + B22)$
   $P7 = (A11 - A21) \times (B11 + B12)$
3. # Compute the resulting submatrices
   $C11 = P5 + P4 - P2 + P6$
   $C12 = P1 + P2$
   $C21 = P3 + P4$
   $C22 = P5 + P1 - p3 - p7$
4. # Combine the submatrices into the result matrix C
   $C = \begin{bmatrix} C11 & C12 \\ C21 & C22 \end{bmatrix}$
5. **return** C

Example: To understand Matrix multiplication, we take an example where matrices $A = \begin{bmatrix} A11 & A12 \\ A21 & A22 \end{bmatrix}$ and $B = \begin{bmatrix} B11 & B12 \\ B21 & B22 \end{bmatrix}$. Let first we use standard matrix multiplication and then Strassen's matrix multiplication. We split the matrices A and B into the following submatrices: $A11 = 2, A12 = 3, A21 = 4, A22 = 1$ and $B11 = 1, B12 = 5, B21 = 6, B22 = 7$. In Standard matrix multiplication, calculate the four quadrants of the result matrix C:

$$C11 = A11 \times B11 + A12 \times B21 = 2 \times 1 + 3 \times 6 = 20$$
$$C12 = A11 \times B12 + A12 \times B22 = 2 \times 4 + 3 \times 7 = 31$$
$$C21 = A21 \times B11 + A22 \times B21 = 4 \times 1 + 1 \times 6 = 10$$
$$C22 = A21 \times B12 + A22 \times B22 = 4 \times 5 + 1 \times 7 = 27$$

Finally, the resulting matrix $C = \begin{bmatrix} C11 & C12 \\ C21 & C22 \end{bmatrix}$. We repeat the same example for Strassen's matrix multiplication. Here we first calculate the seven products, $P1$ to $P7$ as:

$$P1 = A11 \times (B12 - B22) = 2 \times (5 - 7) = -4$$

$P2 = (A11 + A12) \times B22 = ((2 + 3) \times 7) = 35$
$P3 = (A21 + A22) \times B11 = ((4 + 1) \times 1) = 5$
$P4 = A22 \times (B21 - B11) = (1 \times (6 - 1)) = 5$
$P5 = (A11 + A22) \times (B11 - B22) = ((2 + 1) \times (1 + 7)) = 24$
$P6 = (A12 - A22) \times (B21 + B22) = ((3 - 1) \times (6 + 7)) = 26$
$P7 = (A11 - A21) \times (B11 + B12) = ((2 - 4) \times (1 + 5)) = -12$

Next, calculate the four quadrants of the result matrix C:

$C11 = P5 + P4 - P2 + P6 = 24 + 5 - 35 + 26 = 20$
$C12 = P1 + P2 = -4 + 35 = 31$
$C21 = P3 + P4 = 5 + 5 = 10$
$C22 = P5 + P1 - P3 - P7 = 24 - 4 - 5 + 12 = 27$

Finally, the resulting matrix $C = \begin{bmatrix} 20 & 31 \\ 10 & 27 \end{bmatrix}$

The example illustrates that the standard matrix multiplication requires 8 multiplications, while Strassen's matrix multiplication requires 7 multiplications. This reduced number of multiplications in Strassen's algorithm is one of its key advantages, making it more efficient.

Time Complexity Analysis: The recurrence equation for Strassen's Matrix Multiplication can be expressed as follows: $T(n) = 7T(n/2) = O(n^2)$. In this relation, $T(n)$ represents the time required to multiply two matrices of size $n \times n$ using Strassen's algorithm. The term $7T(n/2)$ accounts for the seven recursive multiplications performed on smaller submatrices, and $O(n^2)$ represents the time needed for additional operations like additions and subtractions. In the Master Theorem, the recurrence relation is typically in the form $T(n) = aT(n/b) + cn^2$. In the case of Strassen's Matrix Multiplication, the values of a and b are 7 and 2, respectively. By utilizing Case 2 of the Master Theorem, we can conclude that binary search has a time complexity of $O(n^{2.81})$.

8.4.4 Finding the Median

Order statistics is the problem of finding the smallest or largest element in a set of N linearly ordered elements, a challenge encountered in various applications. The algorithm of choice depends on the values of i and N, leading to distinct scenarios and computational complexities. For instance, discovering the smallest element, when i equals 1, is a simple task, requiring a single pass through the list and $N - 1$ comparisons, resulting in a time complexity of $O(N)$. Similarly, for the largest element $(i = N)$, scanning the list once and tracking the maximum element leads to a time complexity of $O(N)$.

Finding the median is more intricate, contingent on the values of N and i. When N is even and $i = N/2$ or $N/2 + 1$, the conventional approach involves sorting the list, necessitating $O(Nlog_2N)$ comparisons. When N is odd and the objective is the $[(N + 1)/2]$th element, the true median, sorting still requires $O(Nlog_2N)$ comparisons. Nevertheless, there exist more efficient algorithms for this specific case. When i is not a constant, the complexity of finding the ith order statistic increases. Specialized algorithms are essential in such scenarios. Notably, the QuickSelect algorithm efficiently finds the ith order statistic with an expected linear time complexity of $O(N)$. Built upon the QuickSort method, QuickSelect partitions elements around a pivot, progressively reducing the problem size in each iteration. Another valuable algorithm, sometimes referred to as the *Blum-Floyd-Pratt-Rivest-Tarjan* or *BFPRT* algorithm, is employed to locate the kth smallest element in an unsorted list. This algorithm, rooted in the *median of medians* technique, proves particularly advantageous when determining the median. This section will delve into the intricacies of the *BFPRT* algorithm.

Blum-Floyd-Pratt-Rivest-Tarjan (BFPRT) algorithm for finding the median: The *BFPRT* algorithm, also known as the *Median of Medians* algorithm, is used to find the kth smallest element in an unsorted list arr. The following $BFPRT(arr, k)$ algorithm illustrates the step-by-step explanation of how it works. Initially, the input array arr is divided into subarrays, each containing five elements. These subarrays are chosen as the pivot for median calculations. Next, for each subarray, it calculates the median. Recursively call the *BFPRT* algorithm on the *medians* list to find the *median of medians*, which is the median element of the *medians* list. This step is the key to selecting an efficient pivot for partitioning. The input array arr is partitioned into two subarrays: $left$ and $right$, based on the $median\_of\_medians$. Elements less than $median\_of\_medians$ go into $left$, while elements greater than $median\_of\_medians$ go into $right$. The algorithm compares the value of k with the number of elements in $left$. If k is equal to the number of elements in $left$ plus one, it means $median\_of\_medians$ is the kth order statistics, so the algorithm returns $median\_of\_medians$. If $\mathbf{k}$ is less than the number of elements in $left$, it means the kth order statistic is in the $left$ subarray, so the algorithm recursively calls *BFPRT* on $left$ with the same value of k. If k is greater than the number of elements in $left$, it means the kth order statistic is in the $right$ subarray, so the algorithm recursively calls *BFPRT* on $right$ with the adjusted value of k.

```
BFPRT(arr, k)
    if length(arr) ≤ 5
        Sort the array arr
        return the kth element in the sorted array (arr[k − 1])
    Divide the input array arr into subarrays of size 5
    medians = []
    for each subarray:
        Compute the median and add it to the medians list
    median_of_medians = BFPRT(medians, length(medians)/2)
    Partition the input array arr based on the median_of_medians
    Let left be the elements less than median_of_medians
```

```
Let right be the elements greater than median_of_medians
if k == length(left) + 1
    return median_of_medians
else if k ≤ length(left)
    return BFPRT(left, k)
else:
    return BFPRT(right, k − length(left))
```

Example: Let us consider an example to understand the $BFPRT$ algorithm. We will take the input as a list of Indian currency notes, which are initially unordered, *i.e.*, $arr = 2,1,20,50,5,10,100,2000,500$. Our objective is to find the median of the input arr.

- Length of $arr = [2,1,20,50,5,10,100,2000,500]$ is 9.
- Divides arr into subarrays of size 5: [2,1,20,50,5] and [10,100,2000,500]
- Median of each subarray: medians [5,500]
- Median of medians: 5 (since length of median is 2, and we take the middle element)
- Partition arr based on the (which is 5):[2,1][20,50,5,10,100,2000,500]
- Compare $k(4)$ with the length of $left(2)$. Since $4 > 2$, we recursively call *BFPRT* on the $right$ subarray with $= 4 - 2 = 2$.
- The right subarray is: [20,50,10,100,2000,500]. Since the $length > 5$, we divide it into subarrays of size 5: [20,50,10,100,2000] and [500].
- Median of each subarray: medians [50,500] and $median\_of\_medians$: 50
- Partition the right subarray based on the $median\_of\_medians$ (which is 50): [20,10] and [100,2000,500].
- We compare $k(2)$ with the length of $left(2)$ therefore we recursively call *BFPRT* on the $left$ subarray with $k = 2$.
- The $left$ subarray is: [20,10]. Since the length ≤ 5, we sort this subarray: Sorted left subarray: [10,20]
- The kth smallest element in this subarray is the element at index $k - 1 = 2 - 1 = 1$.
- Thus, *BFPRT* returns the element 20 as the 4th smallest element in the original arr.

8.4.5 Closest Pair Problem

The Closest pair problem is a fundamental computational challenge that revolves around the task of identifying the pair of points with the smallest distance between them within a given collection of N points. This problem finds relevance and application across various domains, from computational geometry to pattern recognition and beyond. The choice of the most suitable algorithm to tackle this problem depends on two crucial factors: the specific value of N, representing the number of points in the set, and the desired outcome, which could involve finding the actual distance, the point coordinates, or both. As we navigate through this problem, we encounter a spectrum of scenarios and computational intricacies, all of which stem from the variable N and the specific requirements of the task at hand. The larger the N, the more complex the problem becomes, and the choice of algorithm becomes critical to achieve efficient solutions.

In the realm of brute-force approaches, it is evident that the Closest Pair Problem can be solved in $O(N^2)$ time. This section delves into the intricacies of a divide-and-conquer-based algorithm that has been specifically crafted to address the Closest Pair Problem in a more efficient and effective manner. This algorithm optimizes the search for the closest pair of points, significantly reducing the time complexity, especially when N is substantial.

Divide-and-conquer algorithm for solving closest pair problem: The central concept involves divide-and-conquer based algorithms for solving closest pair problems by dividing the set of points in half and recursively searching for the closest pair of points within each half. To comprehend the solution approach more thoroughly, we'll explore it from three different perspectives: the 1-dimensional (1D), 2-dimensional (2D), and d-dimensional (dD) closest pair problem.

The 1D closest pair problem is concerned with a set of N points, as depicted in Figure 8.3. We initiate the process by partitioning the set of points, denoted as N, into two distinct subsets: $N1$ and $N2$. This partition is executed based on a specific x-coordinate value, ensuring that for every point p in $N1$ and every point q in $N2$, p is less than q in terms of their x-coordinates. Subsequently, we proceed with a recursive approach, computing the closest pair within each of these subsets. Specifically, we identify the closest pair $(p1, p2)$ within $N1$ and $((q1, q2))$ within $N2$. Throughout this process, we maintain a record of the smallest separation encountered up to that point, represented as δ. This value is determined as $\delta = min(|p2 - p1|, |q2 - q1|)$. The closest pair could be one of the following combinations: $\{p1, p2\}, \{q1, q2\}$ or, in certain cases, a pair $\{p3, q3\}$, where $p3$ is a member of $N1$, and $q3$belongs to $N2$. The following $1D\_CLOSEST\_PAIR(N)$ algorithm illustrates the steps of finding the closest pair using divide-and-conquer technique.

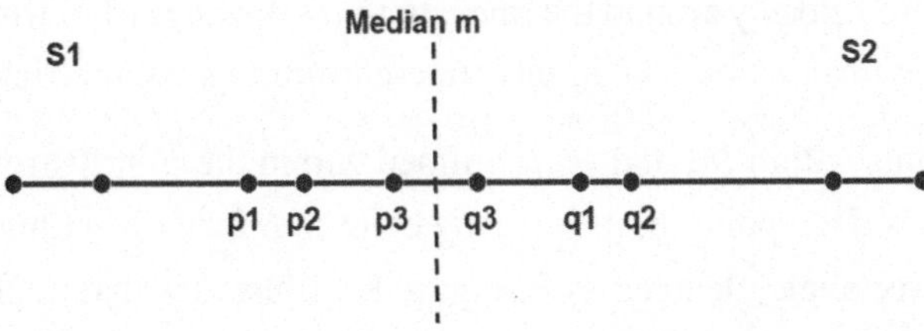

Figure 8.3: 1D closest pair problem is concerned with a set of points.

```
1D_CLOSEST_PAIR(N)
  1.  if the size of set N is 1, the output is δ = ∞
```

2. **if** the size of set $N$is 2, the output is $\delta = |p2 - p1|$
3. **for** larger sets:
   m =Compute the median of x-coordinates
   Divide N into two subsets, $N1$ and $N2$, at m.
   Compute $\delta1$ as $1D\_CLOSEST\_PAIR(N1)$
   Compute $\delta2$ as $1D\_CLOSEST\_PAIR(N2)$
   Determine $\delta12$ as the minimum distance across the cut.

   return $\delta = min(\delta1, \delta2, \delta12)$and corresponding pair

The recurrence equation for the 1D closest pair problem can be expressed as follows $T(n) = 2T(n/2) + O(n)$. In this relationship, $T(n)$ denotes the time required to solve the 1D closest pair problem for a set of n points. The term $2T(n/2)$ accounts for the two recursive closest pair computations performed on smaller subproblems. When analyzing the recurrence relation, it is typically expressed in the form $T(n) = aT(n/b) + cn$. In this case, a and b take the values 2 and 2, respectively. By applying Case 2 of the Master Theorem, we can conclude that the time complexity of the algorithm is $O(n \log n)$, particularly for binary search.

The 2D closest pair problem resembles a puzzle with a sheet of paper bearing scattered dots, each representing a point in a 2D space. The challenge lies in pinpointing the pair of dots closest to each other within this 2D realm, and we approach this puzzle systematically. To start, we partition the dots, referred to as N, into two distinct groups, $N1$ and $N2$, using a vertical line denoted as I. The placement of this line is strategic, ensuring a roughly equal distribution of dots on both sides, and it is positioned based on the median x-coordinate of all the points. Within each of these groups, $N1$ and $N2$, we initiate a search for the closest pair of dots. Essentially, we are on a quest to identify the two dots in each group that are closest to each other. The smallest distance found in $N1$ is labeled $\delta1$, while in $N2$, it is $\delta2$. Subsequently, we compare $\delta1$ and $\delta2$ and choose the smaller of the two, which we designate as δ. This δ serves as a representation of the minimum distance between any two points within our entire set of dots. However, the 2D realm introduces a unique challenge. It is entirely plausible that all the dots in both $N1$ and $N2$ are clustered closely around the line l, within a distance of δ from it. In such a scenario, examining all possible point pairs would be highly time-consuming and inefficient.

We recognize that the points within $N1$ and $N2$, confined within the δ-strip around the line I, exhibit a distinct pattern. Let us consider a point, p, in $N1$. Any point in $N2$ that is within a distance of δ from p must lie within a $\delta \times 2\delta$ rectangle, denoted as R. Figure 8.4 illustrates that in 2D space, the number of such rectangles is limited, with at most six potential candidate rectangles. To identify potential mates of p in $N2$, we project p and all $N2$ points onto the line I. We then select points whose projection is within a distance of δ from p, which amounts to at most six points. We can perform this process efficiently for all points in $N1$ by navigating through pre-sorted lists of $N1$ and $N2$.

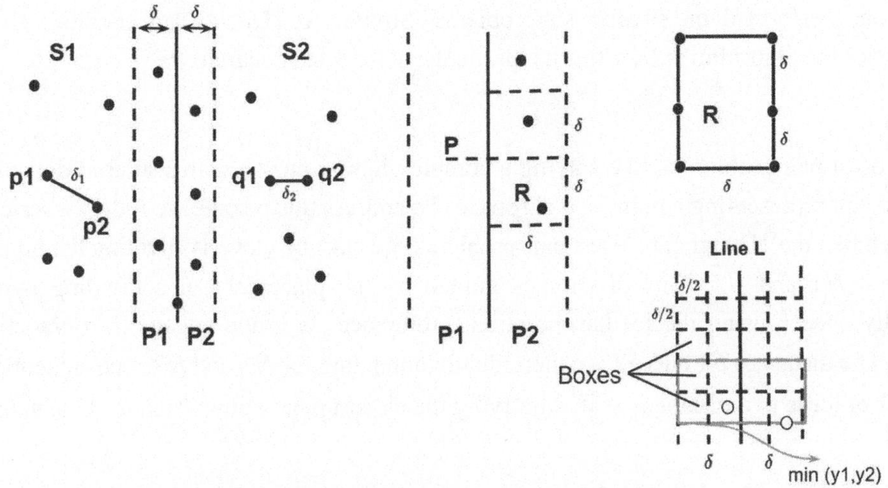

Figure 8.4: An illustration of 2D closed path.

```
2D_CLOSEST_PAIR(N)
if the size of set N is 1, the output is δ = ∞
if the size of set N is 2, the output is δ = |p2 − p1|.
for larger sets:
    m-Compute the median of x-coordinates
    Divide N into two subsets, N1 and N2, at m
    Compute δ1 as 2D_CLOSEST_PAIR(N1)
    Compute δ2 as 2D_CLOSEST_PAIR(N2)
    δ = min(δ1, δ2)
δ_min = δ
Sort all points in the strip δ by their y-coordinates, forming q1 ··· qk, k ≤ N
for i = 1 to k − 1
    j = i − 1
    while j ≥ 0 and y[i] − y[j] < δ   // Let y[i] be the y-coordinate of qi
        distance =distance between qi and qj
        if distance < δ_min:
            δ_min = distance
        j = j − 1
return δ_min and corresponding pair
```

The time it takes to solve this 2D closest pair problem follows a pattern described by a recurrence relation $T(n) = 2T(n/2) + O(n)$. In this relationship, $T(n)$ denotes the time required to solve the 2D closest pair problem for a set of $\boldsymbol{n}$ points. The term $2T(n/2)$ accounts for the two recursive closest pair computations performed on smaller subproblems. Similar to 1D, we can conclude that the time complexity of the algorithm is $O(n \log n)$, particularly for binary search.

The dD closest pair problem is like solving a complex jigsaw puzzle with scattered dots on a sheet of paper, each dot representing a point in a dD space. To address this puzzle, we follow a series of elegant steps. Much like the 1D and 2D closest pair problems, we start by cleverly dividing the input set N into two subsets, $N1$ and $N2$. This division is guided by the placement of a dividing hyperplane H, thoughtfully chosen using the median point as a reference. We then engage in a graceful dance of recursion. The distances $\delta 1$ and $\delta 2$ are individually computed for $N1$ and $N2$. Subsequently, we select the smaller of these two distances as δ, signifying the closest pairs within each of these subsets.

Now, envision a δ thick slab surrounding the dividing hyperplane H, aptly named $N0$. Within this slab, a remarkable inheritance emerges—the δ-sparsity condition. This condition arises from the density of points within a δ distance from H. In this context, any point p can be contained within a δ-cube, with L representing the set of points within this cube. Picture placing a ball with a radius of $\delta/2$ around each point in L. Surprisingly, the volume of the cube C that accommodates this dance is $(2\delta)^d$. Consequently, the maximum number of balls, or points, within C is limited to a mere $c4^d$, translating to an $O(1)$ quantity. This stands as proof of the sparsity of points in this domain.

The complexity is then elegantly transferred to a dimension one less than before. For $N0$, we apply the same divide-and-conquer strategy recursively, gracefully peeling away yet another layer of intricacy. Here's where the elegance truly shines. By harnessing the $\boldsymbol{\delta}$-sparsity condition, we efficiently prune down the number of pairs that require examination within $N0$. Since there are just $O(N)$ points within the δ-thick slab, we are blessed with the luxury of streamlined pair examination, gracefully sidestepping the peril of an exponential surge in potential pair comparisons.

Solving the dD closest pair problem unfolds in a manner that adheres to a recurrence relation $T(n, d) = 2T(n/2, d) + T(n, d-1) + O(n)$. This relationship quantifies the time complexity required to navigate the intricacies of dD space and pinpoint the closest pairs among a set of n points. The $2T(n/2, d)$ the term embodies the recursive nature of the algorithm, where the problem is recursively divided into smaller subproblems in both the number of points (n) and the dimensionality (d). Meanwhile, the $O(n)$ term encompasses the time invested in various operations not directly related to the recursive calls. An interesting parallel can be drawn between the dD closest pair problem and its 2D counterpart. Just as in the 2D case, we can deduce that the time complexity of the algorithm adheres to the pattern of $O(n\,(logn)^{d-1})$. This we derived as $T(n, d) = 2T(n/2, d) + T(n, d-1) + O(n) = 2T(n/2, d) + O(b\,(logn)^{d-2}) + O(n) = O(n\,(logn)^{d-1})$.

$dD\_CLOSEST\_PAIR(N)$

1. **If** the size of set N is 1, the output is $\delta = \infty$
2. **If** the size of set N is 2, the output is $\delta = |p2 - p1|$
3. **for** larger sets:
4. m=Compute the median of x-coordinates
5. Divide N into two subsets, $N1$ and $N2$, at m
6. Compute $\delta 1$ as $dD\_CLOSEST\_PAIR(N1)$
7. Compute $\delta 2$ as $dD\_CLOSEST\_PAIR(N2)$
8. $\delta = min(\delta 1, \delta 2)$
9. strip = PointsWithinStrip(N, m, δ) #Create strip of points within δ from m
10. SortPoints(strip, dimension= 1) # Sort the points in the strip
11. δ_{min} =ClosestPairInStrip(strip,δ) #Calculate minimum distance δ_{min} within strip
12. **return** δ_{min} and corresponding pair

UNIT SUMMARY

- Divide-and-Conquer is a powerful algorithmic paradigm that breaks down complex problems into smaller, more manageable sub-problems to facilitate efficient and systematic problem-solving.
- Characteristics of Divide-and-Conquer involve three main steps: breaking the problem into sub-problems (divide), solving each sub-problem independently (conquer), and combining the solutions to the sub-problems to solve the original problem (merge).
- Design Strategies of Divide-and-Conquer include recursion, where the problem is solved by solving smaller instances of the same problem, and combining, which involves merging the solutions of sub-problems to obtain the solution for the original problem.
- Divide-and-Conquer finds wide-ranging applications across various domains, including computer science, mathematics, and optimization problems, owing to its ability to efficiently tackle complex and computationally intensive tasks.
- One of the classic examples of Divide-and-Conquer, Merge Sort efficiently sorts a list by recursively dividing it into smaller sub-lists, sorting them, and then merging the sorted sublists to obtain the final sorted list.
- Another fundamental application, Binary Search employs the Divide-and-Conquer strategy to locate a target element within a sorted collection, repeatedly dividing the search space until the element is found or determined to be absent.
- Divide-and-Conquer can be applied to matrix multiplication, breaking down the matrix multiplication into smaller sub-multiplications and combining their results to obtain the final product, providing computational efficiency for large matrices.

- The Divide-and-Conquer approach is instrumental in finding the median of a set of elements by recursively partitioning the elements, narrowing down the search space until the median is identified or approximated.
- The Divide-and-Conquer paradigm inherently promotes efficiency and scalability in problem-solving, as it enables the handling of larger and more complex problems by breaking them into smaller, manageable components.
- Divide-and-Conquer remains a foundational concept in algorithmic design, continuously inspiring researchers and practitioners to explore new applications and refine existing strategies for addressing complex computational challenges.

MULTIPLE CHOICE QUESTIONS

1. What is the primary objective of the divide-and-conquer methodology?
   a. To increase computational complexity
   b. To simplify intricate problems by breaking them into manageable subproblems
   c. To introduce redundancy in algorithms
   d. To complicate problem-solving processes
2. In traditional long multiplication, what is the time complexity for multiplying two -digit numbers?
   a. O(n)
   b. O(n log n)
   c. O(n^2)
   d. O(2^n)
3. Which algorithm is more efficient for multiplying large numbers compared to traditional long multiplication?
   a. DC-MULTIPLICATION
   b. Bubble Sort
   c. Insertion Sort
   d. QuickSort
4. What are the key characteristics of divide-and-conquer algorithms?
   a. Absorb, Scatter, Integrate
   b. Divide, Unite, Conquer
   c. Divide, Conquer, Combine
   d. Divide, Multiply, Subtract
5. Which step in the divide-and-conquer approach involves solving subproblems independently?
   a. Divide
   b. Conquer

c. Combine
d. Recursive

6. Which algorithm is NOT mentioned as an example of an efficient divide-and-conquer algorithm?
   a. Merge Sort
   b. Binary Search
   c. Bubble Sort
   d. Matrix Multiplication
7. What is NOT a design strategy of divide-and-conquer algorithms?
   a. Base Case Identification
   b. Problem Division
   c. Recursion Depth Analysis
   d. Loop Unrolling
8. What is the time complexity of Merge Sort?
   a. O(n)
   b. O(n log n)
   c. O(n^2)
   d. O(2^n)
9. What algorithm efficiently finds the ith order statistic with an expected linear time complexity of O(N)?
   a. Merge Sort
   b. QuickSort
   c. Bubble Sort
   d. QuickSelect
10. In Strassen's Matrix Multiplication, how many multiplications are required compared to the standard matrix multiplication algorithm?
    a. More
    b. Less
    c. Equal
    d. Variable
11. Which algorithm efficiently reduces the time complexity for the Closest Pair Problem, especially for large datasets?
    a. QuickSort
    b. Merge Sort
    c. Binary Search
    d. Divide-and-Conquer

12. What is the time complexity of solving the 1D closest pair problem using the divide-and-conquer approach?
    a. O(n)
    b. O(n^2)
    c. O(n log n)
    d. O(2^n)

13. What technique is used to efficiently locate potential mates of a point in the 2D closest pair problem?
    a. Probing
    b. Projection
    c. Permutation
    d. Percolation

14. In the dD closest pair problem, what condition arises due to the density of points within a certain distance from the dividing hyperplane?
    a. Sparse Point Condition
    b. Dense Point Condition
    c. Sparsity Condition
    d. Density Condition

15. Which algorithm is used to find the kth smallest element in an unsorted list in the BFPRT algorithm?
    a. QuickSort
    b. Merge Sort
    c. Binary Search
    d. HeapSort

Solution of MCQ:

1	2	3	4	5	6	7	8	9	10	11	12	13	14	15
b	c	a	c	b	c	d	b	d	b	d	c	b	c	d

SHORT AND LONG ANSWER TYPE QUESTIONS

1 What are the three main steps involved in the Divide-and-Conquer algorithmic paradigm?

2 Explain the significance of recursion and combining in the design strategies of Divide-and-Conquer.

3 Provide a concise overview of Merge Sort and how it applies the Divide-and-Conquer strategy in sorting lists.

4. How does Binary Search utilize Divide-and-Conquer to efficiently locate a target element in a sorted collection?

5. In what way does Divide-and-Conquer enhance computational efficiency in matrix multiplication, especially for large matrices?

6. How does the Divide-and-Conquer approach contribute to finding the median of a set of elements?

7. Discuss how Divide-and-Conquer promotes efficiency and scalability in problem-solving.

8. What is the foundational role of Divide-and-Conquer in algorithmic design?

9. Provide examples of the ongoing inspiration and exploration driven by Divide-and-Conquer in the field of algorithmic design.

10. Explain how Divide-and-Conquer remains relevant and influential in addressing complex computational challenges.

11. What are the three main steps involved in the Divide-and-Conquer algorithmic paradigm, and how do they contribute to efficient problem-solving?

12. Explain the design strategies associated with Divide-and-Conquer, focusing on recursion and combining. How do these strategies facilitate the solution of complex problems?

13. Provide detailed examples of the applications of Divide-and-Conquer in computer science, mathematics, and optimization problems. How does it address computational challenges in each domain?

14. Illustrate the process of Merge Sort as a classic example of Divide-and-Conquer. How does Merge Sort efficiently sort a list, and what are the advantages of using this algorithm?

15. Explore the application of Binary Search as a Divide-and-Conquer strategy. How does it efficiently locate a target element in a sorted collection, and what makes it a fundamental algorithm for search operations?

16. Discuss the application of Divide-and-Conquer in matrix multiplication. How does it break down the problem, solve sub-multiplications, and combine results to enhance computational efficiency, especially for large matrices?

17. Examine how Divide-and-Conquer is instrumental in finding the median of a set of elements. Provide details on how the algorithm recursively partitions elements to identify or approximate the median efficiently.

18. Evaluate the role of Divide-and-Conquer in promoting efficiency and scalability in problem-solving. How does this paradigm enable the handling of larger and more complex problems by breaking them into manageable components?

19 Highlight the foundational significance of Divide-and-Conquer in algorithmic design. How has it influenced the development of new applications and the refinement of existing strategies for addressing complex computational challenges?

20 Explore the ongoing inspiration provided by Divide-and-Conquer for researchers and practitioners. How does this paradigm continue to drive exploration into new applications and the improvement of existing strategies in the field of algorithmic design?

KNOW MORE

Online courses/materials/resources [Accessed May 2024]:

- https://www.geeksforgeeks.org/introduction-to-divide-and-conquer-algorithm-data-structure-and-algorithm-tutorials/
- https://en.wikipedia.org/wiki/Divide-and-conquer_algorithm
- https://www.javatpoint.com/divide-and-conquer-introduction
- https://www.coursera.org/learn/algorithms-divide-conquer
- https://web.stanford.edu/class/archive/cs/cs161/cs161.1138/lectures/06/Small06.pdf
- https://github.com/topics/divide-and-conquer
- https://medium.com/codex/divide-and-conquer-algorithm-f766640ef038

REFERENCES

[1] Lew, Art, and Holger Mauch. Dynamic programming: A computational tool. Vol. 38. Springer, 2006.

[2] Apostolico, Alberto, and Concettina Guerra. "The longest common subsequence problem revisited." Algorithmica 2 (1987): 315-336.

[3] OpenAI. (2023). ChatGPT (Mar 14 version) [Large language model]. https://chat.openai.com/chat

9 NP-Completeness

UNIT SPECIFICS

This unit covers the following aspects:

- *About foundations of computational complexity*
- *Introduces the classes P and NP problem*
- *Delves into NP-Completeness, including Cook's theorem, and its implications.*
- *NP-Completeness demonstrats through Independent Set, Clique, Vertex Cover problems*

This unit will explore the foundations of computational complexity, starting with an introduction to the fundamental concepts. Moving forward, it delves into various computational problems, providing insights into their nature and characteristics. Then introduces the classes P and NP problem and delves into NP-Completeness. The exploration continues with specific examples where NP-Completeness is demonstrated through Independent Set, Clique, and Vertex Cover problems. By studying these concrete instances, the unit aims to provide a comprehensive understanding of computational complexity and the challenges associated with solving certain types of problems efficiently. The link given in the QR code provides this unit is supplementary material.

RATIONALE

The rationale for integrating the design and analysis of algorithms into this unit is to introduce and delve into the concept of P and NP problems, with a particular emphasis on exploring NP-Completeness as a problem-solving technique. This approach aims to provide a comprehensive understanding of how algorithms function, their distinctive characteristics, and their diverse applications across various domains. By incorporating algorithmic design and analysis, the unit aims to equip learners with valuable insights into computational problem-solving strategies and their relevance in real-world scenarios.

PRE-REQUISITES

Prerequisites for this unit include a fundamental understanding of data structures and proficiency in complexity analysis. Learners are expected to have a basic knowledge of how data is organized and manipulated, as well as the ability to analyze the efficiency and performance of algorithms in terms of time and space complexity.

UNIT OUTCOMES

The outcomes of the Unit are as follows:

U9-O1: Understand computational problems, exploring their fundamental concepts

U9-O2: Introduce Class P and NP problems, distinguishing between efficient and non-deterministic polynomial time algorithms.

U9-O3: Explore NP-Completeness, understanding the challenges in solving complex problems efficiently, including Cook's theorem.

U9-O4: Investigate NP-Completeness through Independent Set, Clique, and Vertex Cover problems, gaining practical insights into computational complexities

Unit-9 Outcomes	***EXPECTED MAPPING WITH COURSE OUTCOMES*** *(1- Weak Correlation; 2- Medium correlation; 3- Strong Correlation)*				
	CO-1	***CO-2***	***CO-3***	***CO-4***	***CO-5***
U9-O1	-	-	2	3	2
U9-O2	-	-	2	3	2
U9-O3	-	1	2	3	2
U9-O4	1	1	2	3	2

9.1 Introduction

Previous units have explored various problems and ways to create algorithms to solve them. The main focus of the algorithms is on coming up with practical and effective solutions that make problem-solving easier and more understandable. We have used the keyword $efficient$ multiple times in terms of the effectiveness of the algorithms. Figure 9.1 illustrates that when the value of the input size n is small, both 2^n and n^2 are acceptable. However, for larger values of n neither is sufficient and leads to high running time. It is crucial to grasp the meaning of efficiency in terms of solving a given problem [1-3].

We start the algorithm design with a simple approach known as the brute force searching algorithm. This method searches for the solution among all feasible options. The worst-case running time for such algorithm is an exponential function of the input size n. Generally, an algorithm is considered to run in exponential time if it takes at least $\Omega(c^n)$ for a constant $c > 1$. In contrast to the brute force algorithm, other algorithms are based on strategies like divide-and-conquer, dynamic programming, and network flow. Their worst-case running time is a polynomial function of the input size n denoted as $O(n^c)$, where constant $c > 1$. Figure 9.1 highlights that $O(n\ logn)$ is a polynomial time complexity, as it is a logarithmic factor multiplied by a linear factor (n). This contrasts with exponential functions, such as $O(c^n)$, where the running time grows exponentially with the input size. The significance of $O(n\ logn)$ being polynomial is particularly evident in the efficiency of algorithms commonly encountered in practice. Sorting algorithms like Merge Sort and Heap Sort, for example, have a worst-case time complexity of $O(n\ logn)$. This efficiency is crucial in scenarios where large datasets need to be processed, and polynomial time complexities ensure that the algorithms scale well with increasing input sizes. In general, the worst-case running time of algorithms falls into two categories: polynomial or exponential. Algorithms for solving the given problems can be classified based on these categories. Returning to our keyword $efficient$ algorithms with polynomial worst-case running times are easier to solve compared to exponential times for a given input n. These algorithms are efficient, regardless of whether the constant c of the polynomial is 1 or 10000.

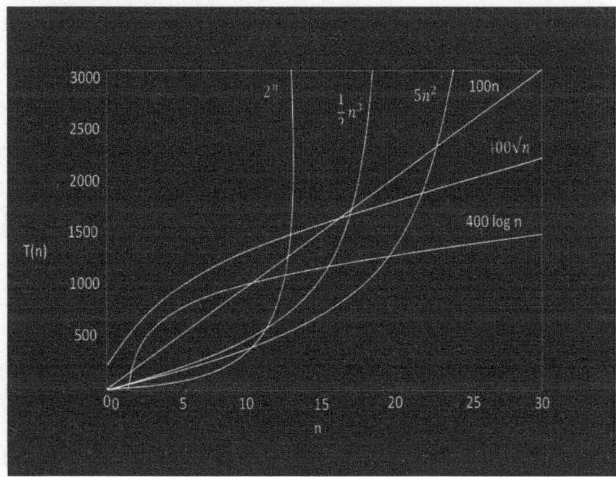

Figure 9.1: Illustration of required operations with increasing input size.

The remainder of this unit is dedicated to a comprehensive exploration of computational problems, delving into specific classes. In Section 9.3, we initiate this unit by examining Class P and NP problems, making a clear distinction between efficient and non-deterministic polynomial-time algorithms. Establishing a solid foundation, Section 9.4 ventures into the intricate domain of NP-Completeness, shedding light on the inherent complexity of select problems. Subsequently, Sections 9.5, 9.6, and 9.7 focus on concrete examples of NP-Completeness, specifically delving into Independent Set (IS), Clique (CLIQUE), and Vertex Cover (VC) problems. Through these examples, the unit aims to provide practical illustrations that reinforce the theoretical concepts under discussion.

9.2 Computational Problems

A computational problem is defined with the objective of identifying an algorithm that transforms the given input into the specified output. An instance of a computational challenge is the Traveling Salesman Problem, wherein the input consists of a group of cities and the distances between every pair of cities. The goal is to identify the most efficient route that visits each city precisely once and returns to the starting city. The complexity of these problems can vary, covering a broad range of domains. They manifest in different types, such as decision problems, where the answer is binary (yes or no), and search problems, where the goal is to discover a solution meeting specific criteria. This section specifically explores the following computational problems: decision problem, language recognition, and search problem.

Decision problem: Computer science and mathematics identify decision problems as inquiries that can be distilled into a yes/no format [2]. The response to such problems typically boils down to a binary choice of yes or no. For instance, in the sorting of given elements, a decision problem might ask, "Are the elements sorted?" Here, the answer is a direct yes or no. These problems assume a critical role in computational complexity theory, where researchers delve into the intricacies of algorithmic problem-solving. Another example of a decision problem is let a set of strings, denoted as X. A string s represents an instance of this problem, and an algorithm, labeled as A, determines the solution to problem X: $A(s) = yes$ if and only if $s \in X$. In preceding units, we have encountered various optimization problems, such as determining the shortest path or finding the minimum-cost spanning tree. The transformation of a problem into a decision problem occurs when its output is simplified to a binary yes or no. For instance, consider the minimum spanning tree decision problem formulated as follows: "Given a weighted graph G and an integer z, does G possess a spanning tree with a weight no greater than z?". In certain cases, the transition to a decision problem may seem less complex. For instance, the aforementioned minimum spanning tree decision problem doesn't necessitate knowledge of the exact weight or specific edges of the minimum spanning tree. However, it underscores that certain problems lack efficient solutions. If efficiently solving the simple decision problem proves challenging, it implies that the broader optimization problem also lacks an efficient solution.

Language recognition: The challenge of language recognition revolves around ascertaining the membership of a given input within a specified language. The primary objective of language recognition is to determine whether a given string, representing an input, belongs to a pre-established language. It is worth noting that a decision problem can be construed as a language recognition problem. To represent a computational problem in the framework of language recognition, the input must be encoded as a string. For instance, when encoding a graph, one can create a string that encapsulates crucial details such as the labels or identifiers of its vertices, the relationships between these vertices represented by edges, and any additional relevant information like weights or costs associated with the edges. This string representation essentially serves as a compact and standardized way to convey the intricate structural and informational aspects of the graph. Employing this methodology, the language that encodes the Minimum Spanning Tree (MST) problem is formulated as:

$$MST = \{serialize(G, z) \mid G \text{ has a minimum spanning tree of weight at most } z\}$$

where, the function $serialize(X)$ is defined to map any combinatorial structure X into a string. Solving the decision problem involves determining whether a specific input string $x = serialize(G, z)$ belongs to MST. The algorithm would answer yes if $x \in MST$, indicating that G has a spanning tree of weight at most z, and no otherwise. Acceptance or rejection of the input is contingent on the algorithm's decision, making decision problems equivalent to language-recognition problems.

Search problem: The primary objective of searching problem is to computationally derive a relevant answer based on a provided input, given that such an answer exists. To illustrate, let us delve into the search version of $3 - coloring\ problem$. In this scenario, given an undirected graph $G = (V, E)$, the task is to discover, if possible, a coloring $c: V \rightarrow \{1,2,3\}$ of the vertices. This coloring must satisfy the condition that for every pair of vertices $(u, v) \in V$, the color assigned to u must be different from the color assigned to v $(color(u) \neq color(v))$. Distinguishing itself from its decision-making counterpart, the search version of this problem unveils layers of intricacy. Beyond the binary determination of the mere existence of a valid coloring, this variant mandates the actual construction of the coloring if indeed a solution prevails. In essence, it extends its inquiry beyond the realm of possibility to the tangible realization of the solution. The challenge, therefore, involves not only affirming the feasibility of a solution but also articulating the specific details encapsulated within that solution. This nuanced aspect of the search problem transforms it into a multifaceted journey of computational discovery, adding a layer of complexity that goes beyond the binary nature of decision problems.

9.3 Class P and NP Problems

In this section, we discuss complexity classes P and NP in detail with examples. A complexity class is the set of all computational problems that can be solved using a specific amount of computational resources.

9.3.1 Complexity Class P

It is time to introduce some important concepts. As we have discussed, a standard convention is to call an algorithm $efficient$ if its worst-case running time is a polynomial function of the input size n denoted as $O(n^c)$, where c is a constant greater than 1. **P** be the class of decision problems that are solvable in polynomial time or there is a polynomial-time algorithm. More formally, the definition of a problem in **P** class is as follows:

P is a set of all languages L for which there exists an algorithm A and a constant $c > 1$, such that A decides L and the worst-case runtime of A is $O(n^c)$.

To establish that problem L belongs to the complexity class **P**, a structured approach is essential. First, create an algorithm that accepts an instance of problem L as input and gives a definite yes or no answer. Next, make sure this algorithm is correct by proving it consistently gives the right answer for both yes and no instances of problem L. In simple terms, if the algorithm says yes for a yes situation (or no for no situation), it should always be right. Finally, validate the efficiency of the algorithm by proving that its worst-case runtime is constrained by a polynomial function of the input size. This involves scrutinizing the time complexity of each algorithmic step and illustrating that the cumulative time complexity remains polynomial. Successfully completing these steps provides compelling evidence that problem L falls within the complexity class **P**.

Let us take an example to understand this process better. Imagine we want to know if a given number is prime (Let us call this problem L). For L to be in **P** complexity class, there should be an algorithm that can quickly decide if a number is prime or not. A simple algorithm could start by checking if the number is 1 or 2, and then look at possible divisors up to the square root of the number. If it finds a divisor, it says no meaning the number is not prime. If it doesn't find any, it says yes meaning the number is prime. This plan follows our rules - it gives the right answer for both yes and yes or no situations. The algorithm has a worst-case runtime bounded by a polynomial function of the input size. Describe an algorithm for L, the algorithm correctly decides L, and the worst-case run time of the algorithm is polynomial proves that the problem L is in **P**.

9.3.2 Verification Algorithms

The core of a language recognition problem involves making a decision about whether a given input string belongs to a specific language or not. In many cases, determining membership in a language requires intricate analysis and may involve complex patterns, structures, or relationships within the strings. Many language recognition problems are challenging to solve, but they share the property of being easily $verifiable$ implies that while determining membership in certain sets (language recognition problems) might be computationally demanding or time-consuming, verifying whether a particular item belongs to these sets is a comparatively simple task.

We consider an example to understand the above discussion. Consider the Hamiltonian cycle problem, where the task is to determine if a given undirected graph possesses a cycle that visits each vertex exactly once. Solving this problem is challenging. However, verifying a claimed Hamiltonian cycle is comparatively simple. If someone provides a sequence of vertices asserting it forms a Hamiltonian cycle, we can easily verify it by ensuring the sequence contains all graph vertices, has no repeated vertices, and exhibits connected edges between consecutive vertices, forming a valid cycle. This verification process, checking conditions in polynomial time, contrasts with the complexity of finding a Hamiltonian cycle. While discovering such a cycle is challenging, confirming its existence, given a potential solution, can be efficiently achieved through verification, highlighting the distinction between problem-solving difficulty and solution verification efficiency.

Formally, for a given language L, where x is an instance and y is a certificate, verification is an algorithm capable of confirming that x belongs to language L with certificate y. If x is not in L, there is nothing to verify. If a verification algorithm exists that runs in polynomial time, we say L can be verified in polynomial time. A verification algorithm takes two inputs: An ordinary string x (the actual input) and a certificate y (proof that the correct answer for x is yes). The verification algorithm A produces one of two outputs: yes or no The **language verified** by a verification algorithm is denoted as

$$L = \{x| \; there\; exists\; y\; for\; which\; A(x, y)\; output\; yes\}$$

Verification algorithms are significant for several reasons. They can prove that a problem is in the complexity class **P** because any problem verifiable in polynomial time is in **P**. Additionally, verification algorithms efficiently check the correctness of solutions to problems. Constructive verification algorithms construct a solution based on the certificate, while non-constructive verification algorithms solely check the validity of the certificate, returning yes or no accordingly. Constructive algorithms are typically more efficient, but non-constructive algorithms prove useful for verifying problems lacking efficient constructive solutions.

Let us take some examples of verification algorithms. Verification for the PATH problem involves a simple algorithm that takes a weighted directed graph G, a vertex pair u and v belonging to edges of the graph $E(G)$, and a number k. Additionally, it considers an ordered list of vertices $(v_1, \ldots, v_m)$. The algorithm outputs yes if the first vertex in the list, v_1, matches u, the last vertex, v_m, matches v, the directed edges (v_i, v_{i+1}) exist for each i, where $1 \leq i < m$, and the total weight of these edges is at most k. In case any of these conditions are not met, the algorithm outputs no. This succinct verification algorithm ensures that the provided list of vertices forms a valid path in the directed graph, with the output indicating the validity based on the specified criteria. Not all languages can be easily verified for membership. For example, the language $UHC = \{G| \; G\; has\; a\; unique\; Hamiltonian\; cycle\}$. There is no known quick way (polynomial-time algorithm) to check if a graph G is in this language. Even if someone shows us one Hamiltonian cycle in G, it is uncertain whether they can provide easily verifiable information to prove it is the only one. Another example is the language $TAUTOLOGY = \{\varphi| \; \varphi\; is\; a\; propositional\; tautology\}$. While recognizing a tautology is simple (a formula is always true), confirming that a given formula is not a tautology is challenging. This is due to the potential infinite counterexamples (truth assignments making the formula false), making a thorough check impractical. These examples highlight the diversity in the ease of verifying membership for different languages.

9.3.3 Complexity Class NP:

Building upon our introduction to complexity class **P**, we now delve into the concept of complexity class **NP** (NP is an abbreviation for **n**ondeterministic **p**olynomial time) encompasses the set of all languages for which membership can be efficiently verified in polynomial time. In other words, **NP** comprises the collection of problems for which yes answers can be validated within a polynomial time constraint. Let n be the size of input, **NP** is defined as

> **P** is a set of all languages L for which there exists an algorithm A and a constant $c > 1$, such that A decides L and the worst-case runtime of A is $O(n^c)$.
>
> **NP** is a set of all languages L for which there exists a verification algorithm A and a constant $c > 1$, such that A verifies L and the worst-case runtime of A is $O(n^c)$.

This implies that the verification process for any problem in **NP** can be accomplished within a reasonable time frame, even for large inputs. Consider the following scenario: you are presented with a problem and a solution. You can quickly verify whether the provided solution is correct. However, you cannot think of any efficient way to find the solution yourself, even with the assistance of the verification process. This scenario illustrates the relationship between complexity classes **P** and **NP**, where **P** represents problems that can be efficiently solved, and **NP** represents problems for which solutions can be efficiently verified. It is evident that if a problem can be efficiently solved without a certificate, it can also be solved with the additional aid of a certificate. Therefore, the set of problems in **P** is a subset of the set of problems in **NP**, implying that **P** ⊆ **NP**. However, the intriguing question remains: are **P** and **NP** equivalent? In other words, does the ability to efficiently verify a solution imply the ability to efficiently find the solution? This question, known as the **P** versus **NP** problem, has been one of the most challenging and enduring unsolved problems in computer science for over 50 years.

A Language is in NP: Proving that a problem L belongs to the complexity class **NP** involves establishing that its solutions can be efficiently verified. First step is to define a certificate for each yes instance of problem L. This certificate should be concise, verifiable, and contain sufficient information to validate the instance as a yes instance. Second, a verification algorithm must be designed that takes an instance of L and a corresponding certificate as inputs. This algorithm should efficiently examine the certificate and determine whether it validates the instance as yes instance. The algorithm should be able to handle both valid and invalid certificates, as well as no instances of problem L. Third, the correctness of the verification algorithm must be verified. This involves demonstrating that the algorithm correctly distinguishes between yes and no instances. Specifically, for any yes instance with a valid certificate, the algorithm should return yes. For any yes instance with an invalid certificate or any no instance, the algorithm should return no. Finally, the polynomial time complexity of the verification algorithm must be proven. This implies that the verification process can be performed efficiently even for large inputs. By successfully completing these steps, one can establish that problem L belongs to the complexity class **NP**. This means that even though finding solutions to problem L might not be efficient, the solutions can be efficiently verified once they are found. The following L_NP(L) illustrates the steps for proving a given problem L is in **NP**.

L_NP (L):

1. Define a certificate for each YES instance of problem L

2. Design a verification algorithm with inputs (an instance of L and certificate)
3. Correctness of the verification algorithm
4. **Return** Yes if instance and certificate are correct for a YES instance
5. **Return** No if the instance and certificate are not correct
6. **Return** No if it is a NO instance.
7. Prove polynomial worst-case run time of algorithm

Example: Let us take an example to prove a given problem L "Determine whether a given graph has a Hamiltonian cycle" is in **NP**. As discussed above, we first define a certificate. In this example, the certificate is "A Hamiltonian cycle in the graph". The verification algorithm takes inputs as given a graph G and a Hamiltonian cycle H and checks whether H is indeed a Hamiltonian cycle in G. If all of the checks pass, then the certificate is valid and the graph has a Hamiltonian cycle. Otherwise, the certificate is invalid or the graph does not have a Hamiltonian cycle. The correctness is for a graph with a Hamiltonian cycle, providing the actual Hamiltonian cycle as a certificate will always result in the verification algorithm returning yes. For a graph without a Hamiltonian cycle, no certificate exists that can make the verification algorithm return yes. Finally, the verification algorithm's worst-case runtime is bounded by $O(n^2)$, where n is the number of vertices in the graph. Therefore, the problem of determining whether a given graph has a Hamiltonian cycle belongs to complexity class **NP**.

9.4 NP-Completeness

This section begins by discussing the concept of reductions, followed by polynomial-time reducibility, then **NP**-hardness and **NP**-completeness. Finally, we delve into proving the Cook-Levin Theorem.

9.4.1 Reductions

The concept of reducing one problem to another plays a crucial role in solving various challenging problems. Let us delve into the intricacies of this process using an example scenario. Consider a problem $P2$ for which a solution is well-established through the application of algorithm $A2$. Now, suppose you encounter another problem $P1$, that exhibits similarities to $P2$. In approaching the resolution of $P1$, you are presented with several strategic options. Firstly, you could opt to solve $P1$ independently, starting from scratch. This involves devising a solution strategy tailored specifically to the unique characteristics of $P1$. Alternatively, you might choose to capitalize on the knowledge and methodology embedded in algorithm $A2$. In this case, you would borrow relevant elements from $A2$ and adapt them to suit the nuances of $P1$. However, a particularly powerful and efficient approach is to explore the possibility of a *reduction* from $P1$ to $P2$. This method involves establishing a connection between the two problems, demonstrating that $P1$ can be transformed into a variant of $P2$. The key steps in this reduction process are as follows:

- Transformation of Inputs: Inputs for problem $P1$ are systematically transformed into inputs suitable for problem $P2$. This conversion is a critical step in aligning the two problems.
- Utilization of $A2$ as a Black-Box: Algorithm $A2$, known to effectively solve problem $P2$, is employed as a 'black-box.' This implies treating $A2$ as a self-contained system without delving into its internal workings.
- Execution of $A2$ to Solve $P2$: The transformed inputs for $P2$ are processed through $A2$ to arrive at a solution for $P2$. As $A2$ is a well-established algorithm for $P2$, it operates as a reliable tool in resolving this interconnected problem.
- Interpretation of Outputs: The outputs generated by $A2$ in solving $P2$ are interpreted and mapped back to provide answers to the original problem, $P1$. This step involves understanding how the solution to $P2$ translates into a meaningful solution for $P1$.

In essence, a reduction from $P1$ to $P2$ leverages the existing solution for $P2$ to efficiently address the analogous problem $P1$. This strategy harnesses the power of established algorithms and their solutions, facilitating a more streamlined and effective problem-solving process. In a more formal sense, problem $P1$ is considered reducible to problem $P2$ if there exists a function, denoted as f, which can take any input x belonging to $P1$ and convert it into an input $f(x)$ for $P2$. Crucially, this transformation ensures that solving $P2$ on the input $f(x)$ provides the solution to $P1$ on the input x. Figure 9.2 illustrates the reduction from P1 to P2.

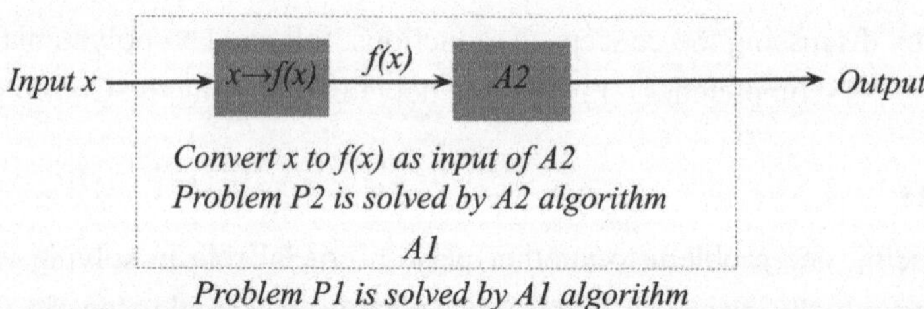

Figure 9.2: Illustration of the reduction from P1 to P2.

Example: Suppose you have a well-established algorithm that effectively solves the problem of matrix multiplication. This algorithm is designed to take two matrices, Let us call them $M1$ and $M2$, as inputs and produces the result of multiplying them together as the output. The general form of this problem can be stated as follows:

- $P2$: *Matrix Multiplication*
- *Inputs*: *Two matrices*, $M1$ *and* $M2$*Matrix Multiplication*
- *Output*: *Multiplying* $M1$ *and* $M2$ *together*

Now, you are faced with a new problem that requires squaring a matrix. The problem statement is as follows:

- $P1$: *Squaring of a Matrix*
- *Inputs*: *A matrix M*
- *Output*: *Squaring M*

Since you already have an algorithm $A2$ for matrix multiplication $P2$, you can leverage it to solve $P1$. The key lies in recognizing the connection between $P2$ and $P1$. You can use $A2$ as follows: The inputs for $A2$: $M1 = M$ (the given matrix) $M2 = M$ (the same matrix). The output of $A2$: The result of multiplying M by itself, which is the squared matrix. By utilizing $A2$ design for matrix multiplication, you effectively address the problem of squaring a matrix. This is an example of problem reduction, where the solution to a known problem (matrix multiplication) is adapted to solve a related problem (matrix squaring). It highlights the efficiency gained by reusing established algorithms in tackling similar computational challenges. Figure 9.3 illustrates how to solve problem $P1$.

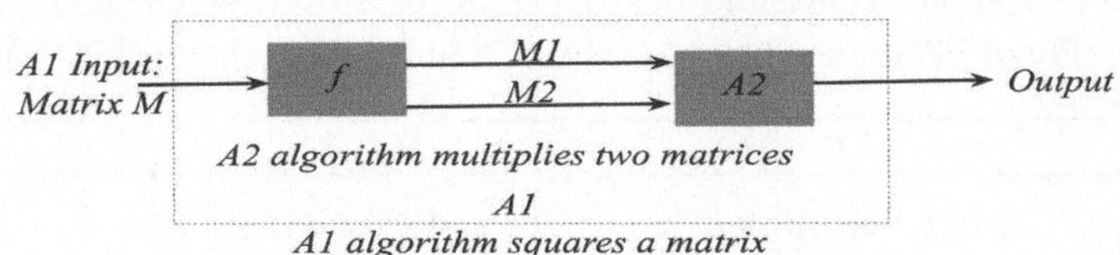

Figure 9.3 Illustrates the solution to problem P1.

9.4.2 Polynomial-Time Reducibility

The concept of reductions proves particularly valuable within Complexity Theory, especially when we can establish a constraint on the computational complexity of the transformation function f as shown in the previous section. Consider a scenario where we have insights into the polynomial time complexity of f. The polynomial-time reducibility, stating that a problem $P1$ is polynomial-time reducible to a problem $P2$ if there exists a function f, computable in polynomial time, which takes any input x associated with $P1$ and transforms it into an input $f(x)$ for $P2$. Importantly, the solution to $P2$ on $f(x)$ is identical to the solution to $P1$ on x. To state this more formally, Polynomial-Time Reducibility:

- Problem $P1$ is polynomial-time reducible to problem $P2$.
- There exists a computable function f, with a polynomial time complexity, such that for any input x in $P1$, f transforms it to an input $f(x)$ in $P2$.
- The solution to $P2$ on $f(x)$ is equivalent to the solution to $P1$ on x.

This concept carries significant implications. For instance, if $P1$ is polynomial-time reducible to $P2$, it implies that the intractability of $P1$ cannot coexist with the tractability of $P2$. In simpler terms, $P2$ is considered as hard as $P1$. It suggests that the difficulty level of solving $P2$ is at least as challenging as solving $P1$. Furthermore, the relationship implies that if $P2$ is tractable, meaning it can be solved efficiently, then $P1$ is also tractable. Conversely, in the contrapositive sense, if $P1$ is proven to be intractable, then $P2$ is also established as intractable. This interconnection between the tractability or intractability of two problems through polynomial-time reducibility sheds light on the relative complexities of these problems within the realm of computational theory.

Theorem: If $P1$ is polynomial-time reducible to $P2$ ($P1 \rightarrow_P P2$) and $P2$ is tractable, then $P1$ is also tractable.

Proof: Let we consider the efficiency of solving $P2$, denoted by the existence of a polynomial-time algorithm $A2$. The polynomial-time reducibility $P1 \rightarrow P2$ allows us to establish a polynomial-time algorithm $A1$ for solving $P1$. The proof unfolds as follows as: The transformation function f, mapping instances from $P1$ to $P2$, operates in polynomial time. Concurrently, the polynomial-time algorithm $A2$ effectively solves $P2$. By constructing $A1$ through the sequential application of function f followed by $A2$, both operating in polynomial time, we ensure that $A1$ also maintains polynomial time complexity. Consequently, $A1$ efficiently solves $P1$. In conclusion, the tractability of $P2$, combined with polynomial-time reducibility $P1 \rightarrow_P P2$, establishes that $P1$ is also tractable. This streamlined presentation emphasizes the derivation of a polynomial-time algorithm for $P1$ based on the tractability of $P2$ and the polynomial-time reducibility relationship.

Lemma: If polynomial-time reducibility $L1 \rightarrow_P L2$ **and** $L2 \in P$ **then** $L1 \in P$
Lemma: If polynomial-time reducibility $L1 \rightarrow_P L2$ **and** $L1 \notin P$ **then** $L2 \notin P$.
Lemma: If polynomial-time reducibility $L1 \rightarrow_P L2$ **and** $L2 \rightarrow_P L3$ **then** $L1 \rightarrow_P L3$

9.4.3 NP-hard

A problem earns the classification of being **NP**-hard when every problem within the complexity class **NP** can be efficiently reduced to it through polynomial-time reducibility, also known as polynomial-time transformation [2-3]. This reduction implies the existence of an algorithm capable of converting an instance of one problem into an instance of another within polynomial time. In the context of a language $L2$ being **NP**-hard, the criterion is established by stating that for every language $L1$ in **NP**, there exists a polynomial-time reduction from $L1$ to $L2$.

A language $L2$ is **NP**-hard if $L1 \rightarrow_P L2$, for all $L1 \in NP$

To prove the NP-hardness of a given problem $L2$, a systematic approach can be adopted. Begin by selecting another problem $L1$ already known to be **NP**. Develop an algorithm that effectively transforms an instance of $L1$ into an instance of $L2$. Crucially, ensure the correctness of the reduction algorithm, verifying that it accepts an instance of $L1$ as input. Demonstrate that the algorithm is indeed a reduction, confirming that it generates a *yes* instance of $L2$ when provided with a *yes* instance of $L1$ and a *no* instance of $L2$ when given a No instance of $L1$. Finally, establish that the worst-case runtime complexity of the algorithm is polynomial. This comprehensive proof strategy underscores the NP-hardness of the given problem L through a carefully crafted reduction process and runtime analysis.

9.4.4 NP-Complete

NP-complete problems are considered to be among the most challenging problems within the **NP** class. In essence, an **NP**-complete problem is one that is at least as hard as the hardest problems in **NP**. A language L is NP-complete if it is **NP**-hard and $L \in NP$ as shown in Figure 9.4.

> A language L is **NP**-complete if $L \in NP$-hard and $L \in NP$

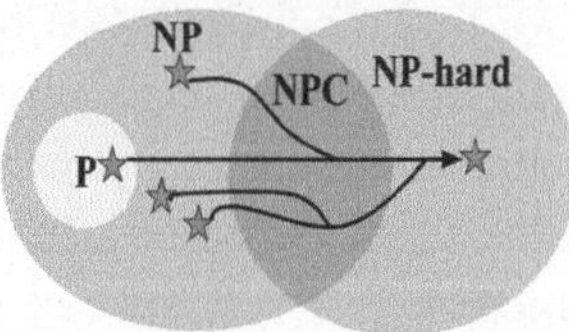

Figure 9.4: Illustration of **P**, **NP**, **NP**-complete (**NPC**), and **NP**-hard.

> **Lemma:** Let a language $L2$ is NP-complete if the following conditions are met:
>
> - $L2 \in NP$: The language $L2$ belongs to the class NP, meaning that given a potential solution, it can be verified efficiently
> - $L1 \rightarrow_P L2$ for some known NP-complete language $L1$: There exists a polynomial-time reduction from a known NP-complete language $L1$ to $L2$. This means that any instance of $L1$ can be transformed into an instance of $L2$ in polynomial time.

The lemma essentially establishes a kind of "hardness" relationship between $L2$ and a known **NP**-complete language $L1$. If we can efficiently solve $L2$, we can also efficiently solve $L1$, and since $L1$ is **NP**-complete, every problem in NP can be reduced to $L1$. However, proving the NP-completeness of a specific problem is an intricate challenge. This complexity arises from the requirement to show that every problem in **NP** can be transformed into the given problem—a criterion set by the definition of **NP**-completeness. This demanding task makes it challenging to assert the **NP**-completeness of a problem directly, contributing to the intricate nature of these proofs. Figure 9.5 illustrates the concept of **NP**-completeness.

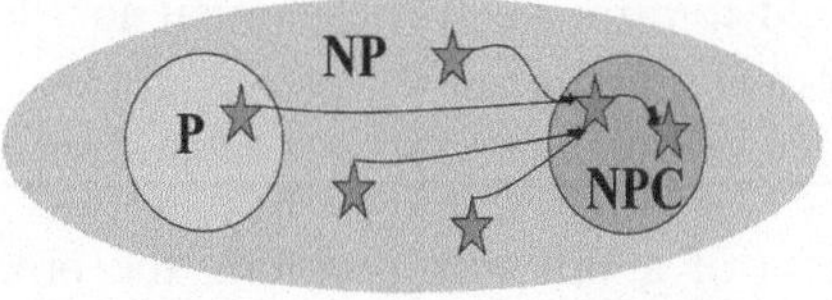

Figure 9.5: Illustrates the concept of **NP**-completeness.

The Cook-Levin Theorem: Before delving into Cook's theory, it is essential to explore a foundational problem known as SAT, which stands for Boolean satisfiability [1-3]. A propositional logic formula φ is in conjunctive normal form (CNF) if it is the many-way AND (conjunction) of clauses. An example of such a boolean formula is $\varphi = (x \vee x \vee x) \wedge (y \vee \neg y \vee \neg x) \wedge (x \vee y \vee \neg y)$, where x and y are literals. A propositional formula is in 3-CNF if it is in CNF and every clause has exactly three literals. The language 3-SAT is defined as follows: $\{\langle\varphi\rangle \mid \varphi$ is a satisfiable 3-CNF formula$\}$. The central question posed by the 3SAT problem is whether there exists an assignment of $True$ or $False$ values to the variables that result in the entire formula evaluating to $True$. In other words, the 3-SAT problem seeks a solution to the question: "Can we find a configuration of $True$ and $False$ assignments to the variables in φ that makes the entire formula true?" This seemingly simple question conceals a significant computational challenge, as finding such a satisfying assignment becomes increasingly complex with larger and more intricate Boolean formulas. Cook demonstrated the existence of a problem known as 3-SAT, establishing its status as NP-complete.

Theorem (Cook-Levin): Boolean satisfiability is **NP**-complete.

Proof Sketch: The initial condition for NP-Completeness is that the problem belongs to **NP** [1-3]. To establish this for 3SAT, it is necessary to show that 3SAT is in **NP**. The approach involves non-deterministically guessing truth values for variables. In the verification context, the certificate comprises the assignment of values to the variables. Subsequently, these values are applied to the formula, and the evaluation process is conducted. It is evident that this entire procedure can be executed within polynomial time.

Moving on to the **NP**-hardness condition, Cook's reasoning unfolds as follows: Any **NP** problem can be encoded as a polynomial-time program with non-deterministic guesses. Considering this program's polynomial runtime, its execution on a specific input can be represented as a linear program without loops or function calls, featuring a polynomial number of lines of code in a chosen programming language. Each line of code undergoes compilation into machine code, and subsequently, each machine code instruction is converted into an equivalent boolean circuit. Each of these circuits is then expressed as a boolean formula, where non-deterministic choices are represented as boolean variables taking values of 0 and 1. Following the definition of non-determinism, the program produces a yes output when there exists a set of decisions that lead to a positive outcome. This signifies the presence of variable assignments, where boolean variables are assigned values of 0 or 1, resulting in the circuit producing an output of 1. This output indicates the fulfillment of the corresponding boolean formula. Consequently, establishing the satisfiability of this formula in polynomial time would confirm whether the initial non-deterministic program generated a positive result within a polynomial timeframe.

To establish the **NP**-completeness of a different problem, the process involves two key steps as illustrated in Figure 9.6 [2-4]. Firstly, demonstrates that the problem is within the class NP, implying its reducibility to the SAT. Secondly, illustrates that SAT (or another known **NP**-complete problem) can be effectively reduced to our chosen problem. This establishes a crucial equivalence between our problem and SAT in terms of solvability within polynomial time. In essence, proving a problem's NP-completeness involves linking it to SAT through reductions, highlighting the inherent complexity and interrelated nature of these computational problems.

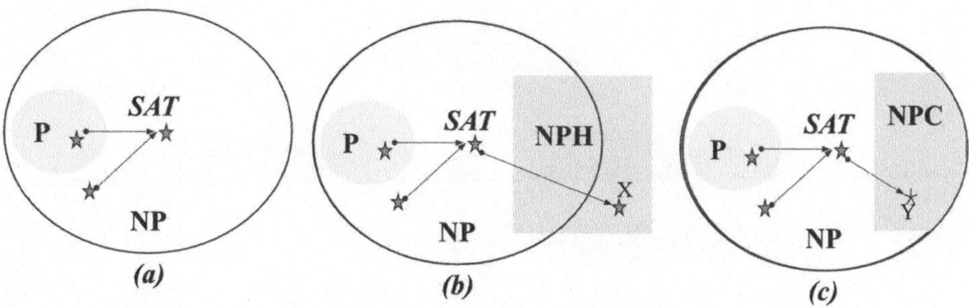

Figure 9.6: Illustration of the structure of NP-completeness (NPC) and reductions. Parts (a)-(c) show that all problems in **NP** are reduciable to SAT, problem X is **NP**-hard (NPH) becasue $SAT \rightarrow_P X$, and Y is **NP**-Complete (NPC) because $SAT \rightarrow_P Y$ and $Y \in NP$, respectively.

Figure 9.7 visually represents the intricate connections and reducibility among various problems falling under the umbrella of NP-completeness. The array of problems considered includes circuit-SAT, SAT, 3-CNF SAT, clique problem, subset problem, vertex cover problem, Hamiltonian cycle, and the traveling salesman problem. As previously discussed, circuit-SAT is a decision problem aiming to ascertain the existence of a valid assignment of truth values to boolean inputs that yields a true output for a given boolean circuit. SAT, another decision problem, explores whether a truth value assignment to boolean variables exists that satisfies a given boolean formula. 3-CNF SAT is a specific case of SAT, where boolean formulas are restricted to clauses with precisely three literals joined by AND operators. Expanding beyond boolean satisfiability, the clique problem, as elaborated in earlier sections, centers on identifying the largest complete subgraph or clique within an undirected graph. The Subset Problem, a decision problem, involves determining if there exists a subset within a given set whose elements sum up to a specified target value. The vertex cover problem revolves around identifying the smallest subset of vertices in an undirected graph, ensuring that each edge is incident to at least one vertex in the subset. The Hamiltonian cycle, a decision problem, inquires whether a given graph contains a cycle that visits each vertex exactly once. Finally, the traveling salesman problem poses an optimization challenge, seeking to find the most efficient, or shortest, closed tour that visits a set of given cities and returns to the starting city. Figure 9.7 goes further to showcase how the traveling salesman problem can be derived from the SAT problem via 3-CNF SAT, clique problem, vertex cover problem, and Hamiltonian cycle. This representation underscores the complex connections and reducibility inherent among these **NP**-complete problems, offering valuable insights into their computational intricacies and shared characteristics.

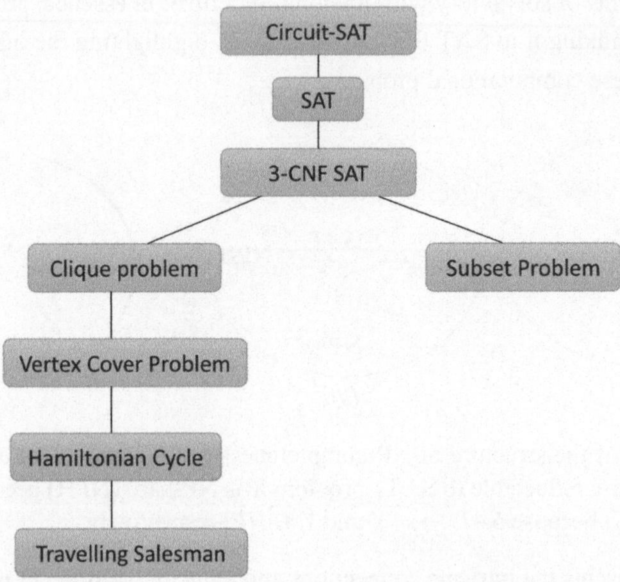

Figure 9.7: Illustrates the reducibility of one problem to another for **NP**-complete.

9.5 NP-Completeness-Independent Set (IS)

Before delving into the **NP**-Completeness of the Independent Set (IS), it is essential to understand the Independent Set problem itself. The IS problem is formulated as follows: given an undirected graph $G = (V, E)$ and an integer k, the question is whether G contains a subset V' of k vertices such that no two vertices in V' share an edge. To illustrate, consider the graph G depicted in Figure 9.8 [2-4]. It possesses an independent set (depicted with shaded nodes) of size 4, but there is no independent set of size 5. Thus, $(G, 4) \in IS$ while $(G, 4) \notin IS$. The independent set problem is relevant in scenarios involving selection, where certain pairs are mutually restricted, preventing simultaneous selection.

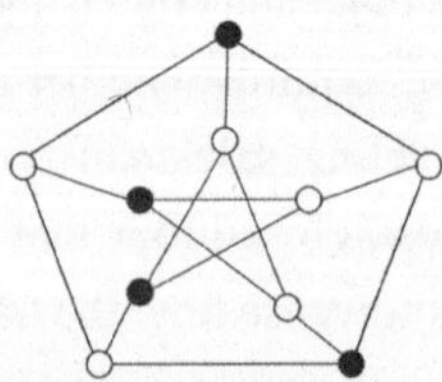

Figure 9.8: Illustrates a graph featuring an independent set of size $k = 4$.

Theorem: Independent Set (IS) is **NP**-complete.

Proof: To prove IS problem is **NP**-complete, we need to show that IS is **NP** and **NP**-Hard [3-6].

- Demonstrate that IS is in **NP**: Initially, IS falls within **NP** because we can efficiently verify whether any given set S is independent and has a cardinality of k in polynomial time. In instances where the answer is yes, we can simplely employ an independent set of size k. Conversely, in cases of no instances, it is evident that no such set exists. Consequently, IS resides in **NP**.
- Pick a known **NP**-complete problem: We already seen that 3SAT is **NP**-Hard. Now we will show that IS is **NP**-Hard via reduction to 3SAT. Suppose we have an instance $F = C_1 \land C_2 \land \ldots \land C_m$, where C_i is the disjunction of three variables, drawn from $x_1, x_2, \ldots, x_n$ and their negations $x'_1, x'_2, \ldots, x'_n$. We create the graph G as follows: For every variable present in each clause, generate a node and assign it the variable's name. Consequently, there might be several nodes labeled x_i or x'_i if these variables appear in multiple clauses. For each clause, establish an edge connecting the three nodes corresponding to the variables within that clause, referring to these nodes and edges as a *clause gadget.* Lastly, for all i, create an edge between every pair of nodes—one labeled x_i and the other labeled x'_i. Utilize our IS black box to determine whether there exists an independent set of size m in G. If such a set is present, respond with yes; otherwise, respond with no.

Therefore we have shown that $3SAT \rightarrow_p IS$. Thus IS is NP-hard, and since we have shown IS to be in NP, IS is **NP**-complete.

9.6 NP-Completeness-Clique (CLIQUE)

The clique problem is a fundamental question in graph theory and computational complexity. It is formally defined as follows: Given an undirected graph $G = (V, E)$ and an integer k, the task is to determine whether the graph G possesses a subset V_0 of k vertices such that, for every pair of distinct vertices u and v within V_0, the edge $\{u, v\}$ is an element of the edge set E. In simpler terms, the objective is to ascertain the existence of a k-vertex subset in G, where the induced subgraph formed by these vertices is complete, meaning that there is an edge between every pair of distinct vertices within the subset.

The CLIQUE problem exhibits a close relationship with two other well-known graph problems: the independent set and the vertex cover problem. Figure 9.9 illustrates of a Clique, independent set, and the vertex cover of the same graph [2-4]. While the connection with independent set is evident, as it involves identifying a subset of vertices that are completely disconnected, the link to the vertex cover problem might not be immediately apparent.

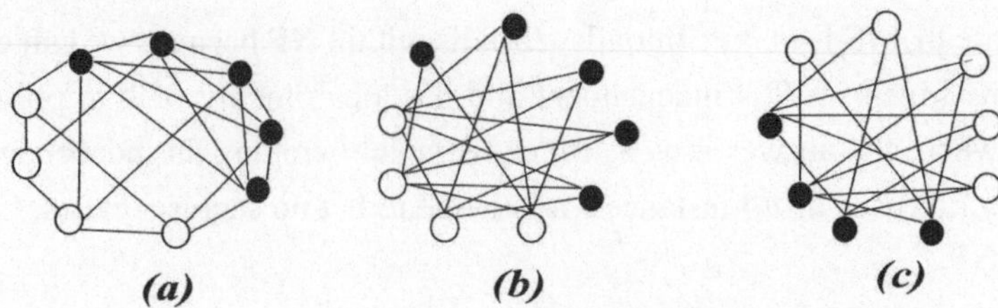

Figure 9.9: Illustrates of a Clique, Independent set, and Vertex Cover. Filled node and connected edges are indicates G' graph of G. Parts (a)-(c) are the V' is a clique of size k in G', V' is a independent set of size k in G, and $V\backslash V'$ is a vertex cover of size $n - k$ in G, respecitvely.

Let G be a graph and G' be the complement graph of G denoted. The edges and non-edges in G' are reversed, meaning that two vertices are connected by an edge in G' if and only if they are not connected by an edge in G. With these definitions in mind, consider the operation $A\backslash B$, denoting the set resulting from removing the elements of B from A. The lemma states that a subset of vertices V' forms a clique in G if and only if its complement $(V\backslash V')$ forms a vertex cover in G'. In other words, a group of vertices that form a complete subgraph in G corresponds to a set of vertices in G' that collectively cover all edges, thus forming a vertex cover. This insightful lemma establishes a bridge between the CLIQUE problem and the Vertex Cover problem, shedding light on the interrelated nature of these fundamental graph problems.

Lemma: Let $G = (V, E)$ be an undirected graph with n vertices, and consider a subset V' of size k. The following conditions are equivalent:

i. V' forms a clique of size k in the complement graph G'.

ii. V' constitutes an independent set of size k in graph G.

iii. The complement of V' in V, denoted as $V\backslash V'$, serves as a vertex cover of size $k - n$for G (where $n = |V|$).

Proof:

(i) ⇒ (ii): Suppose V' is a clique in G'. For every pair of vertices $u, v \in V'$, the existence of $\{u, v\}$ as an edge in G' implies the absence of $\{u, v\}$ as an edge in G [2-4]. This observation verifies that V' constitutes an independent set in G.

(ii) ⇒ (iii): If V' is an independent set in G, then for any pair of vertices $u, v \in V'$, $\{u, v\}$ is not an edge in G. Consequently, each edge in G must have at least one endpoint in $V\backslash V'$, indicating that $V\backslash V'$ serves as a vertex cover for G.

(iii) ⇒ (i): Assuming $V\backslash V'$ is a vertex cover for G, for any pair of vertices $u, v \in V'$, there is no edge $\{u, v\}$ in G, implying the presence of an edge $\{u, v\}$ in G. This establishes that V' forms a clique in G.

The lemma demonstration of the equivalence between the three conditions: forming a clique in the complement graph, constituting an independent set in the original graph, and the complement of the set serving as a vertex cover.

Theorem: CLIQUE is **NP**-complete.

Proof: To prove CLIQUE problem is **NP**-complete, we need to show that CLIQUE is **NP** and $IS \rightarrow_p CLIQUE$.

- $CLIQUE \in \boldsymbol{NP}$: For a given instance (G, k) of the CLIQUE problem, we can efficiently verify membership in **NP**. We non-deterministically guess the k vertices that may form the clique, and these vertices serve as the certificate. The verification process involves checking, in polynomial time, that all pairs of vertices in the guessed set are adjacent, typically accomplished by inspecting $O(k^2)$ entries of the adjacency matrix. If this verification succeeds, the algorithm outputs yes; otherwise, it outputs no. If G indeed possesses a CLIQUE of size k, one of the guesses will be correct, and G will be correctly classified as having a clique of size k. Conversely, if no such CLIQUE exists, all guesses will fail, correctly classifying G as lacking a clique of the specified size.
- $IS \rightarrow_p CLIQUE$: To demonstrate that the IS is polynomial-time reducible to the CLIQUE problem, we introduce the reduction function f. For an instance (G, k) of IS, the function inputs G and k and outputs the pair (G, k). This reduction can be accomplished in polynomial time, as it involves a simple transformation. According to the previously established lemma, this instance is equivalent to the CLIQUE problem.

9.7 NP-Completeness-Vertex Cover (VC)

Vertex Cover (VC) refers to a crucial concept in the context of an undirected graph $G = (V, E)$. In this scenario, a vertex cover is precisely defined as a subset of vertices, denoted as $V' \subseteq V$, such that every edge in the graph has at least one of its endpoints within this selected subset V'. The VC presents a specific computational challenge and can be precisely formulated as follows:

Instance: In the context of a given undirected graph G and an integer k,

Question: Is it the case that G contains a vertex cover, represented by a subset of vertices, with a cardinality of exactly k?

Theorem: Vertex Cover (VC) is **NP**-complete.

Proof: To prove VC problem is **NP**-complete, we need to show that VC is **NP** and $IS \rightarrow_p VC$

- $VC \in NP$: For a given instance (G, k) of the VC problem, the algorithm within the class **NP** involves a nondeterministic guessing strategy. In this process, k vertices are hypothesized to form the sought-after vertex cover (acting as a certificate). To validate this hypothesis, the algorithm undertakes the following steps: First, the algorithm non-deterministically guesses the k vertices that constitute the proposed vertex cover. Next, the algorithm verifies the validity of the guess by ensuring that every edge in the graph G is incident to at least one of the guessed vertices. Finally, if the verification step confirms that the guessed vertices indeed form a vertex cover, the algorithm outputs yes. Conversely, if the verification fails for any reason, the output is no. The rationale behind this approach is that if there exists a vertex cover of size k for the given graph G, one of the non-deterministic guesses will succeed, correctly classifying G as possessing a vertex cover of size k. On the contrary, if there is no such vertex cover, all guesses will fail during the verification process, leading to the correct classification of G as lacking a vertex cover of the specified size.

- $IS \rightarrow_p VC$: Our objective is to demonstrate that, for a given instance of the IS represented by (G, k), we can efficiently transform it into an equivalent instance of the VC problem using a polynomial-time reduction. The reduction function, denoted as f, takes the input (G, k). The process initially computes number of vertices: The function calculates the number of vertices in the graph G, denoted as n. Next, generate vertex cover instance. Here, the output of the function, denoted as $(G, n - k)$, forms the equivalent instance for the VC problem. This reduction process is accomplished in polynomial time, as it involves a series of computations that can be executed in polynomial time with respect to the input size. Therefore, the transformation from an IS instance to an equivalent VC instance, as facilitated by the function f, is a polynomial-time reduction.

UNIT SUMMARY

- Develop a comprehensive understanding of computational problems, exploring fundamental concepts.
- Introduce Class P and NP problems, distinguishing between efficient and non-deterministic polynomial time algorithms.

- Explore NP-Completeness, understanding challenges in efficient problem-solving within computational complexity.
- Investigate NP-Completeness through concrete examples like Independent Set, Clique, and Vertex Cover problems, gaining practical insights.
- Gain proficiency in analyzing algorithmic efficiency and complexities.
- Understand the theoretical foundations of NP-Completeness, including Cook's theorem, and its implications.
- Apply problem-solving skills to various domains by relating algorithmic concepts to real-world scenarios.
- Develop critical thinking and creativity in approaching complex computational challenges.
- Prepare for advanced topics in computer science with a solid understanding of algorithm design and analysis.

MULTIPLE CHOICE QUESTIONS

1. What is the primary objective of a computational problem?
   a. To confuse the solver
   b. To identify an algorithm that transforms input into output
   c. To generate random outputs
   d. To create complexity without solution
2. Which problem involves determining the most efficient route to visit each city precisely once and return to the starting city?
   a. Sorting problem
   b. Minimum spanning tree problem
   c. Traveling Salesman Problem
   d. Language recognition problem
3. What type of problem boils down to a binary choice of yes or no?
   a. Optimization problem
   b. Search problem
   c. Decision problem
   d. Language recognition problem

4. In language recognition, what represents an instance of the problem?
   a. A set of strings
   b. A binary tree
   c. A directed graph
   d. A matrix

5. What problem involves finding a relevant answer based on a provided input?
   a. Decision problem
   b. Language recognition problem
   c. Search problem
   d. Optimization problem

6. Which complexity class includes problems that can be solved in polynomial time?
   a. P
   b. NP
   c. NP-hard
   d. NP-complete

7. What is the set of all languages for which there exists a verification algorithm that runs in polynomial time?
   a. P
   b. NP
   c. NP-hard
   d. NP-complete

8. Which concept states that if a problem P1 can be reduced to problem P2, then P2 is at least as hard as P1?
   a. NP-hardness
   b. Polynomial-time reducibility
   c. NP-completeness
   d. Complexity class

9. What classification is given to a problem that is NP-hard and in NP?
   a. P
   b. NP-hard
   c. NP-complete
   d. NP

10. What problem involves determining if a given graph has a Hamiltonian cycle?
    a. Traveling Salesman Problem
    b. Clique problem
    c. Vertex Cover problem
    d. Hamiltonian cycle problem

11. What is the formal definition of the Clique problem?
    a. Finding the largest complete subgraph within a graph
    b. Determining if a graph has a unique Hamiltonian cycle
    c. Identifying a subset within a set whose elements sum up to a specified target value
    d. Checking if a graph has a subset of vertices forming a complete subgraph

12. What is the primary objective of the Vertex Cover problem?
    a. To find the largest subset of vertices in a graph
    b. To determine if a graph has a Hamiltonian cycle
    c. To verify if a given solution is correct
    d. To find a subset of vertices covering all edges in a graph

13. Which problem exhibits a close relationship with the Vertex Cover problem?
    a. Independent Set problem
    b. Clique problem
    c. Traveling Salesman Problem
    d. Hamiltonian cycle problem

14. What does NP-completeness imply about a problem?
    a. It is the easiest problem in NP
    b. It is as hard as the hardest problems in NP
    c. It can be solved in polynomial time
    d. It is not a decision problem

15. What concept states that if a problem is NP-complete, every problem in NP can be efficiently reduced to it?
    a. Polynomial-time reducibility
    b. NP-hardness
    c. NP-completeness
    d. Complexity class

Solution of MCQ:

1	2	3	4	5	6	7	8	9	10	11	12	13	14	15
b	c	c	a	c	a	b	b	c	d	d	d	a	b	c

SHORT AND LONG ANSWER TYPE QUESTIONS

1 Define Class P and briefly explain its significance in algorithmic efficiency.

2 What does NP-Completeness signify, and why is it a crucial concept in computational theory.

3 Provide a concise explanation of the Independent Set (IS) problem in the context of NP-Completeness.

4 What computational problem does Vertex Cover (VC) address, and how does it relate to NP-Completeness.

5 Explain the concept of computational problems and their significance in computer science. How do they lay the foundation for the study of algorithmic complexities?

6 Elaborate on the distinctions between Class P and NP problems outlined. How does this classification contribute to our understanding of algorithmic efficiency.

7 Discuss the implications of NP-Completeness in algorithmic theory. Provide examples and explain why NP-Completeness is a fundamental aspect of understanding computational complexity.

8 Explore the challenges associated with solving the CLIQUE problem. How does this problem exemplify the concept of NP-Completeness, and what are its real-world applications.

9 Explain the key elements of NP-Completeness, its significance in algorithmic analysis, and its role in classifying computational problems.

10 Explain the NP-Completeness of the following problems: Subset Sum, Hamiltonian Cycle, Traveling Salesman Problem, Knapsack Problem, and Partition Problem. Include key concepts, such as problem definitions, transformations, and their interconnectedness within the NP-Complete class.

11 Examine two decision problems, X and Y. Demonstrate that if X is NP and Y is polynomial-time reducible to X, then Y belongs to the class NP.

12 Demonstrate that the task of locating a satisfying assignment in a Boolean formula is decision-reducible. Specifically, prove that the problem of finding a satisfying assignment for a Boolean formula can be polynomially reduced to the problem of determining whether such an assignment exists.

13 Demonstrate that any two NP-complete problems exhibit polynomial Turing equivalence.

14 Develop an algorithm that can solve SAT-2-CNF in polynomial time.

15 Examine the task of determining the satisfiability of Boolean formulas in 3-CNF, where each clause precisely contains three literals. Establish the NP-completeness of this problem by demonstrating a reduction from SAT-3-CNF to it.

16 Demonstrate that performing a polynomial number of polynomial-time operations can be accomplished in polynomial time.

KNOW MORE

Online courses/materials/resources [Accessed May 2024]:

- https://www.geeksforgeeks.org/introduction-to-np-completeness/
- https://en.wikipedia.org/wiki/NP-completeness
- https://www.javatpoint.com/daa-np-completeness
- https://www.britannica.com/science/NP-complete-problem
- https://www2.seas.gwu.edu/~ayoussef/cs6212/npcomplete.html
- https://www.tutorialspoint.com/what-is-np-completeness-in-toc
- https://www.coursera.org/courses?query=np%20complete
- https://web.stanford.edu/class/archive/cs/cs103/cs103.1156/lectures/26/Small26.pdf

REFERENCES

[1] Thomas H. Cormen, Charles E. Leiserson, Ronald L. Rivest, and Clifford Stein, 2009. Introduction to Algorithms, Third Edition (3rd. ed.). The MIT Press.

[2] David M. Mount, "Notes of Design and Analysis of Computer Algorithms", https://www.cs.umd.edu/class/spring2022/cmsc451/ (accessed Nov.10, 2023).

[3] ChatGPT (Nov 14 version) [Large language model]. https://chat.openai.com/chat, 2023.

[4] James Aspnes, "Notes on Randomized Algorithms", https://www.cs.yale.edu/homes/aspnes/classes/469/notes.pdf (accessed Nov.10, 2023).

[5] Avrim Blum and Anupam Gupta, "Notes of Algorithms", https://www.cs.cmu.edu/~avrim/451f13/ (accessed Nov.10, 2023).

[6] Stephen A. Fenner, "Notes of Analysis of Algorithms", https://cse.sc.edu/~fenner/csce750/ (accessed Nov.10, 2023).

[7] Brassard Gilles and Bratley Paul. 1996. Fundamentals of Algorithmics, Prentice Hall Englewood Cliffs.

10 Advanced Topics in Algorithms

UNIT SPECIFICS

This unit covers the following aspects:

- *Algorithm design techniques*
- *Addressing algorithm complexity and determinateness*
- *Introduction to advanced algorithmic paradigms: Approximation algorithms and randomized algorithms*
- *Application of approximation algorithms in optimizing challenging problems*
- *Exploration of the effectiveness of randomized algorithms using the example of the random version of quicksort*

This unit will explore fundamental algorithm design techniques, covering various approaches to solving computational problems. Starting with a comprehensive introduction, we'll delve into specific classes of challenges, such as approximation algorithms and their associated ratios. A detailed examination of an approximation algorithm tailored for vertex cover problems will follow. The unit will also explore randomized algorithms, including an introduction, an example algorithm, discussions on randomness and classification methodologies, and various approaches. Lastly, the focus will shift to the randomized version of quicksort, covering both deterministic and randomized versions, along with an analysis of their expected running times. The link given in the QR code provides this unit is supplementary material.

RATIONALE

The rationale of this unit, in conjunction with the design and analysis of algorithms, lies in cultivating a profound understanding of fundamental techniques essential for effective problem-solving in computational domains. By exploring diverse algorithmic design approaches, including approximation algorithms and randomized strategies, this unit aims to equip learners with versatile tools to tackle a wide array of computational challenges. The comprehensive introduction establishes a foundation for the subsequent in-depth discussions on specific classes of problems. The unit seeks to bridge theory and practical application, fostering critical thinking and analytical skills in algorithmic problem-solving.

PRE-REQUISITES

Basic understanding of algorithm design

Familiarity with fundamental algorithmic concepts

Proficiency in problem-solving strategies

Readiness to explore advanced algorithmic techniques

UNIT OUTCOMES

The outcomes of the Unit are as follows:

U10-O1: Understand the concept of advanced topics in algorithms

U10-O2: Discuss design strategies of approximation algorithms

U10-O3: Apply approximation algorithms to solve an NP-Complete problem

U10-O4: Discuss design strategies of randomized algorithms

U10-O5: Apply randomized algorithms to solve a sorting problem

Unit-10 Outcomes	EXPECTED MAPPING WITH COURSE OUTCOMES (1- Weak Correlation; 2- Medium correlation; 3- Strong Correlation)				
	CO-1	CO-2	CO-3	CO-4	CO-5
U10-O1	2	2	2	2	3
U10-O2	-	-	2	2	3
U10-O3	-	-	2	2	3
U10-O4	-	-	2	2	3
U10-O5	-	-	2	2	3

10.1 Introduction

The preceding units have discussed a range of algorithm design techniques, including divide-and-conquer, dynamic programming, and greedy strategies, addressing the intricacies and determinateness inherent in algorithms. Although the methods for solving specific problems may vary, they share commonalities: each algorithm furnishes an exact solution achieved through systematic and well-defined processes. Nevertheless, not all problems are simple and may present complexities in designing a solution. Advanced algorithm design techniques exist that, while not ensuring optimal solutions, offer efficient and often practical approaches for addressing complex problems. Let us delve into some of these standard approaches that can be applied to tackle intricate problems. Each approach caters to different aspects of problem-solving, providing diversity and allowing for customization based on the specific characteristics of the given problem [1-5]. The following are some common strategies:

- The first strategy to handle complex problems is by taking advantage of special problem structure, which means identifying simpler and more manageable aspects of a problem to solve. Let us break down this concept with a simple example. Imagine you're planning a full-day trip. Instead of trying to solve the entire day's plan all at once, it is beneficial to focus on smaller parts, like finding the best route for each segment of the journey. By dividing the larger problem into more manageable subproblems, you can tackle each part separately. This approach makes the overall task less daunting and more achievable.
- Brute-force search is another important approach, generally applicable only to small input sizes (e.g., when input size $n \leq 20$). It involves exhaustively examining all possible solutions. While this approach is simple, it becomes computationally impractical as the input size increases.
- Heuristic methods involve devising strategies to generate valid solutions, even though there is no guarantee of optimality. These techniques prioritize efficiency and practicality over exhaustively exploring all possibilities, making them suitable for large-scale problems.
- Powerful algorithms such as branch-and-bound, Metropolis-Hastings, simulated annealing, and genetic algorithms offer versatile solutions for general combinatorial optimization problems. Their effectiveness varies across problems and instances, with some demonstrating notable performance under specific conditions.
- Approximation algorithms aim to find solutions within polynomial time, providing a valuable compromise between efficiency and optimality. The key feature of approximation algorithms is that they guarantee a solution within a certain factor of the optimal solution. While not guaranteeing optimality, they offer a reasonable trade-off in terms of computational complexity and solution quality.

The selection of an appropriate approach depends on various factors, such as the problem's characteristics, size, and the desired trade-off between solution quality and computational efficiency. These diverse strategies underscore the dynamic and multifaceted nature of computational problem-solving in the face of complexity. This unit explores approximation algorithms and randomized algorithms, delving into advanced topics that go beyond traditional algorithmic paradigms.

Approximation algorithms are particularly valuable for tackling optimization problems that present challenges in achieving precise and deterministic solutions. These types of problems, as previously explored in the unit on NP-completeness, frequently find solutions through the application of advanced algorithmic techniques. In our continued exploration, we narrow our focus to a specific NP-complete problem—vertex cover—as we delve deeper into its intricacies. By applying approximation algorithms to vertex cover, we aim to uncover effective strategies that provide near-optimal solutions, contributing to the broader understanding of how these algorithms can address real-world complexities in computational problem-solving.

Randomized algorithms introduce an additional layer of flexibility to conventional deterministic algorithms, augmenting their capacity to navigate and solve complex problems. Setting themselves apart from deterministic approaches, randomized algorithms stand out as strategic tools that inject an element of creativity into the problem-solving process. In this unit, our exploration extends to the random version of quicksort, providing insights into the efficacy of randomized algorithms. Specifically, we delve into the nuanced understanding of how randomness can significantly improve the worst-case complexity, thereby fortifying the algorithm's resilience against adversarial input data. This examination not only sheds light on the technical intricacies of randomized algorithms but also underscores their practical utility in addressing real-world computational challenges.

The remainder of this unit is dedicated to thoroughly exploring computational problems, specifically honing in on distinct classes. Section 10.1 initiates the unit with a comprehensive introduction, laying the groundwork for subsequent discussions. Section 10.2 further delves into the domain of approximation algorithms, offering an initial overview and scrutinizing the approximation ratio of such algorithms. Progressing forward, Section 10.3 examines an approximation algorithm tailored for vertex cover problems. The exploration then broadens to encompass randomized algorithms in Section 10.4, which kicks off with an introductory segment followed by an example of a randomized algorithm, an examination of the role of randomness, discussions on classification methodologies, and various approaches within this context. Lastly, Section 10.5 concentrates on the randomized version of quicksort, covering deterministic quicksort, randomized quicksort, and an analysis of the expected running time of randomized quicksort.

10.2 Approximation Algorithms

NP-completeness finds utility in solving various complex problems and holds significant implications in the field of computational complexity theory, particularly concerning optimization problems. Examples of such problems include the Traveling Salesman Problem, Knapsack Problem, and Graph Coloring Problem, among others. These problems are ubiquitous in various domains, including logistics, finance, telecommunications, and manufacturing. As we saw in the previous unit, NP-complete problems are computationally difficult and lack a known polynomial-time algorithm for their solution. This has profound implications for various real-world optimization problems that fall into the NP-complete category.

Optimization problems involve finding the best solution from a set of feasible solutions, often in terms of maximizing or minimizing an objective function. The statement that these problems are likely to be hard to solve exactly stems from the fact that, as of our current understanding of computational complexity, there is no known algorithm that can solve NP-complete problems in polynomial time. Polynomial time is generally considered efficient in the context of algorithmic time complexity, and problems that can be solved in polynomial time fall within the class P. This point motivates and initiates consideration of approximation algorithms for problems where polynomial-time solutions do not exist or have high algorithmic complexity. In many real-world scenarios, finding good approximations or heuristic solutions becomes a pragmatic approach. While exact solutions may be computationally intractable for large instances of NP-complete problems, heuristic algorithms and approximation techniques can often provide reasonably good solutions within acceptable time frames.

10.2.1 Introduction to Approximation Algorithms

An approximation algorithm emerges as a strategic response to the challenges posed by NP-completeness in the realm of optimization problems. In the face of the theoretical hardness associated with finding optimal solutions within polynomial time, approximation algorithms offer a pragmatic approach. While they do not ensure the identification of the absolute best solution, their primary objective is to achieve solutions that come as close as possible to the optimal solution within a reasonable computational timeframe. These algorithms are often interchangeably referred to as approximation algorithms or heuristic algorithms. Key Features of approximation algorithms are as follows:

- A key characteristic of approximation algorithms is their ability to run within polynomial time with respect to the input size. Despite the inherent complexity of the underlying optimization problem, these algorithms are specifically designed to ensure computational efficiency, rendering them suitable for real-world applications.
- Although approximation algorithms do not guarantee the most effective solution, they commit to delivering solutions of high accuracy and quality. The approximation algorithm is designed to provide a solution with high accuracy. Typically, these algorithms strive to produce solutions that are within a certain factor or percentage of the optimum. For instance, they might aim to find solutions within 1% of the optimal solution, striking a balance between computational tractability and solution quality.
- The primary goal of approximation algorithms is to strike a delicate balance between time complexity and solution precision. These algorithms are crafted to provide solutions that

closely approach the optimal solution, often meeting predefined accuracy criteria. This precision, while not guaranteeing optimality, is crucial for practical problem-solving.

- Approximation algorithms find application in addressing optimization problems by efficiently generating solutions that are near-optimal within polynomial time. These problems span various domains, including logistics, resource allocation, scheduling, and network design, where finding exact solutions is often computationally intractable.

- An important example of an approximation algorithm is used to solve the Travelling Salesman Problem (TSP), a classic optimization challenge. Christofides' Algorithm stands out as an approximation algorithm for the metric TSP, providing a solution within 3/2 times the length of the optimal route [1-6]. In the realm of combinatorial optimization, the Knapsack problem finds a practical approximation solution through a greedy approach, sorting items by their value-to-weight ratio. The vertex cover problem, seeking the smallest set of vertices covering all edges in a graph, is tackled by the greedy vertex cover algorithm, ensuring a solution no more than twice the size of the optimal cover [1]. For the Max-Cut problem, randomized rounding employs randomness in rounding fractional solutions, yielding an approximate solution. The last example is the Greedy Set Cover algorithm efficiently addressing the Set Cover Problem by iteratively selecting sets to cover uncovered elements.

10.2.2 Approximation Ratio of Approximation Algorithms

An approximation algorithm is a computational method that provides a valid or feasible solution to an optimization problem, although it does not necessarily guarantee an optimal solution in terms of size, weight, or cost. The effectiveness of an approximation algorithm is measured by its approximation ratio, defined as the worst-case ratio between the solution produced by the algorithm and the optimal solution. For minimization problems, the ratio is expressed as approximation/optimal, while for maximization problems, it is expressed as optimal/approximation. A lower ratio is indicative of better performance [1-3]. Approximation algorithms support the following performance ratios:

- Appropriate ratio-$P(n)$: In scenarios where the optimization problem involves costs associated with potential solutions, and the goal is to find a near-optimal solution. Consider a problem of size n where C and C^* denote the cost of the solution and the optimal solution for that particular problem, respectively. An algorithm is considered to have an appropriate ratio of $P(n)$ if, for any input size n, the cost C of the solution produced by the algorithm is within a factor of $P(n)$ of the cost C^* of an optimal solution. This is expressed as $max(C/C^*, C^*/C) \leq P(n)$.

- $P(n)$-Approximation algorithm: An algorithm is termed a $P(n)$-approximation algorithm if it achieves an approximation ratio of $P(n)$. In the context of a maximization problem, where $0 < C < C^*$, the value of C^*/C indicates how much larger the cost of an optimal solution is compared to the approximate algorithm's solution. For a minimization problem, where $0 < C^*$

$< C$, the ratio C/C^* signifies how much larger the cost of an approximate solution is compared to an optimal solution.

The approximability of NP-complete problems, which are equivalent in terms of exact solvability within polynomial time in the worst case, exhibits considerable variability. Here are some potential scenarios:

- Inapproximable problems: Certain NP-complete problems fall into the category of inapproximable problems, presenting a formidable challenge in terms of finding approximation solutions within polynomial time. In these cases, no algorithm exists that can achieve a ratio boun, indicative of the quality of the approximate solution, smaller than infinity unless the P versus NP question is resolved in favor of P = NP. This theoretical restriction underscores the inherent complexity and difficulty in obtaining near-optimal solutions for these problems. Two notable examples that belong to this class of inapproximable problems are the independent set problem and the graph coloring problem. In the independent set problem, the goal is to find the largest set of non-adjacent vertices in a graph, and in the graph coloring problem, the objective is to determine the minimum number of colors needed to color the vertices of a graph such that no two adjacent vertices share the same color. Despite numerous attempts and extensive research, the nature of these problems implies that no polynomial time algorithm can achieve a ratio bound smaller than infinity unless a breakthrough occurs in resolving the P versus NP question. This intriguing aspect of inapproximable problems underscores the theoretical limits and complexities inherent in finding efficient solutions for certain classes of optimization problems within the realm of NP-completeness.
- Variable ratio bounds (Function of n): In the realm of NP-complete problems, there exists a subset for which approximation solutions are achievable, but the quality of these solutions is intricately tied to the input size, denoted as n. This class of problems exhibits variable ratio bounds, where the approximation ratio is expressed as a function of the input size. One illustrative example of this category is the set cover problem. The set cover problem is a classic optimization challenge wherein the goal is to identify the minimum number of sets needed to cover all the given elements. Although this problem is NP-complete and, in general, challenging to solve optimally, approximation algorithms provide a practical avenue for obtaining near-optimal solutions. In the case of the set cover problem, the ratio bound, indicating the factor by which the approximate solution may deviate from the optimal solution, is expressed as $O(\log n)$. The logarithmic dependence on the input size is a key characteristic of this variable ratio bound. Importantly, this specific bound is widely believed to be the best possible achievable ratio for approximating the set cover problem within polynomial time. This insight highlights the nuanced nature of approximability in the context of NP-complete problems. While the set cover problem can be tackled with approximation algorithms, the quality of the obtained solutions is intricately linked to the size of the input. The logarithmic dependence suggests that as the input size grows, the ratio between the approximate and

optimal solutions increases in a controlled manner, reflecting a trade-off between computational efficiency and solution quality. This delicate balance exemplifies the intricacies involved in addressing NP-complete problems with variable ratio bounds.

- Constant ratio bounds: In the intricate landscape of NP-complete problems, there exists a noteworthy subset that allows for approximation solutions with a constant ratio bound. This implies that, regardless of the input size, the approximation algorithm guarantees a solution that deviates from the optimal solution by a fixed, unchanging factor. The vertex cover problem serves as an illustrative example of such problems, where approximation within a factor of *2* is achievable. The vertex cover problem involves identifying the smallest set of vertices in a graph such that each edge is incident to at least one vertex in the set. This problem, like many NP-complete problems, is known for its computational complexity in finding an optimal solution. However, the fascinating aspect lies in the fact that, despite the NP-completeness, a constant ratio bound approximation algorithm exists for vertex cover. In this context, the constant ratio bound is set at *2*. This means that the size of the vertex cover produced by the approximation algorithm is guaranteed to be at most twice the size of the optimal vertex cover. In practical terms, this represents a remarkable achievement, providing a computationally efficient algorithm that consistently delivers solutions of reasonably high quality, even for large instances of the problem. The ability to achieve a constant ratio bound, exemplified by the vertex cover problem, showcases a unique aspect of certain NP-complete problems. Despite their inherent complexity, these problems allow for approximation algorithms that strike a stable balance between computational efficiency and solution quality. The constant ratio bound serves as a beacon of reliability, offering a dependable factor by which the approximate solution may deviate from optimality, irrespective of the input size.

- In the realm of NP-complete problems, there exists a remarkable subset that allows for approximation solutions with an unprecedented level of flexibility—problems that can be approximated arbitrarily well. This means that irrespective of the inherent complexity of these problems, approximation algorithms exist that can achieve solution quality as close to optimal as desired, contingent on a user-provided parameter $\varepsilon > 0$. The concept of approximating arbitrarily well is encapsulated in the ratio bound $(1 + \varepsilon)$, where ε serves as a measure of the precision desired in the approximation. As the user tunes ε to smaller values, the algorithm endeavors to provide solutions that approach optimality more closely. Importantly, if such an algorithm runs in polynomial time for any fixed ε, it earns the distinguished title of a polynomial time approximation scheme (PTAS). One illustrative example of a problem in this category is the Euclidean traveling salesman problem (TSP). In the Euclidean TSP, the objective is to find the shortest possible tour that visits a given set of points in the Euclidean plane. Despite the NP-completeness of the general TSP, a PTAS exists for the Euclidean variant. This means that, for any user-specified precision ε, the algorithm can produce a tour whose length is at most $(1 + \varepsilon)$ times the length of the optimal tour, all within polynomial time. The significance of approximating arbitrarily well lies in its adaptability to the user's specific requirements. Whether a tight approximation is needed or a more relaxed one suffices, the algorithm can accommodate different levels of precision, offering a solution quality that aligns with the user's preferences. This characteristic is particularly valuable in practical applications where the trade-off between precision and computational efficiency is crucial. In essence, the existence of polynomial time approximation schemes for certain NP-complete problems, exemplified by the Euclidean TSP, challenges the conventional notion of intractability. It underscores the potential for achieving highly accurate solutions in polynomial time, showcasing the dynamic and nuanced nature of approximability within the rich tapestry of computational complexity theory.

10.3 Approximation Algorithm for Vertex Cover

In graph theory, a fundamental optimization problem is the vertex cover problem, which involves identifying a minimum-size vertex cover for an undirected graph. A vertex cover is a subset of vertices in the graph such that every edge in the graph is incident to at least one vertex from the subset. In other words, for every edge (u, v), either vertex u or vertex v (or both) must be included in the vertex cover. Consider an undirected graph $G = (V, E)$ where V is the set of vertices and E is the set of edges. The optimal solution to the vertex cover problem for graph G is the smallest set of vertices that covers all edges. Figure 10.1 illustrates an example of an optimal solution for the vertex cover problem. The dark vertices represent the minimum size of the vertex cover.

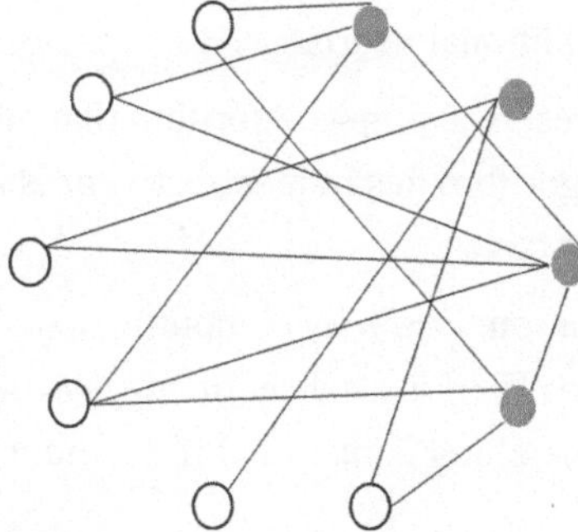

Figure 10.1: Illustration of the optimal solution of Vertex cover problem.

The Vertex Cover problem is categorized as an NP-complete problem, indicating that, based on the current understanding in computational complexity theory, no known polynomial-time algorithm exists to solve vertex cover unless P equals NP. Its NP-completeness implies that finding the optimal solution for large instances of the vertex cover becomes computationally infeasible with current algorithms. Despite the NP-completeness, signifying the lack of a polynomial-time exact solution, there are approximate polynomial-time algorithms that offer solutions with guaranteed bounds on their quality.

In this exploration, we delve into the realm of approximation algorithms, aiming to find a vertex cover with a specified ratio bound, such as *2*. To begin, we aim to develop an approximation algorithm for the Vertex Cover problem with a ratio bound of *2*. This signifies that the algorithm's solution will be, at most, twice the size of the optimum vertex cover. This ratio bound serves as a performance guarantee, allowing us to efficiently find solutions that, while not necessarily optimal, are within a controlled factor of the optimum. The process of finding approximation algorithms involves a systematic approach:

- Greedy Heuristics: One common approach is to employ a greedy heuristic. Greedy algorithms make locally optimal choices at each step, and while not guaranteed to be optimal, they often perform well in practice. In the context of the vertex cover problem, a greedy algorithm might start with an empty vertex cover and iteratively add vertices to cover uncovered edges until all edges are covered.
- Approximation ratios: The notion of an approximation ratio is crucial. We have a ratio bound of *2* means that the size of the vertex cover it finds will be, at most, twice the size of the optimal vertex cover.
- Analysis and proof of approximation: The effectiveness of the algorithm lies in proving its approximation guarantee rigorously. Mathematical analysis is employed to demonstrate that the algorithm's solution is indeed close to optimal. The analysis involves bounding the size of the produced vertex cover in relation to the size of the optimum vertex cover.
- Iterative improvement: Refinement of the algorithm often involves iterative improvement. By analyzing the algorithm's performance and identifying potential shortcomings, adjustments can be made to enhance its effectiveness. Iterative refinement may include modifying the greedy strategy or incorporating additional heuristics.

For the vertex cover problem, we present a simple algorithm that guarantees an approximation within a factor of *2*. The simplicity of this algorithm lies in its effectiveness in finding a solution that is, at most, twice the size of the optimum vertex cover.

- Maximal matching computation: Begin by computing a maximal matching for the given graph. A matching for a graph $G = (V, E)$ is a subset of edges $M \subseteq E$, where each vertex is incident to at most one edge in M. A matching is maximal if it cannot be expanded by adding more edges to it.
- Maximal matching process: Iteratively find unmarked edges (u, v) in the graph. Add the found edge to the matching. Mark all edges incident to either u or v to ensure they are not included in subsequent matchings.
- Vertex cover construction: To obtain a vertex cover from the maximal matching, recognize that for every edge (u, v) in any matching, either u or v must be included in any valid vertex cover. Consequently, a simple strategy is to add both u and v to the vertex cover, ensuring coverage of all edges in the matching.

The summary of the algorithm is as VC_approx(V, E) where V is the set of vertices and E is the set of edges [1-3]. Here, VC_approx algorithm initializes with an empty set C. It then iteratively selects any unmarked edge (u, v) from a maximal matching, adds u and v to the cover set C, and deletes all edges incident to either u or v. This process continues until there are no more unmarked edges. The algorithm returns the set C as the approximate vertex cover for the given graph.

```
VC_approx(V, E)
  1. C = empty set
  2. Set all edges as uncovered
  3. While (there exists an unmarked edge (u, v)):
     // (u, v) is in a maximal matching
          Pick any {u, v} in E
          Add u and v to C
          Delete all eges incident to either u or v
  4. Return C as the approximate vertex cover
```

In Figure 10.2, we observe the step-by-step execution of the VC_approx (V, E) algorithm for the vertex cover problem. The algorithm initiates with a graph $G = (V, E)$ containing vertices and edges. In the first stage, the algorithm selects one edge and its connected vertices, adding them to the vertex cover set C. Simultaneously, it marks and excludes all edges connected to these vertices. This process repeats in Stages 2 and 3 until all edges are marked. The resulting illustration in Figure 10.2 showcases the final solution, where six vertices, distinguished by a dark color, form the approximate vertex cover. These selected vertices effectively cover all edges in the graph, demonstrating the algorithm's efficiency in providing a practical solution to the vertex cover problem.

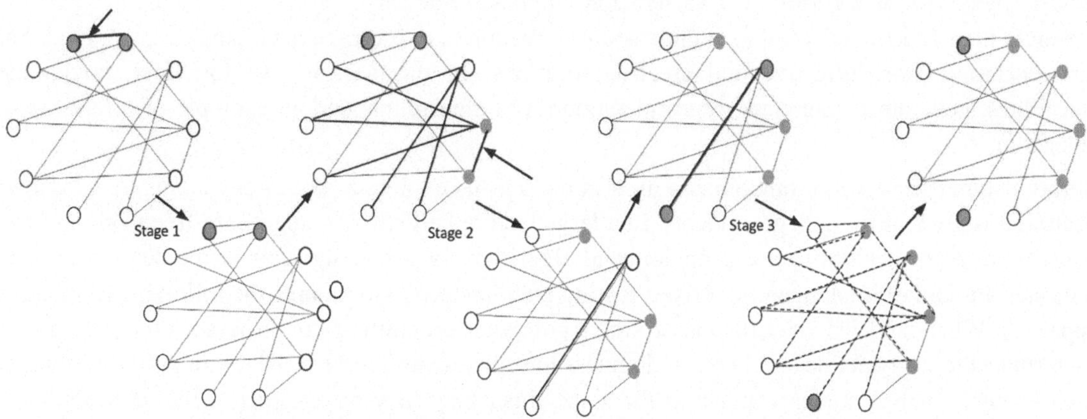

Figure 10.2: Illustration of the solution of the vertex cover problem.

Lemma: VC_approx(V, E) algorithm achieves an approximation ratio of 2.

Proof: The proof for the VC_approx(V, E) algorithm achieving an approximation ratio of *2* unfolds through a systematic analysis of the matching and vertex cover produced by the algorithm. Let us denote the set of edges identified by the algorithm as *M* and the set of endpoints of these edges as *C*. If we define *k* as the cardinality of the matching ($|M|$), it follows that, due to the nature of maximal matching, every edge contributes two distinct endpoints to *C*, resulting in $|C| = 2k$. Importantly, since *M* is a maximal matching, it cannot be expanded further, ensuring the maximality of the selected edges. The proof establishes that *C* serves as a vertex cover of size *2k*, as every edge in the graph is incident to at least one endpoint in *C*. Furthermore, any valid vertex cover must include at least one endpoint from each edge in *M*. Since no two edges in *M* share the same endpoint, the size of any vertex cover must be at least *k*. Therefore, the conclusion emerges that *C* is within a factor of *2* of the optimum size, solidifying the *2*-approximation ratio of the algorithm for the vertex cover problem.

10.4 Randomized Algorithms

Randomized algorithms redefine the landscape of decision-making by seamlessly integrating an inherent element of chance or randomness, dynamically introduced through actions like coin tossing during execution [3-4]. This injection of randomness not only sets these algorithms apart from their deterministic counterparts but also heralds a paradigm shift in problem-solving methodologies. This deliberate inclusion of randomness represents more than a departure from traditional, rigid methodologies; it signifies a proactive embrace of adaptability and flexibility in the decision-making processes of algorithms. This dynamic approach not only enhances their functionality but also underscores a readiness to leverage uncertainty as a strategic tool for generating more effective and creative solutions. In this section, we introduce randomized algorithms, generate randomness, types of randomized algorithms, and an example of a randomized algorithm.

Before delving further into randomized algorithms, Let us explore a day-to-day example: Classroom Seating Assignment for college students. In a large lecture hall where students are free to choose their seats, a professor decides to use a randomized algorithm for assigning seats at the beginning of the semester. Instead of implementing a fixed seating plan, the professor adopts the following randomized approach: When students enter the classroom, a computer program or the professor randomly assigns each student to an available seat. The randomness introduces variability in the seating arrangements for each lecture. Even if students arrive at the same time, they may be assigned different seats. Using randomness helps distribute students evenly across the room, avoiding potential biases or patterns that might emerge with a deterministic seating plan. The random assignment encourages students to interact with different peers throughout the semester, fostering a more diverse and dynamic learning environment. This example demonstrates how randomized algorithms can be applied in practical situations to enhance fairness, encourage interaction, and simplify the process of seat assignments, especially in settings where a deterministic approach might lead to suboptimal outcomes.

10.4.1 Introduction to Randomized Algorithms

When evaluating randomized algorithms, a critical aspect to consider is the examination of their expected worst-case performance. This metric delves into measuring the average time or resource utilization across all conceivable inputs of a specified size. The relevance of this analysis intensifies due to the influence of randomness, introducing variability in the algorithm's behavior contingent on the outcomes of coin flips. The utilization of expected values takes this evaluation to a more nuanced level, involving the computation of average performance across all potential random outcomes. This process provides a comprehensive understanding of the algorithm's behavior, accommodating the inherent variability introduced by the random choices made during execution. While the worst-case analysis remains crucial, the expectation factor brings insight into the spectrum of possibilities introduced by randomness.

In sharp contrast to deterministic algorithms, which adhere strictly to predetermined sequences of steps for a given input, randomized algorithms embody a more adaptive and flexible approach. By infusing randomness into their decision-making mechanisms, these algorithms tap into the power of uncertainty, introducing variability that can lead to more agile and innovative solutions. This distinctive feature opens up new avenues for addressing complex problems. Instead of following a predefined set of instructions, randomized algorithms leverage randomness to explore diverse courses of action. This exploratory nature empowers randomized algorithms to navigate intricate problem spaces with a level of versatility and adaptability that deterministic algorithms may lack, showcasing the transformative potential of embracing randomness in algorithmic decision-making.

Randomized algorithms have found applications in a myriad of domains, showcasing their versatility and potential to address complex challenges. In addition to optimization problems, algorithmic game theory, and machine learning, these algorithms have made significant contributions to fields such as cryptography, data analysis, and network design. Their capacity to harness randomness frequently results in the development of innovative and efficient solutions, contributing to advancements in various fields. However, it is important to note that the probabilistic nature of these algorithms does not assure optimal results in every run. Instead, their value lies in their expected performance, making them particularly beneficial in scenarios where the focus is on average-case behavior rather than the worst-case scenario. These algorithms exhibit both positive and negative attributes. On the positive side, their flexibility in leveraging randomness allows for the exploration of solution spaces in ways that deterministic algorithms might overlook. This adaptability often leads to creative and novel problem-solving approaches, especially in scenarios characterized by uncertainty or dynamic environments. However, the inherent randomness introduces an element of unpredictability. While this can be advantageous in some cases, it also means that the same randomized algorithm may yield different outcomes in different runs. This variability can pose challenges in applications where consistency or deterministic results are critical. Additionally, the reliance on randomness makes it challenging to guarantee optimal solutions for every execution, introducing a degree of risk in scenarios where precision is paramount.

10.4.2 An Example of Randomized Algorithm

Let us delve into an example to illustrate the impact of randomized algorithms. Consider the task of searching for an element in an unsorted array, where the element's presence in the array is known. If we were to adopt a deterministic approach and systematically scan the array, regardless of the order in which we examine the array locations *(a[1], a[2], ..., a[n])*, the worst-case scenario occurs when the target element is situated at the last position. In such a case, we would need to read all n locations. To mitigate this potential inefficiency, we introduce randomness into the algorithm. Instead of deterministically scanning from left to right or right to left, we make this decision by flipping a coin. Suppose the target element is at position k. In this randomized approach, resulting in an average of $(n + 1)/2$ locations read. This randomized strategy significantly reduces the expected time compared to the deterministic algorithm, effectively cutting it in half. When considering constant factors, the introduction of randomness provides us with demonstrably more computational power than a non-random approach. To put this into numerical perspective, Let us say we have an array of size 10 ($n = 10$). In the worst case, the deterministic approach may require reading all *10* locations. However, the randomized algorithm, on average, would only need to read $(10 + 1)/2 = 5.5$ locations. This illustrates the tangible efficiency gains achievable through the judicious use of randomness in algorithmic decision-making.

In the formalization of a randomized algorithm, we conceive of a computational entity denoted as M, operating through the execution of computations represented by $M(x, r)$ as shown in Figure 10.3. Here, x signifies the problem input, and r is a sequence of random bits. The chosen machine model is the random-access machine, a standard model in computer science. In this model, the memory space scales polynomially with the size of the input, denoted as n. Within the model, fundamental operations such as reading from or writing to a memory location and performing arithmetic operations on integers with a bit size of up to $O(\log n)$ transpire in constant time. The procedural steps of randomized algorithm is shown as M(input x, random bits r) pseudocode.

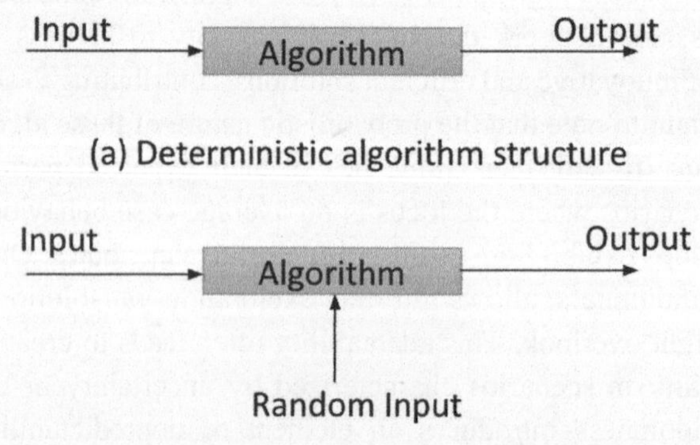

Figure 10.3: Illustration of randomized algorithm structure.

```
M(input x, random bits r):
   // Initialize any necessary variables or data structures
   initialize_variables()
   // Process the input using the supplied random bits
   result = process_input_with_randomness(x, r)
   // Return the computed result
   Return result

initialize_variables():
  // Function for processing input with randomness

process_input_with_randomness(x, r):
   // Perform computations based on the input and random bits
   // Example: Generate a random integer of size O(log n)
   random_integer = generate_random_integer(O(log n))
   // Example: Read the next O(log n)-sized value from the random input
   next_value = read_next_random_value(O(log n), r)
   Return processed_result

read_next_random_value(bit_size, r):
   // Read the next O(log n)-sized value from the random input
   Return read_value
```

10.4.3 Randomness

Contemplating the intriguing question of where the element of randomness originates in a randomized algorithm, we often assume access to genuinely random bits denoted as r. However, the method of obtaining these random bits is not often explored in great detail. In practical applications, three distinct avenues, varying in strength and cost, come to the forefront:

- **Natural Randomness:** In the pursuit of efficiency, strategic approaches delve into tapping into amplified quantum noise and observing physical processes inherently infused with anticipated randomness. This exploration extends to phenomena such as intervals between keyboard presses or the seek times of hard drive heads. Within these scenarios, a meticulous process unfolds, extracting a sequence of random bits that vividly demonstrates effective unpredictability firmly grounded in plausible physical assumptions. Within this domain, the system keenly observes the intervals between keyboard presses, captures the subtleties of mouse movements, and notes the temporal gaps between various user interactions. Furthermore, it delves into the timing intricacies of data read and write operations on a hard drive. These diverse activities collectively paint a nuanced and unpredictable pattern, intricately influenced by individual user behaviors. In doing so, they infuse a distinctive element of natural randomness into the system. This strategic utilization of natural randomness not only embodies cost-effectiveness but also exemplifies a refined understanding of the intricacies of user-machine interactions. The system transforms seemingly routine actions, such as typing on a keyboard or moving a mouse, into a wellspring of organic unpredictability, enhancing the overall robustness of digital systems through the infusion of dynamic and inherently unpredictable patterns.

- **Secure Pseudorandomness:** This method involves finding a function capable of producing such values based on a seed. The key criterion is that, if the seed is chosen uniformly at random—perhaps utilizing a physical random number generator—no polynomial-time program should successfully distinguish the resulting sequence from an actual random sequence with non-trivial probability. This intricate process serves as a robust foundation for cryptographic applications, ensuring that the generated pseudorandom values possess qualities akin to true randomness. The expense associated with this approach reflects the computational complexity and resources required to meet stringent cryptographic standards.
- **Verified Pseudorandomness:** This method directs attention towards functions that successfully pass rigorous statistical tests, particularly those gauging *k*-wise independence of consecutive outputs. The selection of a specific pseudorandom number generator (PRNG) often hinges on factors such as convenience and prevailing trends. However, a cautious approach is advised, especially when dealing with older standard libraries that might harbor PRNGs with suboptimal characteristics. The hallmark advantage of statistical pseudorandomness lies in the swift execution of many PRNGs, ensuring minimal impact on program performance. The speed at which these generators operate is a notable asset. Yet, a caveat emerges in the form of potential reliance on the program's activities to inadvertently conceal any weaknesses inherent in the chosen PRNG.

10.4.4 Randomized Algorithm Classification

In the intricate domain of randomized algorithms, nuances emerge in the assurances they provide concerning correct output and the intricacies of time. These guarantees, which bear recognized names in the literature and align with specific complexity classes in complexity theory, form the bedrock of algorithmic decision-making.

- **Las Vegas:** In the Las Vegas algorithms, the infusion of probability introduces a unique dimension, both acknowledging the potential for failure and presenting distinctive characteristics. The hallmark of Las Vegas algorithms lies in their capacity to discern instances of failure, fostering a strategic response to challenges. If a failure occurs during the algorithm's execution, the unique feature of Las Vegas algorithms emerges—the ability to rerun the algorithm. This iterative approach ensures eventual success, embodying a probability of *1*. This resilience in the face of failure adds a positive layer to Las Vegas algorithms, promising reliable outcomes over multiple runs. However, this resilience comes at a cost. The potential downside is the prospect of an unbounded running time. While the algorithm guarantees success eventually, the time required for this success becomes unpredictable. This inherent variability in running time poses a challenge, particularly in scenarios where time constraints are paramount. A example illustrating Las Vegas algorithms is QuickSort. Renowned for its efficiency and correctness, QuickSort epitomizes the discernibility of failure instances. If a failure occurs, the algorithm can be rerun, eventually achieving success. Despite its reliability, the trade-off lies in the unpredictable running time, prompting the need to carefully quantify and set bounds on the expected running time.

- **Monte Carlo:** In the Monte Carlo algorithms, the element of probability is ever-present, but the crucial differentiator lies in the enigmatic nature of when failure might materialize. As these algorithms yield a *yes/no* answer, a nuanced dance unfolds between failure probability and the potential for success through iterative runs, bringing both positive and negative dimensions to the fore. The distinctive strength of Monte Carlo algorithms emerges when the failure probability is significantly less than *1/2*. In such scenarios, the algorithm's resilience is evident through repeated runs. By favoring the majority answer over multiple iterations, the overall probability of failure can be systematically mitigated. This adaptability to uncertainty adds a positive layer to Monte Carlo algorithms, making them particularly valuable in situations where failure can be minimized through strategic repetition. A quintessential example that captures the essence of Monte Carlo algorithms is the polynomial equality-testing algorithm. Despite featuring a fixed running time, this algorithm introduces an element of randomness into correctness. The certainty of correctness is subject to the unpredictable nature of random outcomes. This inherent uncertainty forms the negative aspect of Monte Carlo algorithms, requiring a careful balance between their utility and the potential drawbacks associated with randomness in correctness.

In choosing between Las Vegas and Monte Carlo algorithms, our preference generally leans towards Las Vegas algorithms. Why? Because with Las Vegas algorithms, we know for sure when we've succeeded. It is like having a clear signal that things worked out. However, there are situations where we have to settle for Monte Carlo algorithms. These can still be quite handy, especially when we can make the chance of failure very small. Think of it like playing the odds in your favor. Let us break it down with an everyday example. Imagine you're trying to figure out the average opinion of a group of people—maybe their views on a political matter. If you take a sample (like asking a few people), you're essentially running a Monte Carlo algorithm. Sure, there's a small chance that your sample doesn't really represent the whole group, but you would not know for sure unless you already have the complete information. In simpler terms, Las Vegas algorithms are like getting a clear "success" signal, while Monte Carlo algorithms are like making educated guesses and hoping they work well, especially when the chances of being wrong are very low.

10.4.5 Different Methodologies for Randomized Algorithms

Randomized algorithms represent a versatile array of methodologies meticulously crafted to capitalize on the inherent unpredictability of randomness in problem-solving. The first strategic approach, avoiding worst-case inputs, addresses scenarios where algorithm performance faces severe compromise. The primary objective is to counteract scenarios where the algorithm's performance is severely compromised. The rationale behind this approach lies in the assumption that potential adversaries may supply input to the algorithm. In such cases, revealing the precise plan of the algorithm can be exploited by adversaries to their advantage. To address this vulnerability, the strategy involves concealing algorithmic details through the introduction of randomness. This substitution replaces a predictable deterministic algorithm with a quasi-random selection from a pool of different deterministic algorithms.

The key benefit of this approach is that it keeps adversaries uncertain about the specific algorithm in use, thereby preventing them from strategically selecting inputs that exploit the algorithm's vulnerabilities.

Moving on to sampling, this methodology strategically employs randomness to acquire representative examples from a given population. This process is essential for various purposes, including estimating average values or selecting crucial elements within algorithms, such as choosing a pivot in quicksort. The underlying rationale for incorporating randomness in sampling is to thwart adversaries from directing the selection process toward non-representative samples. By introducing this element of randomness, the sampling method remains unbiased, ensuring that the selected examples accurately reflect the broader characteristics of the entire population under consideration.

In the realm of hashing, the objective is to assign a concise name (hash) to large objects through a dedicated hash function. This process finds utility in various scenarios, notably in tasks like load balancing or file fingerprinting. The pigeonhole principle acknowledges the inevitability of collisions, where multiple objects may map to the same name. Randomization is introduced in the selection of the hash function to address this challenge. This intentional unpredictability acts as a safeguard, preventing adversaries from influencing the selection of objects based on observed hash functions. The randomized nature of the hash function selection adds a layer of complexity that enhances the security and integrity of the hashing process.

The goal of building random structures involves leveraging the probabilistic method to showcase the existence of structures with specific properties, commonly applied to graphs with interesting characteristics. The rationale behind this approach involves demonstrating that within a particular class, randomly generated structures possess a nonzero probability of having the sought-after property. This method, rooted in probability theory, serves as a powerful tool for establishing the presence of desired properties in structures. The transformation of the probabilistic method into a randomized algorithm occurs when efforts focus on substantially enhancing the probability of the randomly generated structures exhibiting the targeted property. This transition from probability theory to practical algorithmic application highlights the versatility and efficacy of randomized algorithms in constructing structures with predefined characteristics.

Lastly, symmetry breaking in distributed algorithms with multiple processes aims to overcome deadlocks caused by simultaneous identical actions. The primary objective is to introduce variability and disrupt the synchronous actions among processes. Randomization becomes a key tool in this context, serving as a mechanism to break deadlocks by injecting unpredictability into the system. The rationale behind employing randomization for symmetry breaking lies in its ability to introduce variability in the actions of multiple processes, preventing them from getting stuck in synchronized patterns. This deliberate disruption proves instrumental in scenarios where symmetry among processes hinders the desired outcome, enabling progress through the introduction of controlled randomness.

10.5 Randomized Version of Quicksort

Quicksort consists of unique features compared to other sorting techniques, such as in-place sorting, divide-and-conquer, and an efficient average-case time complexity [3-4]. It does not require additional space for sorting the elements and can simultaneously solve the sorting problem. The in-place and divide-and-conquer properties of quicksort make them efficient across diverse input cases. The pivot element in quicksort plays a crucial role in improving the algorithm's effectiveness. The quicksort algorithm finds two variations based on the selection of the pivot element. Deterministic quicksort uses a predetermined strategy to select the pivot element, often opting for the middle element of the array. While this deterministic approach ensures predictability, it may encounter challenges in specific input scenarios. Unlike deterministic quicksort, randomized quicksort introduces randomness in selecting pivot elements. Such selection gives a probabilistic guarantee to improve the algorithm's complexity and reduces the likelihood of encountering worst-case scenarios. It also helps to enhance resilience against adversarial input data. While deterministic quicksort uses a fixed pivot element selection strategy, randomized quicksort uses randomness to select the pivot element to support the overall efficiency of the algorithm across diverse input cases. The rest of this section will discuss the deterministic quicksort and randomized quicksort algorithm.

10.5.1 Deterministic Quicksort

Quicksort is a widely used sorting algorithm renowned for its efficiency and simplicity. Operating on a divide-and-conquer approach, the algorithm selects a pivot element to partition the given array into subarrays. Elements smaller than the pivot are placed to its left, and those greater are placed to its right. The algorithm then recursively applies this process to the subarrays until the entire array is sorted. The selection of the pivot element plays a vital role in the effective execution of the algorithm. The pivot element operates on a comparison basis, where other elements are classified as either less than or greater than the pivot element. The above steps, selecting the pivot element and dividing the array, undergo a recursive sorting process. Observing the quicksort process reveals that it does not require any additional storage, showcasing its remarkable capability to handle sizable inputs efficiently.

The following Deterministic_quicksort(A, p, r) illustrates the procedure of the algorithm, where A is the array, and p and r represent the indices delimiting the segment of the array intended for sorting. The difference between the indices p and r indicates the length of the segment being sorted within the array A. In other words, if p starts with 1, then r will be the length of array A. The base case is first to check whether the array contains any elements. This can easily be checked by examining p and r. The partition function Partition (A, p, r) returns the partitioning index, denoted as q, which divides the array A into two subarrays: ($A, p, q-1$) and ($A, q+1, r$). The partition function processes the elements so that all elements of subarray ($A, p, q-1$) are less than q, and the elements of subarray ($A, q+1, r$) are greater than q. Each subarray recursively calls the procedure until reaching the base case.

```
Deterministic_quicksort(A, p, r)
   if (p < r) then // Base case: If the subarray has more than one element
       q = Partition(A, p, r); // Find the partitioning index, q
       Deterministic_quicksort(A, p, q-1); // Recursively sort left subarray A[p..q-1]
       Deterministic_quicksort(A, q+1, r); // Recursively sort right subarray A[q+1..r]

Partition(A, p, r)
```

1. Element r of A serves as the pivot element.
2. Initialize an index i to start before the first element (p - 1).
3. Iterate through the array from p to r - 1 by using index j.
4. If an element (A[j]) is less than or equal to the pivot,
5. increment i and swap elements at indices i and j.
6. After the iteration, swap the pivot element (A[r]) with the element at index i + 1.
7. **Return** the index i + 1, representing the pivot's sorted position.

The deterministic quicksort ensures a predefined strategy for pivot element selection and a deterministic approach to sorting. As we have seen in earlier units, the worst case of a sorting algorithm is to give the input array in reverse order. The worst-case scenario for quicksort occurs when the partition index *q* is the nth index of an array of *n* elements. Such worst-case partitioning in the algorithm results in a partitioning that yields one subproblem with *n-1* elements and another with *0* elements. This leads to a recurrence relation for the running time, where $T(n) = T(n-1) + T(0) + \Theta(n)$. Simplifying, we get $T(n) = T(n-1) + \Theta(n)$, ultimately resulting in a time complexity of $\Theta(n^2)$. The best case partitioning scenario generates two subarrays of approximately equal size. The recurrence relation of the best case for the running time is $T(n) \leq 2T(n/2) + \Theta(n)$, leading to $T(n) = O(nlogn)$. In this case, the partition index *q* is the center element of the given input array. Therefore, the best case requires that index *q* be the center element or the median. This is possible if the partition function uses a linear-time algorithm to find the median.

10.5.2 Randomized Quicksort

The deterministic quicksort employs a fixed strategy for selecting the pivot element. In contrast, randomized quicksort, while similar to the deterministic version, introduces randomness in the selection of the pivot element during the partitioning process. We maintain our earlier notations, where *A* is the input array, and *p* and *r* denote the indices marking the segment of the array designated for sorting. The algorithm initiates by verifying the termination condition and checking if there are any remaining elements to process.To do this, it checks if *p* is less than *r*. If this condition is met, it proceeds to execute a randomized partition process, Randomized-Partition(*A, p, r*), on *A* within the specified range *p* and *r*. Following the partitioning, randomized quicksort recursively applies itself to the left subarray (*A, p, q-1*) and the right subarray (*A, q+1, r*). Incorporating randomness reduces the likelihood of worst-case scenarios, enhancing average-case performance and making the algorithm more resilient to various input distributions. The Randomized-Partition procedure introduces an element of chance into the selection of the pivot during the partitioning process. Given an array *A* with indices *p* and *r*, Randomized-Partition(*A, p, r*) begins by choosing a random index *i* within the range of *p* to *r* (inclusive). The pivot element is then used to divide the input array *A* into two subarrays, improving the time complexity of the algorithm. Subsequently, it swaps the element at index *i* with the rightmost element (*A[r]*). Following this step, it invokes the standard partition procedure, as seen in deterministic quicksort, using the randomly selected element as the pivot. The pseudocode for the randomized quicksort algorithm is provided as follows:

```
Randomized-quicksort(A, p, r)
if (p < r) then // Base case: If the subarray has more than one element
    q := Randomized-Partition(A, p, r); // Find the randomized partitioning index, q
    Randomized-quicksort(A, p, q-1); // Recursively sort the left subarray A[p..q-1]
    Randomized-quicksort(A, q+1, r); // Recursively sort the right subarray A[q+1..r]

Randomized-Partition(A, p, r)
i := Random(p, r); // Choose a random index within the range [p, r]
swap(A[i], A[r]); // Swap the randomly selected element with the rightmost element
Partition(A, p, r); // Apply standard partition algorithm with random element as the pivot
```

10.5.3 Analyzing the Expected Running Time of Randomized Quicksort

We present two different methods for analyzing the expected running time of the randomized quick-sort algorithm [4].

(a) Direct analysis using recursion: Consider n as the size of the input array A to be sorted. For an index k in the range of *0* to *n-1*, $i.e. 0 \le k \le n-1$, we define the indicator random variable X_k:

$$X_k = \begin{cases} 1 & \text{If partition generates a k:n-k-1 split} \\ 0 & \text{Otherwise} \end{cases}$$

It indicates that if a partition is generated at index k, X_k is set to 1, indicating a successful event; otherwise, it is set to 0, signifying an unsuccessful event. The expected value of a random variable represents the average value one would expect to obtain if the random variable were repeatedly sampled multiple times. Since we consider at random during the split and therefore, all splits are equally likely, assuming elements are distinct. The expected value of X_k is given by

$$E[X_k] = Pr[X_k = 1] = \frac{1}{n}$$

The running time of randomized quicksort is denoted by $T(n)$. It can be determined by exploring all possible split options, where $0,1,2,\ldots n-1$ elements of A are in one subarray, and the remaining elements are in the other. This can be rewritten as:

$$T(n) = \begin{cases} T(0) + T(n-1) + \Theta(n) & \textit{If 0 : n-1 split}, \\ T(1) + T(n-2) + \Theta(n) & \textit{If 1 : n-2 split}, \\ \vdots & \\ T(n-1) + T(0) + \Theta(n) & \textit{If n-1 : 0 split}, \end{cases}$$

We can summarise and rewrite $T(n)$ as

$$T(n) = \sum_{k=0}^{n-1} X_k(T(k) + T(n-k-1) + \Theta(n)).$$

The above $T(n)$ sum up the values for k from 0 to $n-1$ of all three terms, term $T(k)$ represents the running time of the algorithm for the subarray of size k on the left side of the pivot. The term $T(n-k-1)$ represents the running time of the algorithm for the subarray of size $n-k-1$ on the right side of the pivot. Finally, the term $\Theta(n)$ represents the time spent on the partitioning step (choosing the pivot and rearranging elements) for the current array of size n. By using the running time of randomized quicksort $T(n)$ and the expected value of variable X_k, we can rewrite as

$$E[T(n)] = E\left[\sum_{k=0}^{n-1} X_k(T(k) + T(n-k-1) + \Theta(n))\right]$$

Rearranging the expected of each component, it can be rewritten as

$$E[T(n)] = \frac{1}{n}\sum_{k=0}^{n-1} E[T(k)] + \frac{1}{n}\sum_{k=0}^{n-1} E[T(n-k-1)] + \frac{1}{n}\sum_{k=0}^{n-1} \Theta(n)$$

After summations of identical terms, we have

$$E[T(n)] = \frac{2}{n}\sum_{k=1}^{n-1} E[T(k)] + \Theta(n)$$

The expected value $E[T(k)]$ can be replaced by $ak\ lg\ k$ and therefore

$$E[T(n)] \le \frac{2}{n}\sum_{k=2}^{n-1} ak\ lg\ k + \Theta(n)$$

Substitute inductive hypothesis $\sum_{k=2}^{n-1} ak\ lg\ k \le \frac{1}{2}n^2 lg\ n - \frac{1}{8}n^2$ and we have

$$E[T(n)] \le \frac{2}{n}\sum_{k=2}^{n-1} ak\ lg\ k + \Theta(n),$$

$$= \frac{2a}{n}\left(\frac{1}{2}n^2 lg\ n - \frac{1}{8}n^2\right) + \Theta(n),$$

$$= anlg\ n - \left(\frac{an}{4} - \Theta(n)\right),$$

$$\le an\ lg\ n.$$

When the constant a is large enough, then $E[T(n)] = \Theta(n)$.

(b) Indirect analysis via counting the number of comparisons: Indirect analysis of quicksort via counting the number of comparisons involves understanding the average-case behavior of the algorithm based on the expected number of key comparisons performed during the sorting process. This approach employs probabilistic reasoning and mathematical analysis to determine the average or expected number of comparisons required for sorting a randomly shuffled array. By analyzing the algorithm's behavior in terms of comparisons, one can gain insights into its efficiency and performance characteristics, particularly in scenarios where input data is randomly distributed. Similar to the Direct analysis using recursion, we consider *n* as the size of the input array *A* to be sorted. For an index *k* in the range of *0* to *n-1*. Let z_i denote the i-th smallest element of *A*. If we arrange the elements of *A* in sorting order, then $< z_0, z_1, \ldots, z_{n-1} >$. Let us consider a new variable $Z_{ij} = \{z_i,...,z_j\}$, denoting the set of elements between z_i and z_j, including these elements. We also consider an indicator random variable X_{ij} for the event that the i-th smallest and j-th smallest elements of *A* are compared in the execution of quicksort. Since each pair of elements is compared at most once by quicksort, the number *X* of comparisons is given by

$$X = \sum_{i=0}^{n-2} \sum_{j=i+1}^{n-1} X_{ij}$$

The expected number of comparisons is therefore

$$E[X] = \sum_{i=0}^{n-2} \sum_{j=i+1}^{n-1} E[X_{ij}] = \sum_{i=0}^{n-2} \sum_{j=i+1}^{n-1} Pr[z_i \text{ is compared to } z_j]$$

The comparison of z_i and z_j is possible when the first element of Z_{ij} to be picked as pivot element is contained in $Z_{ij} = \{z_i,z_j\}$. The probability of either z_i or z_j being the first pivot chosen from Z_{ij} is the sum of the probability of z_i and z_j being the first pivot chosen from Z_{ij}, i.e.,

$$Pr[z_i \text{ or } z_j \text{ is the first pivot chosen from } Z_{ij}] = \frac{1}{j-i+1} + \frac{1}{j-i+1} = \frac{2}{j-i+1}.$$

By using the above probability, the expected number of comparisons is therefore,

$$E[X] = \sum_{i=0}^{n-2} \sum_{j=i+1}^{n-1} \frac{2}{j-i+1}$$

$$E[X] = \sum_{i=0}^{n-2} \sum_{k=1}^{n-i} \frac{2}{k+1}$$

$$E[X] < \sum_{i=0}^{n-2} \sum_{k=1}^{n} \frac{2}{k}$$

$$E[X] = \sum_{i=0}^{n-2} O(\log n)$$

$$E[X] = O(\log n)$$

The above final expression $O(\log n)$ signifies that, in terms of algorithmic complexity, the expected performance of the algorithm grows logarithmically with respect to the size of the input *n*.

UNIT SUMMARY

- Explored algorithm design techniques for exact solutions. . The exploration aimed to address intricacies and determinateness inherent in algorithms, emphasizing commonalities across various solution methodologies.
- Introduced practical solutions for NP-complete problems, addressing the computational complexity of finding optimal solutions. The focus was on approximation algorithms, offering feasible and efficient approaches to tackle complex optimization challenges within polynomial time.
- Defined the approximation ratio, delving into its significance as the worst-case ratio between algorithmic solutions and optimal solutions. The discussion encompassed appropriate ratios, exploring various NP-complete problem classes and shedding light on the nuanced aspects of *approximability.*
- Examined a constant ratio bound approximation algorithm tailored for the vertex cover problem, showcasing its ability to consistently provide solutions no more than twice the size of the optimal cover. This exploration demonstrated a stable balance between computational efficiency and solution quality for a specific NP-complete problem.
- Explored the integration of randomness in decision-making, emphasizing the strategic use of randomized algorithms to enhance problem-solving capabilities. This investigation aimed to uncover creative and flexible approaches in algorithmic decision processes.
- Discussed the versatility of randomized algorithms, highlighting their applicability across diverse domains such as optimization, cryptography, and game theory. Explored how the introduction of randomness enhances algorithmic strategies in addressing complex challenges in these fields.
- Explored methods of obtaining random bits, encompassing sources like natural randomness, secure pseudorandomness, and verified pseudorandomness. The examination aimed to understand diverse approaches for generating randomness and their applications in algorithmic processes.
- Differentiated Las Vegas and Monte Carlo algorithms by highlighting their distinctions in handling failure and the predictability of running time. Explored how these algorithmic paradigms offer varying trade-offs in terms of reliability and efficiency in different computational scenarios.
- Discussed the integration of randomness in the QuickSort algorithm as a strategy to enhance its efficiency. Explored how introducing randomness contributes to improved performance and resilience against adversarial input data in the sorting process.

MULTIPLE CHOICE QUESTIONS

1. What are the shared commonalities among various algorithm design techniques discussed in the preceding units?
    a. They provide approximate solutions
    b. They guarantee optimal solutions
    c. They furnish exact solutions through systematic processes
    d. They prioritize efficiency over accuracy

2. Brute-force search is generally applicable for:
    a. Large input sizes
    b. Small input sizes
    c. Medium input sizes
    d. All input sizes

3. What is the primary objective of heuristic methods in algorithm design?
    a. Guaranteeing optimality
    b. Prioritizing efficiency and practicality
    c. Exhaustively exploring all possibilities
    d. Providing exact solutions

4. Which algorithms offer versatile solutions for general combinatorial optimization problems?
    a. Brute-force algorithms
    b. Heuristic algorithms
    c. Branch-and-bound algorithms
    d. Dynamic programming algorithms

5. Approximation algorithms aim to find solutions within:
    a. Exponential time
    b. Polynomial time
    c. Constant time
    d. Linear time

6. What is a key feature of approximation algorithms?
    a. They guarantee optimality
    b. They provide solutions within a certain factor of the optimal solution
    c. They are computationally impractical
    d. They prioritize solution quality over efficiency

7. The selection of an appropriate algorithmic approach depends on factors such as:
    a. Problem size only
    b. Problem characteristics, size, and desired trade-off between solution quality
    c. Desired trade-off between solution quality and accuracy

d. Availability of computational resources

8. What is the primary characteristic of NP-complete problems?
   a. They are computationally easy
   b. They lack known polynomial-time algorithms for solution
   c. They have deterministic solutions
   d. They are always solvable in constant time

9. In the realm of NP-complete problems, what does an approximation ratio measure?
   a. The time complexity of the algorithm
   b. The ratio between solution produced by algorithm and the optimal solution
   c. The number of iterations required for convergence
   d. The efficiency of the algorithm

10. Which problem is used as an example of a problem with a constant ratio bound approximation algorithm?
    a. Independent set problem
    b. Graph coloring problem
    c. Traveling Salesman Problem
    d. Vertex cover problem

11. What does the term "PTAS" stand for?
    a. Polynomial Time Approximation Scheme
    b. Perfect Time and Accuracy Solution
    c. Probabilistic Time and Accuracy Scheme
    d. Practical Time and Accuracy Solution

12. What role does randomness play in randomized algorithms?
    a. It ensures deterministic outcomes
    b. It introduces variability and flexibility
    c. It guarantees optimal solutions
    d. It slows down the algorithm

13. Which methodology for randomized algorithms involves selecting a quasi-random algorithm from a pool of different deterministic algorithms?
    a. Avoiding worst-case inputs
    b. Hashing
    c. Moving on to sampling
    d. None of the above

14. What is the primary characteristic of deterministic quicksort?
    a. It requires additional storage
    b. It is not efficient for large inputs
    c. It operates on a divide-and-conquer approach
    d. It guarantees an optimal solution

15. What is the key consideration when evaluating randomized algorithms?
    a. Worst-case performance
    b. Average-case performance
    c. Best-case performance
    d. None of the above

Solution of MCQ:

1	2	3	4	5	6	7	8	9	10	11	12	13	14	15
c	b	b	c	b	b	b	b	b	d	b	a	a	c	b

SHORT AND LONG ANSWER TYPE QUESTIONS

1 What are common strategies for handling complex problems in algorithm design?

2 Explain the randomized version of Quicksort and how the introduction of randomness enhances its performance compared to the deterministic version. Highlight key steps in the algorithm and discuss its expected time complexity and advantages over the deterministic Quicksort?

3 Discuss the trade-offs involved in the use of approximation algorithms, emphasizing their role in finding solutions within polynomial time while compromising optimality?

4 Briefly explain why heuristic algorithms and approximation techniques are often employed for NP-complete problems in real-world scenarios?

5 Define the approximation ratio of an algorithm and its significance in the context of optimization problems?

6 Discuss the characteristics and objectives of approximation algorithms, emphasizing their role in tackling NP-complete problems. Provide examples to illustrate how these algorithms strike a balance between solution quality and computational efficiency?

7 Explain the concept of approximation ratio and how it is used to measure the effectiveness of approximation algorithms. Discuss the different performance ratios and their implications for the quality of approximate solutions?

8 Explore the approximability of NP-complete problems, considering inapproximable problems, those with variable ratio bounds, and those with constant ratio bounds. Provide specific examples for each category and discuss the theoretical and practical implications of their approximability?

9 What is the primary objective of approximation algorithms, and how does the VC_approx algorithm for the Vertex Cover problem contribute to achieving this objective?

10 How does the use of randomness in randomized algorithms contribute to addressing challenges in algorithmic decision-making?

11 How does Christofides' Algorithm address the Travelling Salesman Problem (TSP), and what distinguishes it as an effective approximation algorithm for this classic optimization challenge?

12 Can you elaborate on the significance of the approximation achieved by Christofides' Algorithm for the metric TSP, specifically in providing a solution within 3/2 times the length of the optimal route?

13 How does the greedy approach, specifically sorting items by their value-to-weight ratio, contribute to finding a practical approximation solution for the Knapsack Problem in the realm of combinatorial optimization?

14 What are the key advantages and potential limitations associated with using a greedy approach to solve the Knapsack Problem, considering the sorting of items based on their value-to-weight ratio?

15 How does the Greedy Vertex Cover algorithm approach the vertex cover problem, and how does it guarantee a solution no more than twice the size of the optimal cover?

16 How does randomized rounding utilize randomness to round fractional solutions for the Max-Cut problem, and how does this approach contribute to yielding an approximate solution?

17 In the context of approximation algorithms, how does the Greedy Set Cover algorithm efficiently address the Set Cover Problem, and what is the key strategy involved in iteratively selecting sets to cover uncovered elements?

Know More

Online courses/materials/resources [Accessed May 2024]:

- https://web.cse.ohio-state.edu/~dey.8/course/6332/
- https://ocw.mit.edu/courses/6-854j-advanced-algorithms-fall-2008/pages/syllabus/
- https://www.cs.cmu.edu/~15850/notes/cmu850-f20.pdf
- https://onlinecourses.nptel.ac.in/noc23_cs63/preview
- https://github.com/topics/advanced-algorithms
- https://www.geeksforgeeks.org/learn-data-structures-and-algorithms-dsa-tutorial/

References

[1] Thomas H. Cormen, Charles E. Leiserson, Ronald L. Rivest, and Clifford Stein. 2009. Introduction to Algorithms, Third Edition (3rd. ed.). The MIT Press.

[2] David M. Mount, "Notes of Design and Analysis of Computer Algorithms", https://www.cs.umd.edu/class/spring2022/cmsc451/ (accessed Nov.10, 2023).

[3] ChatGPT (Nov 14 version) [Large language model]. https://chat.openai.com/chat, 2023.

[4] James Aspnes, "Notes on Randomized Algorithms", https://www.cs.yale.edu/homes/aspnes/classes/469/notes.pdf (accessed Nov.10, 2023).

[5] Brassard Gilles and Bratley Paul. 1996. Fundamentals of Algorithmics, Prentice Hall Englewood Cliffs.

[6] Goodrich, Michael T. and Tamassia, Roberto (2015), "18.1.2 The Christofides Approximation Algorithm", Algorithm Design and Applications, Wiley, pp. 513–514.

Annexure: List of Experiments

Experiments with solution approaches

Experiment 1: Implement Insertion sort and demonstrate the best, average, and worst cases through the input. (Reference: Unit 2)

Solution approach: Let us implement Insertion Sort using Indian currency notes denominations as an example, and we'll demonstrate the best, average, and worst cases:

```
# Run on https://colab.research.google.com/ dated Feb-2024
import time
def insertion_sort(arr):
  Function to perform insertion sort on an array.
  Parameters:
     arr (list): The input list to be sorted.
  Returns:
     int: The number of comparisons made during sorting.
  comparisons = 0  # Initialize comparison counter
  for i in range(1, len(arr)):
     key = arr[i]
     j = i - 1
     while j >= 0 and key < arr[j]:
        arr[j + 1] = arr[j]
        j -= 1
        comparisons += 1  # Increment comparison counter
     arr[j + 1] = key
  return comparisons

def generate_input(case):
  Function to generate input arrays for different cases.
  Parameters:
     case (str): The type of case - "best", "average", or "worst".
  Returns:
     list: The input list for the given case.

  if case == "best":
     return [5, 10, 20, 50, 100, 200, 500]  # Already sorted
  elif case == "average":
     return [100, 10, 500, 20, 50, 200, 5]  # Random order
```

```
  elif case == "worst":
    return [500, 200, 100, 50, 20, 10, 5]  # Reverse sorted
def test_sorting_case(case):
  """
  Function to test sorting for a specific case.
   Parameters:
    case (str): The type of case - "best", "average", or "worst".
  Returns:
    tuple: A tuple containing the number of comparisons made and the time taken for sorting.

  arr = generate_input(case)
  start_time = time.time()  # Start time for measuring sorting time
  comparisons = insertion_sort(arr)
  end_time = time.time()    # End time for measuring sorting time
  return arr, comparisons, end_time - start_time
# Test cases
cases = ["best", "average", "worst"]
for case in cases:
  sorted_notes, comparisons, elapsed_time = test_sorting_case(case)
  print(f"{case.capitalize()} case - Comparisons: {comparisons}, Time: {elapsed_time:.6f} seconds")
  print("Sorted Indian currency notes denominations:", sorted_notes)
  print()
```

Input and output:

Best case - Comparisons: 0, Time: 0.000006 seconds

Sorted Indian currency notes denominations: [5,10,20,50,100,200,500]

Average case - Comparisons: 12, Time: 0.000011 seconds

Sorted Indian currency notes denominations: [5, 10,20,50,100,200, 500]

Worst case - Comparisons: 21, Time: 0.000013 seconds

Sorted Indian currency notes denominations: [5,10,20,50,100,200,500]

Experiment 2: Implement Θ notation for $f(n) = 3n^2 + 3n + 1$ *and* $g(n) = n^2$ with constants c_1 and c_2 . (Reference: Unit 2)

Solution approach: The following code finds the value of n_0 and generates a plot for Θ notation for the given $f(n)$ *and* $g(n)$ with fixed values of c_1 and c_2 . The output shows that at $c_1 = 3, c_2 = 4,$ *and* $n_0 = 4$ satisfies theta notation.

```
# Run on https://colab.research.google.com/ dated Feb-2024
import matplotlib.pyplot as plt
# Define functions
def f(n):
  return 3 * n ** 2 + 3 * n + 1
def g(n):
  return n ** 2
def c1_g(n, c1):
  return c1 * g(n)
def c2_g(n, c2):
  return c2 * g(n)

# Define constants c1 and c2
c1 = 1
c2 = 4
def determine_constants():
  for n0 in range(1, 20):
     c1 = min(f(n0) // g(n0),3)
     c2 = c1 + 1
     if c1 * g(n0) <= f(n0) <= c2 * g(n0):
        return c1, c2, n0
c1, c2, n0 = determine_constants()
print("c1:", c1)
print("c2:", c2)
print("n0:", n0)
# Generate data points
n_values = list(range(1, 7))
f_values = [f(n) for n in n_values]
c1_g_values = [c1_g(n, c1) for n in n_values]
c2_g_values = [c2_g(n, c2) for n in n_values]
# Plot the graph
plt.figure(figsize=(10, 6))
plt.plot(n_values, f_values, label='f(n)')
plt.plot(n_values, c1_g_values, label='c1 * g(n)')
plt.plot(n_values, c2_g_values, label='c2 * g(n)')
plt.xlabel('n')
plt.ylabel('Values')
plt.title('Graph of f(n), c1 * g(n), and c2 * g(n)')
```

```
plt.legend()
plt.grid(True)
plt.show()
```

Input and output:

c1: 3
c2: 4
n0: 4

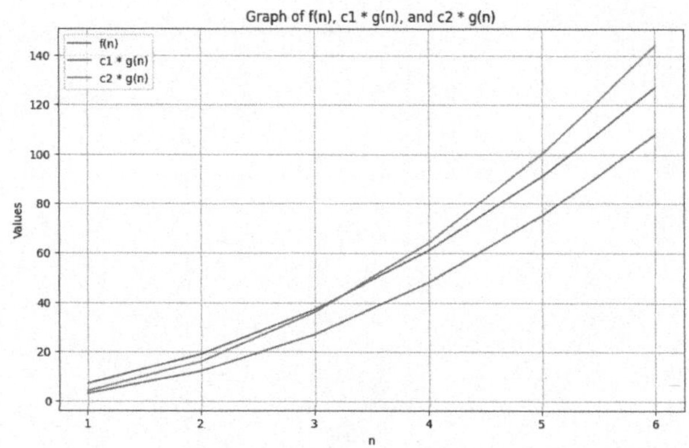

Experiment 3: Implement and analyze Substitution method recursive algorithm using recurrence relations (Reference: Unit 3)

Solution approach: We write a program to implement the Fibonacci series using the substitution method and recursive algorithm. The program takes the number of terms in the series as input and outputs the Fibonacci numbers for those terms.

```
# Run on https://colab.research.google.com/ dated Feb-2024
def fibonacci(n):
  """
  Function to calculate the n-th Fibonacci number using recursion.
  Args:
  - n: An integer representing the position in the Fibonacci sequence.
  Returns:
  - The n-th Fibonacci number.
  """
  # Base cases: F(0) = 0 and F(1) = 1
  if n <= 1:
    return n
  else:
    # Recursive step: F(n) = F(n-1) + F(n-2)
```

```
    return fibonacci(n-1) + fibonacci(n-2)
# Test the function
n = 10  # Calculate Fibonacci sequence up to the 10th number
print("Fibonacci sequence up to", n, ":")
for i in range(n):
  # Print each Fibonacci number up to the n-th number
  print(fibonacci(i))
```

Input and output:

Fibonacci sequence up to 10 :
0
1
1
2
3
5
8
13
21
34

Experiment 4: Write a program to solve given recursive function:

$$x(n) = x(n - 1) + 5 \; for \; n > 1$$
$$x(1) = 0$$

Further, analyze the time complexity of the algorithm (Reference: Unit 3)

Solution approach: The following code calculates the value of $x(n)$ for a given integer n using a recursive function and measures the time complexity of the calculation.

```
# Run on https://colab.research.google.com/ dated Feb-2024
def x(n):
  """
  Recursive function to calculate x(n) = x(n-1) + 5 for n > 1.
  Args:
  - n: An integer representing the position in the sequence.

  Returns:
  - The value of x(n).
  """
  global count
   # Base case
  if n == 1:
```

```
        return 0
    else:
        # Recursive step
        return x(n - 1) + 5
def analyze_time_complexity(n):
    """
    Function to analyze the time complexity of calculating x(n).
    Args:
    - n: An integer representing the position in the sequence.
    Returns:
    - The value of x(n), the count of recursive calls, and the time taken to calculate x(n) in seconds.
    """
    start_time = time.time()
    x_n = x(n)
    end_time = time.time()
    return x_n, count, end_time - start_time
# Test the function
n = 15  # Calculate x(n) for n = 5
x_n, count, time_taken = analyze_time_complexity(n)
print("Loop round={} times, O(n)=Constant*{}, Output of function x({}) = {}, Time taken: {:.6f} seconds".format(n, n,n,x_n,time_taken))
```

Input and output:

Loop round=15 times, O(n)=Constant*15, Output of function x(15) = 70, Time taken: 0.000005 seconds

Experiment 5 (a): Write a program to implement the DFS algorithm for a given graph. (Reference: Unit 4)

Solution approach: The below Python program illustrates DFS starting from IITBHU.

```
# Run on https://colab.research.google.com/ dated Feb-2024
from collections import defaultdict
import networkx as nx
import matplotlib.pyplot as plt
class Graph:
    def __init__(self):
        self.graph = defaultdict(list)
        self.vertices = set()

    def add_edge(self, u, v):
        self.graph[u].append(v)
```

```
        self.vertices.add(u)
        self.vertices.add(v)
def dfs_visit(graph, u, time, colors, discovery_time, finish_time, parent, path):
    time += 1
    discovery_time[u] = time
    colors[u] = 'GRAY'

    for v in graph[u]:
        if colors[v] == 'WHITE':
            parent[v] = u
            path[v] = path[u] + [v]  # Update the path from 'u' to 'v'
            time = dfs_visit(graph, v, time, colors, discovery_time, finish_time, parent, path)
    colors[u] = 'BLACK'
    time += 1
    finish_time[u] = time
    return time

def dfs(graph, start_vertex):
    colors = defaultdict(lambda: 'WHITE')
    discovery_time = {}
    finish_time = {}
    parent = {}
    path = {v: [] for v in graph.vertices}  # Initialize path for all vertices
    time = 0
    time = dfs_visit(graph.graph, start_vertex, time, colors, discovery_time, finish_time, parent, path)
    print("Vertex\tDiscovery Time\tFinish Time\tParent\t\tPath from 'IITBHU'")
    for v in graph.vertices:
        print(f"{v}\t\t{discovery_time.get(v,        'NIL')}\t\t{finish_time.get(v,        'NIL')}\t\t{parent.get(v,
'NIL')}\t\t{path.get(v, 'NIL')}")
    # Visualize the original graph
    G = nx.DiGraph(graph.graph)
    plt.figure(figsize=(8, 4))
    pos = nx.spring_layout(G)
    nx.draw(G,    pos,    with_labels=True,    node_color='lightblue',    node_size=1500,    font_size=12,
font_weight='bold', arrows=True)
    plt.title("Original Directed Graph")
    plt.show()
    # Visualize the DFS traversal graph
```

```
    dfs_edges = [(parent[v], v) for v in graph.vertices if parent.get(v) is not None]
    dfs_G = nx.DiGraph(dfs_edges)
    plt.figure(figsize=(8, 4))
    nx.draw(dfs_G, with_labels=True, node_color='lightblue', node_size=1500, font_size=12,
font_weight='bold', edge_color='red', arrows=True)
    plt.title("DFS Traversal Directed Graph")
    plt.show()
# Test the DFS algorithm
g = Graph()
g.add_edge('IITK', 'IITD')
g.add_edge('IITBHU', 'IITK')
g.add_edge('IITD', 'IITG')
g.add_edge('IITG', 'IITBHU')
g.add_edge('IITBHU', 'IITM')
g.add_edge('IITM', 'IITR')
g.add_edge('IITG', 'IITR')
start_vertex = 'IITBHU'
print(f"Depth First Search (starting from vertex {start_vertex}):")
dfs(g, start_vertex)
```

Input and output:

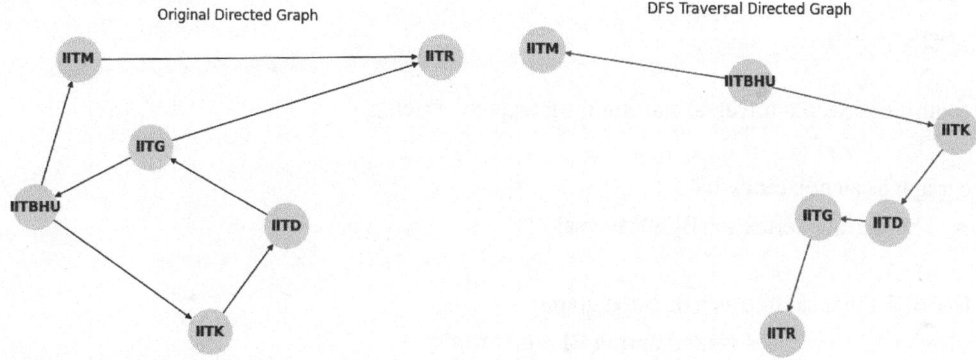

Depth First Search (starting from vertex IITBHU):

Vertex	Discovery Time	Finish Time	Parent	Path from 'IITBHU'
IITG	4	7	IITD	['IITK', 'IITD', 'IITG']
IITBHU	1	12	NIL	[]
IITD	3	8	IITK	['IITK', 'IITD']
IITM	10	11	IITBHU	['IITM']
IITK	2	9	IITBHU	['IITK']
IITR	5	6	IITG	['IITK', 'IITD', 'IITG', 'IITR']

Experiment 5 (b): Write a program to implement the BFS algorithm for a given graph. (Reference: Unit 4)

Solution approach: The below Python program illustrates BFS starting from IITBHU.

```
# Run on https://colab.research.google.com/ dated Feb-2024
from collections import defaultdict, deque
import networkx as nx
import matplotlib.pyplot as plt
class Graph:
  def __init__(self):
    self.graph = defaultdict(list)
    self.vertices = set()
  def add_edge(self, u, v):
    """
    Add an edge between vertices u and v.
    Args:
    - u: Source vertex
    - v: Destination vertex
    """
    self.graph[u].append(v)
    self.vertices.add(u)
    self.vertices.add(v)
def bfs(graph, start_vertex):
  """
  Perform Breadth-First Search traversal starting from a given vertex.
  Args:
  - graph: The graph as an adjacency list
  - start_vertex: The starting vertex for BFS traversal
  Returns:
  - bfs_tree: The BFS traversal tree as a directed graph
  - bfs_order: The order of vertices visited during BFS traversal
  """
  visited = set()
  queue = deque([start_vertex])
  visited.add(start_vertex)
  bfs_tree = nx.DiGraph()
  bfs_tree.add_node(start_vertex)
  bfs_order = []  # To store the order of traversal
  while queue:
```

```
        vertex = queue.popleft()
        bfs_order.append(vertex)  # Append vertex to bfs_order
        for neighbor in graph[vertex]:
            if neighbor not in visited:
                queue.append(neighbor)
                visited.add(neighbor)
                bfs_tree.add_edge(vertex, neighbor)
    return bfs_tree, bfs_order
# Test the BFS algorithm
g = Graph()
g.add_edge('IITK', 'IITD')
g.add_edge('IITBHU', 'IITK')
g.add_edge('IITD', 'IITG')
g.add_edge('IITG', 'IITBHU')
g.add_edge('IITBHU', 'IITM')
g.add_edge('IITM', 'IITR')
g.add_edge('IITG', 'IITR')
g.add_edge('IITR', 'IITR')  # Self-loop for IITR
start_vertex = 'IITBHU'
print(f"Breadth First Search (starting from vertex {start_vertex}):")
bfs_tree, bfs_order = bfs(g.graph, start_vertex)
print("BFS Traversal Order:", bfs_order)
# Visualize both the original directed graph and the BFS traversal tree side by side
plt.figure(figsize=(15, 6))
# Plot the original directed graph
plt.subplot(1, 2, 1)
G = nx.DiGraph(g.graph)
pos = nx.spring_layout(G)
nx.draw(G, pos, with_labels=True, node_color='lightblue', node_size=1500, font_size=12,
font_weight='bold', arrows=True)
plt.title("Original Directed Graph")
# Plot the BFS traversal tree
plt.subplot(1, 2, 2)
pos = nx.spring_layout(bfs_tree)
nx.draw(bfs_tree, pos, with_labels=True, node_color='lightblue', node_size=1500, font_size=12,
font_weight='bold', arrows=True)
plt.title("BFS Traversal Tree")
plt.show()
```

Input and output:

Breadth First Search (starting from vertex IITBHU):
BFS Traversal Order: ['IITBHU', 'IITK', 'IITM', 'IITD', 'IITR', 'IITG']

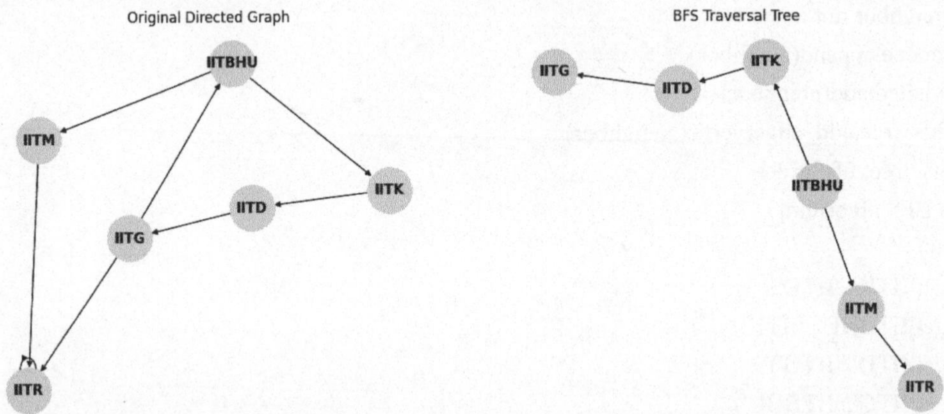

Experiment 6 (a): Write a program and analyze Prim's algorithm to generate minimum cost spanning tree. (Reference: Unit 4)

Solution approach: This Python program implements Prim's algorithm to generate a minimum cost spanning tree. It defines a graph class to represent the graph and contains methods to add edges, apply Prim's algorithm, and construct the minimum spanning tree. The test case provided demonstrates the usage of the algorithm on a sample graph.

```
import networkx as nx
import matplotlib.pyplot as plt
class Graph:
  def __init__(self, vertices):
    """
    Initialize the graph with the given number of vertices.
    Parameters:
    - vertices: An integer representing the number of vertices in the graph.
    """
    self.V = vertices
    # Initialize the adjacency matrix with all zeros
    self.graph = [[0 for _ in range(vertices)] for _ in range(vertices)]
  def add_edge(self, u, v, weight):
    """
    Add an edge between vertices 'u' and 'v' with the given weight.
    Parameters:
    - u: The source vertex.
    - v: The target vertex.
```

```
        - weight: The weight of the edge.
        """
        if u >= self.V or v >= self.V:
            print("Error: Vertex index out of range")
            return
        # Update the adjacency matrix for both directions since it is an undirected graph
        self.graph[u][v] = weight
        self.graph[v][u] = weight
    def prim_mst(self, start_vertex):
        """
        Apply Prim's algorithm to find the minimum spanning tree (MST).
        Parameters:
        - start_vertex: The starting vertex for the algorithm.

        Returns:
        - A list of edges representing the minimum spanning tree.
        """
        key = [float('inf')] * self.V
        parent = [-1] * self.V
        mst_set = [False] * self.V
        key[start_vertex] = 0
        mst_edges = []
        for _ in range(self.V):
            min_key = float('inf')
            min_index = -1
            for v in range(self.V):
                if not mst_set[v] and key[v] < min_key:
                    min_key = key[v]
                    min_index = v
            mst_set[min_index] = True
            for v in range(self.V):
                if (
                    self.graph[min_index][v] != 0
                    and not mst_set[v]
                    and self.graph[min_index][v] < key[v]
                ):
                    key[v] = self.graph[min_index][v]
                    parent[v] = min_index
```

```
        return self.construct_mst(parent)
    def construct_mst(self, parent):
        """
        Construct the minimum spanning tree from the parent array.
        Parameters:
        - parent: An array representing the parent of each vertex in the MST.
        Returns:
        - A list of edges representing the minimum spanning tree.
        """
        mst_edges = []
        for i in range(1, self.V):
            mst_edges.append((parent[i], i, self.graph[i][parent[i]]))
        return mst_edges

def draw_graph(graph, title):
    """
    Draw the graph using NetworkX and Matplotlib.

    Parameters:
    - graph: The graph adjacency matrix.
    - title: The title of the graph.
    """
    G = nx.Graph()
    for u in range(len(graph)-1):
        for v in range(len(graph[u])):
            if graph[u][v] != 0:  # Edge exists
                weight = graph[u][v]
                G.add_edge(u, v, weight=weight)
    pos = nx.spring_layout(G)  # Define node positions using spring layout
    nx.draw(G, pos, with_labels=True, node_size=700, node_color='skyblue', font_size=12,
font_weight='bold', edge_color='gray')
    nx.draw_networkx_edge_labels(G, pos, edge_labels={(u, v): graph[u][v] for u in range(len(graph)) for v
in range(len(graph[u])) if graph[u][v] != 0})
    plt.title(title)
    plt.show()

# Test the Prim's algorithm
g = Graph(4)
```

```
g.add_edge(0, 1, 3)
g.add_edge(1, 0, 3)
g.add_edge(0, 3, 1)
g.add_edge(3, 0, 1)
g.add_edge(3, 2, 2)
g.add_edge(2, 3, 2)
g.add_edge(2, 1, 4)
g.add_edge(1, 2, 4)

mst_edges = g.prim_mst(0)  # Starting vertex is 0 (A)
print("Minimum Spanning Tree using Prim's algorithm:")
print("Edges of MST:", mst_edges)

# Draw the original graph
draw_graph(g.graph, "Original Graph")
```

Input and output:

Minimum Spanning Tree using Prim's algorithm:
Edges of MST: [(0, 1, 3), (3, 2, 2), (0, 3, 1)]

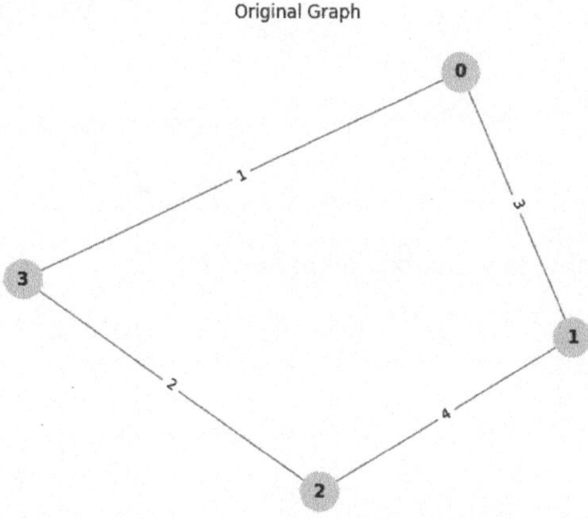

<u>Experiment 6 (b):</u> Write a program and analyze Kruskal's algorithm to generate minimum cost spanning tree. (Reference: Unit 4)

Solution approach: This Python program implements Kruskal's algorithm to generate a minimum cost spanning tree. It defines a graph class to represent the graph and contains methods to add edges, apply Kruskal's algorithm, and construct the minimum spanning tree. The test case provided demonstrates the usage of the algorithm on a sample graph.

```
import networkx as nx
import matplotlib.pyplot as plt
class Graph:
  def __init__(self, vertices):
    self.V = vertices
    self.graph = []
  def add_edge(self, u, v, w):
    self.graph.append([u, v, w])
  def find(self, parent, i):
    if parent[i] == i:
      return i
    return self.find(parent, parent[i])
  def union(self, parent, rank, x, y):
    x_root = self.find(parent, x)
    y_root = self.find(parent, y)
    if rank[x_root] < rank[y_root]:
      parent[x_root] = y_root
    elif rank[x_root] > rank[y_root]:
      parent[y_root] = x_root
    else:
      parent[y_root] = x_root
      rank[x_root] += 1
  def kruskal_mst(self):
    result = []
    i, e = 0, 0
    self.graph = sorted(self.graph, key=lambda item: item[2])
    parent = [i for i in range(self.V)]
    rank = [0] * self.V
    while e < self.V - 1:
      u, v, w = self.graph[i]
      i += 1
      x = self.find(parent, u)
      y = self.find(parent, v)
      if x != y:
        e += 1
        result.append([u, v, w])
        self.union(parent, rank, x, y)
    return result
```

```
    def get_edges(self):
        edges = [(u, v, {'weight': w}) for u, v, w in self.graph]
        return edges
# Function to draw a graph
def draw_graph(graph_edges, title):
    G = nx.Graph()
    G.add_edges_from(graph_edges)
    pos = nx.spring_layout(G)
    nx.draw(G, pos, with_labels=True, node_size=700, node_color='skyblue', font_size=12,
font_weight='bold', edge_color='gray')
    labels = nx.get_edge_attributes(G, 'weight')
    nx.draw_networkx_edge_labels(G, pos, edge_labels=labels)
    plt.title(title)
    plt.show()
# Test the Kruskal's algorithm and draw graphs
g = Graph(4)
g.add_edge(0, 1, 3)
g.add_edge(1, 0, 3)
g.add_edge(0, 3, 1)
g.add_edge(3, 0, 1)
g.add_edge(3, 2, 2)
g.add_edge(2, 3, 2)
g.add_edge(2, 1, 4)
g.add_edge(1, 2, 4)
original_graph_edges = g.get_edges()
mst_edges = g.kruskal_mst()
mst_graph_edges = [(u, v) for u, v, _ in mst_edges]
print("Minimum Spanning Tree using Kruskal's algorithm:")
print("Edges of MST:", mst_edges)
# Draw the original graph
draw_graph(original_graph_edges, "Original Graph")
# Draw the minimum spanning tree (MST)
draw_graph(mst_graph_edges, "Minimum Spanning Tree (MST)")
```

Input and output:

Minimum Spanning Tree using Kruskal's algorithm:
Edges of MST: [[0, 3, 1], [3, 2, 2], [0, 1, 3]]

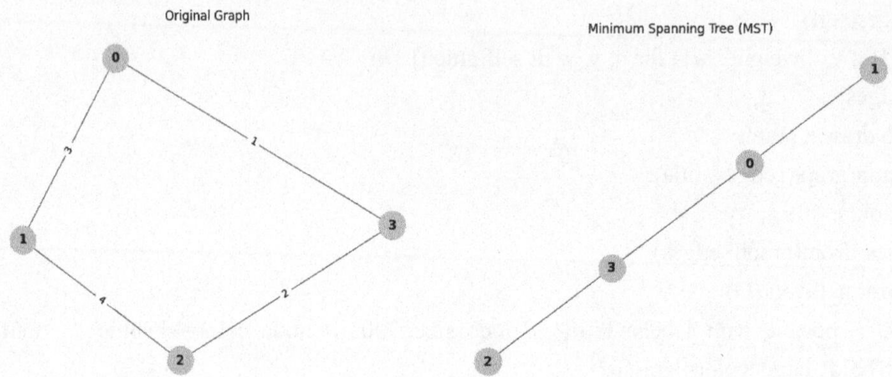

Experiment 7: Implement Floyd's algorithm for the all pairs shortest path problem. (Reference: Unit 4)

Solution approach: This Python program implements Floyd's algorithm to generate all pairs shortest paths as follows:

```
def floyd_warshall(graph):
  """
  Floyd-Warshall algorithm to find the shortest paths between all pairs of vertices.
  Args:
  - graph: Adjacency matrix representing the weighted graph.
  Returns:
  - A: Matrix representing the shortest distances between all pairs of vertices.
  """
  n = len(graph)
  A = [[0 if i == j else graph[i][j] for j in range(n)] for i in range(n)]
  # Draw the original matrix
  print("Original Matrix (k = 0):")
  draw_matrix(A)
  for k in range(n):
     for i in range(n):
        for j in range(n):
           # Update the shortest path if there is a shorter path through vertex k
           A[i][j] = min(A[i][j], A[i][k] + A[k][j])
     # Draw the matrix after each iteration
     print(f"\nAfter iteration k = {k + 1}:")
     draw_matrix(A)
  return A
def draw_matrix(matrix):
```

```
    """
    Helper function to draw a matrix.
    """
    for row in matrix:
        print(row)
# Example usage:
graph = [
    [0, 2, 5,float('inf')],
    [0, 0, 1, float('inf')],
    [float('inf'), 2, 0, float('inf')],
    [float('inf'), float('inf'), 1, 8]
]
shortest_paths = floyd_warshall(graph)
```

Input and output:

Original Matrix (k = 0):
[0, 2, 5, inf]
[0, 0, 1, inf]
[inf, 2, 0, inf]
[inf, inf, 1, 0]

After iteration k = 1:
[0, 2, 5, inf]
[0, 0, 1, inf]
[inf, 2, 0, inf]
[inf, inf, 1, 0]

After iteration k = 2:
[0, 2, 3, inf]
[0, 0, 1, inf]
[2, 2, 0, inf]
[inf, inf, 1, 0]

After iteration k = 3:
[0, 2, 3, inf]
[0, 0, 1, inf]
[2, 2, 0, inf]
[3, 3, 1, 0]

After iteration k = 4:
[0, 2, 3, inf]
[0, 0, 1, inf]
[2, 2, 0, inf]
[3, 3, 1, 0]

Experiment 8: Write a program to implement greedy algorithms for knapsack problems. (Reference: Unit 6)

Solution approach: This Python program implements greedy algorithms for knapsack problems as follows:

```
# Structure for an item which stores profit and weight
class Item:
  def __init__(self, profit, weight):
     self.profit = profit  # profit of the item
     self.weight = weight  # weight of the item

# Comparison function to sort Item according to profit/weight ratio
def cmp(item):
  return item.profit / item.weight  # calculate profit-to-weight ratio

# Main greedy function to solve problem
def fractional_knapsack(W, items):
  # Sorting items based on profit/weight ratio
  items.sort(key=cmp, reverse=True)  # sort items in descending order of profit-to-weight ratio

  final_value = 0.0  # initialize final value to 0
  selected_items = []  # list to store selected items

  # Looping through all items
  for item in items:
     # If adding item would not overflow, add it completely
     if item.weight <= W:
        W -= item.weight  # reduce knapsack capacity
        final_value += item.profit  # add full profit of the item
        selected_items.append((item.profit, item.weight, 1))  # add item to selected items list
     # If we can't add current item, add fractional part of it
     else:
        fraction = W / item.weight  # calculate fraction of item to be added
        final_value += item.profit * fraction  # add fraction of profit
        selected_items.append((item.profit, item.weight, fraction))  # add item to selected items list
        break  # knapsack capacity exhausted

  # Returning final value and selected items
```

```
    return final_value, selected_items

# Driver code
if __name__ == "__main__":
    W = 10  # knapsack capacity
    items = [Item(20, 4), Item(18, 3), Item(14, 2), Item(30, 5)]  # list of items

    # Function call
    final_value, selected_items = fractional_knapsack(W, items)  # solve fractional knapsack problem

    # Print result
    print("Total value of selected items:", final_value)
    print("\nTable of items selected:")
    print("Profit\tWeight\tFraction")
    for item in selected_items:
        print(f"{item[0]}\t{item[1]}\t{item[2]}")
```

Input and output:

```
Total value of selected items: 62.0
Table of items selected:
Profit   Weight  Fraction
14       2       1
18       3       1
30       5       1
20       4       0.0
```

Experiment Exercise

1.	Write a program to find the shortest path for a multistage graph. (Reference: Unit 4)
2.	Write a program for string matching considering two strings of 13 and 8 characters. (Reference: Unit 5)
3.	Write a program to implement brute force method for subset generation. (Reference: Unit 5)
4.	Write a program to implement brute force method for travelling salesman problem. (Reference: Unit 5)
5.	Implement Huffman Coding (Reference: Unit 6)
6.	Write a program to implement a greedy algorithm for job sequencing with deadlines. (Reference: Unit 6)
7.	Implement a dynamic programming algorithm for the 0/1 Knapsack problem. (Reference: Unit 7)
8.	Implement a backtracking algorithm for the N-queens problem. (Reference: Unit 7)
9.	Implement methods for fibonacci number generation. (Reference: Unit 7)
10.	Implement chained matrix multiplication. (Reference: Unit 7)
11.	Write a program for longest common subsequence. (Reference: Unit 7)
12.	Write a program to implement merge sort. (Reference: Unit 8)
13.	Write a program to implement binary search. (Reference: Unit 8)
14.	Write a program to implement matrix multiplication. (Reference: Unit 8)
15.	Write a program to implement a close pair problem. (Reference: Unit 8)

CO and PO Attainment Table

Course outcomes (COs) for this course can be mapped with the programme outcomes (POs) after the completion of the course and a correlation can be made for the attainment of POs to analyse the gap. After proper analysis of the gap in the attainment of POs necessary measures can be taken to overcome the gaps.

Table for CO and PO attainment

Course Outcome	Expected Mapping with Programme Outcomes (1- Weak Correlation; 2- Medium correlation; 3- Strong Correlation)											
	PO-1	PO-2	PO-3	PO-4	PO-5	PO-6	PO-7	PO-8	PO-9	PO-10	PO-11	PO-12
CO-1												
CO-2												
CO-3												
CO-4												
CO-5												

The data filled in the above table can be used for gap analysis.

INDEX

Insertion Sort 16
Interval Scheduling 181
Kadane's Algorithm 48
Knapsack Problem 165
Little o Notation 34
Little Omega Notation 34